MACMILLAN EXAMS

Ready for
First

coursebook with key

3rd Edition

Roy Norris

Updated in line with Cambridge English: First (FCE) 2015 revisions

MACMILLAN

Contents map

Introduction

Welcome to *Ready for First*, a course which is designed to help you prepare for the *Cambridge English: First* examination, also known as *First Certificate in English (FCE)*.

This book contains a wide range of activities aimed at improving your English and developing the language and skills which you will need to pass the examination. As well as providing relevant practice in reading, writing, listening and speaking, each unit of *Ready for First* includes one or more Language focus sections, which revise the main grammar areas, together with Vocabulary slots which will help you to increase your word store.

A significant feature of the Use of English syllabus in the book is the systematic approach to Word formation. At regular intervals you will find special sections which focus on the most important aspects of word building, ensuring that you are properly prepared for this part of the examination. There are also sections, in Units 7, 10 and 13, devoted to the important skill of paraphrasing and recording new vocabulary.

At the end of every unit there is a two-page Review section, which enables you to revise and practise the new language you have encountered in the unit.

Throughout the book you will find the following boxes, which are designed to help you when performing the different tasks:

What to expect in the exam: these contain useful information on what you should be prepared to see, hear or do in a particular task in the examination.

How to go about it: these give advice and guidelines on how to deal with different task types and specific questions.

Don't forget!: these provide a reminder of important points to bear in mind when answering a particular question.

Useful language: these contain vocabulary and structures which can be used when doing a specific writing or speaking activity.

Further information and advice on each of the papers in the *Cambridge English: First* exam is included in the five supplementary 'Ready for ...' units. These are situated at regular intervals in the book and can be used at appropriate moments during the course. The Ready for Writing unit contains model answers for each of the main task types, together with advice, useful language and further writing tasks for you to complete.

At the end of the book you will find detailed explanations of the grammar areas seen in the units in the Grammar reference, together with a topic-based Wordlist and the Listening scripts.

Overview of the Examination

The *Cambridge English: First* examination consists of four papers, as shown below. The Writing, Listening and Speaking papers each carry 20% of the total marks; the Reading and Use of English paper carries 40% (20% for the Reading tasks and 20% for the Use of English tasks). A low mark in one paper does not necessarily mean a candidate will fail the examination; it is the overall mark which counts.

Reading and Use of English   1 hour 15 minutes

There are seven parts to this paper: Parts 1 to 4 are grammar and vocabulary tasks; Parts 5 to 7 are reading tasks. For the Use of English tasks, each correct answer in Parts 1 to 3 receives one mark; each question in Part 4 carries up to two marks. For the reading tasks, each correct answer in Parts 5 and 6 receives two marks, and there is one mark for each question in Part 7. For more information on this paper, see the Ready for Use of English unit on pages 42 to 45 and the Ready for Reading unit on pages 82 to 87, as well as the relevant sections in the main units of the book.

Part	Task Type	Number of questions	Task Format
1	Multiple-choice cloze	8	A text with 8 gaps; there is a choice of 4 answers for each gap.
2	Open cloze	8	A text with 8 gaps, each of which must be completed with one word.
3	Word Formation	8	A text containing 8 gaps. The task is to complete each gap with the correct form of a given word.
4	Key word transformations	6	Gapped sentences which must be completed using a given word.
5	Multiple Choice	6	A text followed by multiple-choice questions with four options.
6	Gapped Text	6	A text from which sentences have been removed. Candidates replace each of these in the appropriate part of the text.
7	Multiple Matching	10	A text preceded by multiple-matching questions which require candidates to find specific information in a text or texts.

Writing   1 hour 20 minutes

There are two parts to this paper, each of which carries the same number of marks. Part 1 is compulsory, so must be answered by all candidates, whereas in Part 2 candidates choose one from three tasks. You are required to write between 140 and 190 words for each part. For more information and advice on the questions in this paper, see the Ready for Writing unit on pages 192 to 201, as well as the relevant sections in the main units of the book.

Part	Task Type	Number of Tasks	Task Format
1	Essay	1 (compulsory)	Candidates are given an essay title and notes to guide their writing.
2		3 (candidates choose one)	A writing task with a clear context, purpose for writing and target reader. Candidates write one of the following: article, email/letter, report, review.

Listening   about 40 minutes

This paper consists of four parts with a total of 30 questions, each of which carries one mark. Each part contains one or more recorded texts, which are heard twice. Candidates are tested on their ability to understand, for example, opinions, gist, the main points or specific information. For more information on this paper, see the Ready for Listening unit on pages 124 to 127, as well as the relevant sections in the main units of the book.

Part	Task Type	Number of Questions	Task Format
1	Multiple choice	8	Short unrelated extracts of approximately 30 seconds each with one or more speakers. There are 3 options for each question.
2	Sentence completion	10	A monologue lasting approximately 3 minutes. Candidates write a word or short phrase to complete sentences.
3	Multiple Matching	5	Five short monologues, each lasting approximately 30 seconds. The extracts are all related to a common theme. Candidates match extracts with prompts.
4	Multiple choice	7	An interview or conversation between two or more speakers lasting approximately 3 minutes. There are 3 options for each question.

Speaking   14 minutes

There are four parts to this paper. There are usually two candidates and two examiners. Candidates are given marks for range and correct use of grammar and vocabulary, pronunciation, discourse management (the ability to organize language and produce extended responses) and interactive communication. For more information on this paper, see the Ready for Speaking unit on pages 164 to 167, as well as the relevant sections in the main units of the book.

Part	Task Type	Time	Task Format
1	Interview	2 minutes	Candidates give personal information in response to questions from the interviewer.
2	Talking about photographs	4 minutes	Each candidate talks about two pictures for about 1 minute, and comments briefly on the other candidate's pictures.
3	Collaborative Task	4 minutes	Candidates are given instructions with written prompts which they use for discussion. Candidates speak for about 3 minutes in total; the giving of instructions takes about 1 minute.
4	Further discussion	4 minutes	The interviewer leads a discussion which is related to the topic of Part 3.

Roy Norris

①Lifestyle

Actor

Potter

Vocabulary 1: Lifestyle

1 **a** Look at the verbs and adjectives that can all be used with the noun *lifestyle* to form collocations. Collocations are pairs or groups of words that are often used together.

		alternative	luxurious	
have		busy	quiet	
live	a/an	chaotic	relaxing	lifestyle
lead		comfortable	sedentary	
		exciting	simple	
		healthy	stressful	

Underline those adjectives which could be used to describe *your* lifestyle.

b   Work in pairs. Compare your adjectives with your partner, explaining your choices.

Example:

*I **have** quite **a healthy lifestyle** at the moment. I'm eating sensibly and doing a lot of exercise.*

2   Discuss the following questions. As in other parts of this book, common collocations are shown in **bold**.

- Would you like to **change your lifestyle**? Why/Why not?
- Do you **lead an active social life**? What kinds of things do you do?
- What do you think is meant by the **American way of life**? How would you describe the **way of life** in your country to a foreigner?
- What are some of the positive and negative aspects of our **modern way of life**? In what ways, if any, was the **traditional way of life** in your country better?
- Why are people so interested in the **private lives** of celebrities? Do they interest you?

6

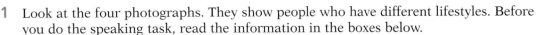

Speaking
Part 2

Talking about photos

1 Look at the four photographs. They show people who have different lifestyles. Before you do the speaking task, read the information in the boxes below.

Student A Compare photographs **1** and **2** and say what you think the people might find difficult about their lifestyles.

Student B When your partner has finished, say which lifestyle you would prefer to lead.

2 Now change roles. Follow the instructions above using photographs **3** and **4**.

How to go about it

Student A

● In Part 2 of the speaking exam you are not asked to describe the photographs in detail, but to compare them. When doing this, comment on the similarities and differences:

Similarities: *Both pictures show …*

Differences: *In the first picture … **whereas** in the second one …*

● When talking about what the people might find difficult about their lifestyles, give reasons for your opinions. You could comment on some of the following:

daily routine	working hours	leisure time	type of home	friends
eating habits	health	travel	family life	

Student B

● In the exam you have time to develop your answer fully and give reasons for your choice.

Useful language

*I **get the impression** it's a stressful life.*
*I **expect/imagine** she has to get up early.*
*He **probably** spends a long time away from home.*
*I **doubt that** she has much time for a social life.*
***Perhaps** he doesn't see his family very often.*
*She **might/may** get lonely during the day.*

What might the people find difficult about their lifestyles?

Farm vet

Fisherman

Multiple matching

You are going to read an article in which four people talk about their lifestyles. For questions **1–10**, choose from the people (**A–D**). The people may be chosen more than once.

How to go about it

- Read all the questions to see the kind of information you are looking for.
- Read section A, then look again at the questions, answering any that you can.

  To help you, one part of section A has been underlined. Match this part to one of the questions. Then look in the rest of section A for any more answers.
- Do the same for the other three sections. Underline the relevant parts of the text as you answer the questions.
- If there are any questions you have not answered, scan the whole text again looking for the information you need.

Which person

admits to having an untidy house?	1
could not imagine doing any other type of work?	2
likes the unpredictable nature of their work?	3
is not particularly keen on taking exercise?	4
says they start the day like many other people?	5
does not have to go far to get to their place of work?	6
never has any trouble getting to sleep?	7
used to feel lonely while working?	8
says that people have the wrong idea about their work?	9
would prefer to go to bed earlier on many occasions?	10

This is your life

Four more personal accounts in our series on different lifestyles

A Colin Dobson: television and stage actor

Normally I get out of bed around midday. <u>I'll sometimes go for a run after I get up, though it's not really my idea of fun. I'm not a fitness fan,</u> but I realize it's important.

5   When I'm not rehearsing or on tour, afternoons usually involve reading scripts or learning lines. My wife and two sons are also actors, so at home there are usually scripts lying all over the place. It's a bit of a mess, I'm ashamed to say. I'm passionate about history, and if
10   I'm working away from home, I spend the afternoons in museums or historic buildings. I always get to the theatre at the last minute, which annoys my co-actors, but I don't like arriving anywhere early.

  After a performance I eat and spend a few hours
15   unwinding, so bedtime is often two or three in the morning. I always fall asleep as soon as my head hits the pillow.

B Jodie Miller: potter

Before I started renting the workshop at the open-air museum, I would crawl out of bed in the morning, get
20 dressed and go straight into the garage, which I'd converted into a studio. Now I get the train and a bus, so I have to get up early and my morning routine is dull and conventional, the same one that's played out in millions of households.

25 On the plus side, though, I get to meet lots of people: there are the museum visitors that come into the workshop every day to watch me working, the other craftspeople – the broom maker, the blacksmith or the glassblower – and I also give classes. Working at
30 home was a solitary business and I hated the fact that I would often go for days without speaking to anyone.

I get lots of requests for personalized mugs, and evenings are spent packaging up orders to send out the next day. I often get to bed later than I would like.

C Janie Collins: farm vet

35 I used to have a dog and we'd go running together most mornings, but I gave him to my mum in the end. I tend to be out all day visiting farms and it wasn't fair to leave him alone. So now I don't get as much exercise as I'd like to.

40 I love my job, especially the variety and not knowing what you'll be doing from one day to the next. But being a vet – any type of vet – is not what people think. It's not all cuddly lambs and cute little pigs. We have to do some pretty unpleasant things sometimes,
45 things which would put you off working with animals for life.

My mum wants to know when I'm going to settle down with someone, but there's no room for a dog in my life, so I don't see how I'll be able to fit marriage in.

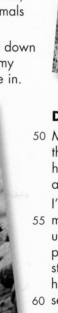

D Mark Fudge: fisherman

50 My flat overlooks the port, so it's just a short walk to the *Ellie May*. That's our boat, the place I think of as home. I get lonely if I'm away from her for longer than a week or so – the crew is like a family to me.

I'm one of four deckhands, which means that the first
55 mate – the second in command after the captain – gets us to do cleaning and maintenance work as well as pulling in the nets, then washing, salting, icing and storing the fish. We work hard – six hours on, six hours off, six hours on, six hours off – every day for
60 seven weeks. It's tough, but I can't see myself in any other profession. There's nothing else I'd rather do.

 Reacting to the text

If you had to choose, which of the four people would you prefer to change places with for a month? Why?

Language focus 1: Habitual behaviour

A General tendencies

1 Which of the alternatives in this sentence is not possible?

*I **tend to be**/**use to be**/**am usually** out all day visiting farms.*

 Look at the Grammar reference on page 209 to see how *tend to* is used.

2 Make three general statements about some of the following groups of people in your country using *tend to*.

- football players
- teenagers
- elderly people
- teachers
- people in cities
- people in villages

Example:
The best football players in my country tend to go abroad. They can earn much more money playing for foreign clubs.

B Frequency adverbs

1 a Look at the following extracts from the reading text. In what position is the frequency adverb placed in relation to the verb?

I'll **sometimes** go for a run after I get up.

At home there are **usually** scripts lying all over the place.

I **always** get to the theatre at the last minute.

b In this sentence, two of the adverbs are in the correct position and two are not. Cross out the two incorrectly placed adverbs.

Normally/Always/Sometimes/Never I get out of bed around midday.

 Check your ideas in the Grammar reference on page 209.

2 For sentences **1–6**, decide if the position of the adverb is possible. If it is not possible, correct the sentence.

1 I rarely go out on weekday evenings.
2 I have usually my dinner in front of the television.
3 Never I spend more than ten minutes doing my English homework.
4 Companies are always phoning me in the evening, trying to sell me something – I get so annoyed.
5 Hardly I ever play computer games – I prefer reading.
6 It's rare for me to go to bed before midnight, and quite often I'll stay up until two in the morning.

3 Say whether or not the sentences in exercise **2** are true for you. Use frequency adverbs and the alternatives in the Grammar reference on page 209.

Example:
*1 It's rare for me to stay at home **on weekday evenings**. I usually do **some type of sport**; I tend to go **running if it's not raining, and if it is**, I'll often go **swimming or play badminton**.*

C *Used to* and *would*

1 *Used to* and *would* can be used to talk about past habits. Look at these sentences from the reading text and answer the question.

a *I **would** crawl out of bed and go straight into the garage.*
b *I **would** sometimes go for days without speaking to anyone.*
c *I **used to** have a dog and we'd go running together most mornings.*

In all three sentences, *used to* could be used instead of *would*/*'d* before the verbs *crawl* and *go*, but in sentence **c**, it is **not** possible to say *I would have a dog*. Why is this?

 Check your ideas on page 209 of the Grammar reference.

2 In the following paragraph, decide whether the underlined verbs can be used with:

a both *used to* and *would*
b only *used to*
c neither *used to* nor *would*

In the bad old days my mum **(1)** had an executive position in a pharmaceutical company. She often **(2)** worked long hours and sometimes **(3)** went away on business trips for two or three days at a time. Our dear old gran **(4)** looked after us on those occasions, but it wasn't the same as having a mum around. My brother and I **(5)** didn't like her being away from home, but we never once **(6)** said anything, because we always **(7)** thought she was happy in her work. Then one day she **(8)** announced she was giving up her job to spend more time with her family. We **(9)** were delighted at the change in lifestyle, but I'm not sure about my mum: she often **(10)** said afterwards that being a full-time mother was harder than being a business executive!

3 Write six sentences comparing your life now with your life five years ago. Write about things which have changed.

Example:
I didn't use to have a job, but now I work on Saturdays so I have more money.

Vocabulary 2: *Get*

1 **a** Look at these sentences from the reading text on pages 8 and 9 and try to remember who said each one. The first one has been done for you.

   a I **get to meet** lots of people. *the potter*
   b Normally I **get out of bed** around midday.
   c I don't **get** as much **exercise** as I'd like to.
   d I **get lonely** if I'm away from her for longer than a week or so.
   e I **get the train** and a bus.
   f I always **get to the theatre** at the last minute.
   g The first mate **gets us to do** cleaning and maintenance work …
   h I **get** lots of **requests** for personalized mugs.

   Check your answers on pages 8 and 9.

   b What is the meaning of the words in **bold** in sentences **a–h** above?

   Example: a have the opportunity to meet

2 The following sentences all contain phrasal verbs or expressions with *get*. Underline the correct alternative. There is an example at the beginning **(0)**.

   0 That jumper looks so old and dirty. When are you going to **get** *away/along/lost/rid* **of** it?
   1 Here's my telephone number. If you have any problems, just **get in** *talk/speak/touch/tact* **with** me.
   2 I heard she was a lovely woman. Unfortunately I never **got the** *occasion/event/ability/chance* **to** meet her.
   3 I asked him how much he **got** *paid/earned/money/salary* but he refused to tell me.
   4 Come on, hurry up and **get** *moved/ready/ordered/fit*! Your bus leaves in five minutes.
   5 His parents are concerned about his behaviour. He's always **getting into** *problem/trouble/punishment/damage* at school.
   6 His girlfriend left him in March and he still hasn't **got** *past/off/by/over* it.
   7 I can't speak French very well, but I always manage to **get** *across/through/by/over* with a dictionary and a few gestures.
   8 They wanted to get to the opera house but they **got** *up/out of/on/off* the wrong bus and ended up at the football stadium.

3 Discuss the following questions.

   • How quickly do you **get ready for school/work** in the morning?
   • How do you **get to school/work**? How long does it take you to get there?
   • Did/Do you often **get into trouble** at school? What was the worst thing you ever did?
   • Did/Do your parents ever **get you to do any jobs** around the house? How did/do you feel about this?
   • What sort of things do you do when you **get angry**? How quickly do you **get over your anger**?

Vocabulary 3: Clothes

1 How many of the items of clothing in the photographs can you name?

2 The following adjectives can be used to describe clothes. Which of them can you match to the photographs?

tight-fitting	formal	tasteful	trendy
baggy	colourful	unfashionable	scruffy
casual	plain	smart	sleeveless

Listening 1
Part 3

Multiple matching 1.1–1.5

You will hear five different people talking about occasions when a person's clothes and appearance caused surprise or concern. For questions **1–5**, match the speaker to the correct occasion in the list **A–H** on page 13. Use the letters only once. There are three extra letters which you do not need to use.

Before you do the task …

Prediction

guest
spectator
audience
competitor
witness
star
candidate
host
invigilator
opponent

1 Match each of the people in the box to the appropriate occasion **A–H** in the listening task on page 13. More than one word may be used for each occasion and some words may be used twice.

  e.g. A wedding: guest, witness

What other people might you also find in each of the situations?

  e.g. At a wedding the people who get married are the bride and groom.

2 Where does each occasion take place?

  e.g. A wedding usually takes place in a church or a registry office.

3 What clothes would you personally wear on the occasions **A–H** mentioned in the listening task on page 13?

  e.g. If I was going to a wedding, I would buy an expensive dress. I would probably wear high-heeled shoes.

Now you are ready to do the task.

What to expect in the exam

- You will have 30 seconds to read the eight options. Use this time to try to predict some of the ideas and language you might hear, as you did on page 12.

- Some of the extracts may contain distractors (key words or expressions which could cause you to make the wrong decision). Pay close attention both times you hear the recording.

A a wedding

B a friend's birthday party

C a classical ballet

D a sporting event

E a film premiere

F an examination

G a job interview

H a special family meal

Speaker 1 ☐ 1

Speaker 2 ☐ 2

Speaker 3 ☐ 3

Speaker 4 ☐ 4

Speaker 5 ☐ 5

 Have you ever been in a situation where someone's appearance caused surprise?

Language focus 2: *Be used to, get used to* and *used to*

1 Look at the following sentences from the listening. In which of them does *used to*

a mean 'accustomed to'?

b refer to a past state which has now finished?

1 *Her unconventional, yet practical clothing shocked spectators, who **were used to** seeing women play in the long, heavy dresses which were typical of that period.*

2 *And he **used to** live in France, which means he probably wouldn't mind changing countries if we needed him to.*

3 *…he will have to **get used to** wearing something a little more formal.*

2 What is the difference in meaning between *be used to* and *get used to*?

3 What form of the verb is used after *be used to* and *get used to*?

Check your answers on page 209 of the Grammar reference.

4 Talk about all the things you have to *get used to* in the following situations:

- you get your first job
- you become famous
- you go on a diet
- you get married
- you have children
- you retire

Example:
In a new job, you might have to get used to working together with other people.

5 a If you went to live in Britain, what aspects of life there would you find it difficult to *get used to*?

b Read the following text about Juan, who moved from Spain to live in England. Ignore the gaps for the moment. How many of the things which you spoke about in **a** are mentioned?

Now that Juan has been living in England for five years he **(0)** _is_ used to _doing_ (do) things differently, but it hasn't always been the case. When he first moved there he couldn't **(1)** _____ used to _____ (have) lunch at 1pm, so he often **(2)** _____ used to _____ (cook) for himself in his flat and eat at 3pm, as his family does in Spain. Even now I don't think he **(3)** _____ used to _____ (eat) English food, because when he comes home to Madrid, he buys Spanish 'delicacies' to take back with him.

I remember how he **(4)** _____ used to _____ (write) to me and complain about the shop closing times. It took him a long time to **(5)** _____ used to not _____ (be) able to buy anything after about five o'clock. Most shops in Spain close at eight or nine in the evening.

He bought an English car a year ago, so he should **(6)** _____ used to _____ (drive) on the left by now. I wonder if he'll ever be able to **(7)** _____ used to _____ (drive) on the right again when, or if, he comes back to live in Spain!

c Read the text again.

In the first gap write either *be, is, get,* or leave it blank.
In the second gap write the correct form of the verb in brackets.
There is an example at the beginning **(0)**.

d What do you think a British person coming to your country might find it difficult to *get used to*?

Writing
Part 2

Informal letter

1   Read the following letter, which you have received from your English friend, Mark.

What two things does he ask you to tell him?

Would you accept Mark's invitation? Why/Why not?

> Dear _____ ,
>
> **a)** <u>Many thanks for your last letter.</u> The new house sounds brilliant – how are you settling in? **b)** <u>I'm sorry I haven't written sooner,</u> but I've been really busy helping my parents out on the farm.
>
> It's great fun, though I still haven't got used to getting up at six every morning to milk the cows! We often have the radio on while we're doing it, so it's not too bad. Then, once we've had breakfast, we tend to spend the rest of the day outside, either in the fields or looking after the sheep.
>
> **c)** <u>That reminds me,</u> do you remember Lady, our oldest sheepdog? Well, she's just had puppies! If you're free in the summer, you could come and see them all and help with the harvest as well. **d)** <u>Let me know</u> if you can make it – we'd love to see you again.
>
> Anyway, **e)** <u>I must go,</u> as it's getting late and tomorrow we've got another early start. **f)** <u>Can't wait to hear from you.</u>
>
> **g)** <u>Best wishes</u>
>
> Mark

2   What is the purpose of each of the four paragraphs?

Example:

Paragraph 1: To say thank you for the letter and to apologize for not writing before.

3   Match each underlined expression **a–g** from Mark's letter with an appropriate alternative from **1–10**. Which three phrases cannot be used and why are they inappropriate?

Example: 1 e)

1 I'd better close now   6 I would be most grateful if you could inform me

2 Thanks a lot for the letter   7 I look forward to your prompt reply

3 Yours sincerely   8 Please write and tell me

4 By the way   9 I'm sorry it's taken me so long to write to you

5 All the best   10 I'm looking forward to hearing from you

Notice the use of contractions in Mark's letter: *I'm, it's* and *haven't*. These are typical of informal writing.

4   Find and circle the following linking words in Mark's letter. Then use an appropriate linker from the box to complete the gaps in sentences **1–5** on page 15. Each linker can be used more than once.

but   while   so   and   as well   as

1 You'll never guess what happened to me _____ I was shopping in the centre of town the other day!

2 I'm writing to ask you to do me a favour _____ I've got myself into trouble.

3 We're having a party next Saturday _____ we were wondering if you'd like to come. Bring a friend _____ .

4 I'd love to accept your invitation, _____ I'm afraid I'm going to be busy.

5 I haven't got any plans _____ I'll certainly be able to go.

5 Read the following instructions.

Six months ago you moved to a new house in another part of your country. Write a reply to Mark's letter giving news about how you are settling in to your new surroundings and what a typical day is like. You should also say whether or not you can accept his invitation to go and stay on his farm in the summer.

Write your **letter** in **140–190** words.

How to go about it

- Begin by referring in some way to the letter you have received from Mark.
- Use some of the informal language and linkers that you have just studied.
- Organize your letter into logical paragraphs, as in the letter from Mark.

Listening 2 | **Part 1**

Multiple choice ◉ 1.6–1.13

You will hear people talking in eight different situations. For questions **1–8**, choose the best answer (**A, B** or **C**).

What to expect in the exam

- The eight recorded extracts are either monologues or conversations. You hear each one twice.
- You will hear distractors. Listen carefully both times to the whole of each extract.

1 You hear two people talking about a friend of theirs. What does the woman say about the friend?

A He talks a lot about his lifestyle.

B He leads a comfortable lifestyle.

C He may change his lifestyle.

2 You overhear a man talking to a friend on his mobile phone. Why is he phoning?

A to persuade his friend to do something

B to ask for some information

C to change an arrangement

3 You hear a woman talking about her family's financial situation. What is she going to do?

A ask someone to help her

B try to find a job

C sell something valuable

4 You overhear a man and a woman talking about their morning routine.
How does the man feel about his mornings?

A He hates travelling to work.

B He does not like getting up early.

C He finds it difficult to talk to other people.

5 You hear a woman on the radio talking about her experiences in a foreign country.
What surprised her about the people?

A the importance they give to clothes

B the type of food they eat

C their attitude to work

6 You turn on the radio and hear the following.
What is it?

A a review

B a news report

C an advertisement

7 You hear two people talking about the village they both live in.
What does the woman think of the village?

A People are not always very friendly.

B Some of the roads are dangerous.

C There are not enough children.

8 You hear a man talking about his job.
Who is the man?

A a hotel doorman

B a hotel receptionist

C a hotel manager

Transformations

For questions **1–6**, complete the second sentence so that it has a similar meaning to the first sentence, using the word given. **Do not change the word given.** You must use between **two** and **five** words, including the word given. Here is an example **(0)**.

0 How long was your journey from London to Manchester?

TAKE

How long ___*DID IT TAKE YOU TO*___ get from London to Manchester?

Write the missing words **IN CAPITAL LETTERS**.

What to expect in the exam

- The second sentence of a transformation is a paraphrase of the first sentence; it expresses the same idea but with different words.
- Transformations test your knowledge of grammar, vocabulary and collocation.

  In the transformations below, all the language which is tested appears in Unit 1, including the Grammar reference on page 209.

- More than one feature of grammar and/or vocabulary may be tested in a single transformation.

  In number **1** below, for example, consider:

  – the verb and preposition used with the word *rid*.

  – the form of the verb after *How about*.

1 Why don't you throw away that old blouse?

RID

How about _____ that old blouse?

2 I still find it strange to wear glasses.

USED

I still haven't _____ glasses.

3 He never asks when he borrows my things!

ALWAYS

He is _____ asking!

4 Simon doesn't usually drink coffee.

UNUSUAL

It _____ drink coffee.

5 Helen is not usually so pessimistic.

LIKE

It is _____ so pessimistic.

6 I can't wait to see you again.

FORWARD

I'm really _____ you again.

Vocabulary

A Adjectives

For questions **1–6**, decide which of the three words is not normally used with the word in capitals at the end of the line. The first one has been done for you.

1 evening	<u>afternoon</u>	fancy	DRESS
2 high-heeled	expensive	tasteful	HAT
3 scruffy	plain	tight-fitting	SCARF
4 unfashionable	sleeveless	trendy	SHOES
5 stressful	baggy	chaotic	LIFESTYLE
6 long-sleeved	modern	traditional	WAY OF LIFE

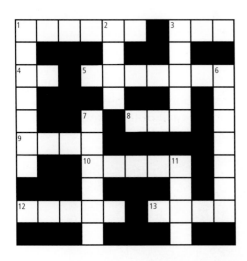

B Expressions crossword

Expressions for use in informal letters

Across

1 Many _____ for your letter.
5 I'm looking _____ to hearing from you.
8 By the _____ , how did the exam go?
9 Write back soon.

_____ ,
Susie

12 I'm sorry it's _____ me so long to write to you.

Down

2 Let me _____ if you can make it.
7 Anyway, I'd _____ close now.
11 Can't wait to _____ from you.

Expressions with *get*

Across

3 Chewing gum is forbidden in class – get _____ of it now!
4 If you don't get _____ the train now, it'll leave without you!
10 They said they'd get in _____ with me, but so far they haven't written or phoned.
13 How much do you get _____ a week in your job?

Down

1 He's always getting into _____ with the police.
3 Turn off the television right now and get _____ for school.
6 I had a shower, got _____ and then went out for a walk.

C People

Each of the words for people **1–6** has a relationship of some kind with one of the words **a–f**. Match the words and then use them to complete the sentences below. You may need to use plural forms.

1 invigilator   a groom
2 host   b spectator
3 bride   c patient
4 competitor   d audience
5 performer   e candidate
6 doctor   f guest

1 The youngest _____ in the stadium surprised the _____ by winning the 400 metres in record time.
2 The only person I recognized at the party was the _____ ; I didn't know any of the other _____ .
3 The _____ and _____ looked very happy as they walked back down the aisle after the ceremony.
4 Many members of the _____ left the theatre before the end of the play, disappointed at the acting of some of the _____ .
5 After a thorough examination the _____ could find nothing wrong with his _____ .
6 One of the _____ was caught cheating in the exam by the _____ .

Writing

Write a short article of **140–190** words about your lifestyle. Use texts **A–D** in the article on pages 8 and 9 as models. Include some of the vocabulary and grammatical structures you have studied in this unit.

2 High energy

Reading and Speaking

Look at the photos on pages 18 and 19 and read about the shows. Talk with your partner about how much you think you would enjoy each of the shows, giving reasons. Then agree on one show which you could both see together.

Pagagnini

An innovative musical show that brings to life some of the world's best-loved pieces of classical music. But *Pagagnini* is more than just a concert: the musicians dance, laugh, cry and generally clown around in one of the most original comedy acts of the moment.

Rhythm of the Dance

This two-hour dance and music extravaganza contains a wealth of Irish talent. The show relives the journey of the Irish Celts throughout history, combining traditional dance and music with the most up-to-date stage technology.

Vocabulary 1: Music

1   a How many of the musical instruments in the photographs can you name?

b All the words in each of the groups below can be used in combination with one of the words in the box. Write an appropriate word from the box in each of the gaps. There is an example at the beginning **(0)**.

| play (v) |
| rock |
| lead (adj) |
| on |
| in |
| instrument |
| live (adj) |
| a song |
| musician |

0		band	3	talented	6		album
	rock	singer		rock			performance
		star		session			music
1		vocalist	4		tour	7		the charts
	_____	singer		_____	stage		_____	concert
		guitarist			the radio			tune
						8	percussion	
2	sing		5		a track		wind	_____
	perform	_____		_____	a tune		stringed	
	mime				a record			

2   Study the word combinations in exercise **1b** for two minutes. Then cover the exercise. How many word combinations can you remember?

3   Work in small groups. You are on the organizing committee for a local charity and you want to raise money. Here are some events which have been suggested.

- A classical music concert given by a local orchestra
- A sale of second-hand CDs and records
- A talk given by a local jazz musician
- A series of music workshops led by local musicians.
- The auction of an electric guitar donated by a world famous rock star

Discuss how successful you think each event would be. Then decide which two events would raise the most money.

Cirque Éloize – *iD*
Sixteen artists on stage, thirteen circus disciplines, and a world of urban dances such as breakdance and hip-hop. The rock, electronic and poetic music, together with the presence of video, highlight the show's playful, energetic, and youthful aspects.
Jeannot Painchaud (Director)

Tap Dogs
Tap Dogs are currently taking the world by storm with their tap show that combines the strength and power of workmen with the precision and talent of tap dancing.

Sentence completion 🔘 1.14

1 **a** Read these Listening Part 2 instructions and the What to expect in the exam box.

You will hear a radio presenter called Jim Dunne talking about local entertainment options. For questions **1–10**, complete the sentences.

What to expect in the exam

- The words you *read* in the question may not be the same as the words you *hear* in the recording, e.g. Question 1:
  You **read**: *Jim recommends Pagagnini to …*
  You **hear**: *I can guarantee … will enjoy watching these four guys.*
- However, the word(s) you need to write are actually heard in the recording.

- You may hear information which could fit the gap but does not answer the question.
  e.g. In question 2 below you will hear the names of two places mentioned. Listen carefully to ensure you choose the right one.
- You do not need to write more than three words for each answer.
- Minor spelling errors can be made (*e.g. musicall*) but the words must be recognizable.

b 🔘 Read questions **1–10** and, as you do so, discuss the type of information you might need to write for each one.

Example: 1 This is probably a person or a group of people.

c Listen to the recording twice and complete the sentences.

Jim recommends *Pagagnini* to the **(1)** ...whole family...

Jim saw a *Pagagnini* concert last year in **(2)** ...Mexico... (based in Madrid)

As well as classical music, *Pagagnini* play rock, blues and **(3)** ...country western...

Jim says the *Pagagnini* show has no **(4)** ...interval / interlude...

The first performance of *Rhythm of the Dance* was in **(5)** ...1999... in Norway.

More than **(6)** ...4 million... people have seen *Rhythm of the Dance* live on stage. (44 countries)

Jim suggests listeners look at the section entitled **(7)** ...photo gallery... on the *Rhythm of the Dance* website.

The name of the first show that the Cirque Éloize performed at the Regent Theatre was **(8)** '...Rain...'

Some performers in *iD* appear on **(9)** ...bikes... and Rollerblades™.

One review of *iD* says it is full of originality, energy and **(10)** ...excitment...

2 🔘 Having listened to Jim Dunne, do you feel the same about the different shows as when you did the Reading and Speaking activity on page 18? Why/Why not?

Language focus 1: Indirect ways of asking questions

1 Compare these two ways of asking the same question:

Direct: *What time does the Pagagnini concert start?*

Indirect: *Could you tell me* what time the Pagagnini concert starts?

Asking questions in a more indirect way, using expressions such as *Could you tell me,* can make them sound more polite. Write the direct form of the following questions:

1 <u>I'd be interested to know</u> when Rhythm of the Dance started performing.

When _____ ?

2 <u>Would you mind telling me</u> why you call the show *iD*?

_____

3 <u>I'd like to know</u> if the Tap Dogs are planning to come here.

_____

2 Compare the direct and the indirect questions in exercise **1** above and answer the following questions:

a In numbers **1** and **2**, what happens to the **auxiliary verbs** *did* and *do* when the indirect question form is used? How are the main verbs *start* and *call* affected?

b In number **3**, what differences are there between the **word order** of the direct question and that of the indirect question?

c In number **3**, where **no question word** (*when, how, what, where* etc) appears in the direct question, which word has to be added in the indirect question?

🅖 Check your ideas on page 209 of the Grammar reference.

3 Questions **a–f** were prepared by a music journalist planning to interview one of the members of *Pagagnini.* Rewrite them to make them indirect. If possible, choose a different phrase from the box to begin each one.

I'd be interested to know …   Could you explain … Would you mind telling us …   We'd like to know … Could you tell me …   I was wondering if you could tell me …

a Why are you called 'Pagagnini'?

_____

b When did you start performing together?

_____

c Have you ever toured outside of Europe?

_____

d What type of music do you prefer playing?

_____

e How many hours do you practise your instrument each day?

_____

f Do you clown around when you're off stage as well?

_____

4 a Student A: Write six indirect questions which you could ask a member of *Rhythm of the Dance.*

Student B: Write six indirect questions which you could ask a member of *Cirque Éloize.*

b 🔘 Take turns to roleplay an interview in which your partner answers the questions you have prepared in **a**.

Writing 1
Part 2

Letter of application

1 a Read the following Writing Part 2 instructions.

You see the following advertisement in your local English-language newspaper:

> ## MUSICIANS AND DANCERS REQUIRED
>
> We need teaching assistants for the music and dance activities at our English-language summer school for young children.
>
> If you can speak English and believe you have the right skills to teach music and/or dance to young people, you are the right person for us.
>
> Write to the director, Paul Beacon, and explain why you would be a suitable person for the job.

Write your **letter of application**.

b Read the letter of application on page 21. Ignore the words and expressions in **bold** (**1–10**) and answer the following question.

Do you think the applicant would be suitable for the job which is advertised? Give reasons for your answer.

Dear (1) **Paul**

(2) **I've had a look at** your advertisement in the latest edition of 'English Weekly' and (3) **I want to ask** for a job as a music and dance teacher at your summer school.

I am a twenty-year-old music student in my second year at university and can play several instruments, including piano, violin and clarinet. (4) **I've also been going to** a local dance academy for the past twelve years and am a member of a modern-dance group called 'Pasos'.

Although (5) **I've never done any jobs** working with groups of children, I teach piano and violin to (6) **quite a lot** of young private students. In addition, I choreograph many of the dances for 'Pasos' and teach the steps to the other members of the group.

(7) **I reckon** I would be (8) **really good at** this job, as I am a very calm and patient person. My whole life is devoted to music and dance and (9) **it'd be great if I could** pass on my skills to other people.

(10) **Can't wait to hear** from you.

Yours sincerely

Sandra Agar

2   When writing a letter of application to the director of a summer school, a formal style is appropriate. However, in Sandra Agar's application above, the words and expressions in **bold** (1–10) are more appropriate to an informal letter. Replace each one with a formal alternative from the box below.

   Example: 1 Mr Beacon

I have no experience	I would like to apply	I feel
I look forward to hearing	I have seen	well-suited to
I have also been attending	~~Mr Beacon~~	a number
I would love to have the opportunity to		

3   Which linking words does Sandra use in her letter.
   Example: also

4   What is the purpose of each of the four main paragraphs in Sandra's letter?
   Example: Paragraph 1: Her reason for writing

5   Read the How to go about it box on page 202 before you do the following Writing Part 2 task.

   You see the following advertisement in your local English-language newspaper:

   # ARE YOU A MUSIC FAN?

   We require English-speaking volunteers to help at a four-day international pop and rock music festival aimed at raising money for charity.

   • What relevant music-related interests do you have?

   • Do you have experience of working with people?

   • How would you benefit from helping at this event?

   Write to Paul Groves at *Music for Life* explaining why you would be suitable as a volunteer.

   Write your **letter of application** in 140–190 words.

Gapped text

1 ⬤ You are going to read an article about the game of rugby. Look at the photographs, which show men and women playing rugby, and discuss the following questions.

How much do you know about rugby? What are some of the rules of the game?

The article you are going to read says that '*rugby is rather like chess*': why do you think it makes this comparison?

2 Read through the base text (the main text with the gaps). Are any of your ideas from exercise **1** mentioned?

3 Six sentences have been removed from the article. Choose from the sentences **A–G** the one which fits each gap (**1–6**). There is one extra sentence which you do not need to use.

How to go about it

- Check that the whole sentence fits in with the meaning of the text before *and* after the gap.

  To help you do this, some words and phrases are written in **bold**. These show connections between the language in the text and the language in the missing sentences. A number of grammatical words such as *them, this* and *these* are written in *italics* to show further connections.

  Note: these connections are not shown in the *First* examination.

- Now look at gap number **1**. The words in **bold** before and after the gap indicate that the missing sentence:

  a refers <u>back</u> to the words *uncomplicated* and *get points*

  b refers <u>forward</u> to the different ways of getting points.

  When you think you have found the sentence, read the whole paragraph again to check that it fits.

- Now complete each of the remaining gaps with an appropriate sentence. Do not choose a sentence simply because it contains a word which also appears in the base text. For example, the word *obstacles,* before gap number **2**, is repeated in sentence **G**, but this does not necessarily mean that **G** is the correct answer.

- When you have finished, check that the sentence which you have not used does not fit into any of the gaps.

How to play ... rugby

Welcome to a sport which will enchant and excite you, and take you to the heights and the depths of human emotion. Learn the rules and you will be unable to resist it.

Rugby is a game of 40-minute halves with the most **uncomplicated** of objectives – to **get** more **points** than your opponent. [1   ] You either **touch the ball down over your opponents' line**, known as a try, for
5 five points, or **kick the ball over your opponent's posts;** three points for a dropped goal and a penalty, two points for a conversion (kicking the ball between the posts after a try).

The complexities in rugby arise as a result of the **obstacles** which are put in every rugby player's path to make it **harder** for him to score points. [2   ] **This can be done in three ways**: by **throwing you to the ground**, by teaming up with other players to **push against you** when you have the ball in your hands or by
10 **pushing against you** when the ball is on the ground.

There is also the **law** that says **the ball can only be passed backwards**. [3   ] **This is clearly rather difficult to do when you have fifteen very large opponents standing in front of you** ready to throw you to the floor if they get anywhere near you.

Each team is made up of eight forwards and seven backs. The job of the forwards is to get the ball for the
15 quicker, lighter backs to score. **Rugby is rather like chess:** chess pieces have special functions, in the same way that rugby players have specific tasks to perform. Within these roles they both employ various moves to get to the other side. [4   ] **Rugby is a game in which all the players work together**, and the better their relationships and understanding of one another, the better their chances of getting one of their team to the try-line.

20 [5   ] The tools you need to **overcome them** are simple: time and space. When you hear commentators talking of tactics or strategies, they're just talking about the various ways in which you 'create space' or 'make time'. For example, if the backs keep passing along the line they will eventually run into problems, as the last player has no one else to pass to, and no space to run in. He'll get thrown off the pitch by the opposition, and the ball will go to them.

25 There are **tactics like miss-moves** (missing someone out in the line so that a defending player runs the wrong way and leaves a gap) **and dummies** (pretending to pass so the opposition runs the wrong way). [6   ]

There are a few other things which could be mentioned, but basically, rugby is nowhere near as complicated as it looks. It is, after all, just a game.

A The point at which rugby becomes **much more fun than a board game** is in its **team dynamics**.

B **However, this complexity in the rules** of rugby does not make the game any less exciting to play, or indeed, to watch.

C **The methods of scoring** are **equally simple**.

D Because of *this* **rule, players have to run forwards** or they'll end up back on their own line.

E *These strategies* are *both* **ways of tricking the opposition** into opening up a gap in the defence for you to run through before you run out of space.

F *One such* **difficulty** is that the opposing team can **physically stop you from scoring**.

G **Now we know the aim** of playing rugby, **and the nature of the obstacles** that stand in the way, we need to look at **how to deal with these obstacles**.

⬤ Reacting to the text

Would you be interested in watching or playing rugby? Why/Why not?

Are there any sports you have not played but would like to try out? If so, which one(s)?

Language focus 2: Gerunds and infinitives

1 Look at the underlined words in the following extracts from the reading text. For each one, explain why a gerund, an infinitive without *to*, or an infinitive with *to* is used.

Example:
a <u>to make</u>: *the infinitive with to is used to express purpose, the reason why something is done.*

a ... *the obstacles which are put in every rugby player's path <u>to make</u> it harder for him <u>to score</u> points*
b *This can <u>be done</u> ... by <u>throwing</u> you to the ground.*
c ... *the backs keep <u>passing</u> along the line ...*
d ... *we need <u>to look</u> at how to deal with these obstacles.*

2 Some verbs can be followed by a gerund and some others can be followed by an infinitive with *to*. Complete each of the following sentences using the correct form of the verb in brackets. One verb in each sentence will be a gerund, the other an infinitive with *to*.

1 When I **suggested** _____ (go) skiing at the weekend she was extremely enthusiastic and we **arranged** _____ (meet) at seven o'clock on Saturday morning.
2 I **can't help** _____ (smile) when I see my dad playing tennis. He's had hundreds of lessons but he still hasn't **learnt** _____ (hit) the ball properly.
3 Paul **seems** _____ (enjoy) playing golf. He's even **considering** _____ (buy) his own set of clubs.
4 One of my cousins has **promised** _____ (take) me windsurfing as soon as I've **finished** _____ (study).
5 At first my parents **refused** _____ (let) me go to karate lessons, but I **kept** _____ (ask) and eventually they agreed.

3 Some verbs can be followed by more than one verb form. Underline the correct alternatives in the following sentences. In some sentences more than one alternative is correct.

1 It **started** *rain/to rain/raining* so they had to postpone the match.
2 I only **stopped** *have/to have/having* a rest once during the whole marathon.
3 Jones **continued** *play/to play/playing* football professionally until he was forty.
4 These exercises should **help** you *run/to run/running* faster.
5 **Remember** *drink/to drink/drinking* water before the race.
6 Sally **tried** *use/to use/using* a heavier racket, and she played a little better.

 Read the Grammar reference on pages 209–10 and check your answers.

4 The verbs in the box can be used to talk about our likes and dislikes. They are all usually followed by the gerund.

Write each verb in an appropriate place on the line below according to the strength of its meaning.

really enjoy	don't mind	quite like
detest	can't stand	don't like
love	absolutely adore	hate

STRONG DISLIKE ⊢―――――――――――⊣ **STRONG LIKE**
detest   *absolutely adore*

5 Certain adjectives followed by a preposition and the gerund can also be used to talk about what does and doesn't interest you. Study the following table and complete each space with a preposition from the box. The first one has been done for you.

at	in	~~on~~	about	with	of

	adjective + preposition	noun or gerund
I'm (really)	keen ___on___	sport/cinema etc
I'm not (really)	interested _____	listening to ... etc
I've never been	fond _____	watching ...
I've always been	good/bad _____	playing ...
I get (really)	bored _____	doing ...
I never get	excited _____	going ...

6 Write eight sentences about your likes and dislikes using the language you have just studied.

Examples:
Preposition + gerund: *I never **get excited** about going to the cinema.*

Verb + gerund: *I quite **like listening** to jazz.*

Gerund as subject: ***Collecting** postcards is one of my favourite pastimes.*

7  Compare your sentences with your partner's. Ask questions about each other's likes and dislikes.
Example:
A: *I've always been keen on going to the cinema.*

B: *How often do you go?*

A: *I tend to go once every two weeks or so.*

B: *And what are your favourite films?*

A: *Well, I really enjoy watching science fiction, but I don't like films with a lot of violence. I get bored very easily if there are lots of deaths.*

You may be asked to talk about your interests in Part 1 of the Speaking test. Make sure you develop your answers, explaining and justifying your opinions.

Vocabulary 2: Sport

1 Underline the correct alternative in these extracts from the reading text on page 23.

a You *foot/kick/give/fire* the ball over your opponent's *sticks/poles/pillars/posts*.

b ... obstacles which are put in every rugby player's path to make it harder for him to *do/goal/score/mark* points ...

c ... the ball can only be *given/presented/passed/changed* backwards.

d ... chess *pieces/parts/packs/portions* have special functions ...

e He'll get thrown off the *court/pitch/track/camp* by the opposition ...

Check your answers on page 23.

2 Can you name all the sports in the pictures? Write the name of each sport next to the verb which it is used with. The first one has been done for you.

do _____*athletics*_____.

go _____

play _____

3 **a** Write the name of the sport with which each group of four nouns is associated. The first one has been done for you.

1 _*tennis*_	court	net	racket	backhand
2 _____	pitch	referee	corner	foul
3 _____	course	green	clubs	hole
4 _____	slope	sticks	run	goggles
5 _____	track	field event	lane	meeting
6 _____	saddle	helmet	pedals	peloton

b Add each of these nouns to the appropriate group in **a**.

red card	fairway	gears	lift	service	triple jump

4 **a** Complete each gap with a verb from the box.

beat	draw	hit	take	take	win

1 Which sports _____ **place** on an ice rink?

2 Which country's football team _____ Holland to win the 2010 World Cup Final?

3 Which **medal** does a runner-up _____ ?

4 In which sports do you _____ **the ball** with a racket?

5 How many players from each team can _____ **part** at one time in a game of basketball?

6 If two hockey teams _____ **nil–nil**, how many goals are scored?

b  Answer the questions in **a**.

5 Work in pairs.

Student A Choose a sport and explain the rules to your partner.

Student B Imagine that you are not familiar with your partner's sport. Ask your partner any questions that are necessary to help you fully understand the rules.

When you have finished, change roles.

Listening 2
Part 4

Multiple choice ● 1.15

1 ● Look at the photographs of unusual sports. What do you think contestants have to do in each one?

2 You will hear a man talking on the radio about unusual sports. For questions **1–7**, choose the best answer (**A, B** or **C**).

What to expect in the exam

- Look at question **1** below and the following extract from the listening script. The underlined sections contain words which are the same or similar to words in all three of the possible answers **A**, **B** and **C**. Only one of these sections matches an answer; the others are distractors. Decide which is the correct answer and say why the others are incorrect.

Now you may think this is just a bit of fun, but when I watched two men competing in a televised match last year, _I was amazed by their level of skill in each of these two very different disciplines_. After all, _boxing is such an aggressive, violent sport_ – it's about using the body, whereas chess is all about using the brain.

- Although a particular option may be true, it may not be the correct answer to the question you are asked. In question **2**, all three statements are true but only one is something that _Mike finds it difficult to believe_.

1 When Mike saw a chess boxing match, he was surprised by
  - **A** how skilled the competitors were at both parts of the sport.
  - **B** how much fun the competitors were having.
  - **C** how aggressive the competitors were.

2 Having read about octopushing, Mike finds it difficult to believe that
  - **A** players do not have to hold their breath for long intervals.
  - **B** a high level of fitness is not required to play it.
  - **C** it is an exciting sport to watch.

3 What does Mike say about wife carrying?
  - **A** Male competitors must not be over a certain weight.
  - **B** The name of the sport is not entirely appropriate.
  - **C** The sport has a lot of complicated rules.

4 What is Mike's criticism of sports like wife carrying?
  - **A** They are not suitable for young children.
  - **B** They should not really be called sports.
  - **C** They are not worth taking seriously.

5 What do we learn about the organizers of toe wrestling?
  - **A** They apply what they learn from international competitions.
  - **B** They have arranged a number of events in schools.
  - **C** They made a request which was rejected.

6 How does Mike feel about the human triumphs in the Man Versus Horse Marathon?
  - **A** They are very surprising.
  - **B** They deserve more recognition.
  - **C** They are unlikely to be repeated.

7 Why did Mike give up running?
  - **A** He was injured.
  - **B** He lost interest.
  - **C** He had no time.

3 ● Would you be interested in taking part in or watching any of the sports Mike mentions? Why/Why not?

Do you have any strange sports in your country? What do the competitors do?

Word formation: Affixes

1 Add an appropriate suffix, **-or, -er** or **-ant**, to each of the verbs in the box to form nouns for the people who perform these actions. You may need to make further spelling changes to the verbs.

Example: win – winner

win	box	play	spectate	compete	participate
listen	organize	run	ride	contest	

Check your answers in the listening script on pages 223–4.

2 Add either **-ist, -eer, -ee** or **-ian** to the pairs of words below to form the nouns for the corresponding people. Use the same suffix for both words in each pair. You may need to make further spelling changes.

employ/train   electric/politics   novel/science   mountain/engine

3 In **1–7** below, use the same prefix from the box with all three adjectives to make them negative. The first one has been done for you.

dis-	un-	in-	ir-	il-	im-

Adjectives   **Negative**

1 lucky/concerned/reliable   *unlucky/unconcerned/unreliable*
2 experienced/competent/tolerant   _____
3 legal/logical/legible   _____
4 moral/mature/modest   _____
5 practical/patient/perfect   _____
6 regular/responsible/relevant   _____
7 honest/obedient/satisfied   _____

4 What meaning do the prefixes in bold have in the following words?

undercook   **over**eat   **pre**historic   **post**graduate   **hyper**market
microelectronics   **mis**spell   **re**write   **ex**-wife   **extra**terrestrial

Writing 2
Part 2

Article

Read the following Writing Part 2 instructions.
You have just seen this advertisement.

Write your **article** in **140–190** words.

INTERNATIONAL SPORTS WEEKLY

• What is your favourite sport?
• Why do you like it?
• What advice would you give to someone who wants to take it up?

We are looking for short articles answering these questions and we will publish some of the best articles next month.

How to go about it

• Before you write your article, read the model and analysis on page 202.
• To help you plan your article, answer the following questions and make notes.

Paragraph 1:
What is your favourite sport?
What is special about it?

Paragraph 2:
Why do you like it?
What are the benefits of doing it?

Paragraph 3:
What advice can you give to people who want to take it up?
Are any special qualities, equipment or clothes needed?

Paragraph 4:
What final encouragement can you give?

• Give your article a title and include some of the features of style from page 202.

Word formation

1 In **1–6** below, one of each of the four words is not normally used. Underline the word.

1 undercook	undercharge	underestimate	undersleep
2 overgrown	overweight	overlittle	overcrowded
3 overeat	oversing	oversleep	overwork
4 misbehave	misunderstand	misspell	missucceed
5 dislove	dishonesty	disappearance	disobedience
6 uncommon	unselfish	unglad	unreliable

2 For questions **1–6**, complete each of the gaps with the correct form of one of the words from exercise **1**.

1 These jeans should have cost £70, but the assistant made a mistake and _____ me. I only paid £50 for them.

2 The house has been abandoned for years. That's why the garden is looking so _____ .

3 I'm sorry I'm late. My alarm didn't go off, so I _____ .

4 You've _____ my surname. There are two 't's in Hutton, not one.

5 Police are investigating the _____ of confidential documents from the Prime Minister's office.

6 Paul comes to school tired, and it is not _____ for him to fall asleep in class.

3 Now write five sentences of your own using some of the other words from exercise **1**. Leave a space in each sentence where the word should be and ask another student to complete them.

Reading and Use of English
Part 3

Word formation

For questions **1–8**, read the text below. Use the word given in capitals at the end of some of the lines to form a word that fits in the space **in the same line**. There is an example at the beginning **(0)**. Write your answers **IN CAPITAL LETTERS.**

The Celebrated Pedestrian

Pedestrianism, an early form of racewalking, was an **(0)** ___EXTREMELY___ popular   **EXTREME**
sport in 18th- and 19th-century Britain, attracting huge crowds of **(1)** _____ .   **SPECTATE**
Individuals would either aim to walk a certain **(2)** _____ within a specified   **DISTANT**
period of time or else compete against other pedestrians. Cash prizes were offered
but **(3)** _____ could also earn substantial amounts from the money gambled   **PARTICIPATE**
on events.

Perhaps the most famous **(4)** _____ was Captain Robert Barclay Allardice,   **WALK**
whose **(5)** _____ achievements earned him the title of 'The Celebrated   **ORDINARY**
Pedestrian'. The Scotsman's most memorable **(6)** _____ took place in 1809,   **PERFORM**
when he walked 1000 miles (1609 kilometres) in 1000 hours for a bet of 1000
guineas. Many considered it **(7)** _____ that he would complete the challenge,   **LIKELY**
which required him to walk a mile an hour, every hour, for forty-two days and
nights. He proved them wrong, though the task was so **(8)** _____ demanding   **PHYSICAL**
that by the end of the walk he had lost nearly fifteen kilos in weight.

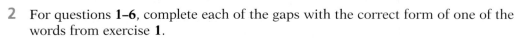

CAPTAIN BARCLAY

Gerunds and infinitives

Complete each of the gaps below with the correct form of the verb in brackets.

1 I've been meaning _____ (write) to you for ages but I just haven't had the time.

2 If we go skiing tomorrow, it'll mean _____ (get) up early. The slopes get crowded very quickly.

3 I wish you'd stop _____ (tap) your foot!

4 These long car journeys make me really hungry. Can we stop _____ (have) lunch soon?

5 When I tell you to be quiet, why must you always go on _____ (talk)?

6 After looking at verbs which take the gerund, we went on _____ (study) those which are followed by the infinitive.

7 I tried hard _____ (open) the window, but I couldn't move it. It was stuck.

8 These plants look as if they need a lot more light. Try _____ (put) them a little closer to the window.

Vocabulary

A Sport

Complete each gap with a suitable word.

1 Our hotel was right next to the golf _____ we played on every morning. In fact, our room overlooked the fairway of the eighteenth _____ .

2 The _____ blew his whistle to signal the end of the football match and hundreds of jubilant United fans ran onto the _____ to congratulate their players.

3 I'm useless at tennis: I can't even _____ the ball over the net with the _____ .

4 The _____ taking us to the top of the steepest ski _____ broke down halfway up and we were left hanging in the air for over an hour.

5 Over three thousand runners will take _____ in this year's marathon, which for the first time ever takes _____ on a Sunday.

6 Barcelona _____ Valencia 3–2, while Real Madrid could only _____ 1–1 at home to Rayo Vallecano.

B Music

Complete each of the gaps below with an appropriate word combination from page 18 of this unit. You may need to use nouns in the plural. There is an example at the beginning (0).

0 I never buy _live albums_ . You don't get the same quality of sound as you do with a studio recording.

1 Adele's latest album sounds great. I heard a couple of tracks _____ last night.

2 I spend all my time in piano lessons practising the scales. I still haven't learnt to

_____ .

3 Her last record only got as far as number ten _____ .

4 When groups make a record they often have to employ _____ to play some of the instruments.

5 That guitar sounds awful! Are you sure it's _____ ?

6 I hate it when they _____ on the TV. It's so obvious they aren't really singing.

7 The band is going _____ again next year. They'll be playing in nine European countries in three months.

8 Next on Capital Radio we're going to _____ from the latest 'Sidewinder' album. It's called _Ready for love_ – I hope you like it.

Vocabulary: Technology

1 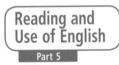 Look at the choices below. For each one, discuss the following questions, giving reasons for your answers:

Which, if any, of the alternatives do you tend to do more?

Would you prefer to do any of the other alternatives?

- phone people using a landline phone, a mobile phone or a personal computer
- use a hand-held mobile phone or a hands-free mobile phone with a headset or remote control
- use a tablet, personal computer, netbook, laptop, smartphone, or other device to log on to the Internet
- communicate with friends via email, text, chat rooms or social networking sites
- use textspeak or whole words when texting people
- buy CDs or download music
- watch films online, on DVD, TV or another device
- take photos with a digital camera, mobile phone, tablet or other device

2 Underline the correct alternative to complete the meanings of the items of textspeak. The first one has been done for you.

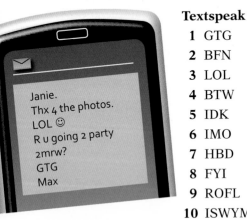

Textspeak	Meaning
1 GTG	glad/*got*/green to go
2 BFN	best/bye/break for now
3 LOL	laugh off/over/out loud
4 BTW	by/back/beyond the way
5 IDK	I don't kiss/know/kick
6 IMO	in my opinion/it's my office/I'm moving out
7 HBD	home before dark/happy birthday/had a big dinner
8 FYI	find your identity/free young individuals/for your information
9 ROFL	rolling on/off/out (the) floor laughing
10 ISWYM	I shop with your mum/I see what you mean/I still want your mobile

Reading and Use of English
Part 5

Multiple choice

1 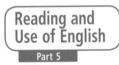 Read the following short paragraph and discuss the question.

You are going to read an article by Australian journalist Susan Maushart about her book *The Winter of Our Disconnect*. The book is an account of what she calls 'The Experiment', a six-month period during which she and her three teenage children stopped using most of their electronic media, such as computers, televisions, games consoles and mobile phones.

What effects do you think The Experiment had on the writer's family?

2 Read through the article quite quickly. Which, if any, of your ideas in exercise **1** are mentioned?

Digital detox: Why I pulled the plug on my family

There were lots of reasons why we pulled the plug on our electronic media ... or, I should say, why I did, because my children would rather have volunteered to go without food, water, or hair products. At ages 14, 15, and 18, my daughters Sussy and Anni and my son Bill don't use media. They inhabit media. And they do so
5 exactly as fish inhabit a pond. Gracefully and without consciousness or curiosity as to how they got there. They don't remember a time before email, or instant messaging, or Google.

When my children laugh, they don't say 'ha ha'. They say 'LOL'. They download movies and TV shows and when I remind them piracy is a crime, they look at one
10 another and go 'LOL'. These are children who shrug indifferently when they lose their iPods, with all 5000 tunes plus video clips, feature films, and 'TV' shows (like, who watches TV on a television anymore?). 'There's plenty more where that came from,' their attitude says. And the most infuriating thing of all? They're right. The digital content that powers their world can never truly be destroyed.

15 As a social scientist, journalist, and mother, I've always been an enthusiastic user of information technology. But I was also beginning to have doubts about the power of media to improve our lives – let alone to make them 'easier'. I'd noticed that the more we seemed to communicate as individuals, the less we seemed to function together as a family. And on a broader scale, that the more facts we have at our fingertips, the less we seem to know. That the 'convenience' of messaging media (email, SMS, IM) consumes ever larger amounts of our time. That as a culture we are practically swimming in entertainment, yet remain more depressed than any people who
20 have ever lived.

Our family's self-imposed exile from the information age changed our lives infinitely for the better. I watched as my children became more focused, logical thinkers. I watched as their attention spans increased, allowing them to read for hours at a time; to hold longer and more complex conversations with adults and among themselves; to improve their capacity to think beyond the present moment. They probably did no more homework during The
25 Experiment than they had done before, but they all completed it far more efficiently and far more quickly.

The older children took the opportunity to go out more – shopping, visiting, or clubbing in Anni's case, and hanging out at the pool or playing saxophone in somebody's garage in Bill's. The Experiment forced us to notice food more. Before, eating had been a side dish. Now it was the main course, or at least one of them. Our approach to cooking changed, too, especially for the girls. They'd started out as reasonably competent cooks,
30 but by the end of The Experiment they were capable of turning out entire meals with ease.

The Experiment also confirmed my strong suspicion that media had been robbing Sussy of sleep for years. She'd been our family's most militant multitasker, and the one who'd been attracted by a digital lifestyle at the youngest age. Unplugged, the changes to her sleep patterns, energy levels, and mood were correspondingly dramatic. The evidence strongly suggests she is no isolated case. One study found that children who spend more time online
35 also drink more caffeinated beverages, with a resulting effect on their prospects of sleeping well. 'Subjects who slept the least also multi-tasked the most,' the authors concluded.

No amount of talking to Anni, Bill, and Sussy could ever have persuaded them of the extent of their media dependence as eloquently as even a week without information technology. But by six months, the time had come to return to what our culture (rightly or wrongly) has decided is 'normal'.

3 Read the article again. For questions **1–6** on page 32, choose the answer (**A, B, C** or **D**) which you think fits best according to the text.

How to go about it

- Read the article first for an overall understanding. (You did this in exercise **2**.)
- Find the part of the article which relates to the question you are answering. As in the exam, the questions for this article appear in the same order as the information in the text.
- Eliminate the options which are clearly wrong, then check the option or options you have not eliminated.
- If you still cannot decide, choose one of the options. Marks are not deducted for incorrect answers.

1 The writer says her children 'inhabit media … as fish inhabit a pond' to show that
  A they have little interest in the outside world.
  B electronic media are a natural part of their lives.
  C electronic media have made them less intelligent.
  D their memory has been affected by using electronic media.

2 How does the writer describe her children's reaction to losing their iPods?
  A tearful
  B amused
  C indignant
  D unconcerned

3 What does the writer say about information technology in paragraph 3?
  A It has created a number of contradictions.
  B It is the main cause of depression today.
  C It is an unreliable source of information.
  D It has helped to simplify our daily lives.

4 The writer says that the period without electronic media enabled her children
  A to get to know a wide range of people.
  B to pay more attention to news events.
  C to concentrate for longer periods at a time.
  D to devote more time to doing their homework.

5 In what way did the Maushart family's relationship with food change?
  A They ate larger portions of everything.
  B They attached more importance to it.
  C They all took turns to cook meals.
  D They prepared healthier dishes.

6 What does the writer mean by 'she is no isolated case' in line 34?
  A Sussy sleeps better when she shares her bedroom.
  B No one in Sussy's family sleeps very well at night.
  C Sussy prefers using media in the company of other children.
  D Other children who use media suffer in the same way as Sussy.

○ Reacting to the text

What effects might a similar experiment have on you and your family?

Do you think people have become too dependent on information technology? Why/Why not?

What to expect in the exam

In the exam, the six multiple-choice questions may focus on some of the following features:

- the writer's use of comparison, *e.g. question 1*.
- the attitude or opinion of the writer or someone mentioned in the text, *e.g. question 2*.
- the main idea expressed in a paragraph, *e.g. question 3*.
- a detail in the text, *e.g. question 4*.
- the meaning of a word or phrase, *e.g. question 6*.

There may also be a question testing global understanding of a feature of the whole text, such as the writer's reason for writing it or the overall tone of the text. This type of question would come last.

Language focus 1: Comparisons

Complete the following sentences from the text. If a word is given in brackets, write the correct form of that word. You may need to write more than one word.

1 The _____ facts we have at our fingertips, the _____ we seem to know.

2 Their attention spans increased, allowing them … to hold _____ (long) and _____ (complex) conversations with adults.

3 They probably did no _____ homework during The Experiment _____ they had done before, but they all completed it far _____ (efficiently) and far _____ (quickly).

4 She'd been our family's _____ (militant) multitasker, and the one who'd been attracted by a digital lifestyle at the _____ (young) age.

5 Subjects who slept the _____ also multi-tasked the _____ .

Now check your answers in the reading text.

A Comparative and superlative forms

1 Why are the following comparative and superlative forms **not** possible in sentences **2** and **5** above?
more long   complexer   militantest   most young

2 What are the comparative and superlative forms of the following adjectives?
clean   hot   strange   happy
clever   good   bad   far

3 *Easy* and *quickly* both have two syllables and both end in –y. The comparative form of *easy* is *easier*. Why isn't *quicklier* the comparative form of *quickly* in sentence **3**?

4 In sentence **3**, *far* is used with a comparative (*far more quickly*) to talk about a big difference. Which of the following are used before comparatives for big differences and which for small differences?
a bit   much   significantly   a little   slightly   a lot

B Other comparative structures

1 To talk about people or things that are the same in some way we can use *as* + adjective or adverb + *as*.

*They're just **as silly as** each other.*

In negative sentences which talk about differences, *so* can be used instead of the first *as*.

*She's **not so fit as** she used to be.*

Not so becomes *not such* if a noun is used after the adjective.

*Maybe this **isn't such a good idea as** I thought.*

2 *The* + comparative, *the* + comparative

This structure is used to show that two changes happen together. The second change is often the result of the first.

***The more** facts we have at our fingertips, **the less** we seem to know.*

The older he gets, the more slowly he drives.

 Read more about comparisons on pages 210 and 211 of the Grammar reference.

1 Match each sentence **1–6** with a sentence **a–f** which expresses a similar idea. The first one has been done for you.

1 She's far lazier than anyone else.   *c*
2 She works a lot less than she ought to.   ___
3 She's not quite as lazy as she used to be.   ___
4 She doesn't have as many problems as she used to. ___
5 She's the worst student I've ever taught.   ___
6 The more she works, the more success she has.   ___

a She doesn't work nearly as much as she should.
b She has fewer difficulties than before.
c Everyone works much harder than her.
d She's more successful when she works harder.
e She's slightly more hardworking than before.
f I've never had such a bad student in my class.

2 Complete the second sentence so that it has a similar meaning to the first sentence, using the word given. Use between **two** and **five** words, including the word given.

1 The film wasn't nearly as good as I thought it would be.
FAR
The film _____ I thought it would be.

2 I've never had such a boring holiday!
ENJOYABLE
This is _____ I've ever had!

3 There are fewer teachers in my school than there were last year.
NOT
There _____ teachers in my school as there were last year.

4 If you work harder now, you won't have to do so much later.
THE
The harder _____ you'll have to do later.

5 Lucy is as tall as her mother.
HEIGHT
Lucy _____ her mother.

6 Kate has slightly more experience than the others.
QUITE
The others don't have
_____ Kate.

3 a Write down one example for each of the following:
1 The best type of pet.
2 The best smartphone.
3 Your favourite pop or rock group.
4 A film you really enjoyed.
5 A sportsman or woman you admire.
6 A favourite holiday destination.

b Work in small groups. Try to persuade the other members of your group that your choices are better than theirs.

Example:
Student A: Cats are the best pets to have. They're far more independent than most other animals.
Student B: Yes, but cats aren't nearly as playful as dogs. Dogs are a lot more fun.
Student C: You're both wrong. Hamsters are the friendliest pets – much nicer than cats or dogs …

Word formation: Nouns 1

1 Write the correct noun form of the words in brackets to complete these extracts from the reading text on page 31. You may need to use a plural form.

  1 Gracefully and without _____ (conscious) or _____ (curious) as to how they got there.

  2 As a culture we are practically swimming in _____ (entertain).

  3 Their _____ (attend) spans increased, allowing them ... to hold longer and more complex _____ (converse).

  4 The _____ (evident) strongly suggests she is no isolated case.

  Check your answers in the text.

2 Use the suffixes in the box to create nouns from the words in **1–6**. The same suffix is required for all four words in each group. The final word in each group also requires a spelling change. There is an example at the beginning **(0)**.

-ity	-ness	-ion	-ation	-ment	-ence	-ance

  0 object   react   predict   convert
  objection   *reaction*   *prediction*   *conversion*
  1 enjoy   treat   govern   argue
  2 original   popular   major   able
  3 appear   perform   annoy   tolerate
  4 sad   weak   careless   lonely
  5 inform   resign   present   explain
  6 differ   exist   depend   obey

3 Use the word given in capitals at the end of some of the lines to form a noun that fits in the gap **in the same line**. You may need to use a plural or a negative form. The first one has been done for you.

  1 Carla could not hide her ___*amusement*___ at the sight of her father's **AMUSE**
  first ever laptop. He had quite a _____ of what he called **COLLECT**
  'technological antiques' and this was his favourite. It had plenty
  of _____ to her own model, but it was the weight and **SIMILAR**
  _____ of it that caused her to smile. **THICK**

  2 One of the many _____ during our Science Week this year **ACTIVE**
  is a trip to the Technology Museum. A single _____ of £15 **PAY**
  should be made by Friday 7 October. Please also sign the attached
  form giving _____ for your child to attend. **PERMIT**

  3 Aunt Gwen's _____ at Christmas was unquestionable but **GENEROUS**
  it had to be said that most of her present-buying _____ **DECIDE**
  were not the best – a pink jumper and a romantic novel, for example.
  Prepared for _____ , Paul unwrapped her gift and was **DISAPPOINT**
  amazed to find a top-of-the-range smartphone.

  4 I am writing to express my _____ with the speakers I **SATISFY**
  recently ordered from you. There are a number of _____ **DIFFERENT**
  between the _____ of the product on your website and **DESCRIBE**
  the speakers I received. Judging from some of the more negative
  Internet reviews I have read, this is not an isolated _____ . **OCCUR**

Listening 1
Part 4

Multiple choice 1.16

1 Look at the photographs, newspaper headlines and dictionary definition.

What different uses for robots can you think of?

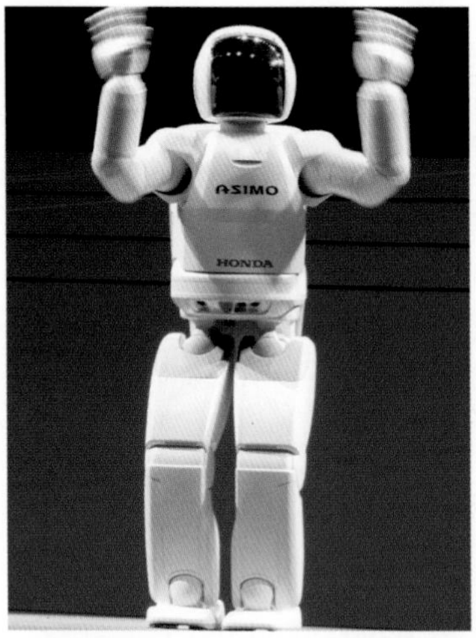

Hospital takes delivery of robot

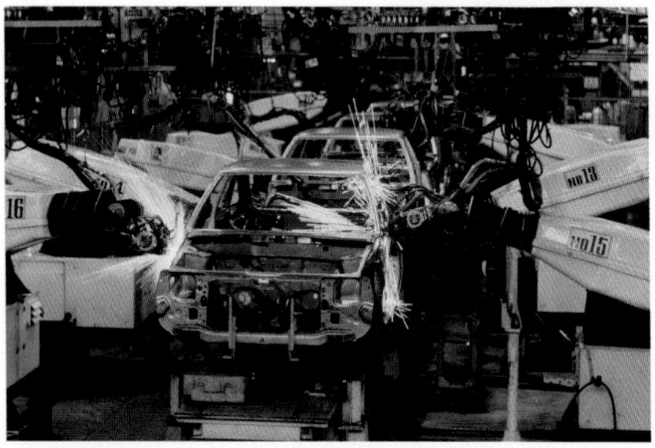

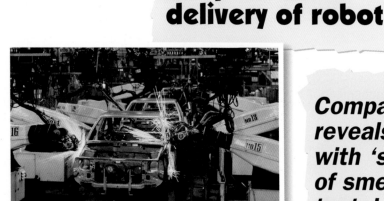

Company reveals robot with 'sense of smell and taste'

robot /ˈrəʊbɒt/ noun [c]:
a a machine that can do work by itself, often work that humans do
b a machine that looks and talks like a human, and can do many of the things humans do

Robot dog – the perfect companion

2 You will hear an interview with a robot scientist.

For questions **1–7**, choose the best answer (**A, B** or **C**).

How to go about it

Underlining key words in the questions or sentence beginnings will help you focus on the information you are required to listen for. The first one has been done as an example.

1 What does Keith say about his <u>company's latest project</u>?
A He does not want to talk about it.
B He is not allowed to talk about it.
C He does not know much about it.

2 How does Keith describe his work?
A monotonous
B tiring
C varied

3 What is the possible result of having robots that can display and detect emotions?
A Robots will become more acceptable to people.
B Robots will be mistaken for humans.
C Robots will age and grow ill.

4 What does Keith say about robots in films?
A They are not always shown in a positive light.
B They often have a good sense of humour.
C They are not particularly well designed.

5 Keith expresses concern that robots might cause us
A to do less physical exercise.
B to become less intelligent.
C to think less for ourselves.

6 Keith says that progress in the robotics industry
A is as fast as that of computers.
B has become faster recently.
C was fast in the early years.

7 What does Keith say about humanoid robots?
A They are unable to perform many tasks.
B Many people consider them to be a toy.
C People are getting used to seeing them.

Do you think that robots will one day be as common in homes as computers? Why/Why not?

Speaking 1
Part 3

Collaborative task ○

Read tasks **1** and **2** below. Then, before you do the tasks, read the information in the boxes at the bottom of the page.

1 Your class has decided to do a project on changes and developments over the last century. Talk with your partner about some of the changes that have taken place in the different areas below.

Education

What changes have taken place in these different areas over the last century?

Communication

Travel and transport

Free time

Medicine

2 Now decide in which two areas the most positive changes have taken place.

How to go about it

● Part 3 is an interactive task. As well as giving your own opinions, ask your partner what they think, and respond to their comments by agreeing, disagreeing, or adding a further comment.

● In task **1** you can talk about the areas in any order you choose. Say as much as you can about each one.

The photographs on this page are there to give you at least one idea for each area. (There are no pictures for Part 3 in the Cambridge English: First exam.)

● Do not start to make your decisions for task **2** while you are doing task **1**. They are two separate tasks.

● In task **2** you do not have to agree with your partner when making your final decision.

● In the exam you have two minutes for task **1** and then about a minute for task **2**. However, allow yourself more time as you practise for Part 3 in the early units of *Ready for First*.

Useful language

Relevant grammar areas

Present perfect: *e.g. Technology **has changed** the way we communicate.*

Past habitual behaviour: *e.g. We **used to play** outside more.*

Present habitual behaviour: *e.g. **It's quite normal for** schools **to** provide laptops now.*

Comparisons: *e.g. We're **a lot healthier** now, thanks to medical advances.*

Asking questions

Can you think of any more changes?

Do you have any other ideas?

Do you agree with me on that?

Agreeing and disagreeing

That's right/true.   I think so, too.
I agree (up to a point).

That's not right/true.   I really don't think so.
I completely disagree.

Speaking 2
Part 4

Further discussion

In Part 4 of the Speaking test the examiner will ask you questions which are related to the topic in Part 3. Discuss the following questions on the topic of change.

How to go about it

- Answer the questions fully, giving reasons for your opinions.
- As well as responding to the examiner, you can also interact with your partner, as in Part 3.

- Do you think the quality of life in general is better now than it used to be?
- Some people say we have too much choice nowadays. What do you think?
- How could the education system in your country be improved?
- If you could change one thing in your life, what would it be?
- Some people don't like change. Why do you think that is?
- What do you think will be the biggest changes in the next 100 years?

Language focus 2: Articles

1 Read the extract from the article entitled 'A century of change', ignoring the spaces for the moment, and answer the following questions.

- Which two areas from the speaking activity on page 36 are mentioned in the extract?
- Which of the changes mentioned in the extract did you discuss in the speaking activity?

2 Now read the extract again and complete each of the gaps with *a, an* or *the*, or leave it blank. There is an example at the beginning **(0)**.

3 🄖 Read the main rules for the use of articles on pages 211–12 of the Grammar reference. Then use them to give reasons for each of the answers in exercise **2**.

Example:
0 Section A4: a specific aspect or part of something, where the noun is followed by of.

A century of change

Since **(0)** _the_ beginning of the last century there have been enormous changes in the way **(1)** ____ people live. **(2)** ____ world has become a much smaller place and **(3)** ____ life is much faster.

In **(4)** ____ first half of the twentieth century, **(5)** ____ horse was gradually replaced by **(6)** ____ motor car as **(7)** ____ most popular form of transport. **(8)** ____ hundred years ago, **(9)** ____ air travel was in its infancy; now there are over 90 000 commercial flights **(10)** ____ day worldwide. In the 1940s, **(11)** ____ steam trains were still a common sight on the world's railways. They have now all but disappeared from mainline routes and in several countries electric-powered high-speed trains can be seen racing across **(12)** ____ countryside at around 300 kilometres **(13)** ____ hour.

And **(14)** ____ information travels faster, too, thanks to developments in information technology, telecommunications and mass media. Having your own computer at **(15)** ____ home was almost unheard of in 1970, but just 40 years later in 2010 there were well over **(16)** ____ billion personal computers in use worldwide. Invented in 1876, **(17)** ____ telephone was already fairly widely in use by 1910, with some seven million installed in **(18)** ____ United States alone. But who could have predicted that a century later an estimated 70 per cent of the world's population would own **(19)** ____ mobile phone? Commercial television did not really take off until just after **(20)** ____ Second World War – and we all know how successful that phenomenon has been!

Another area where enormous changes have taken place is

Listening 2:
Part 3

Multiple matching 👁 1.17–1.21

1 Read the following Listening Part 3 instructions.

You will hear five different teachers talking about changes that have been made in their schools. For questions **1–5**, choose from the list **A–H** what each speaker says. Use the letters only once. There are three extra letters which you do not need to use.

How to go about it

- Underline the key words and phrases in the eight options. The first one (**A**) has been done for you. However, if you hear one of these words or phrases, do not assume that the option which contains them is the answer.
- Listen carefully both times before making your final decision.

A The change has resulted in <u>a number of new problems</u>.
B Too many changes have been introduced.
C The change is insufficient to solve a problem.
D We should have been consulted about the change.
E The change is being made for selfish reasons.
F Most parents support the change.
G The change has brought unexpected benefits.
H Most of the teachers feel the change is unnecessary.

Speaker 1 ☐ **1**
Speaker 2 ☐ **2**
Speaker 3 ☐ **3**
Speaker 4 ☐ **4**
Speaker 5 ☐ **5**

2 Check your answers using the listening script on pages 224–5. Underline those parts of each extract which guide you to the correct answers.

3 One student wrote the following **incorrect** answers.
1 D   2 H   3 C   4 A   5 B
Identify the language in each extract which may have caused the student to choose the wrong answer.

Example: 1 Perhaps I should have spoken out at the consultation meeting.

4 👁 Work in pairs. Tell your partner about two changes which have occurred recently in your life. Describe the reasons for the changes and your attitude towards them.

5 Now turn to page 203 and do the vocabulary exercises.

Writing
Part 1

Essay

1 👁 Read the following Writing Part 1 instructions and the example answer on page 39. Do you agree with the writer's conclusion? Why/Why not?

Your English class has been discussing the effect of technology on sport. Now your English teacher has asked you to write an essay.

Write an essay using **all** the notes and give reasons for your point of view.

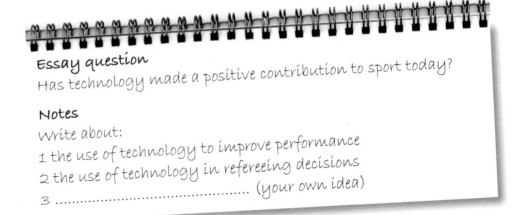

Essay question
Has technology made a positive contribution to sport today?

Notes
Write about:
1 the use of technology to improve performance
2 the use of technology in refereeing decisions
3 .... (your own idea)

Write your **essay** in **140–190** words.

Has technology made a positive contribution to sport today?

Some people feel that technology has helped to improve our enjoyment of sport and they approve of its use. Others, however, point to the negative aspects and would prefer to see its influence limited.

On the positive side, the use of technology in football to decide if a goal has been scored or not, or in tennis to judge whether the ball is in or out, clearly helps to make the games fairer. Communication between football officials via microphones also improves the quality of their decisions. Another positive influence of technology is its role in increasing safety for competitors. Modern helmet design in cycling is an example of this.

On the other hand, the use of technology to improve performance can give some sportspeople an unfair advantage over others. For this reason, full-length swimsuits and so-called 'superbikes' have now both been banned from some swimming and cycling competitions.

To conclude, I think that as long as sporting achievements remain the result of human effort, rather than scientific advances, then the contribution of technology will always be positive.

2 The third note in the question asks for 'your own idea'. What is the writer's own idea in the example answer?

3 What is the purpose of each of the four paragraphs in the example answer?
Example:
Paragraph 1: a general introduction

4 **a** A number of linking devices can be used to express contrasts. Complete the table using an appropriate expression from the example answer.

Expressing contrasts	
Some people	Others, however,
On the negative side	
On the one hand	

b Add the following linking devices to the appropriate column in the table below. The three examples all appear in the example answer.

In addition (to this)   Consequently   On balance   What is more
Furthermore   To sum up   Moreover   As a result   In conclusion
Firstly/Secondly/Finally

Adding information	Expressing result	Concluding
Another positive influence	For this reason	To conclude

5 Do the Writing Part 1 task on page 203.

③ Review

Vocabulary: Technology

Match the words on the left to those on the right to create compound nouns related to technology. The first one has been done for you.

1 web — set
2 lap — book
3 head — page
4 land — tasking
5 down — top
6 net — line
7 multi — load

Expressions with *as ... as*

Complete each gap with an appropriate word.

1 You can go out, as _____ as you do your homework first.
2 As _____ as he got home, he got changed and went back out again.
3 We can throw this vase away, as _____ as I'm concerned. We never use it.
4 As _____ as being an excellent sportswoman, she's also a brilliant scientist.
5 I sometimes receive as _____ as 300 emails in a single day.

Comparisons

1 Complete each gap in the paragraph with a word from the box. You do not need to use all the words.

many	much	most	more	less
lot	little	so	such	nearly
the	of	by	in	to

Max has changed since our days at school together. The older he gets, **(1)** _____ more sociable he seems to be. He was never the **(2)** _____ confident boy **(3)** _____ the class and he didn't have as **(4)** _____ friends as he probably would like to have had. But he's **(5)** _____ less reserved now, and not **(6)** _____ as nervous. Physically, he's different as well. He's quite a **(7)** _____ larger than he used to be and not **(8)** _____ pale and sickly looking. In those days he was **(9)** _____ far the thinnest of my friends, but he's put on a bit of weight and he looks **(10)** _____ delicate now.

2 Complete the following sentences in an appropriate way.

1 The older I get, _____ .
2 The more technological devices you own _____ .
3 The more information you have, _____ .
4 The less you pay for a mobile phone, _____ .
5 The more time I spend online, _____ .

Writing
Part 2

Article

You have seen this announcement in an international magazine.

> ### LIFE CHANGES
>
> Tell us about a time in your life when something changed. Mention the reasons for the change and describe your feelings before and after it.
> We will publish the most interesting articles next month.

Write your **article** in **140–190** words.

For more information on writing articles, see page 196.

40

Articles

1 Read the following text quite quickly. To what extent do you share the writer's views?

   1 I am ↑ self-confessed technophobe. I have come to hate technology and the way it
         a

   2 dominates every aspect of ~~the~~ life. One of the worst offenders is the computer,

   3 which for many has become the most important object both in home and the

   4 workplace, where they spend the more time staring at a screen than interacting

   5 with the people around them. Computers have killed an art of conversation.

   6 Sure, they can be used to write the emails and 'chat' to friends – or even to total

   7 strangers – but isn't it ironic that the more we communicate, less communicative

   8 we seem to become? Equally irritating is mobile phone, or 'cell phone', as it is

   9 also known, perhaps because the people who use one should be put in the

 10 prison cell for doing so. They shout into them on train or send pointless text

 11 messages to one another. I once sat in a bar and watched young couple text each

 12 other from opposite sides of the same table. But it's not just young who are

 13 addicted to these toys: the high percentage of over-60s have joined in the 'fun'.

 14 Indeed, the older you are, the louder you have to shout into the your phone – or

 15 so it seems, anyway. But maybe I'm a one with the problem, maybe I should

 16 just get myself a laptop and a mobile, go away to mountains and then contact my

 17 friends and family from there. I might get to talk to them more that way.

2 Each numbered line in the text has one mistake in the use of articles. You may have to **add, change** or **delete** an article. The first two have been done for you.

Reading and
Use of English
Part 3

Word formation

For questions **1–8**, read the text below. Use the word given in capitals at the end of some of the lines to form a word that fits in the space **in the same line**. There is an example at the beginning (**0**). Write your answers **IN CAPITAL LETTERS**.

Don't forget!

- Read the whole text through once before writing your answers.
- You may need to write the plural form of a noun.

Michael Hart

Michael Hart (1947–2011) was the (**0**) *FOUNDER* of Project Gutenberg,   **FOUND**
one of the (**1**) _____ and longest-lasting online literary projects. His life's   **EARLY**
aim was to digitize the world's literature and make it freely available online. As a
result of his work, he is widely considered to be the (**2**) _____ of the e-book.   **INVENT**
In 1971, Hart typed a copy of the United States Declaration of Independence into
the computer at the University of Illinois, where he was a student. The Internet was
used only by academic and military (**3**) _____ : the world wide web would   **RESEARCH**
not come into (**4**) _____ for another two decades. Yet Hart spent the next   **EXIST**
fifteen or so years typing up historic texts such as the works of Shakespeare and
the American Constitution, using (**5**) _____ he had begged, borrowed or   **EQUIP**
made himself. In 1987, with over 300 books in the online (**6**) _____ , he   **COLLECT**
took on an (**7**) _____ , and together they recruited volunteers worldwide   **ASSIST**
to help with typing and proofreading (**8**) _____ . Project Gutenberg now   **RESPONSIBLE**
offers more than 36 000 free e-books to download in over 60 different languages.

Use of English

Introduction

The first four parts of the **Reading and Use of English** paper are Use of English tasks. In this unit we will look specifically at three of the tasks:

Part 1 Multiple-choice cloze
Part 2 Open cloze
Part 3 Word formation

Information on the content of **Part 4 (Transformations)** appears at frequent intervals throughout this book.

What do you know about the Use of English tasks?

Look at the following statements and decide which are true and which are false. If you think a statement is false, give reasons for your answer.

1 All four Use of English tasks are in the form of a text. _____

2 You should read texts through at least once before you attempt the task. _____

3 One mark is given for each correct answer in the Use of English tasks. _____

4 Parts 1, 2 and 3 each contain eight gaps. _____

5 All four parts of the paper contain an example. _____

6 You should not write the answer for the examples on your answer sheet in the exam. _____

7 In **Part 1** (Multiple-choice cloze), if you are not sure of the answer it is better to leave a blank. _____

8 In **Part 2** (Open cloze), you sometimes have to write two words. _____

9 In **Part 3** (Word formation), an answer is given no marks at all if the word is misspelt. _____

10 In **Part 4** (Transformations), the key word must not be changed in any way. _____

Part 1: Multiple-choice cloze

What to expect in the exam

Part 1 of the **Reading and Use of English** paper focuses mainly on vocabulary. The following examples show some of the different features of the language which are tested in the Multiple-choice cloze.

Look carefully at the words in *italics* and underline the answer A, B, C or D which best fits each gap.

1 **Knowing the meaning of a word.**

If you need anything *during the exam,* you should ask one of the _____ .

A invigilators   B surveyors   C observers   D superintendents

2 **Knowing the grammar of a word.**

His doctor _____ *him to eat* less and do more exercise.

A said   B suggested   C advised   D insisted

3 **Knowing which words go together.**

a The match was postponed because of the _____ *rain*.

A strong   B hard   C forceful   D heavy

b Could you _____ *in touch with* John and arrange a time to meet?

A put   B find   C get   D go

4 **Phrasal verbs**

He was offered the job, but he *turned* it _____ because of the low salary.

A up   B down   C off   D on

5 **Linking words**

We'll let you buy a motorbike _____ you ride it carefully.

A as if   B whenever   C although   D as long as

1 Look at the title of the text below. What do you think you will read about?

Now read the text through quickly, ignoring the gaps, and check your predictions.

2 Read the text again and for questions **1–8**, decide which answer (**A**, **B**, **C** or **D**) best fits each gap. There is an example at the beginning (**0**).

Bookcrossing – the World's Library

If you're walking in your local park and you find a book with a label inside (**0**) ____ 'Read and Release me', don't just treat it as a (**1**) ____ . You've probably come (**2**) ____ an example of 'bookcrossing', a book-sharing movement started in 2001 by American Ron Hornbaker.

Bookcrossers 'release' books either by (**3**) ____ them on to friends, or else by leaving them in public places for others to pick up, or 'catch', and then read, before they in (**4**) ____ release them back 'into the wild'. (**5**) ____ a book has been 'caught', the person finding it is (**6**) ____ to record the event by logging on to the bookcrossing website and entering the book's ID number written on the label. That (**7**) ____ , both the original owner and subsequent readers of the book can keep track of its progress.

Over one million people worldwide participate in bookcrossing, 'releasing' books in a (**8**) ____ range of locations including cafés, airports, bus stations and telephone boxes.

Don't forget!

- Read the sentence before and after the gap.
- Consider both meaning and grammar when making your decisions.

0	**A** telling	**B** <u>saying</u>	**C** talking	**D** writing
1	**A** joke	**B** fun	**C** humour	**D** comedy
2	**A** away	**B** across	**C** aside	**D** along
3	**A** letting	**B** presenting	**C** leaving	**D** passing
4	**A** turn	**B** result	**C** order	**D** part
5	**A** Soon	**B** Since	**C** Once	**D** While
6	**A** animated	**B** suggested	**C** encouraged	**D** promoted
7	**A** time	**B** place	**C** manner	**D** way
8	**A** deep	**B** wide	**C** high	**D** long

Part 2: Open cloze

1  What do you know about the habitat, food and behaviour of wolves?

2 Read the following text. Are any of the points you discussed in exercise **1** mentioned?

Grey Wolves

(0) At one time grey wolves, whose Latin name is *Canis lupus,* could be found over large areas of Europe. Over the last century, however, **(1) their** numbers and range have been considerably reduced, mainly as a result of hunting and the widespread destruction of habitat. Consequently, it is **(2) not** as easy to see them in the wild as it used to be.

There are **(3) a** number of subspecies of grey wolf, including the Italian wolf and the Iberian wolf, **(4) which** inhabits the forests of northern Portugal and northwestern Spain. All wolves hunt for food in small packs, often preying on animals that are much larger **(5) than** themselves. And **(6) although** they will eat almost anything, including deer, sheep, rabbits and even fish and fruit, wolves rarely attack people.

Grey wolves usually give birth **(7) to** between four and seven cubs. The cubs leave the den when they are eight to ten weeks old, after which they **(8) are** cared for by all members of the pack until they reach maturity.

What to expect in the exam

In Part 2 of the **Reading and Use of English** paper there is a text with eight gaps to be filled. This task focuses mainly on grammar. The following are some of the types of words which are omitted. Look at the words in **bold** in the text above and write each one with its number next to the corresponding type. The first one **(0)** has been done for you.

Type of word	Example and number
Articles	
Auxiliary verbs	
Linking words	
Negative words	
Possessive adjectives (my, your, his etc)	
Prepositions	(0) At
Relative pronouns	
Words in comparisons	

3 Read the text below and think of the word which best fits each gap. Use only **one** word in each gap. There is an example at the beginning **(0)**.

Saved by Heavy Metal?

Walter Eikrem was listening to music **(0)** __*on*__ his mobile phone as he made his way home from school in the Norwegian town of Rakkestad. The path leading from the stop **(1)** _____ he catches the school bus to his family's farmhouse crosses a gently sloping hillside. All of **(2)** _____ sudden, he made out something grey on the hillside. 'At first, I thought it might **(3)** _____ been the neighbour's dogs,' he said. **(4)** _____ he actually encountered, though, were four wolves.

'I was afraid they would attack me,' said Walter, but he didn't let his fear show. He pulled the earphones out of his mobile phone, turned the volume all **(5)** _____ way up and blasted heavy metal music over its miniature speakers. **(6)** _____ the same time, he shouted as loud as he could while waving his arms about wildly **(7)** _____ scare off the pack of wild animals.

The plan worked. Eikrem said he was able to drive away the wolves **(8)** _____ playing the song 'Overcome' by the American hard-rock band Creed. 'They just turned around and simply trotted away,' said Walter.

Part 3: Word formation

- Part 3 contains a text with eight gaps, each of which has to be filled with the correct form of a word given in capital letters.
- The missing words are usually nouns, adjectives, adverbs and occasionally verbs. Sometimes the word you write will need to be in the plural, and sometimes a negative form is required. The meaning of the text surrounding the gaps will help you decide.

1 For questions **1–8** use the word given in capitals at the end of each line to form a word that fits in the space in the same line. Use the words in **bold** to help you decide on the correct form of your answer. There is an example at the beginning (**0**).

0 The _length_ of the Channel tunnel is roughly fifty kilometres.	**LONG**
1 His third book is a **lively and** _____ account of family life.	**HUMOUR**
2 The company took on **two thousand new** _____ last year.	**EMPLOY**
3 Rising prices have forced consumers **to** _____ their belts.	**TIGHT**
4 It is **becoming** _____ **difficult** for young people to find work.	**INCREASE**
5 **Unfortunately**, the train was **both noisy and very** _____ .	**COMFORT**
6 Desert animals cope with **the** _____ in a number of ways.	**HOT**
7 **Cook** the mixture on a low heat **in a medium-sized** _____ .	**SAUCE**
8 This _____ **achievement** won her a place in the **record books**.	**ORDINARY**

2 Describe each answer in exercise **1** using the words in the box below.

noun	adjective	adverb	verb
negative	plural	compound	spelling change

Example:

(0) 'Length' is a noun. A spelling change is required to form it: the 'o' in 'long' becomes an 'e' in 'length'.

Don't forget!

Check the spelling of the words you write. No marks will be awarded for a misspelt word.

3 Look at the title of the paragraph below. What do you think the text will say? Read through the text quite quickly, ignoring the gaps, and check your predictions.

4 Now read the text again and for questions **1–8**, use the word given in capitals at the end of some of the lines to form a word that fits in the space in the same line. There is an example at the beginning (**0**).

Careers information: circus performers	
Here is some brief **(0)** _information_ for anyone thinking of following a career in the circus. There is of course a wide range of jobs available: trapeze artists, acrobats, clowns, **(1)** _____ , fire-eaters and tight-rope walkers are all to be found in the big top.	**INFORM** **MAGIC**
A few circuses train their own performers, but usually they are more **(2)** _____ in someone who can already demonstrate a circus-related **(3)** _____ or skill. Circus schools are the best way of obtaining the necessary training, and can be either connected to a large circus or else totally **(4)** _____ . Circus performers need to be physically fit and possess the necessary mental **(5)** _____ to cope with the intense training and obvious demands of the job. They are also flexible and able to adapt **(6)** _____ to new situations, particularly as circuses are frequently on the move.	**INTEREST** **ABLE** **DEPEND** **STRONG** **EASY**
Additionally, for many jobs within the circus, good concentration is essential. Fire-eaters and acrobats cannot afford to be **(7)** _____ as mistakes can have **(8)** _____ consequences.	**CARE** **DISASTER**

4 A good story

Vocabulary 1: Films

1 Look at these film posters. Do you know any of these films? What type of film is each one? Choose from the words in the box.

thriller	horror film	comedy	romance	historical drama
action film	western	fantasy	science fiction film	

2 For exercises **A** and **B**, decide which word best fits each space.

A *terrible*   *terrific*   *terrifying*

1 It was a _____ performance, for which he deserves to win an Oscar.

2 Absolutely _____ ! I've never been so frightened in all my life.

3 This was probably the worst film I've seen all year. The plot was non-existent and the acting was _____ .

B *review*   *criticism*   *critic*

It seems that every **(1)** _____ I read of this film gives a different opinion. For example, the **(2)** _____ who writes for *The Times* is very enthusiastic about it and has nothing but praise for Peter Jackson. The same director, however, comes under strong **(3)** _____ in the magazine *Premiere*.

3 Read the following review of *The Matrix*, which appeared in a student magazine. Does this type of film appeal to you?

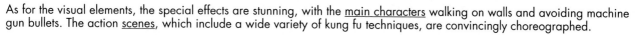

THE MATRIX

The Matrix is one of the most entertaining science fiction films I have seen. It combines frenetic action with terrific <u>special effects</u>, and <u>stars</u> Keanu Reeves as Neo, and Laurence Fishburne in the <u>role</u> of Morpheus.

The film is <u>set</u> in the future, in a world controlled by machines. In order to hide this reality from humans, the machines have constructed the Matrix, a vast virtual reality system resembling Earth at the end of the twentieth century. The <u>plot</u>, which focuses on a revolt led by Morpheus against the Matrix, is complicated and at times confusing. However, the <u>cast</u> is very strong and the film features a surprisingly competent <u>performance</u> from Keanu Reeves.

As for the visual elements, the special effects are stunning, with the <u>main characters</u> walking on walls and avoiding machine gun bullets. The action <u>scenes</u>, which include a wide variety of kung fu techniques, are convincingly choreographed.

I would recommend the film to anyone who likes science fiction. If you ignore the complexities of the plot and just enjoy the action, you will not feel disappointed.

4 Complete each gap in **1–8** using the underlined words from the review of *The Matrix*. Do not change the words in any way. There is an example at the beginning **(0)**.

0 Some of the <u>scenes</u> in *Casablanca* are memorable, particularly when Humphrey Bogart and Ingrid Bergman say goodbye at the end of the film.

1 *War Horse* is _____ in England and Europe during the First World War.

2 The film has an international _____ , with French, Polish and Italian actors.

3 One of my least favourite films is *Notting Hill*, which _____ Julia Roberts as a world-famous film actress. I like the music from the soundtrack, though.

4 I found Hugh Grant irritating in the _____ of a nervous bookseller who has an unlikely romance with the film star.

5 This was not Brad Pitt's most convincing acting _____ .

6 The _____ is straightforward and easy to follow.

7 The _____ are well portrayed by Colin Firth and Geoffrey Rush, and there's a fine supporting performance from Helena Bonham Carter as Queen Elizabeth.

8 SFX is the abbreviation for _____ .

5 ◐ Talk about the following using some of the vocabulary in exercises **1–4**.

- a film you didn't enjoy
- the most frightening film you have ever seen
- your favourite film
- the most gripping film you have ever seen

Language focus 1: *So* and *such*

1 Look at these two sentences.

I was **so** impressed with the soundtrack of the film that I downloaded it as soon as I got home.

She has **such** a wonderful voice that it seems a shame to dub her films into English.

a Why are *so* and *such* used in each of these sentences?
b What types of words follow *so* and *such*?

Ⓖ Check your ideas in the Grammar reference on page 212.

2 For questions **1–4** complete the second sentence so that it has a similar meaning to the first sentence, using the word given. **Do not change the word given.** You must use between **two** and **five** words, including the word given.

1 We decided to see the film as it had such good reviews.
THAT
The reviews for the film _____ we decided to see it.

2 The weather was so bad that we decided to come home.
SUCH
It _____ that we decided to come home.

3 I got so absorbed in the film I forgot to phone Amy.
SUCH
It _____ film I forgot to phone Amy.

4 The party was so crowded we could hardly move.
PEOPLE
There _____ at the party we could hardly move.

Word formation: Adjectives ending in *-ing* and *-ed*

To describe how we feel about something or someone we can use past participles as adjectives.

I got really **frightened** *when I saw the main character being killed.*

To describe the thing or person that produces the feeling we can use present participles as adjectives.

It was an extremely **frightening** *scene.*

Adverbs can be formed from present participle adjectives.

Not **surprisingly**, *we were disappointed that we couldn't get tickets to see the film.*

1 Look back at the review of *The Matrix* and find examples of adjectives and adverbs formed with *-ing* and *-ed*. Note that not all the words ending in *-ing* and *-ed* in the text are adjectives.

2 Put the past participle of each of the following regular verbs in the appropriate group, according to how the *-ed* ending is pronounced.

annoy	frustrate	tire	disappoint	disgust	astonish	terrify
amuse	fascinate	bore	impress	frighten	relax	

/d/	/t/	/ɪd/
surprised	*embarrassed*	*excited*

3 The present participle (*-ing*) form of the verbs in exercise **2** can all be used as adjectives, except in the case of one of the verbs. Which one is it and how is the adjective formed?

4 Complete each gap with the present or past participle form of an appropriate verb from exercise **2**. You may need to use an adverb.

1 Teachers need long holidays. They do a very _____ job.

2 I'm sorry, but I'm just not _____ . I don't find it at all funny.

3 I wish you'd stop whistling. It's extremely _____ !

4 My mark in the exam was _____ low. I thought I had done much better.

5 I've never been very interested in science but this was such a _____ book that I couldn't put it down. I was totally absorbed.

6 I'm not eating that – it smells _____ ! What is it?

7 _____ , she was still alive after spending 20 days buried under a building which had collapsed in the earthquake.

Writing 1
Part 2

Review

Your teacher has asked you to write about a film you have seen recently on DVD for the school's English magazine. Write a review for the magazine, giving your opinions on the film and saying whether you would recommend it.

How to go about it

Here is a paragraph plan for your review. However, the paragraph summaries are not in the correct order. Look again at the review of *The Matrix* and put them in order.

a A brief summary of the plot and comments on the acting, with opinions.

b Recommendations with reasons.

c A general opinion of the film, together with some factual details, e.g. *type of film, actors/actresses, director.*

d Other aspects of the film together with opinions.

• Decide on the film you are going to review and make notes for each of your four paragraphs, using the above plan as a guide.

• Include relevant film vocabulary as well as some participle adjectives to express your opinion.

• Work with a partner and tell each other about your films, following the notes you have made. Have you each included a balance of information and opinions?

Now you are ready to write your **review** in **140–190** words.

Speaking
Part 2

Talking about photos

The following two photographs show different free-time activities.

Student A Compare these photographs and say what you think the people are enjoying about these different activities.

Student B When Student A has finished, say whether you enjoy these different activities.

Don't forget!

Student A
- Compare the photographs. Do not describe them in detail.
- The second part of the task is written as a question above the photographs.

Student B
- Develop your answer fully, giving reasons for your feelings or opinions.

> **What are the people enjoying about these different activities?**

Now change roles. The following two photographs show different types of cinemas.

Student A Compare these photographs and say what the advantages are of watching films in cinemas like these.

Student B When student A has finished, say in which of the places you would prefer to see a film.

> **What are the advantages of watching films in cinemas like these?**

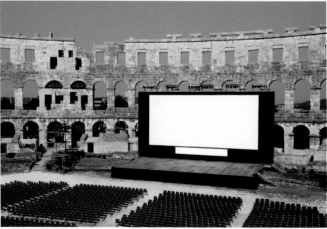

49

Preparing for listening: Focus on distractors

1 Match each sentence beginning **1–5** with an appropriate ending **a–e**.

① My brother was so scared he couldn't watch the film

2 **Although** most critics agree that the novel is her best ever,

3 **Although** snow is now unlikely,

4 My daughter wanted me to help her with her homework

5 **Whereas** in most of his other films he plays the 'baddie',

a we can expect a certain amount of rain later on.

ⓒ **whereas** I didn't find it at all frightening.

b in this one he's definitely the good guy.

d I was rather disappointed by it: the plot is very weak.

e **but** I told her to ask her mother.

2 Now decide on the correct alternative in each of the following interpretations of the sentences in exercise **1**. Give reasons for your answers.

The speaker in sentence …

1 **A** was frightened by the film.   **B** was not frightened by the film.

2 **A** enjoyed the book.   **B** was not enthusiastic about the book.

3 **A** says it will probably rain.   **B** says it will probably snow.

4 **A** helped his daughter.   **B** didn't help his daughter.

5 **A** says the actor is the villain.   **B** says the actor is the hero in the film.

The incorrect answers in exercise **2** are typical of the distractors you might find in a Part 1 Listening task. The ideas in them are similar to the information in exercise **1** but not the same. Note the use of contrast linkers, written in **bold**.

Listening
Part 1

Multiple choice 1.22–1.29

You will hear people talking in eight different situations. For questions **1–8**, choose the best answer, **A**, **B** or **C**.

Don't forget!

In this Part 1 exercise, you will hear distractors of the type you met in the Preparing for listening section.

1 Listen to this woman talking about an actor. What is her opinion of him?
  A He is handsome.
  B He is fashionable.
  C He is rude.

2 You overhear this conversation between two friends. What type of film are they going to see?
  A a historical drama
  B a romance
  C a thriller

3 You hear a man telling a woman about a storytelling course he attended. What does he say about the course?
  A It was better than he expected.
  B It will be useful for his work.
  C It helped build his confidence.

4 You hear an actress talking about her performance in a play. How does she feel?
  A tired
  B disappointed
  C excited

5 You overhear this man talking on the telephone. Who is he talking to?
  A an old school friend
  B a work colleague
  C a relative

6 You hear a young woman talking to her friend about a film. Why didn't she like it?
  A It was too slow.
  B There was too much violence.
  C It was very predictable.

7 You hear a woman telephoning a bookshop. What is she doing?
  A making a complaint
  B making a suggestion
  C apologizing

8 You hear this young man talking on the phone. What does he have in common with his girlfriend?
  A They were born under the same star sign.
  B They share the same taste in music.
  C They have the same sense of humour.

Vocabulary 2: *Take*

A Phrasal verbs with *take*

1 What is the meaning of this phrasal verb from the listening?

*So are you going to be leaving us to **take up** a career as a storyteller, then?*

2 Read the following short story and choose the best title **a–c**.

  a The dangers of Irish dancing   **b** The end of a promising career

  c Winning isn't everything

Roisin always a) <u>took after</u> her dad. Her mother was a calm, laid-back person, but Roisin, like her father, was ambitious. She had to be the best at everything, and that included Irish dancing, which she b) <u>took up</u> at the age of eight. She c) <u>took to</u> it immediately, and knew after just a few lessons, that she wanted to be a world champion. Her teachers were impressed: once she'd learnt a new dance routine, her feet seemed to d) <u>take over</u> and she would move across the floor with incredible agility.

Shortly before her first World Championships in Glasgow, Roisin's teacher e) <u>took</u> her <u>aside</u> during the lesson and reminded her that, whilst she had every confidence in her, the competition would be tough. Full of self-belief, Roisin took no notice and was convinced she would win. When she finished sixth, she was devastated and just couldn't f) <u>take in</u> the fact that she hadn't come first. She never did win a championship, but she eventually learnt to love dancing for itself rather than as a means to be the best. Then, three years ago Roisin's dancing career g) <u>took off</u> when she was h) <u>taken on</u> as a dancer with an Irish dance company that travels the world. There's no competing, only supporting – and she's never been happier.

3 Match each of the underlined phrasal verbs in exercise **2** to one of the meanings in the box below. Use the context of the story to help you.

start to like	employ	resemble	move away from other people to talk
accept as true	gain control	start doing	start to become successful

B Expressions with *take*

1 Complete each gap **1–8** with an appropriate form of the verb *take*. The first one has been done for you.

  A **1** A pair of shoes should last longer than two months. If I were you,
        I <u>*would take*</u> them back to the shop.

      2 My dad used to _____ me to school, but now I have to get the bus.

  B **3** I lost money on that business deal! Of course I regret _____ his advice!

      4 She criticizes everybody else and refuses _____ any of the blame herself.

  C **5** If you _____ more interest in the children, they'd respond better!

      6 The stray cat was looking a lot healthier. It was clear that someone
        _____ pity on it and given it something to eat.

  D **7** It _____ a great deal of courage to sing in front of an audience.

      8 Come on! I can't understand why you _____ so long to do this exercise.

2 In each of the sentences in exercise **1**, underline the expression with *take*.

  Example:
  A pair of shoes should last longer than two months. If I were you, I would <u>take</u> them <u>back to the shop</u>.

3 The expressions in exercise **1** are organized into four groups, **A**, **B**, **C** and **D**. Match each of the following general meanings for *take* to an appropriate group.

  1 to express what is needed or required

  2 to talk about the movement of something or someone from one place to another

  3 to talk about the way people feel or react to others

  4 to accept

4 Which group in exercise **1** do the following expressions belong to?

    take pride in   *be taken to hospital*   *take a joke*   *take the infinitive*

5 Now write a short story of your own using at least three expressions and three phrasal verbs with *take*.

Gapped text

1
  a Match the genres **1–8** to the book covers **A–H**. You may use each genre more than once.

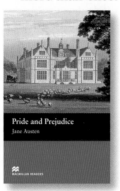

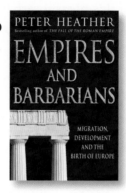

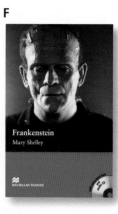

| 1 literary classic | 2 science fiction | 3 crime fiction | 4 thriller |
| 5 romance | 6 horror | 7 historical novel | 8 fantasy |

b What do you enjoy reading most (e.g. books, magazines, newspapers, etc)? Why?

What was the last book you read? Did you enjoy it? Why/Why not?

2 Read the extract from a novel, ignoring the gaps.

  1 Which of the genres from exercise **1** is it?

  2 What has made Graham Holt's daughter angry?

  3 Why does she eventually decide to go to Madrid?

'Enemies? Everyone despised him. I can't think of a man with more enemies.' I sat up. I despised my father, but I didn't like the thought of other people hating him. I don't know why. I suppose because
5 I felt that he must be some part of me. We shared blood, and genes. And we had once shared a life – if only for a very short time.

We were sitting in the café at the top of a department store in the centre of Madrid. Blanca de la Rosa
10 sipped her coffee. I sipped mine. We were next to the window and below us I could see people going in and out of shops. Christmas shopping, perhaps? **1** It was a cold day in early November. The wind moved the clouds, but never enough to open up the sky. It
15 was the kind of day I had never expected to see in Spain.

I rubbed my arms and said: 'But hating someone casually is different from wanting to kill them.' Blanca de la Rosa shrugged. 'I wouldn't know. I don't
20 go in for such emotions.' Blanca de la Rosa was my father's secretary. Or had been, before he died. My father had run a business selling British art. **2** After all, he knew nothing about art.

When I was growing up, he had owned a sports shop.
25 Later, I heard he worked in the music business, as a booking agent or something like that. **3** Since my teens, you see, I had been trying to forget about my father.

I was well on my way to achieving this when I
30 got the phone call that afternoon in September. It was a Sunday and I was in a London pub with some friends. **4** Then there was a click and a woman's voice, half-American, half-something else, said: 'Hello? I am Blanca de la Rosa. I am Graham
35 Holt's secretary. I understand you are his daughter.' 'That's right,' I said. I was already shaking when she dropped her bombshell. 'I'm calling to tell you he was found dead last night,' she went on. 'He was shot.'

40 **5** I was furious that my father had come back into my life. Then I called my mother, who I like to think I take after only slightly more than my father. She laughed and told me to stay away. 'I always knew someone would kill him one day,' she said.
45 'I only wish it had been me.'

I took her advice. I called Blanca de la Rosa and told her to do whatever she felt was appropriate with my father's belongings and money – to keep them or give them to charity if she wanted. And I tried
50 to forget about my father all over again. **6** It just wouldn't go away. In the end, I called Blanca de la Rosa again to ask her whether the police had arrested anyone for his murder.

'The police have more important things to do with
55 their time,' she snorted. My father was a liar and a cheat. He had hurt me in countless ways. But someone had killed him and not been punished, and I had to know why. So I booked a flight to Madrid and arranged to meet Blanca de la Rosa.

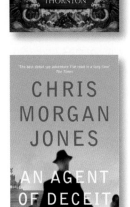

3 Six sentences have been removed from the extract. Choose from the sentences **A–G** the one which fits each gap (**1–6**). There is one extra sentence which you do not need to use.

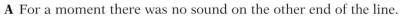

Don't forget!

- For each answer, check that the whole sentence fits in with the meaning of the text before *and* after the gap.
- When you have finished, check your answers by reading through the whole text again to ensure that it makes sense.
- Check that the extra sentence does not fit into any of the gaps.

A For a moment there was no sound on the other end of the line.
B For a week I did nothing.
C I've always been amazed at how he had managed to get into that.
D But he had a business here and someone has to arrange his affairs.
E I'm not really sure, as I never took much notice of what he did.
F But it was too soon for that.
G But over the next few weeks, I couldn't get his image out of my mind.

Reacting to the text

How do you think the story continues?

Language focus 2: Past tenses

1 Look at the following sentences from the extract and name the underlined past tenses. Choose from:

past simple   past continuous

past perfect simple   past perfect continuous

1 in the café at the top of a department store in the centre of Madrid.
2 But someone had killed him and not been punished, and I had to know why.
3 I was already shaking when she dropped her bombshell.
4 Then I called my mother … She laughed and told me to stay away.
5 Since my teens, I had been trying to forget about my father.

2 In which sentence above is the past tense or combination of tenses used to describe:

a a series of actions or events following each other in chronological order?
b an event which occurred before the other past actions in the narrative?
c an action which continued until a specific point in the past?
d a situation which occurred over a period of time and which forms the background to other past actions in the narrative?
e an action which was in progress when another action occurred?

3 Name the tenses in the following pairs of sentences and explain the difference in meaning between each pair.

1a When he was having breakfast, he read the newspaper.
 b When he'd had breakfast, he read the newspaper.
2a I heard about it when I was listening to the news on the radio.
 b I listened to the news on the radio when I heard about it.
3a I lived in Oxford for six years.
 b I had been living in Oxford for six years.

4 In which of the sentences in exercise **3** can *while* be used in place of *when*?

In which sentences can *as soon as* be used in place of *when*?

Do these words change the meaning of the sentences in any way?

5 Complete each of these spaces with either *at the end, in the end* or *at last*.

a I'd like you to hand in your homework _____ of the class.

b We were going to catch a train but _____ we decided it would be cheaper to drive.

c We've found a house we like _____ ! We've been looking for nearly a year.

In which sentence could *eventually* be used without changing the meaning?

Look at page 212 of the Grammar reference for more information about past tenses and time linkers.

6 For each of the sentences **1–6** decide which of the three alternative time expressions fits the gap. Pay attention to both grammar and meaning.

1 He wasn't allowed to go home _____ he'd apologized to the teacher.

 A until   **B** afterwards   **C** as soon as

2 _____ she was coming home, she fell over and hurt herself.

 A After   **B** During   **C** As

3 It can get very hot here _____ the summer.

 A while   **B** during   **C** when

4 First of all he won the 100 metres freestyle competition. _____ he went on to break the record for backstroke and crawl at the same distance.

 A After   **B** After it   **C** Afterwards

5 She got so tired of waiting for him that _____ she just went home.

 A at the end   **B** in the end   **C** at last

6 _____ she'd gone, he started to cry.

 A Eventually   **B** Until   **C** As soon as

7 Read the following texts in which two people tell the story of an embarrassing moment. In each of the spaces write the appropriate past form of the verb in brackets. There is an example at the beginning **(0)**.

Bus blush

Something very embarrassing **(0)** _happened_ (happen) to me while I **(1)** _____ (travel) home from school on the bus one day. We **(2)** _____ (have) a laugh at the back of the bus when I **(3)** _____ (see) a friend from school. She **(4)** _____ (sit) at the front, so I **(5)** _____ (run) up and **(6)** _____ (sit) down behind her, pulling her ponytail and shouting, 'Hi there, Rebecca!' I felt so stupid when a man I **(7)** _____ (never/see) before turned round! 'Actually, my name's Andrew,' he **(8)** _____ (smile). I **(9)** _____ (not/stop) blushing until I **(10)** _____ (get) home.

Face paint

My nephews **(11)** _____ (ask) me for days to take them somewhere, and eventually I **(12)** _____ (agree) to go to the park with them. While they **(13)** _____ (play) football, I **(14)** _____ (fall) asleep in the sun. Later, on our way to the shopping centre, where I **(15)** _____ (arrange) to meet my boyfriend, Paul, they **(16)** _____ (keep) telling me how beautiful I looked. As soon as Paul **(17)** _____ (see) me, he **(18)** _____ (burst) out laughing. 'Have you looked in a mirror?' he said. Catching my reflection in a shop window, I **(19)** _____ (discover), to my horror, that my nephews **(20)** _____ (draw) a huge beard and moustache on my face with crayons. I nearly died of embarrassment.

Writing 2
Part 2

Report

1 Read the following Writing Part 2 instructions then do the exercises in **2–5** below.

> Your local mayor wants to increase the number of visitors to your area. You have been asked to write a report for the mayor on **one** of the following:
>
> - Cinemas, theatres and concert halls
> - Historic buildings and museums
> - Parks and gardens
> - Transport facilities
> - Sports facilities
>
> The report should describe what your area offers visitors and make recommendations for improvements.

2 In **a–c** below and on page 55, there are three possible introductions to the report on *Cinemas, theatres and concert halls*. Complete each gap (**1–8**) with a word from the box, using the words in **bold** to help you. There is an example at the beginning **(0)**.

aim   aims   contains   ~~looks~~   make   order   provide   terms   ways

a This report **(0)** _looks_ **at** some of the entertainment facilities that visitors to this town can find here. It also suggests **(1)** _____ **of** improving these facilities **with the (2)** _____ **of** attracting more visitors.

b This report **(3)** _____ **to** describe what our town offers visitors **in (4)** _____ **of** cinemas, theatres and concert halls. It also **(5)** _____ **recommendations** for improving these facilities so as to encourage more people to visit the town.

c

Introduction

The purpose of this report is to (6) _____ **an overview of** the town's cinemas, theatres and concert halls and **to (7)** _____ **suggestions** on how to improve them **in (8)** _____ **to** attract more visitors.

3 Read the continuation of the report which was introduced in **2c** above. Is the style of the language in the report appropriate? Give reasons for your answer.

Cinemas

There are three cinemas in the town centre, all of which are in poor condition and create a bad impression on anyone visiting our town. The buildings are old, the seats are uncomfortable and each cinema has just one screen, so there is not much choice in terms of films.

Theatres and Concert halls

We are fortunate enough to have three theatres and a large concert hall in our town. Unlike the cinemas, these buildings are well maintained and offer both residents and tourists a wide variety of plays and concerts. However, overseas visitors comment on the high prices of tickets and this prevents many from attending shows.

Recommendations

I recommend that the council should build a new multi-screen cinema complex, showing some original version films, particularly for the benefit of English-speaking tourists to our town. I also suggest offering special discounts on theatre and concert tickets for the many young foreign people who come here to study.

4 The question in **1** says that the report should consider visitors to the area. In each paragraph of the report in **2c** and **3**, how does the writer show the relevance of the report to visitors?

Example:
Introduction: the writer says that suggestions will be made 'in order to attract more visitors'.

5 **a** In the final paragraph of the report in **3**, what structures are used after the verbs *recommend* and *suggest*?

b Underline any other language in **3** which could be used in the different reports for the question in **1**.

Example:
in poor condition

6 Write your own answer for **one** of the other reports in the question in **1** on page 54. Write your **report** in **140–190** words.

How to go about it

- Write a plan for your report.

  Note down positive and negative points about the facilities in your area. For each negative point, consider a recommendation you could make.

- In your plan you could have two or three central paragraphs after the introduction, with a final paragraph containing your recommendations. Alternatively, you could include a recommendation in each paragraph.

- Give each paragraph a short title.

- Follow the instructions in the question carefully.

  Remember to make your report relevant to visitors to your area.

- If you are not sure what to write about, you can invent information.

- Write your report in an appropriate style and use a range of language.

  In this report for the mayor, a formal style is appropriate.

For more information on writing reports, see page 200.

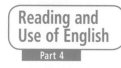

Review

Transformations

For questions **1–6**, complete the second sentence so that it has a similar meaning to the first sentence, using the word given. **Do not change the word given.** You must use between **two** and **five** words, including the word given.

Write the missing words **IN CAPITAL LETTERS**.

1 When the meeting was over, they went out for a drink.

   HAD

   As _____ finished, they went out for a drink.

2 When we eventually arrived at the party, all the food had been eaten.

   GOT

   By _____ the party, all the food had been eaten.

3 He put everything back in its place before he left.

   UNTIL

   He did not _____ everything back in its place.

4 They decided against employing him because of his age.

   TAKE

   They decided _____ because of his age.

5 She is not very interested in my work.

   INTEREST

   She does _____ my work.

6 This is the funniest book I've ever read.

   FUNNY

   I've _____ book before.

Correcting mistakes

In each short text **1–5**, there are two words which should not be there. Find these words and cross them out. The first one has been done for you.

1 At first we weren't sure whether we could afford to go on holiday, but in the end we ~~had~~ felt we ought to spend at least ~~during~~ a week on the coast.

2 I was extremely impressed with the special effects and some part of the action scenes. As for as the acting, though, I felt many amateurs could have done better.

3 Sophie was so much glad after her last exam. 'At the last!' she cried. 'I thought I'd never finish.'

4 When he had came home from work he was made himself a cup of tea and read the newspaper. It had been an exhausting day.

5 I'm really pleased we took to your advice and went to the new Indian restaurant that's just opened. The service was marvellous and it was such a good food.

Vocabulary: Cinema

Complete each gap with **one** word, the first letter of which has been given. You may need to use the plural form of a word.

1 The 2012 film *Cloud Atlas* features **an all-star c_____** including Tom Hanks, Halle Berry, Hugh Grant and Susan Sarandon.

2 Penelope Cruz won an Academy Award for Best Actress in **a Supporting r_____** for her part in the 2008 film *Vicky Cristina Barcelona*.

3 The novel was highly praised by **literary c_____** but the film adaptation received **poor r_____** .

4 It's a well-written thriller, with convincing characters and **a gripping p_____** .

5 One ingredient of a good action film is an exciting and **memorable opening s_____** ; some kind of chase involving cars or helicopters, for example.

Reading and Use of English
Part 3

Word formation

1 Read the following text, ignoring the gaps for the moment. What is the purpose of the text?

Storytime

The *Storytime School of Storytelling* offers a **(0)** __VARIETY__ of courses to anyone **(1)** _____ in the ancient art of storytelling. A wide range of people have studied with us, from tour guides to teachers, lawyers to **(2)** _____ and bankers to business owners.

VARY
INTEREST

LIBRARY

Their motives for attending our courses vary enormously. They may be keen to develop their **(3)** _____ as public speakers, learn how to use stories in the classroom, or activate their **(4)** _____ in a playful environment. Whatever their reasons, participants usually find the experience extremely **(5)** _____ , as you can see from the enthusiastic testimonials on our website. Many of these point to the school visits to give **(6)** _____ to local children as the highlight of their course. Others mention the supportive atmosphere in our school and the quality of the teaching.

CONFIDE
CREATIVE

FASCINATE
PERFORM

Not **(7)** _____ , many people come back to *Storytime* again and again. We offer an almost **(8)** _____ number of courses ranging from *Animal tales* to *Using your voice* or *Creating your own stories*. Why not contact us? We're sure to have a course for you.

SURPRISE
LIMIT

---

2 Read the text again and use the word given in capitals at the end of some of the lines to form a word that fits in the space **in the same line**. There is an example at the beginning **(0)**. Write your answers **IN CAPITAL LETTERS**.

Writing
Part 2

Write an answer to one of the following in **140–190** words.

1 You have seen this notice on the noticeboard of your school's computer club.

> **Reviews wanted: Games based on films**
> Help us to choose games for the club!
> Write us a review of a computer game you play which is based on a film. Tell us about the game's good and bad points and say whether you would recommend it for the computer club games library.

Write your **review**.

2 This is part of a letter you have received from your English friend, Tanya.

> *I'm not sure what to read next. What's the best book you've read recently? Tell me a little bit about the plot (not too much!) and say what you liked about it. If it sounds good, I'll see if I can get a copy in English.*
> *Thanks*
> *Tanya*

Write your **letter**.

 **Doing what you have to**

Talking about photos

1 Look at the four photographs. They show people doing something they should not be doing.

Student A Compare photographs **1** and **2** and say how you think the people are feeling.

How are the people feeling?

Student B Say which of the people you think is behaving worse.

2 Now change roles. Follow the instructions above using photographs **3** and **4**.

Multiple matching

1 What are/were some of the rules at your secondary school?
Which of them do/did you agree or disagree with? Why?
What punishments are/were imposed if you break/broke the school rules?

2 You are going to read an article in which people talk about school rules. For questions **1–10**, choose from the people (**A–D**). The people may be chosen more than once.

Don't forget!

- Read all the statements first, underlining key words.
- Read section A and match any statements you can. Underline the relevant parts of the text as you do so.
- Do the same for the other three sections.
- Scan the whole text again to find information which relates to any remaining statements you have not yet matched.

Which person states the following?

I fail to understand the reason for a rule at my child's school.	1
Something which was forbidden at the school before is actively encouraged now.	2
School rules serve to prepare young people for the future.	3
I disagree with the element of choice offered to my child.	4
I did not realize that I had accepted a rule at my child's school.	5
School rules were clearer and easier to understand when I was at school.	6
Some school rules affected my ability to study.	7
There has been a decline in standards of behaviour at my child's school.	8
I was angry at the way my child was made to feel.	9
I was discouraged from voicing my opinion on a rule at my child's school.	10

How are the people feeling?

School rules

Four parents compare their school rules with those of their children

A Simon

When I was at school – more years ago than I care to remember – far too much emphasis was placed on what we could and couldn't do, and sometimes this got in the way of learning. We had to wear our jacket and tie at all times, no matter what the temperature, and I remember sitting there in the height of summer, sweating profusely as I battled with algebra or struggled with French verb forms.

They didn't let us drink water in the classroom either. That would cause an outrage now. My daughter goes to the same school as I did, and we're asked to provide her with a refillable bottle, which she can take into class with her. They've realized that water improves concentration, so pupils almost *have* to drink it now.

B Jenny

At my son David's school, rule number one of their two-page Mobile Phone Policy states that 'pupils are strongly advised not to bring mobile phones to school'; then there are sixteen more rules describing situations in which they can and cannot be used. It's very confusing – it would be much simpler just to ban them altogether. That's what my old school would have done if mobile phones had been around then. Everything was black and white in those days, just like our school tie.

And that's another thing – David doesn't have to wear a tie if he doesn't want to, even though it's part of the uniform. That's just silly. I almost wrote to the school about it, but my son advised me against it. It seems that school rules are decided on jointly by students and teachers, and as a parent, I don't have any say in the matter.

C Lucy

My sixteen-year-old daughter isn't allowed to wear a nose stud to school on health and safety grounds. Can you believe it? According to the headteacher, in a busy school piercings present 'a very real risk of accidents'. I
35 can't see why – they're no more dangerous than carrying a sharpened pencil in your pocket, and there's no rule against that, as far as I know. I used to wear earrings to school and never had any problems.

It seems I agreed to all this when I signed the school
40 rules document at the beginning of last term, but I honestly wasn't aware of any ban on tiny metal objects in the nose. We were given a couple of warnings, but I was still furious when they made her take it out and sent her home for the day: they humiliated her in front of her
45 classmates and there's no excuse for that.

D Andrew

It's gone from one extreme to the other. When I was a lad, we weren't allowed to have shoulder-length hair at school. The headteacher cut it off in his office if we did, without so much as a phone call home. Now my boy
50 mustn't have his hair cut too short, otherwise he'll be suspended until it grows back to 'a suitable length'. He thinks it's unfair, but ultimately all rules, whatever they are, help to maintain order and get children ready for the real world.
55 As a lawyer, I don't need to be convinced of their importance – they're part of my daily life. If anything, they should tighten the rules up a bit more at my son's place. Discipline there has gone downhill in the last few years and the kids seem to do what they want.

Don't forget!

Develop your answers fully and give reasons for your opinions.

 Reacting to the text

Which of the school rules mentioned in the text do you find the most surprising?
Do you think pupils should be involved in deciding what the school rules are?
Should parents be asked to sign a school rules document?

Language focus 1: Obligation, necessity and permission

1 Look at sentences **1–10** from the reading text and answer questions **a–d** below.

> 1 ... *far too much emphasis was placed on what we <u>could</u> and <u>couldn't do</u>* ...
> 2 *We <u>had to wear</u> our jacket and tie at all times* ...
> 3 *They <u>didn't let us drink</u> water in the classroom* ...
> 4 ... *pupils almost <u>have to drink</u> [water] now.*
> 5 ... *situations in which [mobile phones] <u>can</u> and <u>cannot be used</u>.*
> 6 *David <u>doesn't have to wear</u> a tie if he doesn't want to* ...
> 7 *sixteen-year-old daughter <u>isn't allowed to wear</u> a nose stud to school* ...
> 8 ... *they <u>made her take</u> [the nose stud] out* ...
> 9 *When I was a lad, we <u>weren't allowed to have</u> shoulder-length hair at school*
> 10 *As a lawyer, I <u>don't need to be convinced</u> of their importance* ...

a Which underlined verb phrases talk about what is/was permitted?

b Which verb phrases talk about what isn't/wasn't permitted.

c Which ones express necessity and/or obligation in the present or past?

d Which express a lack of necessity and/or obligation in the present or past?

2 Who might say the following sentences?

a You must hand in your homework tomorrow.

b We have to hand in our homework tomorrow.

Why is *must* used in the first sentence and *have to* in the second?

3 In the following sentences the forms which express obligation, necessity and permission are all used incorrectly.

🅖 Correct the mistakes and then check your answers by reading the Grammar reference on page 213.

1 I have not to tidy my room up today; I did it yesterday.

2 Do you must make such a noise? I'm trying to concentrate!

3 Last week I must went to the hairdresser. Mum said my hair was far too long.

4 Did you be allowed to watch that film on telly last night?

5 They've changed my hours! Now I must start work at 7.30 instead of 8.30.

6 Come shopping with us if you want to. But you mustn't – it's up to you.

7 You need prepare your bags tonight if your train leaves at 6.30 in the morning.

8 You really should to go and see that film.

Make and let

4 Note that both of these verbs in the active are followed by the infinitive without *to*.

a Rewrite the following two sentences from the text in the passive.

1 They didn't let us drink water in the classroom.

We weren't _____ water in the classroom.

2 They made her take the nose stud out.

She was _____ the nose stud out.

b Complete the following sentences using the correct form of *make, let* or *allow*.

1 I wanted to watch the film last night but I wasn't _____ to. I had to go to bed early.

2 I'd love to come but I don't think my boss will _____ me have the day off work.

3 I hate cabbage but my mum _____ me eat it.

5 The advertisement below appeared in an international magazine. Read the advertisement and Tim's email, then complete each gap in the email with a verb from the box. Use each verb **once** only.

| supposed to | have to | don't have to | mustn't |
| need | should | ought | better |

Competition

Why not enter our exciting new writing competition?

The rules are simple: just write a story in no more than 600 words on any theme you like, and you could win an e-book reader.

Send us your entry* by email no later than 31 January. The winning story will appear in the March edition of English Today.

* Entrants must be at least 16 years old.

To: Elisa
Sent: 6 January
Subject: Writing competition

Hi Elisa

Do you remember that writing competition I told you about? Well, my teacher suggested I **(1)** _____ go in for it, so I think I will. I reckon the hardest thing for me will be the fact that you **(2)** _____ write more than 600 words. Once I start writing I just can't stop, so I'll **(3)** _____ to control myself if I want to keep within the limit.

The good thing is you **(4)** _____ write about any specific topic – you can choose that yourself. But I think I **(5)** _____ to write about something I'm familiar with, don't you? I could base it around a fishing trip or a tennis match. The only problem is you're **(6)** _____ be at least 16 to enter. My birthday's not until 4 February, but it would be a bit mean of them not to accept my entry, wouldn't it?

I **(7)** _____ send it in by the end of the month, so I'd **(8)** _____ start writing soon, as I'm going skiing on the 19th.

Wish me luck!

Tim

6 ⬭ Talk about the things you *have to, should* or *ought to* do and those things you *don't have to* or *aren't allowed to* do at:

- home
- school/college/work
- the weekend

> *Example:*
> Home:
>
> *I ought to tidy my room more often, but I never seem to find the time. I don't have to clean it, though. My mother does that for me.*

Word formation: -*en* suffix

> *… they should **tighten** the rules up a bit more at my son's place.*
>
> *… it's no more dangerous than carrying a **sharpened** pencil in your pocket.*

1 **a** Some verbs are formed by adding the suffix –*en* to an adjective (*tight – tighten*) or -*n* if the adjective ends in *e* (*loose – loosen*). Write the verbs formed from these adjectives. You may need to double the final consonant.

weak _____   *sweet* _____   *deaf* _____   *fat* _____
bright _____   *wide* _____   *worse* _____   *sad* _____

b A small number of verbs are formed by adding -*en* to the noun rather than the adjective. Complete the table.

Adjective	Noun	Verb
strong	_____	_____
long	_____	_____
high	_____	_____

2 Complete the gaps with the correct form of one of the words you wrote in exercise **1**. The first one has been done for you.

1 Are there any types of **food** which you know are very ___*fattening*___ but which you can't resist?

2 Do you have many things in your house such as paintings, plants or ornaments to _____ it **up**? How about your bedroom?

3 If you drink **tea or coffee**, how much sugar do you add to _____ it?

4 Do you like listening to _____ **music**? Does it bother you if others play loud music?

5 Which of the following **problems** have _____ in recent years in your country and which have improved? Is enough being done to solve them?

football violence   crime   unemployment   pollution

6 If you were asked to describe your main _____ **and weaknesses** at a job interview, what would you say?

7 If you had to choose, would you _____ **the working/school day** and go to work/school one day fewer each week, or shorten it and go one day more? Why?

8 Do you **have a good head for** _____ or do you hate being at the top of tall buildings?

3 ⬭ Discuss the questions in exercise **2** with your partner.

Open cloze

1 Read the quotations about housework. Which is your favourite? Why?

> Housework is what a woman does that nobody notices unless she hasn't done it.
> **Evan Esar**

> I hate housework! You make the beds, you do the dishes – and six months later you have to start all over again.
> **Joan Rivers**

> My husband and I have figured out a really good system about the housework: neither one of us does it.
> **Dottie Archibald**

> Housekeeping is like being caught in a revolving door.
> **Marcelene Cox**

2 Who does most of the housework in your family?
Which household chores do you do?
How do you feel about doing them? Why?

3 Look at the cover of the book *How to get things really flat*. What sort of advice do you think it includes? Why do you think the author calls it *A Man's Guide*?

4 Read the internet review of the book, ignoring the gaps, then answer these questions. Would you be interested in reading this book? Why/Why not?

How to get things really flat by Andrew Martin

This was by (0) _FAR_ the best present I received last Christmas. It's an informative and amusingly written book, which is (1) _____ funny that it had me laughing out loud (2) _____ a number of occasions. Andrew Martin has managed (3) _____ make the subject of housework entertaining, combining useful information and tips with recollections from his childhood and hilarious scenes from daily family life. (4) _____ it's labelled 'a man's guide', it's intended for any 'person who does not know, or care, (5) _____ day the dustbin men come, or where the bathroom cleaner is kept'.

The title of the book is a reference to ironing. Martin reassures us that this is (6) _____ at all difficult, and he describes the correct order (7) _____ which we should iron the various parts of a shirt. We also learn 'how to load a dishwasher without causing comment', how to vacuum stairs, and why a feather duster (8) _____ from ostrich feathers is better than a synthetic one. An interesting read – highly recommended.

---

5 Read the text again and for questions **1–8**, think of the word which best fits each gap. Use only **one** word in each gap. There is an example at the beginning **(0)**. Write your answers **IN CAPITAL LETTERS**.

How to go about it

- Look at the words both before and after the gap, before you decide what the missing word is.
  For gaps 1–3, as for the example (0), key words have been underlined to help you make your decisions. No words are underlined in the First examination.
- Sometimes you will only be able to make the right decision by reading the whole sentence.
  For gap 4, read the whole sentence before deciding which linker to use.

Listening 1
Part 4

Multiple choice ⦿ 1.30

1 ⬤ Do you think teenagers should be expected to help with the housework? Why/Why not?

2 You will hear an interview with a woman called Deborah Chilton talking about teenagers and housework. For questions **1–7**, choose the best answer (**A, B or C**).

1 Deborah says it is important for parents to understand
   A the reasons for making teenagers do housework.
   B how difficult it is to get teenagers to do housework.
   C the advantages for the whole family of teenagers doing housework.

2 According to Deborah, what is the mistake that many parents make?
   A They expect their children to do too many chores.
   B They tell rather than ask their children to do chores.
   C They wait too long before giving their children chores.

3 Deborah says that parents should give teenagers
   A help when cooking a meal.
   B clear instructions for tasks.
   C more than one task a week.

4 According to Deborah, what should parents do if a teenager fails to do a chore?
   A prevent the teenager from going out
   B give the teenager extra chores to do
   C let the teenager face the consequences

5 What does Deborah recommend parents should do if the situation does not improve?
   A appeal to the teenager's sense of responsibility
   B stop payment of the teenager's pocket money
   C allow the teenager to choose an alternative chore

6 Which aspect of a chore does Deborah feel a teenager could decide?
   A the type of chore
   B the timing of the chore
   C the method of doing the chore

7 Deborah says a positive feature of household chores is that
   A they can be fun if they are done with help from other people.
   B they give teenagers something different to think about.
   C they are very varied.

3 Do you agree that teenagers should not be paid for doing household chores? Why/Why not?

Speaking 2
Part 3

Collaborative task ⬤

1 When a mixed group of teenagers and adults was asked what they thought were the qualities of a good parent, they came up with the following list. Talk to each other about how important it is for a parent to have each of these qualities.

A sense of humour — **How important is it for a parent to have these qualities?** — A sense of fairness

Patience — The ability to listen

Strictness

2 Now decide which two qualities are the most important for a parent to have.

Don't forget!

* Interact with your partner: ask them questions, respond to their answers and give your own opinions.
* In task **2** you do not have to agree with your partner.

Useful language

It's important/essential for a parent to be patient, **otherwise** ...
If parents are not strict enough/too strict with their children, **then** ...
Parents need to show patience/authority/a sense of humour, **because** ...
A good parent is one who listens to their children's problems ...
Parents should always be (firm but) fair towards their children ...
Look again at the Useful language box on page 36.

Vocabulary: The world of work

1 **a** The following verbs can all be used before the countable noun *job*.

get   look for   apply for   ~~be out of~~   go for an interview for

Put the verbs in the boxes below depending on the order they normally occur in.
The first one has been done for you.

| be out of a job | → | | → | | → | | → | |

b The following verbs all indicate ways of ending a job. Put each one into an appropriate gap below.

sacked   made redundant   resigned

1 Because of the economic crisis, 50 workers were _____ in order to ensure the survival of the company.

2 She had become increasingly bored in her job, so she _____ from the company in order to take up a more challenging post.

3 He was _____ for stealing and he's finding it difficult to get another job.

2 **a** Which of the verbs below is not normally used before the countable noun *career*?

to change   to give up your   to devote yourself to your   to study a   to start a

b Which of the nouns below is not normally used after the verb *to earn*?

a high salary   a weekly wage   a good living   a competition   a lot of money

3 Explain the difference in meaning between the two items, **a** and **b**, in **1–3** below.

1 a *to work part time*   **2 a** *to work overtime*   **3 a** *to work flexitime*
   b *to work full time*   **b** *to work long hours*   **b** *to work shifts*

4 **a** Name the jobs in the photographs.

b ⬤ Describe one of the jobs to your partner, but without naming it. Your partner will tell you which one you are describing. Use some of the Useful language from the box.

Useful language

A Skills
You (don't) need *good telephone/computer/artistic/organizational/language* **skills** for this job.
B Adjectives for personal qualities
patient confident intelligent brave well-educated talented
strong creative hard-working polite cheerful fit
C Adjectives for jobs
well-paid responsible satisfying challenging
badly paid tiring unpleasant monotonous

Listening 2
Part 2

Sentence completion ⦿ 1.31

1   ◯   What skills and qualities do you think are required to be a firefighter?
What do you think firefighters do when they are not called out to attend to a fire?

2   You will hear a talk given by Rob Martin, the station manager at Hove Fire Station. For questions **1–10**, complete the sentences.

Don't forget!

Underline the correct alternative in each of the following sentences.

- You *need to/don't need to* write more than three words for each answer.
- You *should/shouldn't* write a word or phrase that you actually hear. You *need to/don't need to* rephrase.

- Minor spellings errors *can/can't* be made, but the words you write *need to/don't need to* be recognizable to the examiner, so you *should/shouldn't* check your spelling.
- You *can/can't* expect to hear the answers in the same order as the questions.

Before you listen to the recording, read through all the questions and try to predict the type of information you will hear for each one.

Potential recruits are not required to have any **(1)** ....

Applicants take a literacy and numeracy test and are also assessed on their **(2)** .... skills.

There are physical tests measuring a candidate's grip and the strength of their **(3)** ....*and*............

Hove fire station currently employs **(4)** .... women.

After working a series of day and night shifts firefighters have a break of **(5)** ....

At the Watch Parade, during the change of shift, firefighters have to **(6)** ....

Firefighters give home safety advice to vulnerable people like the **(7)** ....*and*............

Most call-outs occur during the **(8)** ....

Firefighters can spend **(9)** .... clearing up after a fire.

Rob says that being a firefighter is a dangerous but at the same time very **(10)** .... job.

3   Look at the listening script on page 226 and use the context to help you guess the meanings of the phrasal verbs in bold.

Example:

*A typical shift begins with the Watch Parade, which is where one shift **hands over** to the next.*

Hand over means to give power, control or responsibility to someone else.

4   ◯   Would you be interested in working as a firefighter? Why/Why not?

Language focus 2: Noun phrases

1 Read the following explanations and examples. Then complete the gap in each category with a further example from the box. There is an example at the beginning **(0)**.

a Sunday newspaper	a series of tests	the top of the ladder
workforce	~~fire engine~~	wine bottle	four weeks' work
next Friday's meeting	a candidate's back and legs

There are a number of different ways of combining nouns.

A Noun + noun

Noun + noun is used in a large number of compound nouns to describe a single idea. Some are written as two words:

e.g. *fire station* (0) ___fire engine___

Some are written as one word:

e.g. *firefighter* (1) _____

There are no rules to help you decide whether compound nouns are written as one word or two.

B Noun + *of* + noun

Where no compound noun exists, noun + *of* + noun is often used.

e.g. *an important part of the job* (2) _____

Noun + *of* + noun is used with words like *top, bottom, back, front, beginning, middle, end* to describe parts of things.

e.g. *the end of the week* (3) _____

C Noun + *'s/s'* + noun

When talking about possession by a person, noun + *'s/s'* + noun is used.

e.g. *the firefighter's equipment* (4) _____

D Special distinctions

1 Noun + noun can be used for things which happen or appear regularly.

e.g. *a Saturday job a day shift* (5) _____

Noun + *'s/s'* + noun is used if they happen or appear once:

e.g. *last Saturday's newspaper* (6) _____

or to show duration:

e.g. *a day's journey* (7) _____

2 Noun + noun is used for containers:

e.g. *matchbox* (8) _____

Noun + *of* + noun is used to refer to the contents of the containers:

e.g. *a box of matches*   *a bottle of wine*

2 Complete the sentences using noun phrases formed from the words in brackets.

1 I have a big breakfast at the _____ (day; start) and several _____ (coffee; cups) throughout the morning. I wouldn't be able to work/study if I didn't.

2 I've never had a _____ (job; holiday); my _____ (time; leisure) is too important to me.

3 I'd hate to work a _____ (night; shift); I'd only consider it if they gave me an extra _____ (month; holiday) each year to compensate.

4 My school didn't prepare/hasn't prepared me very well for the _____ (work; world). In fact, most lessons were/are a _____ (waste; time).

5 There aren't many _____ (opportunities; job) for school leavers in my area; a _____ (young person; chances) of finding work are not very good.

6 I think all schools should organize a programme of _____ (experience; work) for their students; that way, they get a taste of what life is like in the _____ (place; work).

3 ⬤ How true for you or your area is each sentence in exercise **2**? Develop your answers, giving reasons and/or examples.

Writing
Part 1

Essay

1 ⬤ Read the following Writing Part 1 instructions. How would you answer the essay question and what could you say for each of the three 'Things to write about' in the Notes?

In your English class you have been talking about the world of work. Your English teacher has asked you to write an essay.

Write an essay using **all** the notes and give reasons for your point of view.

Write your **essay** in **140–190** words.

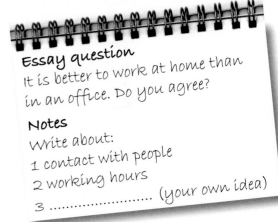

Essay question
It is better to work at home than in an office. Do you agree?

Notes
Write about:
1 contact with people
2 working hours
3 .... (your own idea)

2 Read the answer below to the question in exercise **1** and discuss the following questions with your partner. Give examples from the answer.

a How well has the writer addressed the three points in the notes?

b How varied is the writer's language?

c How appropriate is the style?

d Does the writer use appropriate linking devices?

No, I don't agree. I'd prefer to work in an ofice.

If you work at home you can't talk to anyone – their's only you and the computer. No one else. It's not very helthy if you can't talk to people during the day. You don't hear other people's ideas and oppinions and you get a bit lonley with just the computer to talk to. You might talk to somebody on the phone but it's not the same.

OK, if your at home and you don't have contact with poeple, no one can talk to you and disturb you, so you do more work. So it's better to work at home if you just want to work all the time. But talking to people makes life more intresting and it's pretty boring just working all the time. I think so, anyway.

Anyway, maybe you don't realy have many working hours at home, because you have loads of coffee brakes and no one tells you, 'Come on, do some work'.

So for all these reasons, my own idea is that it is better to work in an office than at home.

3 There are ten spelling mistakes in the answer above. Find the mistakes and correct them.

4 Write an **essay** in **140–190** words on **one** of the following:

a Write your own answer to the question in **1** above.

b Write an answer to the following question.

In your English class you have been talking about the pressures that exist for young people nowadays. Your English teacher has asked you to write an essay.

Write an essay using **all** the notes and give reasons for your point of view.

Don't forget!

- Plan your essay. Consider all three points in the Notes.
- Write in a consistently formal or neutral style.
- Organize your ideas using paragraphs and linking devices.
- Include a suitable introduction and conclusion.
- Use a range of language and avoid repetition.
- Check your answer for accuracy.

Reread the information about writing essays on page 39 in Unit 3.

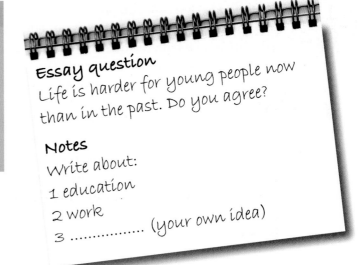

Essay question
Life is harder for young people now than in the past. Do you agree?

Notes
Write about:
1 education
2 work
3 .... (your own idea)

Modal verbs

For Questions **1–8** decide which answer **A, B** or **C** best fits each space.

1 You _____ take an umbrella; it's not going to rain.

   A mustn't   **B** can't   **C** needn't

2 I think we _____ to phone Marta and ask her if she wants to come.

   A should   **B** ought   **C** can

3 The best thing about my job is that I _____ to get up early. I don't start until 10 am.

   A needn't   **B** don't have   **C** am not supposed

4 A 'Non-uniform Day' is a day when we're _____ to wear 'normal clothes' to school if we want.

   A let   **B** made   **C** allowed

5 We'd _____ make too much noise; we might wake the baby up.

   A better not   **B** shouldn't   **C** ought not to

6 Where have you been? You were _____ to be here half an hour ago!

   A allowed   **B** supposed   **C** had

7 The rules are very clear. You know you _____ wear jewellery to school.

   A mustn't   **B** don't have to   **C** don't need to

8 I _____ to stay at my friend's house last night.

   A may   **B** could   **C** was allowed

Reading and Use of English
Part 3

Word formation

For questions **1–8**, read the text below. Use the word given in capitals at the end of some of the lines to form a word that fits in the space **in the same line**. There is an example at the beginning **(0)**. Write your answers **IN CAPITAL LETTERS.**

Boarding schools

Boarding schools are **(0)** _RESIDENTIAL_ schools that provide students with accommodation and food as well as education. The initial separation	**RESIDENT**
from the family can be a traumatic experience, and not **(1)** _____ , homesickness is a common problem.	**SURPRISE**
However, **(2)** _____ of this type of education feel that the advantages	**SUPPORT**
more than outweigh the disadvantages. They believe that boarding schools encourage a sense of discipline and **(3)** _____ ; children are taught to	**RESPONSIBLE**
follow a strict daily routine and obey a clear set of rules, but they are also forced to make many **(4)** _____ on their own, which leads to greater	**DECIDE**
(5) _____ and increased self-confidence. In addition, long periods of	**DEPEND**
time in the company of other children provides the opportunity to form close friendships and helps in the **(6)** _____ of communication and	**DEVELOP**
social skills. Many parents also argue that boarding can **(7)** _____	**STRONG**
family ties; time spent away from home often **(8)** _____ a child's	**HIGH**
appreciation of precious time spent with the family, and teenage anger can be directed at teachers rather than parents.	

Reading and Use of English
Part 1

Multiple-choice cloze

For questions **1–8**, read the text below and decide which answer (**A, B, C or D**) best fits each gap. There is an example at the beginning **(0)**.

A more commercial tune

At the age of 40, Roger Press **(0)** ___ his career. After spending five years as a concert pianist he went into business, **(1)** ___ up his own company.

'After leaving university I decided to **(2)** ___ myself to a career in music. I loved performing but it was very hard **(3)** ___ . I played at concerts in Europe and America, made recordings and got good **(4)** ___ . But unless you're one of the world's top pianists, it's difficult to earn a good **(5)** ___ and I wasn't one of the greatest.

'When I **(6)** ___ up my performing career, I joined a recording company and started its classical video division, producing programmes about famous artists. Then I left and formed my own company, **(7)** ___ in multimedia programmes. Now that I run my own business I am in control of my life. Although the stress is high and I work **(8)** ___ hours, the stress involved in piano playing was much worse.'

	A	B	C	D
0	A moved	B changed	C adjusted	D stopped
1	A giving	B setting	C forming	D bringing
2	A devote	B take	C assign	D employ
3	A job	B effort	C work	D career
4	A reviews	B critics	C reports	D praise
5	A life	B living	C money	D payment
6	A took	B brought	C gave	D put
7	A dedicating	B focusing	C concentrating	D specializing
8	A overtime	B large	C bonus	D long

Reading and Use of English
Part 4

Transformations

For questions **1–6**, complete the second sentence so that it has a similar meaning to the first sentence, using the word given. **Do not change the word given.** You must use between **two** and **five** words, including the word given.

Write the missing words **IN CAPITAL LETTERS**.

1 When I was younger I wasn't allowed to watch much television.

   LET

   When I was younger my parents _____ much television.

2 Paula had to wash up before she could go out.

   MADE

   Paula _____ wash up before she could go out.

3 Why can't we go to the party?

   ALLOWED

   Why _____ go to the party?

4 There's no need for you to hand the homework in until next week.

   NEED

   You _____ in the homework until next week.

5 I think you should see a doctor.

   BETTER

   I think you _____ a doctor.

6 Do you know what the homework is?

   SUPPOSED

   Do you know what we _____ for homework?

Vocabulary 1: Phrasal verbs

What do you think are the ingredients of:

a a good friendship?

b a successful marriage?

A Romance

1 The following sentences tell the unhappy love story of a young couple. Match a sentence beginning **1–6** with an ending **a–f**. The first one has been done for you.

1 Lucy and I started **going**   **a up with** her boyfriend, so I asked her to dance.

2 I saw her smile and **fell**   **b on** well **with** each other. We had good fun together.

3 I heard she had just **split**   **c out with** each other a year ago. We met in a club.

4 We laughed a lot and **got**   **d over** her for a long time. It's going to be very hard.

5 Sadly, last week we **fell**   **e for** her immediately. It was love at first sight.

6 I miss her and won't **get**   **f out with** each other after a row. I think it's all over.

2 Write the infinitive of each of the phrasal verbs from exercise **1** next to its meaning.

1 to stop being friendly with someone because you have had an argument or disagreement with them _____

2 to end a romantic relationship with someone _____

3 to have a romantic relationship with someone _____

4 to have a good relationship with someone _____

5 to fall in love with someone _____

6 to start to forget someone and feel happy again after a relationship has ended

_____

3 Study the sentences in exercise **1** then cover up the endings **a–f**. Take turns with your partner to read out the beginnings **1–6** and complete the sentences from memory.

B Family

1 Use the context in these sentences to help you work out the meaning of the phrasal verbs in **bold**.

1 After Leo's parents died, his aunt **brought** him **up** as if he were her own son.

2 I was born in England but I **grew up** in France; I lived in Paris until I was 18.

3 Parents need great patience to be able to **put up with** teenagers' changing moods.

4 Amy cried when her dad **told** her **off** for breaking a glass; he sounded very angry.

5 My mum is my role model. I **look up to** her because of her kindness and tolerance.

6 Tim's parents felt he had **let** them **down**. He'd repaid their generosity by stealing from them.

2 What is the infinitive form of each of the phrasal verbs in exercise **1**?

3 Write five sentences, each containing one of the phrasal verbs from Vocabulary 1. Leave spaces where the phrasal verbs should be and ask your partner to complete the sentences with the correct phrasal verbs.

Speaking 1
Part 3

Collaborative task

Read tasks **1** and **2** below and the Useful language box. Then do the tasks with another student.

1 Imagine that a magazine for teenagers and young adults is going to publish a series of articles giving advice about relationships. Below are some of the relationships they want to include.

Talk to each other about what problems might arise in these relationships.

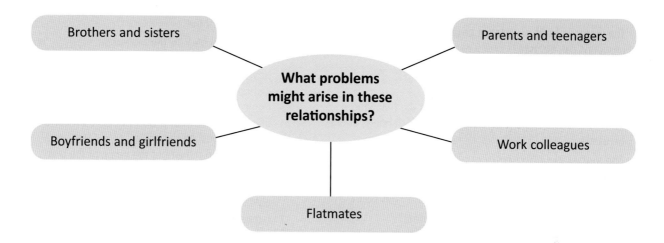

2 Now decide which two relationships teenagers and young adults would be most interested to receive advice on.

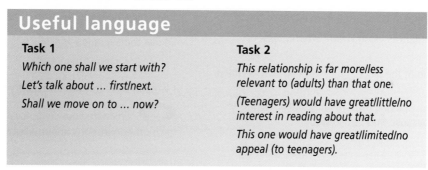

Useful language

Task 1

Which one shall we start with?

Let's talk about ... first/next.

Shall we move on to ... now?

Task 2

This relationship is far more/less relevant to (adults) than that one.

(Teenagers) would have great/little/no interest in reading about that.

This one would have great/limited/no appeal (to teenagers).

Listening 1
Part 3

Multiple matching   1.32–1.36

1 You will hear five different people talking about problems in their relationships with other people. For questions **1–5**, choose from the list (**A–H**) what each speaker says was the cause of the problem. Use the letters only once. There are three extra letters which you do not need to use.

Don't forget!

- Underline key words and phrases in the eight options.
- Listen carefully both times before making your final decision.

A the stress of working long hours

B the other person's general lack of tolerance

C having different ideas about how to keep someone occupied

D the other person's lack of self-confidence

E not having enough time together

F the other person's inability to adapt to a new role

G never having enough money

H the other person's sense of injustice

Speaker 1 [1   ]
Speaker 2 [2   ]
Speaker 3 [3   ]
Speaker 4 [4   ]
Speaker 5 [5   ]

2   Which of the five speakers do you have most sympathy for? Why?

Language focus 1: Defining relative clauses

Defining relative clauses contain information which is essential for our understanding of the whole sentence.

1 Look at these two extracts from the listening exercise and answer the questions.

*I shared a flat once with someone **who** used to get annoyed about the silliest of things.*

*He'd also tell me off for cooking food **that** made the house smell.*

The words in **bold** are relative pronouns. What alternative pronouns can be used?

Can the relative pronoun be omitted from these two sentences? Why/Why not?

2 A relative pronoun has been omitted from the following sentence. Where could it be inserted and which one(s) could be used?

The money we inherited from our grandmother wasn't divided equally between us.

Why is it possible to leave the pronoun out in this case?

3 Which of these two sentences is more formal?

*The woman **to whom** I spoke had no idea what was going on.*

*The woman **who** I spoke **to** had no idea what was going on.*

Can the relative pronoun be omitted from either of them?

4 Complete these sentences using *when, where, why* or *whose*.

   a What's the name of the place _____ we had that accident last year?

   b The reason _____ people from Mediterranean countries live so long is because they eat so well.

   c I'll always remember the day _____ I started my first job.

   d That's the woman _____ husband you spoke to on the phone.

   Check your answers and read more about defining relative clauses on page 214 of the Grammar reference.

5 Complete each of the gaps below with an appropriate relative pronoun or relative adverb. Decide in which sentences there is more than one possibility and whether the word can be left out.

   1 I'd like to go back to the restaurant _____ we celebrated your birthday last year.

   2 Have you been to the new Spanish tapas bar _____ has just opened in the town centre?

   3 Ironic really. The person _____ car they stole had just finished a three-year prison sentence for car theft.

   4 Have you finished the book _____ I lent you?

   5 I wish I could remember the name of the man _____ sold me this computer.

   6 The only thing _____ worries me is the cost. Will we be able to afford it?

   7 Here's that phone number _____ you wanted.

   8 I was born in 1969. That was the year _____ the first man landed on the Moon.

6 Complete the following sentences with your own ideas.

   A good friend is someone who …

   I don't like people that …

   I'd like to have a job which …

   I'll never forget the time when …

   I wouldn't like to live in a country where …

   Compare your sentences with your partner's. Ask each other questions about what you have written.

Speaking 2
Part 1

Interview

In Speaking Part 1 you may be asked to talk about your family and friends. Talk to your partner, taking turns to ask and answer the questions.

> **How to go about it**
>
> - Do not just answer 'yes' or 'no' to the examiner's questions. Develop your answers by giving reasons or examples.
> - Do not learn long pre-prepared answers. You are unlikely to sound natural and you may not answer the questions correctly.

- Do you take after your mother or your father? In what way?
- What types of things do you enjoy doing with your family?
- Describe the relationship you have with one of your family members.
- Do you prefer celebrating your birthday with friends or family?
- Do you spend most of your free time on your own or with friends?
- What do you like most about your best friend?

Reading and
Use of English 1
Part 1

Multiple-choice cloze

1 ◯ Who are the people in the photograph? How do you think they are feeling?

Do you like having your photograph taken? Why/Why not?

2 For questions **1–8**, read the text below and decide which answer (**A, B, C** or **D**) best fits each gap. There is an example at the beginning (**0**).

Example:

0 **A** glanced **B** looked **C** <u>seen</u> **D** stared

All four verbs are related to looking, but *seen* is the only appropriate word in the context. In addition, the other options, *glanced, looked* and *stared* would all be followed by the preposition *at*, which does not appear after the gap.

How to go about it

- Read through the whole text first, ignoring the gaps, to get a general idea of the content.

- When making your decisions, look at the words both before and after the gap.

  In this exercise, relevant words have been underlined in the first paragraph to help you. (No words are underlined in the exam.)

- You should also consider the overall meaning of the whole sentence in which the gap appears.

  For question 7 in this particular exercise, you will also need to consider the meaning of the previous sentence.

Renting family and friends

In recent years Japan has **(0)** ___ <u>the growth of</u> agencies which rent out <u>actors to</u> **(1)** ___ <u>the part of</u> relatives, friends and work colleagues. Social events such as weddings or funerals are generally very formal occasions in Japan, and <u>a large</u> **(2)** ___ <u>of guests</u> is an essential ingredient for many families. But for those <u>unlucky enough to be</u> **(3)** ___ <u>work</u> or only in temporary employment, there are fewer opportunities to make friends, so people like these **(4)** ___ <u>to</u> the growing rent-a-person service sector <u>for help</u>.

At one person's wedding recently, as **(5)** ___ as thirty of the family members, friends and co-workers were fakes, including the boss, as the groom had just been **(6)** ___ redundant. Often, **(7)** ___ just one actor is required, perhaps to impersonate the husband of a single mother who needs help sorting out a problem her son is having at school, or to listen as a friend to a lonely person in **(8)** ___ of conversation.

1	**A** pretend	**B** play	**C** show	**D** be
2	**A** amount	**B** quantity	**C** volume	**D** number
3	**A** out of	**B** away from	**C** over with	**D** off to
4	**A** ask	**B** demand	**C** pay	**D** turn
5	**A** high	**B** soon	**C** many	**D** far
6	**A** made	**B** taken	**C** given	**D** put
7	**A** moreover	**B** however	**C** even	**D** although
8	**A** charge	**B** look	**C** wish	**D** need

3 ◯ How popular would a rent-a-person agency be in your country? Why?

Reading and
Use of English 2
Part 5

Multiple choice

1 ⬤ Describe one of your aunts or uncles. What sort of relationship do you have with him or her?

2 You are going to read a short story about an aunt. For questions **1–6**, choose the answer (**A**, **B**, **C** or **D**) which you think fits best according to the text.

> **Don't forget!**
>
> - Read the whole story first for an overall understanding.
> - For each question, eliminate the options which are clearly wrong, then check the option or options you have not eliminated.
> - If you still cannot decide, choose one of the options.

Aunt Georgia

It was early June and Aunt Georgia, who lived down in London, came to help with the preparations for my sixteenth birthday party. She was the beautiful sister, with thick black
5 hair and eyes the colour of seaweed. She had been a ballet dancer in her youth and had kept her girlish figure. My mother was plump by comparison. Aunt Georgia arrived two days before the party in a fancy convertible sports
10 car with the top down. She had married well and was not one to hide her wealth. She pulled off her silk headscarf, shaking out her long hair, then kissed my mother and me. 'I'm so excited,' she cried. 'Where are we starting?'

15 We started with the glasses. My mother's idea had been to decorate ordinary wine glasses with coloured glass beads. While we sat around the kitchen table gluing the beads to the stems by hand, we talked about my
20 school, in particular my German classes. 'The latest addition to her collection,' my mother announced. The other language in my 'collection', apart from English, was French, which my Parisian father had always spoken
25 to me. My mother was envious because, as she was always saying, she had no gift for languages. 'My French really isn't what it should be,' she said again now – and I thought she looked a little uncomfortable. 'Your Aunt
30 Georgia was always the linguist in the family.'

My aunt nodded and looked through the kitchen window at the garden. After a while, she said. 'I'm not sure about these glasses. They're a little downmarket, don't you think?
35 A bit tacky. Why don't we drive into town today and get some crystal champagne flutes?' My mother smiled. 'Georgia, they're far too expensive. Half of them will get broken anyway. These are fine.' 'They'll be a gift from
40 me,' my aunt said. 'It's Clare's sixteenth after all. We shouldn't cut corners.'

We ate lunch outside and my aunt asked me about my summer holidays. I told her about my planned trip to Hamburg. 'A school trip?'
45 she asked. 'Not exactly,' I said. 'I'm going to stay with my German penfriend, Johann.' Aunt Georgia frowned, and quickly changed the subject, asking my mother how she planned to decorate the garden. My mother told her
50 about the candles we had bought. 'Candles?' my aunt said. 'We can do better than that, surely. We could wrap fairy lights around the trees, like they do in the Caribbean. Let's go into Manchester and look in Gamidges. I'm
55 sure they'll have something tasteful. While we're there, we could look for a dress for Clare.'

'She's already got a dress,' my mother said. Aunt Georgia smiled. 'But is it something she'll want
60 to look at in photos in twenty years? I wish I'd known earlier. I could have had her something made. I've got a wonderful tailor in London.' 'It's fine, really,' my mother said. 'It fits perfectly and it's a lovely colour for her eyes.' My aunt
65 laughed. 'Oh darling,' she said to my mother. 'If only you knew about colour. It's the wrong tone for her skin. Anyway,' she added, looking at her watch, 'we'd better get going.'

My aunt went upstairs to freshen up and I
70 asked my mother: 'Why do you let her speak to you like that? She's been getting at you all morning. You should stand up for yourself.' My mother started to put the wine glasses back in their boxes, avoiding my eyes.

75 'What?' I asked.

'Daddy was Aunt Georgia's French penfriend,' she said. 'They wrote to each other for a year and she was crazy about him.'

'Daddy and Aunt Georgia?' I said, astonished.

80 'That's right. Then, the summer *she* was sixteen he came over to stay. The problem was…'

'He fell in love with you instead.'

My mother nodded. 'We'll get the glasses and the fairy lights, but the dress is up to you.'

1 What does Aunt Georgia's choice of car tell us about her?

   A She did not mind others knowing how rich she was.

   B It was just one of several cars she drove.

   C It enabled her to show off her hair.

   D She enjoyed driving fast.

2 In the second paragraph we learn that the narrator's mother

   A had no interest in learning French.

   B was not a proficient language learner.

   C disapproved of her daughter's German classes.

   D disliked her husband speaking French to their daughter.

3 Why did Aunt Georgia disapprove of the wine glasses?

   A Some of them were broken.

   B Some of them had sharp edges.

   C They seemed to be of low quality.

   D They had been bought in a market.

4 When the narrator mentioned her German penfriend, Aunt Georgia

   A was disappointed she had not been told before.

   B was visibly pleased for her niece.

   C expressed surprise at his name.

   D did not want to talk about him.

5 What did Aunt Georgia suggest when talking about the dress?

   A Her sister had little idea about choosing the right clothes.

   B Her sister should have made the dress herself.

   C Her niece was not a very fashionable teenager.

   D Her niece did not look very good in photographs.

6 What does the narrator's mother suggest is the main cause of Aunt Georgia's behaviour towards her?

   A Aunt Georgia's self-importance

   B Aunt Georgia's feelings of jealousy

   C the mother's poor organizational skills

   D the mother's lack of taste

⬤ Reacting to the text

Why do you think the narrator's mother says *'We'll get the glasses and the fairy lights, but the dress is up to you'*?

Language focus 2: Non-defining relative clauses

1 Look at the following sentence from the reading text.

Aunt Georgia, who lived down in London, came to help with the preparations for my sixteenth birthday party.

This sentence contains two separate ideas.

Main idea: Aunt Georgia came to help with the preparations for my sixteenth birthday party.

Second idea: Aunt Georgia lived down in London.

The information contained in the second idea is not essential to our understanding of the meaning of the main idea. A relative clause which contains non-essential information is called a non-defining relative clause.

2 Underline the correct alternative in the following rules for non-defining relative clauses.

  a *Who* or *which* **can/cannot** be replaced by *that*.
  b The relative pronoun **can/cannot** be omitted.
  c Commas **are/are not** used.

  (G) Check your answers and read more about non-defining relative clauses on page 214 of the Grammar reference.

3 For **1–5**, link the ideas contained in the two sentences to form one sentence. Use an appropriate relative pronoun (*who, which, whose*) or relative adverb (*when, where*) and make any other necessary changes. Don't forget to add commas.

Example:

Main idea: This photograph shows the royal family on the palace balcony.

Second idea: This photograph was taken in 1919.

This photograph, which was taken in 1919, shows the royal family on the palace balcony.

  1 **Main idea:** We spent the weekend in York.
     Second idea: My mother was born in York.

  2 **Main idea:** My best friend has just got married.
     Second idea: My best friend always said she wanted to stay single.

  3 **Main idea:** My oldest sister lives in Munich.
     Second idea: My oldest sister's husband is German.

  4 **Main idea:** The best time to visit Iceland is in summer.
     Second idea: The average temperature in Iceland in summer is around ten degrees.

  5 **Main idea:** He has to work on Saturdays.
     Second idea: He isn't very happy about the fact that he has to work on Saturdays.

Open cloze: Relative clauses

For questions **1–10** read the text below. Complete each of the gaps with either a relative pronoun (*who, which, that, whose*) or a relative adverb (*when, where*). If there is more than one possibility, or the word can be left out, you should also indicate this. There is an example at the beginning **(0)**.

Family members' yawns are most contagious

A phenomenon **(0)** _which/that_ has long perplexed scientists is 'yawn contagion', the impulse **(1)** _____ we feel to yawn when we see other people doing so. Although some suggested the behaviour was a form of social empathy **(2)** _____ helps people connect with one another, it was unclear what determines whether we 'catch' a yawn or not. Now a new study has shown that the biggest factor in whether or not a yawn is contagious is the relationship between the yawner and the person **(3)** _____ hears or sees it. Prof Elisabetta Palagi, **(4)** _____ co-authored the study, said: 'We found that the most important factor is not nationality, the colour of skin, different cultural habits, sex or age of the people involved, but the type of relationship **(5)** _____ linked the two people.'

The study was carried out in Europe, North America, Asia and Africa, **(6)** _____ researchers from the University of Pisa in Italy analysed 480 bouts of yawning among 109 adults over a 12-month period. They found that the people **(7)** _____ yawns we are most likely to catch are close family members, followed by friends, then acquaintances and lastly strangers. The results also showed that the delay in **(8)** _____ a yawn is passed on is longer between strangers than between people **(9)** _____ know each other well. Children do not develop contagious yawning until the age of four or five, **(10)** _____ they also develop the ability to interpret other people's emotions properly.

Vocabulary 2: Describing people

A Personality

1 The following adjectives can all be used to describe a person's character. Which of them are positive and which are negative? Make two groups in your notebook.

sociable	mean	tolerant	patient	sensitive	polite
sincere	selfish	decisive	lazy	reliable	cheerful
practical	mature	bad-tempered	adventurous	moody	sensible

2 Arrange the adjectives in exercise **1** into the columns below according to the prefix which is used to form the negative. If none of the prefixes is used for a particular word, write a new word which expresses the opposite idea.

un-	in-	im-	different word
*un*sociable			*mean – generous*

3 ⬤ Think of two people you know, for example a relative and a friend, and describe what these people are like, using the adjectives you have just studied to help you.

B Appearance

1 One adjective in each group is not normally used before the noun in capital letters.

Underline the adjective which does not fit.

1 flowing   scruffy   bald   shoulder-length   straight   spiky   HAIR
2 dark   hazel   sparkling   almond-shaped   piercing   pierced   EYES
3 wrinkled   freckled   thinning   round   tanned   expressive   FACE
4 smooth   pale   dark   healthy   well-built   spotty   COMPLEXION

Which of these features can you see in the photographs above?

2 What is the difference between the words in each of the following groups?

a fat   plump   overweight   **b** thin   slim   skinny

3 ⬤ Work in pairs. Take it in turns to compare two people in the photographs above and say which of the two people you would prefer to meet and why. As well as describing physical appearance and clothes, you should also talk about personality.

Listening 2
Part 1

Multiple choice 👁 1.37–1.44

You will hear people talking in eight different situations. For questions **1–8**, choose the best answer, (**A**, **B** or **C**).

1 You hear a woman on the radio talking about her father.

What does she say about her father?

A He was not very talkative.
B He was very similar to her.
C He was very sure of himself.

2 You overhear a man talking about a former teacher.

What does the man say about the teacher?

A His teaching style was boring.
B His behaviour was distracting.
C His enthusiasm was contagious.

3 You hear a woman complaining about one of her employees.

What is she complaining about?

A his untidy appearance
B his poor punctuality
C his impolite behaviour

4 You hear part of a radio programme in which a man is giving advice.

Who is he giving advice to?

A parents
B teachers
C teenagers

5 You overhear a woman talking on the phone about some clothes.

What does the woman want to do with the clothes?

A throw them away
B give them to someone
C sell them

6 You hear a man and a woman talking about a person in a photograph.

Who is the person in the photograph?

A the man's sister
B the man's mother
C the man's daughter

7 You hear an elderly woman talking to a man about her new neighbours.

What does she like about them?

A They are often away at weekends.
B They have been very friendly.
C They look after their garden.

8 You hear a man talking on the radio about a musician who influenced him

What was it about the musician that influenced him?

A his fashion style
B his musical style
C his performing style

Language focus 3: Causative passive with *have* and *get*

1 a Complete each gap in the following sentences from the listening with the correct form of the verb in brackets.

Extract 4: ... *they want* **to have their nose** _____ *(pierce) or* **get a tattoo** _____ *(do).*

Extract 6: *She's had it* _____ *(frame) and it's up on the wall in her living room.*

b Check your answers in the relevant extracts of the listening script on page 227. What form of the verb does each of your answers have?
c In **1** and **2** explain the difference in meaning between the two sentences **a** and **b**.
1a He's repaired the car.   **b** He's had the car repaired.
2a He cut his hair.   **b** He got his hair cut.

🔍 Read more about causative passive with *have* and *get* on page 214 of the Grammar reference.

2 In questions **1–6**, write a suitable form of *have* in the first gap and the correct form of the verb in brackets in the second. The first one has been done for you.

1 Would you like __to have__ any part of your body __pierced__ (pierce)?
2 What are the advantages and disadvantages of _ _____ your head completely _____ (shave)?
3 If you could _____ your photo _____ (take) with someone famous, who would you choose?
4 When was the last time you _____ a tooth _____ (fill)?
5 Have you ever considered _____ your hair _____ (restyle)?
6 Do you know anyone who _____ their house _____ (break) into?

3 🔊 Ask and answer questions **1–6** in exercise **2**. Develop your answers.

Example:
A: Would you like to have any part of your body pierced?
B: I wouldn't mind, but I'm a hotel receptionist and I don't think my boss would be very happy if I went into work with a nose stud or a tongue piercing.

Writing
Part 2

Article

1 Read the following Writing Part 2 instructions.
You see this notice on your school noticeboard.

2 Read the model answer below. Which of the three people in the illustrations is most similar to the one described in the answer?

> INFLUENCES
> • Which person has had a big influence on you?
> • How has this person influenced you?
>
> Write us an article for the school magazine describing the person and saying how he or she has influenced you.

'Cheer up, chicken!'

That's what my grandmother, my Nana, says me when things are'nt going well. Then she tells me, 'It'll turn out all right at the end, you'll see.' And she's nearly always right.

So when I'm ill, or I've fell out with a friend or I'm just feeling down, I imagine Nana, with her wrinkled, but smiling face and sparkling blue eyes, saying her words of encouragement to me. And although my problems they don't just magically disappear, they don't seem so bad any more and I'm in better mood to sort them out.

Nana has taught me to be positive in difficult moments. She's had many of them in her long and hard life. But despite this, she has a straight back and a determined look on her face. Always she is cheerful and I've never seen her in a bad temper.

So even though she's nearly half my size and such small that she sometimes wears children's clothes, she's the person I most look up at in my family. She's a little lady with a big influence.

3 The model answer contains eight mistakes. Read the article again and correct the eight mistakes.

4 What techniques does the writer use:

a to attract and interest the reader at the beginning of the article?

b to leave the reader something to think about at the end of the article?

5 Find examples in the model answer of the following features:

a language of description, *e.g. her wrinkled, but smiling face and sparkling blue eyes*

b phrasal verbs, *e.g. cheer up*

c linking words, *e.g. Then*

6 Write your own answer to the question in exercise **1** in **140–190** words.

Don't forget!

- Begin with an interesting opening paragraph.
- Include direct questions or direct speech for a lively article.
- Use contractions and phrasal verbs for an informal style.
- Include a range of descriptive language and linking words.
- Leave the reader something to think about at the end.
- Give your article a catchy title.

6 Review

Relative clauses

Decide whether the relative clause in each of the following sentences is defining or non-defining. If the relative clause is non-defining, add commas in the appropriate place(s). If it is defining, say whether the relative pronoun or adverb can be omitted or not. There are two examples at the beginning (**0** and **00**).

0 My father who works in a chocolate factory never eats sweet things.

Non-defining – add commas after father *and* factory.

00 There'll be a prize for the student who tells the most jokes in five minutes.

Defining – the relative pronoun who *cannot be omitted.*

1 Lady Gaga whose real name is Stefani Joanne Angelina Germanotta was born on March 28 1986.

2 What's the name of the village where you got married?

3 He hasn't given me back the book that I lent him.

4 She told me that Vasilis had failed his driving test which didn't surprise me at all.

5 That song always reminds me of the time when I was working in Brazil.

6 He's the only person in this class whose first name begins with 'Z'.

7 Emma received a phone call from her Managing Director who had been impressed by her sales performance.

8 Few written records have survived so it is a period of history about which we know very little.

Vocabulary

A Describing people

Complete the crossword using the following clues.

Across

1 Someone who doesn't like meeting and spending time with other people is _____ .

3 Hazel eyes are light brown and slightly _____ in colour.

6 'Thank you for your donation to our charity. It was extremely _____ of you.'

8 'He's going to have his left _____ pierced.'

9 negative prefix for *decisive*

10 'She's so _____ : she only ever thinks about herself.'

11 unattractively thin

12 'Unfortunately, he's in a _____ mood today.'

14 Unlike Mediterraneans, people in northern Europe tend to have a rather _____ complexion.

Down

1 negative prefix for *adventurous*

2 'She's such a _____ child: always so happy and positive.'

4 'She looks much nicer with shoulder-length _____ .'

5 opposite of 6 across

7 'Please try to be _____ about this. Think with your head rather than with your heart.

10 attractively thin

11 'He was too _____ to ask her to go out with him, so he got his friend to do it for him.'

13 negative prefix for *honest*

80

B Phrasal verbs

Complete the gaps in sentences **1–8** below with the correct form of an appropriate phrasal verb. Use the verbs and particles from the boxes.

fall	bring	get	look
let	tell	fall	get

out	over	for	off
on	up	down	up

1 When I kept getting into trouble at school, my parents understandably felt I had _____ them _____ .

2 He was _____ _____ for hitting his sister and made to apologize to her.

3 I was _____ _____ by my parents to believe that honesty is the best policy.

4 I was extremely disappointed when I found out that my uncle had spent three years in prison: I had always _____ _____ to him and considered him a role model.

5 I don't _____ _____ very well with my mother-in-law. I don't think she's forgiven me for taking her son away from her.

6 It was love at first sight. I _____ _____ him immediately.

7 They're always _____ _____ over the silliest of things. They'll be talking to each other again tomorrow, you'll see.

8 He wasn't ready for a relationship; he still hadn't _____ _____ his divorce.

Reading and Use of English
Part 4

Transformations

For questions **1–6** complete the second sentence so that it has a similar meaning to the first sentence, using the word given. **Do not change the word given.** You must use between **two** and **five** words, including the word given.

Write the missing words **IN CAPITAL LETTERS.**

1 I won't tolerate your bad behaviour any longer.

PUT

I refuse _____ your bad behaviour any longer.

2 You shouldn't follow Petra's example.

SHOULD

Petra is not a person _____ follow.

3 He is not known for his sincerity as a politician.

MOST

He is not considered to be one _____ politicians.

4 We're getting a friend to repair the roof.

HAVING

We _____ by a friend.

5 They took his tonsils out when he was 11.

TAKEN

He _____ when he was 11.

6 We don't want a complete stranger to do it.

HAVE

We don't want _____ a complete stranger.

Writing
Part 2

Email

This summer you are going to spend one month studying English in an English-speaking country. Read this part of an email you received from your host family and write your reply to them. Write your **email** in **140–190** words.

Don't forget!

You may write a formal or an informal reply, but the style of your email should be consistent.

> We have your personal details but perhaps you could tell us a little more about yourself. How would you describe your personality and what sorts of things would you like to do when you're here?
> Thanks
> Kate and Andy Newson

Introduction

In the **Reading and Use of English** paper there are three reading texts.
Understanding of each of the three texts is tested in a different way with a different
type of task each time.

Part 5: Multiple choice

1 Part 5 consists of a text followed by six multiple-choice questions, each with four
   options. Before answering the questions, you should always read the text through
   quite quickly to get an idea of the overall meaning. Read the text on page 83 and
   answer the following questions:

   What is the purpose of the text?
   Where might you expect to find it?

2 In all of the reading tasks there will inevitably be words you do not know the meaning
   of. On many occasions it is not essential for you to understand these words in order to
   complete the task, and you can ignore them. If necessary, though, you may be able to
   use the context in which the word appears to help you work out the meaning.

   Find the words below in the first three paragraphs of the text, and then use the
   context and the clues below to work out the approximate meaning of each one.
   The number in brackets refers to the line in which the word appears.

(1)	pump (verb	*What does your heart do all the time you are alive?*
(7)	intake (noun)	*This word is composed of two parts: what are they? What does the rest of the paragraph talk about in relation to water?*
(12)	raging (adjective)	*What type of thirst do you develop in high temperatures if you wait for a long time before you have a drink?*
(13)	swig (noun)	*Look at the advice given in the first half of this sentence. What type of action, therefore, is 'to take a swig' of water?*
(15)	palatable (adjective)	*What do you improve by adding fruit juice to water?*

3 Use context to work out the meanings of the words in **bold** in the second column of
   the text on page 83. These words will help when you answer questions **3, 4** and **6** on
   page 83.

4 For questions **1–6** on page 83, choose the answer (**A, B, C** or **D**) which you think fits
   best according to the text.

A walk in the midday sun
When the heat is on, walkers need to be on their guard

Hot weather makes your heart pump harder, and if you're not very fit, you start to understand why the majority of mountain rescue statistics are made up from summer walkers suffering heart attacks. Heat exhaustion is quite easy to get when you're
5 making a great physical effort. It happens where your body can't produce enough sweat to keep you cool.

The answer is to keep up your water intake. It's a good idea to drink a pint of water for every 10 degrees Fahrenheit every 24 hours. So, if the temperature is in the 70s, and you are doing a
10 five-hour walk, you'll need a minimum of around one and a half pints of water. It's vital that you don't wait until you develop a raging thirst before you stop for a drink – keep taking regular swigs from your water bottle.

Many walkers flavour their water with fruit juice, which makes
15 it a lot more palatable. You could even use one of the isotonic drinks made for athletes, which replace the body's salts lost through sweating. Powders such as Dioralyte, which you may have in the house as a treatment for diarrhoea, will do the job just as well, as its main aim is also effective rehydration.

20 Given that evaporation is your body's cooling mechanism, you can help things along with an external application of water. Soaking your hat with water is a great way to cool the head, though if the sun is beating down, it will probably dry off almost immediately. Better still, then, if you can plunge into
25 a river or the sea fully-clothed. And if that's not possible, then at least take off your boots and socks and paddle in a cool stream.

30 Walking in the heat increases the rate at which your feet **swell**, which can lead to them feeling tight in your boots. Cool water from a stream reduces any swelling and helps general foot comfort. At the same time, you can check out your feet for signs of **blisters**. Extra sweating makes the skin softer and increases the chance of blisters forming, in the same way as when water **leaks** into your boots and gets to your feet.

As for what clothing you wear, this should be lightweight and
35 reasonably loose-fitting. Tight clothing will feel uncomfortable and may even lead to the formation of an irritating **rash** known as 'prickly heat' on your skin. The answer, if this does develop, is to try and stay cool as much as possible. Do this by either keeping in the shade, or washing the affected area with cold
40 water, but without soap. But prevention is by far the best approach, so keep your clothing light.

It's understandable to want to remove any extraneous clothing when it's extremely hot, but it doesn't really make much sense to take off T-shirts. The sun's rays can be quite strong, and
45 shoulders are always very sensitive to sunburn. This is the worst place to be red and sore when you are wearing a heavy rucksack on your back. Wearing shorts can also create problems for walkers, as the backs of the legs can catch the sun very easily.

50 In fact, those days when an apparently harmless **breeze** is blowing can be the most **deceptive**. It might not feel so hot, so you probably won't notice the damage being done so soon. As on every other day then, a good strong sun cream should therefore be applied to any skin which is exposed. Make the most
55 of the summer, but treat the sun with the respect it deserves.

1 The writer says that hot weather
   A is the main cause of heart attacks.
   B ensures that mountain walkers stay fit.
   C requires walkers to have frequent drinks.
   D is the worst type of weather for mountain walking.

2 What does the writer say about 'Dioralyte'?
   A It helps to reduce sweating.
   B It prevents the loss of body salts.
   C It will prevent you getting diarrhoea.
   D It works in the same way as an isotonic drink.

3 According to the text, when might your feet suffer?
   A when they are wet
   B when they cool down
   C when your boots are the wrong size
   D when you walk long distances in the heat

4 According to the writer, it is better to wear loose-fitting clothing because
   A it keeps you cool.
   B it is usually very light.
   C it lasts longer than tight-fitting clothing.
   D it is less likely to create problems for your skin.

5 What does the writer mean by 'extraneous' clothing in line 42?
   A clothing which most people would consider unusual in hot weather
   B clothing which is no longer needed to keep you warm
   C clothing which is too heavy to wear
   D clothing which is too tight

6 According to the writer, when are walkers particularly at risk from the effects of the sun?
   A if their sun cream is not strong enough
   B when they are unaware of the heat
   C if they have suffered an injury
   D when there is a strong wind

Part 6: Gapped text

1 Part 6 consists of a text from which sentences have been removed and placed in a different order after the text. You have to decide which part of the text the sentences have been removed from. This task tests your understanding of the way texts are structured, so look carefully at the language both before and after the gap.

What to expect in the exam

Each correct answer in Parts 5 and 6 receives two marks; correct answers in Part 7 receive one mark each.

2 Read the headline and first paragraph of the newspaper article about the Siberian city of Yakutsk. What aspects of life in Yakutsk do you think might be mentioned in the article?

3 Read through the base text (the main text with the gaps). Are any of your ideas from exercise **2** mentioned?

The coldest city on earth

Shaun Walker enjoys a mini-break in deepest Siberia

Yakutsk, in Eastern Siberia (population 200 000), can convincingly claim to be the coldest city on earth. In January, the most freezing month, average 'highs' are around minus 40°C; today
5 the temperature is hovering around minus 43°C, leaving the city covered in a blanket of freezing fog that restricts visibility to 10 metres. I have come here to find out for myself how people manage to survive in the world's coldest place.

10 **Before venturing outdoors for the first time, I put on a suitcase's worth of clothes** to protect me against the cold, including a thermal undershirt, a long-sleeved T-shirt, a tight-fitting cashmere jumper, a padded winter coat with
15 hood, two pairs of gloves and a woolly football hat. **1** The small part of my face that is naked to the elements definitely notices **the cold air**, but on the whole, **it feels fine**. As long as you're dressed right, I think, **this isn't too bad**.

After the gap, 'the cold air' tells us the writer is outside, so the missing sentence will probably serve as a transition from putting on the clothes to going outside.

20 **2** The first place to suffer is the exposed skin on my face, which **experiences shooting pains and goes numb**. Then the cold penetrates the double layer of gloves and sets to work on **chilling my fingers**. The woolly hat and padded
25 hood are no match for minus 43°C either, and **my ears begin to sting**. Finally, I find myself with **severe pain all across my body** and have to return indoors.

In the previous paragraph the writer is untroubled by the cold: 'it feels fine', 'this isn't too bad'. In this paragraph he begins to suffer. The missing sentence will probably refer to this contrast.

Despite the fact that the locals are stoically going
30 about their business, and children are playing in the snow on the central square and laughing merrily, I realize that **I'll need a warm taxi to continue my exploration. 3** **I collapse on the bed in the hotel room, and it takes half an**
35 **hour for my body to feel normal again.**

In the missing sentence the writer may refer to his planned exploration of Yakutsk and/or explain why he collapses on his hotel bed.

4 **Workers continue working on building sites up to minus 50°C, and children go to school unless it's below minus 55°C**. 'Of course it's cold, but you get used to it,' says Nina, a
40 Yakut woman who spends eight hours every day standing at her stall in the fish market. 'Human beings can get used to anything,' she says.

Almost without exception, the women wear fur from head to toe. 'In Europe you have people
45 who say it's not nice to wear fur because they love animals,' says Natasha, a Yakutsk resident, who is wearing a coat made of rabbit and a hat of arctic fox. 'They should come and live in Siberia for a couple of months and then see if they are still so
50 worried about the animals. **You need to wear fur here to survive. 5** '

'For us, the winter is like the working week and the summer is like the weekend,' says local blogger Bolot Bochkarev. The short summer,
55 when the temperature hits 30°C or 35°C for two or three weeks, is a time when **efforts are made to ensure that the region is ready for winter**. **6** **If they fail, those stuck without warmth risk death**. The whole region suffers harsh
60 winters. A few hundred miles away is Oimyakon, known as 'The Pole of Cold'. It was here that the lowest ever temperature in an inhabited place was recorded – minus 71.2°C.

4 Six sentences have been removed from the article. Choose from the sentences **A–G** the one which fits each gap (**1–6**). There is one extra sentence which you do not need to use.

A The thirteen minutes I have spent outside have left me out of breath and aching all over.

B Even wearing glasses gets tricky: the metal sticks to your cheeks and will tear off your skin when you remove them.

C I'm ready to face everything Yakutsk has to throw at me and I stride purposefully out of the hotel door.

D Heating pipes are examined and repaired.

E Locals are a little more skilled at dealing with the cold.

F Nothing else keeps you warm.

G Within a few minutes, however, the icy weather begins to make itself felt.

5 🔘 If you had to live in either extreme heat or extreme cold, which would you choose and why?

Part 7: Multiple matching

1 Part 7 consists of either one continuous text divided into sections, or a number of smaller texts. Ten questions or statements are placed before the text(s). For this task you are asked to find the specific information in the text(s) which matches the questions or statements.

2 ⬤ Look at the book covers and/or the book titles and discuss the following in pairs or small groups:

Which, if any, of them have you read, either in English or your own language?

Have you seen film versions of any of them?

What do you know about the story and/or characters in each one?

3 Read the following Part 7 instructions.

You are going to read an article in which children's writer Leroy Hadley describes his five favourite classic works of children's literature. For questions **1–10**, choose from the books (**A–E**). The books may be chosen more than once.

How to go about it

- Underline key words in the statements before the text. Numbers **1–4** have been done for you.
- Read each of the sections (**A–E**) looking for information which matches that contained in the statements.

  One of the answers (4) for A has been given, with the relevant part of the text underlined.

- There are two more statements which match A; find the statements and underline the relevant parts of the text. Then do the same for B–E.
- If there are any statements you have not matched, scan the text again looking for the information you need.

What to expect in the exam

- The words used in the statements (**1–10**) will not be the same as the words used in the relevant parts of the text, but they do express the same idea, e.g. *4 A*
- The information in a particular section could lead you to make the wrong choice, e.g. *In section **D** 'My mother read this to me when I was ten' might lead you to match it to statement 1, but later in section **D** we read: 'I read it on my own afterwards.'*

Of which book does Leroy Hadley say the following?

I have still <u>not</u> actually <u>read it myself</u>.	1 ☐
<u>A lot of people</u> are <u>surprised</u> by one of its features.	2 ☐
The author shows his <u>main characters</u> in a <u>positive light</u>.	3 ☐
I have <u>not had it for very long</u>.	4 *A*
I read the original version of this story as a child.	5 ☐
It shows a way of life which unfortunately does not exist now.	6 ☐
It reminds me of a certain period of my life.	7 ☐
The story proved to be very educational.	8 ☐
Children will find it easier to read than the other books in this selection.	9 ☐
The beginning of the book gave me ideas for the start of my latest work.	10 ☐

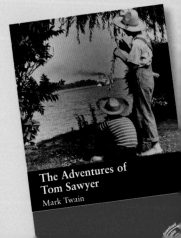

The Adventures of Tom Sawyer
Mark Twain

Children's Classics

Children's author Leroy Hadley picks his five favourite children's classics.

A ***The Call of the Wild*** by Jack London

This book is a recent addition to my collection. I seemed to have missed it as a child and I'd been meaning to read it for years. I ordered it on the Internet a few months ago, together with the audiobook so that my daughters could listen to it in the car. The CD arrived first and we all loved it – the actor reading it really brought the text to life and made us love, admire and feel pity for Buck the dog, who is kidnapped and forced into pulling sledges in the freezing cold Yukon during the Gold Rush in the late 19th century. We learnt a lot about how hard life was for the gold prospectors and the girls were motivated to find out more. In the end I didn't bother with the book – I might do one day.

B ***The Adventures of Tom Sawyer*** by Mark Twain

I love the humour in this book and the great affection with which Mark Twain writes about his protagonists, Tom and his friend Huckleberry Finn, who both come across as cheeky, but likeable rogues. We laugh at the innocence of childhood, as Tom tries to win the affections of Becky Thatcher, we smile nostalgically as he and Huck imagine they are pirates who go digging for treasure, and we hold our breath in fear when Tom and Becky are lost in a cave. Despite the dangers, it's sad to think that young children can no longer play like Tom and his friends, that they no longer have the freedom to go off in search of adventure without the presence of an interfering adult.

C ***The Lion, the Witch and the Wardrobe*** by CS Lewis

Of all the books here that I read when I was growing up, this was the only one which wasn't adapted or abridged in any way. Being more modern than the rest – it was published in 1950 – the language is still fairly accessible for younger readers and there's less danger of them becoming frustrated with the style. It's the perfect fantasy adventure, with daring children, a talking lion and other magical creatures doing battle with the forces of darkness led by the White Witch. I loved it as a child and still find it totally absorbing.

D ***Treasure Island*** by Robert Louis Stevenson

My mother read this to me when I was ten, and rather than being scared by the likes of Long John Silver, Black Dog or Blind Pew, I couldn't help laughing at the hilarious range of voices she gave the different pirates in the book. I laughed, too, when I read it on my own afterwards, my mother's humorous voices still ringing in my ears. Stevenson writes with a good deal of humour anyway, something which many aren't expecting when they read the book for the first time. They are familiar with the story but not the way it is told.

E ***The Wind in the Willows*** by Kenneth Grahame

This lovingly told tale of the adventures of a group of animal friends – Mole, Water Rat, Toad and Badger – brings back memories of my teenage years, when I lived in a house on a river bank. Grahame evokes wonderfully the sounds, sights and smells of the countryside and creates an atmosphere of peace and tranquillity, which is becoming increasingly difficult to find in today's world. I read the book again two years ago, and the first chapter, when Mole first meets Rat, provided the inspiration for the opening of my most recent novel *Harvest Mouse*. I can only dream that it will be as popular as *The Wind in the Willows*.

Call of the Wild
London

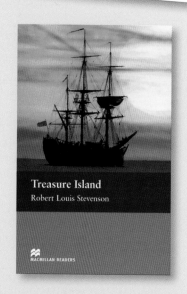

Treasure Island
Robert Louis Stevenson

MACMILLAN READERS

4 Tell each other about any other children's classics you have read, either English ones or ones originally written in your own language.

7 Value for money

Speaking 1
Part 2

Talking about photos ⬤

Why have the people chosen to shop in these different places?

1   Look at the four photographs. They show people shopping in different places.

    Student A Compare photographs **1** and **2** and say why you think the people have chosen to shop in these different places.

    Student B When your partner has finished, say which of these places you would prefer to shop in.

2   Now change roles. Follow the instructions above using photographs **3** and **4**.

Vocabulary 1: Shopping

1   Complete each of the gaps below with a word from the box.

foodstuffs	own-brand	cashier	value	brands
trolley	out-of-town	receipt	convenience	checkout
corner	range	till	aisles	counter

I prefer a trip to a large **(1)** _____ supermarket to shopping in the local **(2)** _____ shop because there's so much more variety. You can choose between all the usual well-known **(3)** _____ , or if you prefer, there are the store's cheaper **(4)** _____ products. As well as tinned and frozen **(5)** _____ food, there's a wide **(6)** _____ of fresh fruit and vegetables, meat, fish and other **(7)** _____ . The household goods are particularly good **(8)** _____ for money, compared to other shops.

Once I've walked down all the **(9)** _____ , filling my **(10)** _____ with enough food to last a month, I head for the cheese **(11)** _____ , where I treat myself to a selection of Roquefort, feta and manchego. When I go through the **(12)** _____ I try hard not to look when the amount I've spent is displayed on the **(13)** _____ , and I try not to listen as the **(14)** _____ reads it out. I hand over my credit card, take the **(15)** _____ and hurriedly put it away in my purse, preferring not to look at it until I get home.

2   ⬤ Do you plan carefully what you are going to buy? Do you ever buy things on impulse? What shops have you been in during the last fortnight? What did you buy?

Why have the people chosen to shop in these different places?

Speaking: Supermarket psychology

Supermarket chains tend to design their stores in a similar way. For example, supermarkets sell a lot of milk, so they usually put it at the back of the store, leading customers to walk past, and hopefully buy, many more products.

In which area of the supermarket would you put the following products? Why?

Products	Areas of the supermarket
confectionery (chocolates and sweets)	at the back of the shop
bread	in the middle of the shop
alcoholic drinks	at the checkouts
fruit and vegetables	near the entrance
fresh meat	near the exit

Listening 1
Part 2

Sentence completion 1.45

1   You will hear part of a radio programme in which a supermarket manager explains how supermarkets are planned. For questions **1–10** below, complete the sentences.

Customers might buy less if the supermarket entrance were located in the
(1) .... of the building.

Fruit and vegetables are situated near the entrance so that customers feel they are entering **(2)** ....

On sale next to the fruit and vegetables are products aimed at keeping
(3) .... interested.

The **(4)** .... counter is usually to be found at the back of the store.

Pre-packed meat prevents customers relating the product to the **(5)** ....

Usually only **(6)** .... are sold in the frozen food section.

Sales of goods at the end-of-aisle areas are often **(7)** .... greater than at other locations.

The **(8)** .... section is situated in the far corner of the supermarket.

The **(9)** .... from this section helps to provide a pleasant atmosphere.

On sale at the checkouts are products which encourage customers to buy
(10) ....

Don't forget!

In the exam you have 45 seconds to read the Part 2 questions. Use this time to try to predict the type of information you might hear.

2   How do your ideas in the speaking task compare with those you have just heard in the listening?

Think of a supermarket you know. Is it designed in the way described in the listening?

89

Reading and
Use of English
Part 6

Gapped text

1 ⬭ Look at the title of the article and read the first paragraph. What reasons do you think the writer will give for hating clothes shopping?

2 Read the base text (the text without the missing sentences). Does the article mention any of the ideas you spoke about in exercise **1**?

3 Six sentences have been removed from the article. Choose from the sentences **A–G** on page 91 the one which fits each gap (**1–6**). There is one extra sentence which you do not need to use.

Why I hate shopping

Football does it to some people. For others it's home improvements. But in my case, when the conversation turns to clothes shopping, my eyes glaze over and I start staring into space,
5 thinking of a hundred and one other topics I'd rather be discussing. Like football, or home improvements.

I've always detested shopping for clothes, ever since the days when I used to get dragged
10 around the town by my mother to hunt down a new pair of school trousers, summer sandals or a winter coat. ⬚1⬚ Believe me, I've tried many times to enjoy the whole shopping experience, but there are just too many reasons to hate it.

15 The first obstacles to overcome are the sales assistants. I can never seem to get rid of them. They are impatient for a sale, hungry for commission, and I feel pressured into trying things on I know I'm not going to like. It's almost
20 a relief to get to the changing room – perhaps they'll find someone else to bother now. ⬚2⬚ It's hot, it's cramped and there's nowhere to sit and nowhere to hang anything up, so the floor becomes a mess of clothing. Loud background
25 music adds to the confusion and I break into a sweat.

Feeling claustrophobic now, I work quickly to put an end to my suffering. But it's never straightforward. ⬚3⬚ Trousers are the worst.

30 Right waist, wrong length. Right length, wrong cut. So I hurriedly put my own clothes back on and head off in search of my size, careful to avoid any assistants as I do so.

When I do find something I'm more or less
35 satisfied with, I often have to leave it in the shop for a week to have it shortened, lengthened, taken in or let out. And when I go to pick it up, I wonder what on earth led me to buy it in the first place. ⬚4⬚ It makes it difficult to
40 appreciate the true colour of the garment, and you can never really know for certain what you've bought until you get it outside in the street.

Part of my problem in all this, I suppose, is that I
45 just can't get excited about clothes. ⬚5⬚ I can wear the same baggy old T-shirt for days on end, or at least until I have to change it for reasons of hygiene. So why would I put myself through the torture of shopping unless it were absolutely
50 unavoidable?

But there is an alternative. I have just taken delivery of a pair of trousers for work, which I ordered online. It's the first time I've bought clothes on the Internet – and it probably won't
55 be the last. ⬚6⬚ Importantly, I don't have to suffer all the hassle of crowded stores, pushy shop assistants, tiny changing rooms and deafening music to do this. A simple trip to the post office is all that's needed. Now that's a
60 shopping experience I'm happy to go through.

A They don't fit, it's true, but I can easily return them and ask for a larger size.

B I'm not bothered if I look scruffy, as long as I feel comfortable.

C Things don't get any better there, though.

D At last they move away and leave me to look around in peace.

E The shop's fluorescent lighting is sometimes to blame for this.

F Why is it that nothing ever fits on the first attempt?

G Now I shop alone, but my heart still sinks when I have to buy new shoes or replace a favourite pair of jeans that have finally fallen apart.

Reacting to the text

Do you share the writer's opinions? Why/Why not?

If you had to write a different article entitled 'Why I hate …', what topic would you write about and what reasons would you give for hating it?

Language focus 1: Present perfect simple

1 The present perfect links **past** events and situations with the **present**. The present perfect is used:

1 to describe something that started in the **past** and continues until the **present**.
I've always detested shopping for clothes, ever since the days when I used to get dragged around the town by my mother …

2 to describe events which occurred at some time between the **past** and the **present** (exactly when they happened is not important).
I've tried many times to enjoy the whole shopping experience, but there are just too many reasons to hate it.

3 to talk about something which occurred in the **past** but in an unfinished time period which includes the **present**.
So far this morning I've bought a pair of jeans, a casual shirt and a jumper. (It is still the morning and I may buy more things.)

4 to talk about recent **past** events with some relevance to the **present**.
I have just taken delivery of a pair of trousers for work, which I ordered online. (I now have the trousers.)

5 to talk about the first, second, third etc time something has occurred between the **past** and the **present**.
It's the first time I've bought clothes on the Internet.

2 Which of the five descriptions above can be used to explain the use of the present perfect simple in these sentences?

   a Your parents have just arrived. I can hear their car.
   b I've known Keith since we started school together.
   c Sue has worked in a number of different countries.
   d That must be the tenth time you've told me that joke!
   e Ben's already sent me fifteen text messages this week.
   f Mrs Avery has lived in that house for over sixty years.
   g This film's very familiar – I think I've seen it before.
   h I've lost my glasses. Can you help me look for them?

3 a Decide which time expressions in the box you would use with the present perfect and which with the past simple. Make two groups of expressions in your notebook.

yet   last summer   in September so far today   in the last few days   since I got up two weeks ago   before I came here   for the last two years over the last week   on my 10th birthday when I was younger   already   this month

   b Choose four expressions from each group in exercise **3a** and write true sentences about yourself, using the appropriate tense.

   Example:
   So far today I've eaten three bars of chocolate.
   I went to see a basketball match on my 10th birthday.

   c Compare your sentences with your partner's. Ask each other questions about what you have written.

   Example:
   Have you eaten anything else?
   Which teams did you see play?

   Read more about the present perfect on page 215 of the Grammar reference.

Vocabulary 2: Paraphrasing and recording

1 If you paraphrase a sentence, you use different words to express the same meaning.

a In **1–8** below, complete each gap with **one** word so that the second sentence has the same meaning as the first. The second sentence is taken from the reading text on page 90. There is an example at the beginning **(0)**. **Do the exercise without looking at the reading text on page 90.**

0 I start to look straight in front of me without looking at anything in particular.
I start **staring into** _____*space*_____. (4)

1 I can never seem to make them go away.
I can never seem to **get** _____ **of** them. (16)

2 I work quickly to stop my suffering.
I work quickly to _____ **an end to** my suffering. (27–28)

3 You can never really be certain about what you've bought.
You can never really **know** _____ **certain** what you've bought. (41–42)

4 I can wear the same baggy old T-shirt for many consecutive days.
I can wear the same baggy old T-shirt **for days on** _____. (45–46)

5 Why would I make myself suffer the torture of shopping?
Why would I **put myself** _____ the torture of shopping? (48–49)

6 A pair of trousers has just been delivered to me.
I have just _____ **delivery of** a pair of trousers. (51–52)

7 The only thing I need to do is go to the post office.
A simple trip to the post office **is** _____ **that's needed**. (58–59)

8 I still get depressed when I have to buy new shoes.
My _____ still **sinks** when I have to buy new shoes. **(G)**

b Check your answers in the reading text on page 90. The numbers in brackets refer to the lines in the text; the letter in **8** refers to the sentence **G**.

2 Paraphrasing is a useful way to record vocabulary. Paraphrase the following sentences from the reading text and record both sentences in your vocabulary notebook. You do not need to change every word in the sentence. The first one has been done for you.

a ... when the conversation turns to clothes shopping ...(2–3)
... when people start talking about clothes shopping ...

b ... I feel pressured into trying things on ... (18–19)

c I break into a sweat. (25–26)

d I head off in search of my size. (32)

e I'm not bothered if I look scruffy ... (**B**)

f The shop's fluorescent lighting is sometimes to blame for this. (**E**)

Multiple choice 1.46

1 What are the advantages and disadvantages of living in the country and living in a city? Which would you prefer?

2 You will hear part of a radio programme in which two people, Rebecca and Greg, are interviewed about their life in the countryside. For questions **1–7**, choose the best answer (**A**, **B** or **C**).

1 Rebecca moved out of the city to escape
 A the traffic.
 B the noise.
 C the pollution.

2 What gives Greg less cause for concern now that he lives in the countryside?
 A his neighbours' opinions
 B the amount of violent crime
 C his children's safety

3 Rebecca regrets the fact that
 A she does not live close to local amenities.
 B she does not have much privacy.
 C she is unable to drive.

4 What does Greg say about buses where he lives?
 A They are too infrequent.
 B They are unreliable.
 C There is no service.

5 How does Greg react to Rebecca's concerns that her children may grow bored?
 A He sympathizes with teenagers who live in the country.
 B He advises her to move back to the city when they are older.
 C He criticizes parents who do not do enough for their children.

6 What does Greg say about the future?
 A He will probably move back to the city.
 B He says that the future is uncertain.
 C He would like to work in an office.

7 What inconvenience does Rebecca mention in relation to her return to work?
 A Her children will have to change schools.
 B She will spend very little time at home.
 C Her journey to work will be time-consuming.

Language focus 2: Expressing preferences

1 The following sentences from the listening show three different ways of expressing preferences.

- *prefer* + gerund/noun + *to* + gerund/noun

  *Now we **prefer living** with less noise (**to living/life** in a noisy city).*

- *would prefer* + infinitive with *to* + *rather than* + infinitive without *to*

  ***I'd prefer to stay** in the village and work at home **rather than do** a nine-to-five job in an office.*

- *would (much) rather* + infinitive without *to* + *than* + infinitive without *to*

  ***I'd rather drive** to work **than go** back to living in the city.*

2 Complete the second sentence so that it has a similar meaning to the first sentence. Use up to five words.

 1 We'd prefer to come back later rather than wait here.
 We'd rather _____ here.

 2 I think it's better to pay by cash than use a credit card.
 I prefer _____ using a credit card.

 3 I'd rather phone him than send an email.
 I'd prefer _____ send an email.

 4 She wants to stay in bed longer.
 She'd rather _____ up until later.

3 a Which of the following do you prefer doing and why?
 - playing sport or watching it
 - downloading music or buying CDs
 - a pizza or having one delivered
 - giving presents or receiving them

 b Which of the following would you rather do if you could or had to choose? Why?
 - learn another language or perfect your English
 - live abroad for five years or stay in your own country
 - go whitewater rafting or do a parachute jump
 - do a poorly paid but stimulating job or earn a high salary doing something dull

Vocabulary 3: Towns and villages

1 **a** Complete each gap with a word from the box to form places you might find in a village, town or city. The first one has been done for you.

building	flats	housing	industrial
office	pedestrian	~~residential~~	shopping

1 This charming three-bedroomed villa is located in a quiet _residential_ **area**.

2 You can't drive down Bromley Way any more – it's a _____ **street** now.

3 My uncle lives on the fifteenth floor of a huge **block of** _____ .

4 I usually buy my clothes at the **indoor** _____ **centre** on the edge of town: there's so much choice under one roof.

5 Most of the _____ **blocks** here are occupied by insurance companies and law firms.

6 Property prices fell and all building work stopped, leaving a number of abandoned _____ **sites** around the town.

7 They knocked down all the houses and built an _____ **estate** for small manufacturing businesses.

8 It's easy to get lost on the _____ **estate** where I live: all the properties look exactly the same.

b Can you think of an example for each of the places in **1a** in the area where you live?

Are they *on the outskirts* of your town or village or *in the centre*?
Are any *within easy walking distance* of your home?

2 The following adjectives can all be used to describe a town or a village. Which of them are positive and which are negative? Make two groups in your notebook.

lively	pleasant	run-down	picturesque	shabby
dull	quaint	depressing	prosperous	bustling

Which adjectives would you use to describe the area where you live?

Speaking 2
Part 1

Interview 〇

In Part 1 of the Speaking exam, you may be asked to talk about where you live. Ask and answer the following questions with your partner.

Don't forget!

Develop your answers by giving reasons or examples.

- What are the amenities like in your local area? (e.g. shops, sports facilities, cinemas, libraries)
- Is everything within easy walking distance?
- What are the good points about living where you do?
- Is there anything you don't like about it?
- What changes have there been in your local area in recent years?
- Have they been changes for the better or for the worse?
- Do you think you will always live in the same area?

Language focus 3: Present perfect continuous

1 The present perfect continuous can be used:

1 to emphasize the duration of a situation or activity.

You've been living in a village for nearly five years now.

2 to suggest that a situation or activity is temporary.

I'm decorating my room so I've been sleeping on the sofa.

3 to suggest that a situation or activity is incomplete.

We've been painting the house. We hope to finish it soon.

4 to focus on the repetition of a situation or activity.

I've been trying to phone Tim all day, but there's no reply.

Like the present perfect simple, the continuous form can be used to talk about the effects in the present of a recent past event.

Continuous: *I think she's been crying. Her eyes are very red.* (activity)

Simple: *You've cut yourself. There's blood on your shirt.* (single action)

However, it is not normally used to talk about the number of things that have been completed.

Continuous: *I've been writing letters this morning.* (focus on the activity)

Simple: *I've written five letters this morning.* (focus on the finished result)

2 For questions **1–4** explain the difference in meaning between sentence **a** and **b** and why the present perfect simple or continuous is used in each case.

1 a I've been reading that book you lent me. I can't put it down.
   b I've read that book you lent me. I really enjoyed it.

2 a They've been going to the supermarket to do their shopping recently.
   b They've gone to the supermarket to do their shopping. They'll be back at 12.00.

3 a I've been baking all day. I'm exhausted.
   b I've baked a couple of cakes. Would you like to try one?

4 a She's been living with her sister since June, just until she finds a place of her own.
   b She's lived with her sister for over 80 years.

3 Complete the gaps in this telephone conversation with the past simple, the present perfect simple or the present perfect continuous form of the verbs in brackets.

Dave: Hi Andy, it's Dave. I **(1)** _____ (just/hear) that you and Sandra are getting married next May. How long **(2)** _____ (you/be) engaged?

Andy: About six months. I **(3)** _____ (propose) to her when we were on holiday in Fiji. We **(4)** _____ (keep) it secret for about a month or so after that, just until we **(5)** _____ (be) sure of the date for the wedding.

Dave: So **(6)** _____ you _____ (make) all the arrangements yet?

Andy: Yes, more or less. Of course, since we got engaged we **(7)** _____ (save) up to buy a flat as well. We **(8)** _____ (both/work) overtime to earn a bit extra. We **(9)** _____ (already/save) enough to pay a deposit. Anyway, how about you? What **(10)** _____ you _____ (do)?

Dave: I **(11)** _____ (study) hard as usual. I **(12)** _____ (fail) a couple of exams in June, so I've got to re-sit them next month.

4 Work in pairs. Read the following then do the roleplay below.

For the last six months, a small group of young people has been living on an otherwise uninhabited tropical island as part of an experiment in survival. They will be there for another six months.

A group of journalists has been allowed to land on the island and interview the young castaways about their experiences since the beginning of the experiment. Here are some examples of what they will ask about:

| finding and preparing food | entertainment | relationships |
| shelter and clothing | health and fitness | other |

Student A

You are a journalist. You should prepare your questions for the interview. Write questions which focus on:

a Activities: *e.g. What have you been using to hunt with?*
b Completed actions: *e.g. Have you caught many fish?*

Student B

You are a castaway. You should prepare some answers for the interview. Write sentences on:

a Activities: *e.g. I've been eating fruit from the trees.*
b Completed actions: *e.g. We've built a very basic kitchen.*

 Now roleplay the interview.

Writing
Part 2

Email

1 Read the two Writing Part 2 tasks and answer the questions for each one. Would a formal or informal style be appropriate in the email you write? Why?

A You have been asked to reply to the following email from the new English director of the language school where you study.

> I plan to arrive on 6 August in order to find some temporary rented accommodation. I would not require anything too expensive, preferably somewhere with good shopping facilities nearby and not too far from the school. Could you recommend two possible areas?
> Best regards
> John Simpson

Write your **email** in **140–190** words.

B This is part of an email you have received from your English friend, Rob.

> I'll be coming to your area on 6 August. I'll need to look for a place to live – somewhere fairly cheap to rent, with shops nearby and reasonably close to the language school where I'll be studying. Can you suggest a couple of areas?
> Thanks
> Rob

Write your **email** in **140–190** words.

2 Read the answer to writing task **A,** ignoring the numbered words, and answer these questions.

a Is the style appropriate and consistent?

b Has the writer addressed all the points in John Simpson's email?

What to expect in the exam

In Part 2 of the Writing paper, one of the options might be a letter or an email. The requirements for emails are similar to those of letters. Answers must be grammatically correct with accurate spelling and punctuation, and written in a style which is relevant to the target reader and the situation. The abbreviated language of textspeak is not appropriate.

A

Dear Mr Simpson

Thank you for (0) **informing** us of the date of your arrival. There is (1) **a wide choice** of reasonably priced rented accommodation available in many parts of the city. Here are just two areas that you might like to (2) **consider**.

Although it is on the outskirts of the city, the pleasant and leafy district of Mirador has very good (3) **rail** connections to the centre and the (4) **journey** to the school would take less than twenty minutes. The shopping facilities are more than (5) **adequate**, including a very large indoor market and four supermarkets.

Another possibility is Justa, which is a (6) **slightly** less expensive neighbourhood than Mirador, (7) **despite** being closer to the centre and having better shopping facilities. (8) **However,** because of its location, there is a great deal of traffic noise. If you can (9) **tolerate** this, I would certainly recommend this very vibrant area, which is within easy walking distance of the school.

I hope you find this information useful. We (10) **look forward** to seeing you in August.

Yours sincerely
Susana Redd

3 a Read the answer to writing task **B**, ignoring the numbered gaps. The style is appropriately informal and, apart from three minor factual differences, the content is the same as the content of the answer to writing task **A** in exercise **2**.

Can you find the three factual differences between answer **A** and answer **B**?

B

Hi Rob

Thanks for letting me (0) _know_ when you're coming. There are (1) _____ of cheap rented flats to choose from all over the city, and here are just a couple of areas worth (2) _____ about.

Mirador is a really pleasant district with loads of trees, and although it's on the edge of the city, you can get a (3) _____ into the centre very easily. It'd take you under thirty minutes to (4) _____ to the school. There are more than (5) _____ shops there, including an enormous indoor market and five supermarkets!

Another possibility is Justa, where rents are a (6) _____ cheaper than in Mirador, even (7) _____ Justa's closer to the centre and there are a lot more shops. (8) _____ of course, being in the centre, there's a lot of noise from the traffic. If you can (9) _____ up with that, though, I'd definitely recommend the area – it's really lively and you can cycle to the school from here.

Anyway, hope this is useful. Can't (10) _____ to see you in August.

All the best

Susana

b Use the numbered words in **bold** in the answer to writing task **A** to help you complete the numbered gaps in the answer to writing task **B** with an appropriate word. Write **one word** in each gap. There is an example at the beginning **(0)**.

4 Read and compare the two answers (**A** and **B**) again. Comment on any further differences you notice between them. Consider:

a differences in the language used to express the same idea.

b differences in the use of punctuation.

c any other differences you notice.

5 Read the following Writing Part 2 instructions and write an email.

This is part of an email you have received from your Irish friend Patrick, who lives in your country.

> Cristina and I are going into town next Saturday. I want to buy a printer for my computer and we both need some casual clothes – good quality but not too expensive. I know you can't come shopping with us but you know the town very well – where do you suggest we should go?
> Thanks
> Patrick

Write your **email** in 140–190 words.

Don't forget!

- Plan your email.
- Include a brief, relevant opening paragraph.
- Use linking expressions.
- Write in a consistently appropriate style.

For more information on writing emails, see page 197.

Useful language

Making suggestions

If I were you, I'd go to …

You could try looking in …

Make sure you have a good look round in …

The best place to buy computer equipment is …

If you want to buy decent casual clothes, you can't go far wrong in …

Talking about price

You can buy decent printers at low/reasonable/ competitive/affordable prices.

Their clothes are cheap/reasonably priced/ affordable/good value for money.

7 Review

Vocabulary: Shopping

1 Complete each of the phrases with an appropriate word from the box. The first one has been done for you.

> meat   range   convenience   ~~walking~~   brand
> out-of-town   own-brand   goods   value   corner

 1 easy _____*walking*_____ distance
 2 wide _____ of products
 3 good _____ for money
 4 local _____ shop
 5 fresh _____ counter
 6 large _____ supermarket
 7 frozen _____ food
 8 cheap _____ goods
 9 well-known _____ of washing powder
 10 household _____ section

2 Write five sentences, each including one of the phrases in exercise **1**.

Example:

There is a very good shopping centre within easy walking distance of our house.

Reading and Use of English Part 2

Open cloze

For questions **1–8**, read the text below and think of the word which best fits each gap. Use only **one** word in each gap. There is an example at the beginning (**0**). Write your answers **IN CAPITAL LETTERS**.

Don't forget!

- Read the whole text through first.
- Look at the whole sentence, not just the words immediately before and after the gap.
- The open cloze focuses mainly on grammar.

Microflats

Many urban centres suffer from a chronic lack **(0)** _OF_ affordable housing. One solution to this problem, particularly for young, first-time buyers, **(1)** ____ the microflat, an apartment which sometimes measures little more **(2)** _____ 15 square metres. With just enough room to enable the occupier **(3)** _____ sleep, eat and wash, microflats represent the ultimate in small-scale city living.

One of the best publicized designs of microflat was that of young architects Stuart Piercy and Richard Conner, **(4)** ____ came up with their idea when they realized they couldn't afford to buy a place to live in London, **(5)** _____ the fact that they were earning reasonable salaries. Their 30-square-metre prototype **(6)** _____ first exhibited in the shop window of Selfridges department store in January 2002.

Teacher Sally Wright has been living in her London microflat **(7)** _____ nearly two years now. 'Naturally, I would much **(8)** _____ live in a bigger flat, but I would have to rent. At least I have a place I can call my own.'

Reading and Use of English
Part 4

Transformations

1 Match each sentence **1–3** with two of the sentences **a–f** which both express a similar idea.

1 I haven't done this before.

2 I haven't done this for five years.

3 I've been doing this for five years.

a It's five years since I started doing this.
b It's five years since I last did this.
c I've never done this.
d The last time I did this was five years ago.
e It's the first time I've done this.
f I began doing this five years ago.

2 Complete the second sentence so that it has a similar meaning to the first sentence, using the word given. **Do not change the word given.** You must use between **two** and **five** words, including the word given.

Write the missing words **IN CAPITAL LETTERS**.

1 I haven't spoken to her since she had her baby.
   LAST
   The _____ her was before she had her baby.

2 I haven't eaten Greek food before.
   TIME
   This is the _____ Greek food.

3 My nephew began to play tennis in 2010.
   SINCE
   My nephew _____ 2010.

4 He hasn't seen his sister for many years.
   AGES
   It's _____ his sister.

5 The last time I went swimming was three months ago.
   FOR
   I _____ three months.

6 I've never seen a supermarket as big as this before.
   EVER
   This is the _____ seen.

Writing
Part 1

Essay

You have recently had a discussion in your English class about the advantages and disadvantages of different places you can go shopping. Now your English teacher has asked you to write an essay.

Write an essay using **all** your notes and give reasons for your point of view.

Write your **essay** in **140–190** words.

Essay question

Is it better to go shopping in small local businesses or large out-of-town shopping centres?

Notes

Write about:

1 where things are cheaper
2 where the service is better
3 .... (your own idea)

1 ⬤ Look at the photograph of the International Space Station (ISS) and read the title and first paragraph of the article.

What would be difficult about each of the following on board the ISS?

How might astronauts overcome these difficulties?

> moving around   eating and drinking   washing
> keeping fit   sleeping   maintaining motivation
> getting on with other crew members

2 Read the rest of the base text (the text without the missing sentences).

Which of the topics in exercise **1** are discussed?

Does the article mention any of the ideas you spoke about?

Life aboard the International Space Station

The first residents arrived at the International Space Station on 2 November 2000, but fewer than 200 people have first-hand knowledge of life on board. Only a fraction have stayed more than six months
5 on the largest orbiting spacecraft ever built.

The images of weightless astronauts doing somersaults and chasing food through the air make it seem as though the space station is floating free from the pull of gravity. **1** ☐ It is forever falling
10 to Earth and would crash-land if it were not moving fast enough to maintain a gentle curve around the planet. In orbit, things are weightless simply because they are all falling at the same velocity.

The space station has a permanent crew of six, so
15 the arrival of new faces is a cause for celebration. **2** ☐ There is a subtle art to moving around without crashing into anything or anyone, knocking computers, equipment and other objects off the walls to which they are attached with Velcro pads.

20 **3** ☐ They can fly down the length of the station, straight as an arrow, without touching anything,

except with their fingertips. People sit in mid air, tapping away at a computer, with only a toe hooked under a wall strap to keep themselves in position.
25 Then, with a slight movement of the hand, they'll float up to another computer and carry on typing there.

In such close quarters personal hygiene is a must, but the weightless conditions make washing a
30 delicate **chore**. Water droplets can **short-circuit** electrical equipment, so many astronauts use wet **wipes**. Hair-washing is **trickier**. **4** ☐ Even Sunita Williams, who spent 195 consecutive days on the space station – a female record – had her long dark
35 hair **chopped** to shoulder length. But it was still problematic. 'Washing took time,' she says. 'I usually did it on a weekend when we didn't have a whole lot of other things to do.'

It takes the space station one and a half hours to
40 fly around the planet. **5** ☐ But after 45 minutes of daylight, a dark line appears on the planet, dividing Earth into night and day. For a couple of seconds, the space station is bathed in a coppery light and then complete darkness. Another 45

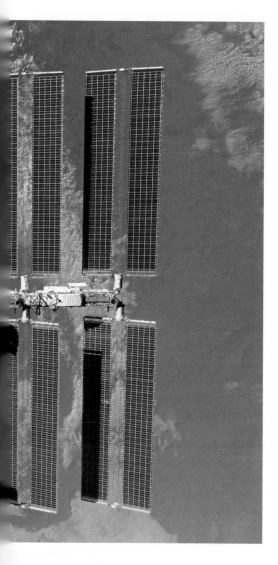

3 Use context to help you work out the approximate meaning of the words and phrases in **bold** around gap 4 in the base text.

e.g. **chore**: *an activity, something you have to do regularly*

4 Six sentences have been removed from the article. Choose from the sentences **A–G** the one which fits each gap (**1–6**). There is one extra sentence which you do not need to use.

Don't forget!

- Before reading sentences **A–G**, try to predict the general content of each gap.

  For example, the sentence before the first gap talks of the appearance of the ISS floating in space, whereas the sentence after the gap explains the reality of the ISS falling fast through space. Perhaps, then, the missing sentence refers to this difference in some way.

- When making your choices, look for connections between the language in the missing sentences and the language in the text, both before and after the gap.

A Men tend to get military cuts before a mission.

B However, even the most welcome visitors can cause chaos if they are inexperienced.

C Because of this, the light has a calming effect on the astronauts.

D Some strap pillows to their heads to make it feel more like lying down.

E Nothing could be further from the truth.

F For half that time, the light can be so blinding that astronauts reach for their sunglasses.

G In time, people improve the skill.

◑ Reacting to the text

Would you enjoy life aboard the International Space Station? Why/Why not?

Vocabulary 1: Sleep

1 **a** Complete each of these extracts from the article with a word from the box. Then check your answers in the last paragraph of the base text.

> falling   snoozing   nodding

1 _____ **asleep** can take some getting used to.
2 Just as you are _____ **off**, you can feel as though you've fallen off a 10-storey building.
3 … anyone still awake after bedtime would see his _____ form drift by.

b Which two words or expressions in the sentences in **a** above mean 'going to sleep'? Which word means 'sleeping'?

2 Now do the exercises on page 204.

---

45 minutes later, and just as abruptly, the sun rises to fill the station with brilliant light again.

Because of the frequency of these apparent days and nights, a bedtime
50 schedule is imposed by mission controllers. Each of the crew has a small cabin where they can hook a sleeping bag to the wall and settle down for the night. [6] ___ Falling asleep can take
55 some getting used to. Just as you are nodding off, you can feel as though you've fallen off a 10-storey building. People who look half asleep will suddenly throw their heads back and
60 put out their arms. It gets easier with time, though. One Russian crew member even goes without a sleeping bag and anyone still awake after bedtime would see his snoozing form drift by, slowly
65 bouncing off the walls.

Language focus: The future

A Making predictions

1 The following sentences all represent opinions, predictions or expectations about the future. Decide which of the words and expressions in **bold** express:
a certainty   **b** probability   **c** possibility
1 The ISS **will probably** still be in operation after 2020.
2 It **may well** continue in orbit until 2028.
3 The American space shuttle programme has finished, but Russian Soyuz capsules **will** continue to take astronauts to the space station.
4 The US space agency NASA **might** one day set up a space station on the moon.
5 They **could** even establish a base on Mars.
6 But this **is not likely to** happen in my lifetime!

What is the negative form of each of the words and phrases in **bold** in **1–5** above?

Example: will probably – probably won't/will not

2 Look at the following predictions for the year 2030. Make your own predictions by completing each gap below with either the positive or the negative form of one of the words or phrases in Section A.
1 Robot pets _____ take over from animals in the home.
2 The car _____ cease to be the main means of transport.
3 Children _____ receive most of their education at home.
4 Books _____ be found only in museums.
5 Scientists _____ have found a cure for cancer and Aids.
6 There _____ be peace throughout the world.

⬤ Discuss your sentences with your partner.

B Other futures

Match each of the future forms **1–9** with an explanation **a–i**.
Example: 1 b
1 I can't talk now. I <u>am</u> just <u>about to go</u> into a meeting.
2 This time next week I'<u>ll be sitting</u> on a beach in Spain.
3 When you come to visit, I <u>will have finished</u> my exams.
4 The train <u>leaves</u> at seven o'clock tomorrow evening.
5 That suitcase looks very heavy. Here, I'<u>ll carry</u> it for you.
6 I'<u>m meeting</u> Susan at eight o'clock.
7 I'<u>m going to try</u> and book a flight to Morocco.
8 Quick, give me a handkerchief! I think I'<u>m going to sneeze</u>.
9 Elisa <u>will be</u> nine years old next Monday.

a a prediction based on present evidence
b an event which is on the point of happening
c a timetabled event
d an event that will be in progress at a certain time in the future
e an event that will be completed by a certain time in the future
f an arrangement made with another person
g a personal intention or planned decision
h a factual statement about the future
i an offer to help; a decision made at the moment of speaking

🔍 Check your ideas in the Grammar reference on pages 215–6.

C Time linkers

Complete each of the following gaps with a word from the box. Use each word only once.

soon   by   when   before   until

1 Make a brief plan _____ you start writing your review.
2 What an awful traffic jam! _____ the time we get to the airport, the plane will have left.
3 Do not unfasten your seat belt _____ the plane has come to a complete stop.
4 I'll phone you as _____ as I hear any news.
5 You may leave the room _____ you have completed the test.

Which tenses are used after the time linkers to refer to the future?

D Further practice

1 In sections **A** and **B** below choose the most likely alternative. For sections **C** and **D** complete the gaps with an appropriate future form of the verbs in brackets.

A

I've just heard on the radio weather forecast that it **(1)** *is raining/is going to rain* tomorrow. That's a real shame because **(2)** *we're going/we'll go* to the countryside for a picnic, and **(3)** *we'll have to/we're having to* eat in the car if the weather's bad.

B

Lola's plane **(4)** *is about to take off/takes off* at six tomorrow morning, so **(5)** *I'll get up/I get up* at four and give her a lift to the airport. While you're still in bed, **(6)** *we'll be driving/we're driving* along the motorway!

C

I should be able to leave work a little early tomorrow. I **(7)** _____ (see) a client at four, but I don't think our meeting **(8)** _____ (last) very long. We **(9)** _____ (only/sign) a few papers so I expect we **(10)** _____ (finish) by half past four.

D

Kath: What time **(11)** _____ (we/meet) tomorrow? What do you think?
Pascal: Well, the film **(12)** _____ (not/start) until four, but we could have a coffee beforehand.
Kath: That's a good idea. In that case, I **(13)** _____ (get) the 2.30 bus and I **(14)** _____ (probably/see) you there at about three. OK?

2 ⬤ Discuss these questions with your partner.
What will you be doing this time tomorrow?
What plans have you made for next weekend?
Are you planning to buy anything special in the near future?
How will your life have changed in ten years' time?

Multiple choice 1.47–1.54

You will hear people talking in eight different situations. For questions **1–8**, choose the best answer (**A, B** or **C**).

1 You overhear this man talking about the hotel where he is staying.
  How does he feel about his room?
  A surprised
  B disappointed
  C angry

2 Listen to this woman talking about a job she has applied for.
  What job has she applied for?
  A a tour operator
  B a travel agent
  C a restaurant manager

3 You hear a woman talking to a tour guide.
  What is the woman's problem?
  A She does not have her passport.
  B She has left her money in the hotel.
  C She thinks she has been robbed.

4 You overhear a man talking about a place he tried to visit on holiday.
  What place is he describing?
  A a cathedral
  B an art museum
  C a castle

5 Listen to this conversation between a man and a teenage boy.
  Who is the man?
  A the boy's father
  B a chemist
  C a doctor

6 You hear a local resident talking about tourists in her town.
  What is she complaining about?
  A They have no money to spend.
  B There are too many of them.
  C They make too much noise.

7 You hear this boy talking to his mother.
  Why is he disappointed?
  A He thinks his parents' idea is boring.
  B His parents had promised to do something else.
  C He's tired of doing the same things.

8 You hear a man talking about a beach he recently visited.
  What did he like about the beach?
  A the quality of the sand
  B the temperature of the sea
  C the closeness of the shops

Vocabulary 2: Travel

1 **a** Complete each of the gaps **1–6** with a word from the box.

> cruise   flight   journey   tour   travel   trip

1 I sometimes read when I **go on a long car** _____ , and I sleep a lot, too.

2 I've never **been on a long-haul** _____ ; the furthest I've flown is from London to Berlin.

3 I'm a huge fan of **rail** _____ ; I'd love to take the Trans-Siberian railway or go from one coast of the United States to the other by train.

4 I wouldn't like to **go on a Caribbean** _____ : I'd probably be seasick and I'd rather get to know one island well than visit lots of different ones.

5 I think the best way to see the sights in a city is to **go on a guided** _____ .

6 When there's a public holiday, I often **go on a day** _____ to the coast or to the mountains with my family.

b How true are sentences **1–6** above for you? Discuss each one with your partner.

2 Underline the correct alternatives. Pay close attention to the words in **bold**.

Last year **we went on (1)** *holiday/holidays* **to** Scotland and booked two weeks **on a (2)** *camping/campsite*, **where we (3)** *stayed/spent* **in a caravan**. We didn't really **(4)** *enjoy/relax* **ourselves** because it was very noisy and it rained nearly every day, too. My sister and I **had a good (5)** *time/fun*, though, splashing around in the puddles, but my dad didn't think it was **much (6)** *funny/fun*. One day we **went on a half-day (7)** *excursion/voyage* **to a castle**, but it was **(8)** *full/crowded* **of** noisy tourists so we were almost glad to get back to the campsite. We're going to **go (9)** *away/out* **for a couple of weeks** with my dad again this summer, but he's promised to take us on a **(10)** *packet/package* **holiday** to a Mediterranean resort to make up for last year's disaster.

Speaking 1
Part 1

Interview

In Part 1 of the Speaking test the examiner might ask you about your holidays.

Student A Imagine you are the examiner. Ask your partner the following questions.
Student B You are the exam candidate. Answer the questions as fully as possible.

- Where do you usually spend your holidays?
- What types of things do you like doing on your holiday?
- Would you enjoy going on holiday on your own?
- What is the best holiday you have ever had? And the worst?
- Is there anywhere you would particularly like to visit? Why?

Now change roles and follow the same instructions again.

Speaking 2
Part 2

Talking about photos ⬤

Before you do the following Speaking Part 2 tasks, study the Useful language box below.

1 Look at photographs **1** and **2**. They show people whose jobs involve working with holidaymakers.

Student A Compare photographs 1 and 2 and say what you think the people enjoy about these different jobs.

Student B When your partner has finished, say which job you would prefer to do.

> What do the people enjoy about these different jobs?

> Why are the people riding motorbikes in a group?

Useful language

Student A

Use a range of structures to speculate about the photographs.

look + adjective	He **looks** underline{interested} in his work.
look like + noun	**They look like** underline{policemen}.
look as if + verb phrase	**He looks as if** underline{he likes} talking to people.
Modal verbs	They **could** be going to an official event.
	He **might** enjoy being outside all the time.
Other verbs	I **imagine/expect** they all know each other.

Student B

Use a range of structures to express preferences.

I**'d prefer to** do this job **rather than** that one.

I **would rather** work here **than** there.

I **would love/hate/be thrilled/be scared to** ride a motorbike.

2 Now change roles and look at photographs **3** and **4**. They show people riding motorbikes in a group.

Student A Compare photographs 3 and 4 and say why you think the people are riding motorbikes in a group.

Student B When your partner has finished, say whether you would enjoy riding a motorbike in a group.

Multiple matching 1.55–1.59

1 When, if ever, do you use a bicycle?
How common is it for people to cycle in the cities in your country? How safe is it?

2 You will hear five different people speaking on the subject of cycling within a city. For questions **1–5**, choose from the list (**A–H**) the phrase which best summarizes what each speaker is talking about. Use the letters only once. There are three extra letters which you do not need to use.

A a move in the right direction

B the consequences of breaking the law   Speaker 1 ☐ 1

C the need to educate the public   Speaker 2 ☐ 2

D a lack of open spaces to cycle in   Speaker 3 ☐ 3

E the problem of pollution   Speaker 4 ☐ 4

F a feeling of freedom   Speaker 5 ☐ 5

G the dangers of not being visible to drivers

H the intolerance of other road users

3 What measures can be taken by the government and/or local authorities in your country to encourage cycling?

Vocabulary 3: Phrasal verbs

1 Use the context to help you work out the meanings of the phrasal verbs in **bold** in these sentences from the listening.

1 I get shouted at by people who still haven't **caught on** that it's me that has right of way, not them.

2 I get off the train, put on my helmet and **head for** the office.

3 Someone in the town hall **came up with** a nice idea to promote cycling in the city.

4 There's a real festival atmosphere now, with thousands of cyclists of all ages **turning out** every month.

5 Sometimes you **come across** some really nasty drivers in the city.

6 People don't generally use a bike to **get about** the city.

2 Discuss the following questions with another student.
Where are you heading for after this class?
Did you come across any friendly people on your last holiday?
What is the best way to get about your town or city?

Word formation: Adjectives

1   Use the word in capitals at the end of each of these sentences from the listening to form a word that fits in the gap **in the same sentence**. There is an example at the beginning **(0)**.

0 There's a cycle path that goes right round the city, and ___VARIOUS___ shorter ones within it.   **VARY**

1 It's pedestrians, not motorists, that have to be _____ they don't wander onto them.   **CARE**

2 And of course, cycling is just so _____ – I've never felt fitter.   **HEALTH**

3 We need a whole series of _____ measures to make this a more cycle-friendly city.   **ADDITION**

4 It's really _____ – sometimes I lose my balance and nearly fall off.   **DANGER**

5 They get _____ if they have to slow down for me.   **PATIENCE**

6 I get beeped and shouted at all the time – it's very _____ .   **PLEASE**

7 It's not an _____ option, really, given the quality of the air here.   **ATTRACT**

8 We're in the middle of a huge _____ area.   **INDUSTRY**

2   **a** Copy the following table with adjective suffixes into your notebook. Complete the table by writing the adjectives you wrote for exercise **1** in the appropriate columns.

-ous	-ful	-y	-al	-ent	-ant	-ive
various						

b Use the appropriate suffixes from **a** to create adjectives from the words in the box. **You may need to make further spelling changes.** Add the words to the table in your notebook. There are **three** words for each column.

Example: ignore – ignorant

ignore	differ	origin	poison	peace	protect	cloud
beauty	hunger	appear	decide	tolerate	mystery	finance
fog	humour	describe	hesitate	benefit	succeed	obey

Reading and Use of English 2

Part 3

Word formation

For questions **1–10**, read the text below. Use the word given in capitals at the end of some of the lines to form a word that fits in the gap **in the same line**. There is an example at the beginning **(0)**. Write your answers **IN CAPITAL LETTERS**.

Monorails

Monorail systems are (0) ___FREQUENTLY___ associated with airports, zoos and amusement parks. They can, however, also be integrated into a city's main transport infrastructure and in recent decades a (1) _____ number have been built around the world for this purpose. In particular, there are (2) _____ examples in Asia, with Japan leading the way. Elsewhere, Sydney, Moscow and Sao Paolo all have modern monorails. Perhaps the most (3) _____ system in operation was also one of the first to be built: the 'Schwebebahn' in Wuppertal, Germany, whose trains are suspended from its track, was opened in 1901. Monorails run over short (4) _____ , providing a quick and efficient method of urban transport. Supporters point to their (5) _____ safety record and the fact that, because they are electrically powered, they have an (6) _____ advantage over other more polluting forms of city transport. They are also (7) _____ to operate. However, among the objections to monorail systems are the high costs of construction and the unpleasant (8) _____ of the elevated tracks.

FREQUENT

SIGNIFY

NUMBER

USUAL

DISTANT

IMPRESS

ENVIRONMENT

EXPENSE

APPEAR

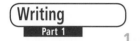

Essay

1  Read the following Writing Part 1 instructions. How would you answer the essay question and what could you say for each of the three 'Things to write about' in the Notes?

In your English class you have been talking about travel and tourism. Your English teacher has asked you to write an essay.

Write an essay using **all** the notes and give reasons for your point of view.

Essay question

Is it better to spend a summer holiday in the countryside or on the coast?

Notes

Write about:

1 leisure options

2 climate

3 .... (your own idea)

2 Read the answer below to the question in exercise **1**.

What is the writer's 'own idea' for number **3** of the Notes section in the question?

How similar is the essay to the one you would have written if you had answered the question?

A summer holiday by the sea

Without doubt, the best place to spend the summer is on the coast, which generally has far more advantages for the holidaymaker than the countryside.

For one thing, in the countryside there is not much to do apart from walking and visiting villages, whereas the coast offers a wider range of possibilities for the tourist. You can stroll around seaside villages, but you can also spend the day on the beach, take part in watersports such as sailing and surfing, eat in a variety of restaurants and go to clubs and bars in the evening.

Secondly, in July and August it is usually cooler on the coast than in the countryside, and therefore much more pleasant. It is not surprising that most people head for the beach during the hot summer months. Another positive point is that, because so many people choose the coast as their holiday destination, there are more opportunities to make new friends than in the countryside.

In my opinion, then, the coast offers the chance of a far more varied and enjoyable summer holiday than the countryside.

3 a What linking devices does the writer use to introduce each of the three points from the Notes section in the question.

e.g. For one thing

b What other linking devices does the writer use?

4 a Read the following Writing Part 1 instructions.

In your English class you have been talking about travel and transport. Your English teacher has asked you to write an essay.

Write an essay using **all** the notes and give reasons for your point of view.

Write your **essay** in **140–190** words.

b Decide on your third point. This will depend on the situation in your area and the answer you give, but here are some possible options:

- comfort
- frequency
- noise and pollution
- parking facilities

c Make a brief plan before writing your essay. Write down ideas for each of the three points in the Notes section. Select those you wish to include and decide how you will organize them into paragraphs.

Now you are ready to write your **essay**.

Essay question
Is it better to use the car or public transport in your town or area?

Notes
Write about:
1 journey times
2 cost
3 .... (your own idea)

Don't forget!

- Include a brief introduction and conclusion in your essay.
- Write in a consistently formal or neutral style.
- Include a range of language and avoid repetition.
- Use appropriate linking devices (see exercise 3 above and page 39 of Unit 3).
- Check your work when you have finished.

Transformations

1 Match each sentence **1–6** with a sentence **a–f** which expresses the same idea. The first one has been done for you.

1 She isn't thinking of going out.
2 She's likely to go out.
3 She's about to go out.
4 She may not go out.
5 She's unlikely to go out.
6 She'll have gone out.

a She'll probably go out.
b She might stay at home.
c She isn't planning to go out.
d She won't be at home.
e She probably won't go out.
f She's on the point of going out.

2 Complete the second sentence so that it has a similar meaning to the first sentence, using the word given. **Do not change the word given.** You must use between **two** and **five** words, including the word given.

Write the missing words **IN CAPITAL LETTERS**.

1 Where are you thinking of spending your summer holiday this year?
   PLANNING
   Where _____ your summer holiday this year?

2 He was about to say something when the phone rang.
   POINT
   He was _____ something when the phone rang.

3 The employment situation will probably improve in the next few months.
   LIKELY
   The employment situation is _____ better in the next few months.

4 I may fall asleep during the film.
   ABLE
   I might _____ awake during the film.

5 The plants will probably be dead when we eventually get home.
   HAVE
   The plants _____ the time we get home.

6 Let me know the moment you think of a solution to this problem.
   COME
   Let me know as _____ with a solution to this problem.

The future

Complete each gap with a word from the box. You do not need to use all of the words. The first one has been done for you.

having	be	is	will	much	well	of	on	out
in	~~about~~	for	during	away	to	a	not	

I'm just **(1)** _about_ to get ready to go **(2)** _____ on a business trip to St Petersburg I'll only be gone **(3)** _____ a couple of days and I'll **(4)** _____ spending nearly all my time there in meetings, so it won't be **(5)** _____ fun. I don't expect **(6)** _____ see **(7)** _____ great deal of the city either, but if I get the chance, I may **(8)** _____ pay a quick visit to the Hermitage Museum. I'm a huge fan **(9)** _____ Leonardo da Vinci, and two of his works are on display there. Being February, it **(10)** _____ likely to be very cold, but I might **(11)** _____ notice that too much as I'll be inside most of the time, so I'm not planning **(12)** _____ taking lots of extra winter clothing with me.

Reading and Use of English
Part 1

Multiple-choice cloze

For questions **1–8**, read the text below and decide which answer (**A, B, C** or **D**) best fits each gap. There is an example at the beginning (**0**).

Seville

Situated on the banks of the river Guadalquivir, Seville (0) ___ the best of Andalusian culture, with its rich Moorish heritage, fine food and passionate flamenco music. Hidden within the narrow streets of its historic centre are beautiful courtyards (1) ___ of flowers, bringing an air of calm to an otherwise vibrant city.

Begin your (2) ___ to Seville with a guided tour aboard an open-top bus or one of the many horse-drawn carriages which (3) ___ off from the cathedral. Then climb the Giralda tower for a spectacular (4) ___ of the city, before strolling around the gardens of the Alcázar palace. Seville, of course, is (5) ___ for its delicious 'tapas', so if you need a break from sightseeing, (6) ___ Triana or Santa Cruz, where you can sample the delights of southern Spanish cuisine.

If you have time, take a (7) ___ out to the Roman ruins of Italica, birthplace of the emperors Trajan and Hadrian. Just a short bus (8) ___ away from the city centre, Italica boasts an impressive Roman amphitheatre and numerous mosaics.

0	**A** discovers	**B** explores	**C** <u>offers</u>	**D** involves
1	**A** plenty	**B** lots	**C** crowded	**D** full
2	**A** stay	**B** visit	**C** sight	**D** arrival
3	**A** set	**B** put	**C** get	**D** give
4	**A** vision	**B** view	**C** aspect	**D** appearance
5	**A** seen	**B** looked	**C** known	**D** heard
6	**A** come across	**B** head for	**C** make up for	**D** put up with
7	**A** travel	**B** trail	**C** track	**D** trip
8	**A** ride	**B** walk	**C** pass	**D** run

Writing
Part 2

Article

You see this announcement in an international magazine.

HOLIDAY COMPETITION

Write an article about a holiday destination you know well, giving details of what tourists can see and do there. The top ten articles will be included in the next edition of our magazine.

Write your **article** for the competition. You should write **140–190** words.

How to go about it

Use the multiple-choice cloze text on Seville above as a model. Consider the following:

- How many paragraphs are there?
- What type of information does each one contain?
- Are there any expressions which you could use in your own article?

9 Mystery and imagination

Multiple choice

1 Do you enjoy reading novels or watching films of mystery and suspense? Why do you think they are so popular?

2 You are going to read an extract from a mystery novel. The scene takes place on 'The Island', not a real island, but a green and rocky headland in St Ives in the south-west of England. Read the extract quite quickly and answer the following questions:

What would you have done if you had been in this situation? Why?

An unusual find

At the end of Porthmeor Beach, Laura climbed the stone steps to the Island and took the path that curved around the edge of it. There were benches dotted along it, and a red plastic box containing a life-
5 rope. Laura had her doubts that the rope would be effective in an emergency. The current that surged up to the black rocks was so brutal that anyone unlucky enough to fall in would be swept out to sea before they had time to draw breath. Laura felt the magnetic pull
10 of the ocean beneath the black cliffs, and goose bumps rose on her arms.

On the north side of the Island, the headland screened out both the town and the beaches. Laura would stop there sometimes and gaze out to sea. If no one
15 was around, she liked to pretend she was alone on a desert island. Today, however, the path had an eerie feel. In the short time since Laura had left the house a sea mist had rolled in, obscuring everything except the grey silhouette of the hill topped by St Nicholas's
20 chapel with its twin crosses. The tide was in and violent waves splattered the path. More than once, Laura had to leap to avoid a drenching.

She might have stepped on the bottle if she had not been skirting a puddle. It was an ordinary glass bottle
25 – the kind used for concentrated juice syrups, but the label had been removed and it had been scrubbed clean. It was lying in the centre of the path, almost as if it had been deliberately placed there. Even before she lifted it, Laura could see there was a note in it.

30 She almost didn't pick it up. The idea of finding a message in a bottle seemed ridiculous, like a joke or something. But curiosity got the better of her. Before she picked it up, she took a good look round in case the person who'd left it there was hanging around to
35 have a laugh. But she was alone.

She bent down and studied the rolled piece of paper through the glass. There was something written on it. Before she removed the lid, she glanced up at the chapel. There was a sudden flash of white, although
40 whether it was someone's shirt or the wing of a gull Laura couldn't tell. For two full minutes she stared upwards, but saw nothing else.

What sort of people put messages in bottles? Pranksters and marooned ancient mariners were the
45 only two categories Laura could think of. Since the bottle was shiny and new and had obviously never been in the sea, old sea dogs could be ruled out. That left a joker with too much time on his or her hands.

The lid twisted off easily. Retrieving the note was
50 trickier. Laura managed it with the aid of a stick. She unrolled the paper, a cream-coloured parchment. There was something old-fashioned about the handwriting, as if the writer had a calligrapher's skills and had used the quill of a feather and a pot of indigo ink. In long,
55 artistic letters were the words: *Can I trust you?*

Laura looked around again. The path was unusually quiet for this time of the morning. Most days it was teeming with dog walkers. She put down the note while she zipped up her coat and pulled her scarf
60 tighter. The mist had whited out the coastline. Clouds of it rolled across the sea, muffling the sound of the waves.

If she had any sense, she'd toss the bottle into the nearest litter bin, hurry along and forget she ever saw
65 it. But *what if?* That's what the voice in her head was saying. What if the writer was someone in real danger? What if she was their only lifeline and she ignored them and walked away?

Laura opened her bag and took out a pen. Beneath
70 the question, *'Can I trust you?'*, she wrote in bright red capitals: YES.

3 For questions **1–6**, choose the answer (**A, B, C** or **D**) which you think fits best according to the text.

1 When Laura reached the Island, she was struck by
  A the length of the life-rope.
  B the colour of the rocks.
  C the power of the sea.
  D the shape of the path.

2 What does 'a drenching' mean in line 22?
  A feeling sick
  B getting wet
  C being seen
  D falling over

3 When Laura saw the bottle on the path, she was
  A amused.
  B annoyed.
  C impressed.
  D suspicious.

4 Before opening the bottle, Laura felt certain
  A the message had not been written by a sailor.
  B the bottle had been left there by mistake.
  C someone was watching her from the chapel.
  D a dog had brought the bottle to the path.

5 After reading the note, Laura took time to
  A listen to the sea.
  B admire the view.
  C keep out the cold.
  D observe some dogs.

6 How did Laura's attitude change towards the end of the extract?
  A She started to fear for her own safety.
  B She pretended to trust the message writer.
  C She began to take the message more seriously.
  D She became irritated with herself for wasting her time.

Reacting to the text

What would you have done if you had found the bottle?
Have you ever found anything unusual, interesting or valuable? What did you do with it?

Vocabulary 1: Ways of looking

1 a Match the words in **bold** in sentences **1–3** from the reading with their meanings **a–c**.

1 *Laura would stop there sometimes and **gaze** out to sea.*
2 *Before she removed the lid, she **glanced** up at the chapel.*
3 *For two full minutes she **stared** upwards, but saw nothing else.*

a have a quick, short look at something
b look somewhere for a long time, especially with interest or admiration
c look directly at something for a long time, e.g. when you are thinking

b Work out the approximate meaning of the words in **bold** in sentences **1–3**.

1 James **peered** through the keyhole and thought he could see something – or someone – lying on the floor.
2 If you stand on a box, you might **glimpse** the President as he drives past.
3 He didn't say anything when I turned up late, but he clearly wasn't pleased: he just stood there **glaring** at me.

2 Complete each gap with the correct form of one of the six verbs from **1a** and **b**.

1 Bored with the lesson, I _____ **quickly** at my watch to see how long was left.
2 Sam _____ **dreamily** at the moonlit sky: it was a wonderful sight.
3 The boy sat _____ **wide-eyed** and **open-mouthed** at the huge cake.
4 I only **caught a brief** _____ of the thief as he ran away.
5 The teacher _____ **angrily** at me, obviously thinking I was making fun of him.
6 The policewoman shone her torch into the room and _____ **cautiously** inside.

113

Language focus 1: Modal verbs for speculation and deduction

1 Here are Laura's possible thoughts, when she was speculating about who had put the bottle on the path. Read them and answer the questions below.

*'I suppose a prankster **might have left** the bottle there, or else it **might have come** from a marooned ancient mariner. Actually, though, the bottle is shiny and new, and has obviously never been in the sea, so it **can't have been** an old sea dog. That means a joker with too much time on his or her hands **must have done** it.'*

1 Which of the forms in **bold** express:
   a possible explanations for who left it?
   b certainty about who didn't leave it?
   c certainty about who left it?
2 Which verb form is used after each of the modal verbs?
3 Which of the following modal verbs can be used in place of *might* in the first sentence above without changing the meaning?

   could   should   can   may

 Check your ideas on page 216 of the Grammar reference and read more about modal verbs for speculation and deduction.

2 Speculate about what might have happened in the following situations. Write two or three sentences for each using modal verbs.

Example: 1

She could have just received some bad news.
She may have had an argument with a friend.
She might have been peeling onions.

1 Angela's crying.
2 Paul's face and hands are very dirty.
3 The kitchen window is broken.
4 There's a red mark on Derek's shirt collar.
5 Lucy was late for school.
6 Nobody in the class did their homework last night.

3 Match each of the sentences **1–6** with a suitable continuation **a–f**.

1 Don't make too much noise.   *b*
2 What do you mean, you don't know what to do? ____
3 Would you lend me yours?   ____
4 I can't find her name on their webpage.   ____
5 You should ask her.   ____
6 I want everyone to search the area.   ____

a She might not be working there any more.
b He might still be asleep.
c He can't have got very far.
d You can't have been listening to my instructions.
e I must have left mine at home.
f You never know; she might be interested.

4 Look at sentences **a–f** in exercise **3** again and for each one decide whether the speaker is talking about the past or present. What form of the verb is used after the modal verb in each case?

5 Use modal verbs to speculate about possible contexts for each of the sentence combinations in exercise **3**.

Example: 1 *This could be a mother speaking to her children. They might be playing in the house and their father may be ill in bed.*

Listening 1
Part 4

Multiple choice ⦿ 1.60

1 ⦿ You are going to listen to a radio interview with a ghost walk guide. What do you think happens on a ghost walk? What does the guide do?

2 Listen to the interview. For questions **1–7**, choose the best answer (**A**, **B** or **C**).

1 Alan says his job as a ghost walk guide has enabled him to
   A become an expert on local history.
   B combine his different talents.
   C improve his acting skills.

2 Alan says that participants in the ghost walks

  A are never disappointed.

  B want to be frightened.

  C laugh at all his jokes.

3 According to Alan, what quality enables a storyteller to frighten audiences?

  A self-confidence

  B a loud voice

  C good timing

4 What type of people do not usually enjoy the ghost walk so much?

  A people who have not been anticipating it

  B people who come as part of a group

  C people who do not like surprises

5 What does Alan say about playing different characters on the ghost walks?

  A Some of the roles help to improve his mood.

  B He dresses up as real people from history.

  C Acting helps maintain the audience's interest.

6 When talking about the possible existence of ghosts, Alan says that

  A he respects other people's belief in ghosts.

  B he believes ghosts are part of people's imagination.

  C he suspects people of inventing stories to impress others.

7 When talking about his favourite ghost story, Alan says that

  A he does not want to give all the details.

  B he does not tell it on many ghost walks.

  C he does not think everyone enjoys it.

3 ● Have you or has anyone you know ever had 'a paranormal experience'?
Do you believe that ghosts and haunted buildings exist?
Would you be interested in going on a ghost walk? Why/Why not?

Word formation: Adverbs

1 In these sentences from the listening, write the adverb formed from the adjective in brackets.

  1 *They all laugh _____ (nervous).*

  2 *These people _____ (usual) respond _____ (extreme) well.*

  3 *_____ (regrettable), I have to say that I haven't seen any on the walks.*

Check your answers in the listening script on pages 229–30. What are the rules for the formation of the adverbs in the above examples?

2 Write the adverbs formed from these adjectives. The same rule applies to both adjectives in each pair.

  ***Example:** beautiful → beautifully   total → totally*

  1 complete _____   sole _____

  2 simple _____   gentle _____

  3 lucky _____   extraordinary _____

  4 scientific _____   dramatic _____

3 Write the adverbs formed from these adjectives. These should be learnt separately.

  1 whole _____   **2** shy _____   **3** full _____

  4 public _____   **5** true _____

4 Complete each gap with an appropriate adverb formed from the noun or verb in capital letters at the end of the line.

  1 Sue's not coming to work today. _____ , she's suffering from stress. **APPEAR**

  2 I _____ deleted all the photos on my camera yesterday. **ACCIDENT**

  3 Cycling is becoming _____ popular in this city. **INCREASE**

  4 This museum was _____ built as a palace. **ORIGIN**

  5 Mike's still in hospital, but his condition is improving _____ . **DAY**

  6 They had been told _____ not to play near the main road. **REPEAT**

  7 Tim was stopped by the police and accused of driving _____ . **CARE**

  8 Lynne does a lot of exercise. However, she eats far too _____ . **HEALTH**

Vocabulary 2: *Give*

A Phrasal verbs with *give*

1 Look at this extract from the listening on page 114. Match the two phrasal verbs in **bold** to their meanings **a** and **b**.

*I particularly like stories which involve smells that some buildings are said to **give off** when ghosts are around. I don't want to **give away** too much here on the programme ...*

a tell information or facts that should be kept secret

b produce and send into the air

2 Work out the meaning of the phrasal verbs in **bold** in the following sentences. Use the context of the sentence to help you.

1 I'm so unfit! I really ought to **give up** smoking.

2 Tired of running, he **gave himself up** at a police station and confessed to the crime.

3 I'm going to **give out** the test papers now but you mustn't begin until I tell you.

4 You should never **give out** your personal details or financial information online.

5 If you **give in** your homework now, I'll mark it tonight and **give** it **back** tomorrow.

6 My parents said no at first, but eventually they **gave in** and let me go to the party.

B Collocations with *give*

1 In sections **A** and **B** below match a sentence beginning on the left with a suitable ending on the right.

A **1** Pat saw the mouse, **gave a piercing**   **a sigh**, and sent her yet another text.

2 Thrilled at the news, he **gave a broad**   **b look**, as if he didn't recognize her.

3 She said goodbye, **gave** him **a tender**   **c smile**, showing all his teeth.

4 He looked at her photo, **gave a deep**   **d scream** and ran out of the room.

5 She waved, but he **gave** her **a blank**   **e kiss** on the cheek and walked away.

B **1** Lovely to see you. **Give my best**   **a shock** when they saw her phone bill.

2 The conference brochure **gives full**   **b performance** in this, her latest film.

3 Your gifts of toys will **give great**   **c speech** on the state of the economy.

4 Lucy's parents were **given a nasty**   **d details** of speakers and their talks.

5 Meryl Streep **gives an impressive**   **e regards** to your family, won't you?

6 The President **gave a lengthy**   **f pleasure** to the orphaned children.

2 The collocations in **bold** in exercise **1A** all refer to *physical actions* of some kind. Match the following general meanings to the collocations in bold in **1B**.

a to cause someone to experience an emotional feeling

b to perform or present something in public

c to communicate information, opinions or greetings

3 Cover up the sentence endings in the right hand column of exercises **1A** and **B** and see how many of the *nouns* you can remember for the corresponding *verb + adjective* combinations on the left.

4 a ◖ Describe situations in which you might:

- give a broad smile
- give a piercing scream
- give a deep sigh
- give a nervous laugh
- give someone a blank look

b ◖ Think of a time when someone or something:

- gave you a nasty shock
- gave you a pleasant surprise
- gave you great pleasure
- gave an impressive performance
- gave a lengthy (and boring!) speech

Example:
You might give a broad smile when you find out you've passed an exam, or you ask someone to go out with you and they say 'yes'.

Open cloze

1 ⬤ Read the examples of sportsmen and women's superstitious rituals on page 204. Do you know any more like this?

2 For questions **1–8**, read the text below and think of the word which best fits each gap. Use only **one** word in each space. There is an example at the beginning **(0)**.

Write your answers **IN CAPITAL LETTERS**.

Sporting superstitions

Most of (0) __US__ have routines, habits and superstitions. We'll wear our lucky shirt to an interview, arrange our cutlery in a particular way or turn the oven off three times, just to (1) ____ sure. In a competitive environment, in (2) ____ athletes are all going for gold, years of training, drastic diets and intense coaching might just (3) ____ be enough. So, sometimes, the Olympians turn (4) ____ luck for extra support.

'Superstition is very common in sport,' says sports psychologist Dr George Sik. 'Athletes use it so they can rely on something else other (5) ____ their own consciousness. Superstition means being in control, adding a safety net. If you convince (6) ____ that you are in luck, you'll boost your confidence and tend to perform better. And if you fail, you can always blame it (7) ____ the luck.'

So, (8) ____ they may know deep down that a 'lucky' pair of socks won't take them over the line any faster, many athletes stick to their rituals for that little bit of confidence, belief and a sense of security.

3 ⬤ How much does superstition affect your behaviour?

Sentence completion ⬤ 1.61

1 You will hear a woman called Sally Hurst talking on the radio about the Superstition Mountain Range in the United States. For questions **1–10**, complete the sentences.

The Superstition Mountains

While she was in the Superstition Mountains, Sally was able to **(1)** ....

Sally does not recommend visiting the area in **(2)** ....

Sally says the mountains were probably given their name by local **(3)** .... in the nineteenth century.

The owner of the lost gold mine was a **(4)** .... immigrant.

The mine owner died in **(5)** .... 1891.

It was estimated at one point that as many as **(6)** .... people every year tried to find the lost mine.

According to one clue, when the sun is **(7)** ...., it shines into the entrance of the mine.

The section on the mine in the Superstition Mountain Museum contains a collection of **(8)** ....

Goldfield is now a **(9)** .... town, visited by many tourists.

Dutchman's Gold is the title of a **(10)** .... about the lost mine.

2 ⬤ Do you know any places with mysteries or legends attached to them?

Language focus 2: Question tags

1 The following sentences from the listening all end with a question tag. Look at the words in **bold**. How are question tags formed?

    1 *It's a bit hot there, though, **isn't it**?*
    2 *Now I bet **you didn't know** that, **did you**?*

2 ⊙ 1.62 Listen to the examples from the recording again. In which of the sentences in **1** is the speaker:

    a asking a real question because he or she is *unsure* if the statement is true or not?

    b expecting agreement to the statement, which he or she feels *sure* is true?

    How can you tell the difference?

    ⓖ Read more about question tags on page 216 of the Grammar reference.

3 Add an appropriate question tag to each of the following statements.

    1 You don't believe him, _____ ?
    2 You won't let me down, _____ ?
    3 You went away for the weekend, _____ ?
    4 He's not playing very well, _____ ?
    5 He's already passed the *First* exam, _____ ?
    6 I'm right about that, _____ ?
    7 You can play chess, _____ ?
    8 Let's phone Paul, _____ ?

    ⊙ 1.62 Now listen and check your answers.

4 Listen to the sentences in exercise **3** again and next to each question tag draw an arrow to show if the intonation is rising ⤴ or falling ⤵ at the end.

5 Practise saying the sentences with the same intonation as the speakers in the recording.

6 Write down four statements about your partner that you are *sure* are true and four that you are *unsure* about, adding a question tag to each one.

    Examples:
    You don't like heavy metal music, do you?
    You went abroad for your holiday last year, didn't you?

7 ⊙ Ask and answer each other's questions, using appropriate intonation.

    Example
    A: *You don't like heavy metal music, do you?*
    B: *No, I don't. You're right. And you went abroad for your*

    holiday last year, didn't you?

    A: *No, I didn't, actually. I went abroad the year before last. Last summer we stayed in our house in the countryside.*

Reading and Use of English 3
Part 7

Multiple matching

1 ⊙ Read the introduction to the reading text Mystery Donors on page 119, as well as the titles of the true stories **A–D**. What do you think happened in each story?

2 Read the text quite quickly and check your predictions in exercise **1**.

3 For questions **1–10**, choose from the stories (**A–D**). The stories may be chosen more than once.

Which story

mentions the desire of some people to thank the donor in person?	1
says that everyone who saw the 'gifts' was positive about them?	2
mentions an unsuccessful attempt by a newspaper to identify the donor?	3
says that people did not expect the 'gifts' to attract so much media attention?	4
mentions speculation about the donor's reasons for leaving the 'gifts'?	5
says that most people did not want it to be known who the donor was?	6
mentions the donor's recent piece of luck?	7
mentions people's worries about possible negative consequences of the 'gifts'?	8
mentions the appropriateness of the 'gifts'?	9
says that one person initially mistook the intentions of the donor?	10

Mystery Donors

Here are four true stories of people who left 'gifts' in public places – and kept their identity a secret

A Book sculptures appear in Edinburgh's cultural centres

Between March and November 2011, a total of ten sculptures, beautifully crafted from books, were left anonymously in various cultural buildings in the city of Edinburgh.

Each was accompanied by a note, which included the words, 'In support of libraries, books, words, ideas and festivals'. There was unanimous approval of the intricate sculptures from all those lucky enough to view them when they were put on display.

Each sculpture was carefully and suitably chosen: a dinosaur for the National Museum, or a tiny cinema for the city's Filmhouse. Despite a strong suggestion in one of the notes that the donor was a woman, a local newspaper said they believed it to be a man. They claimed they had discovered the identity of the sculptor, but kept it quiet, given that the general view was that he or she should remain anonymous.

B New Jersey knitter decorates the town

In January 2010, residents of West Cape May in New Jersey were amused to find that colourful, knitted scarves had mysteriously begun to appear wrapped around the trees and lamp posts in the town's Wilbraham Park. And the fact that the knitter preferred to remain anonymous only added to the fun. What surprised them was the huge interest shown by newspaper and radio journalists, who came from other US states and abroad to report on events.

While most local people reacted positively to the decorations, some residents expressed concern that the scarves might harm the trees and become unattractive with the effects of the weather. Although the scarf wrapping continued and spread to traffic signs and fence posts, by mid-March it was all over. The scarves vanished overnight, as quickly and mysteriously as they had first appeared.

C *Unseen donor gives away large sums of cash*

In March 2012, the German town of Braunschweig began to capture the attention of the world's press. An anonymous benefactor had been donating money to local good causes, each time leaving the recipient an envelope containing €10000 in cash. Among the beneficiaries were the victim of a burglary, a severely disabled boy and a hospice, all of whom had appeared in the local newspaper. A total of nearly €200000 had been donated.

There were a number of theories to explain who the donor was and why they might have given the cash away: an elderly person with no family to leave their money to, a criminal wanting to get rid of stolen money or a lottery winner trying to do some good. Some of the beneficiaries wanted to meet the donor to express their gratitude. However, the local newspaper believed in respecting the donor's desire for anonymity and made no effort to discover their identity.

D Mystery man gives out money in supermarket

Just before Christmas 2011 a man entered a supermarket in Tiverton, England and handed out a number of envelopes, each containing a fifty-pound note, to delighted shoppers. Also inside the envelopes was a message which read: 'Happy Christmas. I have recently been fortunate enough to come into quite a lot of money – more than I need for myself and my family. So I thought that I would share some of it with you.' Believing it to be part of a marketing promotion, one beneficiary nearly threw the blank envelope away. Another went to the bank to check that the note was genuine. The donor's identity remains unknown, in spite of the efforts of one national daily, which asked readers to get in contact if they knew who the mystery benefactor was.

● Reacting to the text

Which story do you like best? Why?

If you unexpectedly came into 'quite a lot of money', would you give some away? If so, who would you give it to, and why? If not, what would you do with it?

Speaking
Part 3

Collaborative task

1 Imagine that a wealthy donor wants to give away large sums of money to different institutions and other places in your community. Below are some of the possible recipients of the donations.

Talk to each other about how these different recipients could spend their donations.

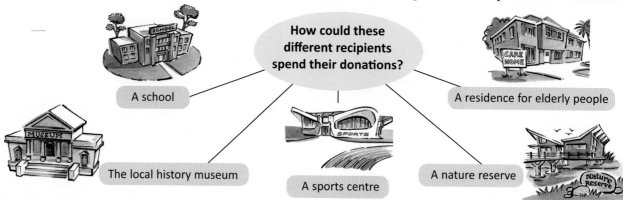

A school — **How could these different recipients spend their donations?** — A residence for elderly people

The local history museum — A sports centre — A nature reserve

2 Now decide which two donations would benefit the community most.

Useful language

Task 1

A Spending the donations

Complete each gap with a word from the box.

for	in	on	on	out

1 *They could* **spend** *it _____ (computers).*
2 *One idea would be to* **invest** *_____ (new equipment).*
3 *They could use the money to* **pay** *_____ (advertising).*
4 *A sensible thing to do would be to (***take** *_____ more staff).*
5 *Another possible way to use the money would be to (***carry** *_____ repairs).*

B Question tags

Complete each gap with an appropriate question tag.

1 *That's not a bad idea, _____ ?*
2 *That would be useful, _____ ?*
3 *Schools here never have enough computers, _____ ?*

4 *We've said all we can about that one, _____ ?*
5 *Let's talk about this one now, _____ ?*

Task 2

Referring back to the discussion in task 1

As I said before, (schools never have enough computers).

You made a good point earlier about (the health benefits of sport).

We both agreed on the importance of (preserving our past).

We should take into account what you said about (the environment).

Comparing the different options

(A museum) wouldn't need financial help as much as (a school).

The more help we give to (elderly people), the better for the community.

The community would benefit far more from a donation to (the nature reserve).

The one most in need of a donation would be (the sports centre).

3 Now do the Speaking Part 4 task on page 204.

Language focus 3: Contrast linkers

1 Use the words in the box to complete the gaps in these extracts from the reading on page 119. More than one answer may be possible.

although	but	despite	however	in spite	while

1 They claimed they had discovered the identity of the sculptor, _____ kept it quiet. (A)
2 _____ a strong suggestion in one of the notes that the donor was a woman, a local newspaper said they believed it to be a man. (A)
3 _____ most local people reacted positively to the decorations, some residents expressed concern that the scarves might harm the trees … (B)

4 _____ the scarf wrapping continued and spread to traffic signs and fence posts, by mid-March it was all over. (B)
5 Some of the beneficiaries would have loved to meet the donor. _____ , the local newspaper believed in respecting the donor's desire for anonymity. (C)
6 The donor's identity remains unknown, _____ of the efforts of one national daily. (D)

2 Check your answers in the relevant story of the reading on page 119.

Ⓖ Read more about contrast linkers on page 217 of the Grammar reference.

Writing
Part 2

Review

1 Read the following Writing Part 2 instructions. What item would you choose to review?

You have seen this notice in your school's English-language magazine.

> **REVIEWS WANTED**
>
> We would like you to write a review of something you have bought recently. It could be a computer game, a book, a magazine, a smartphone … anything you like!
>
> Describe the good and bad points of your purchase and say who you would recommend it to.
>
> The most interesting reviews will appear in next month's edition.

2 Read this review of a music download. The title of the album and the name of the band that recorded it have been covered with ink stains. Can you name either?

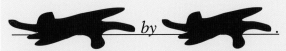
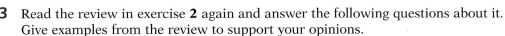
_by_ .

This classic album, named after the band's London recording studio, has been in our family for over forty years. It's my dad's vinyl version, and it's been played so often that it's too scratched to listen to now. So last week I bought the download.

Despite its age, it still sounds as fresh as when it was first released in 1969. Most of the tracks, of course, were composed by Lennon and McCartney, always a guarantee of quality music. However, my favourites are the two written by George Harrison – gentle songs of love and hope.

The Liverpool band's use of vocal harmony on the album is outstanding, and there's a good mix of fast and slow tracks, with one or two humorous ones as well. Ringo's contribution about the octopus is the weakest, but he was always a better drummer than a singer, wasn't he?

The album has songs to suit every generation, from children to grandparents, so I'd recommend it to everyone. Unfortunately, of course, the artwork of the 'Fab Four' on the zebra crossing is tiny on my smartphone, but we still have the cover from the vinyl version!

3 Read the review in exercise **2** again and answer the following questions about it. Give examples from the review to support your opinions.

  a Has the writer described both good and bad points and said who they would recommend it to?

  b Is the review organized into suitable paragraphs?

  c Are ideas connected with appropriate linking words?

  d Is there a good range of vocabulary and structures?

  e Is the style of the review formal, informal or neutral? Is the style appropriate?

4 Use questions **a–e** in exercise **3** to help you plan and write your own answer to the question in exercise **1**. To add an element of mystery, **do not mention the name or title of the item you are reviewing.**

5 Work in pairs.

  a Read your partner's review and try to guess the name or title of the item he or she has written about.

  b Read the review again and give your partner feedback on it, using questions **a–e** in exercise **3**. Give examples from the review to support your opinions.

  c If necessary, rewrite your own review, incorporating the points your partner has mentioned.

Vocabulary: Ways of looking

Match a sentence beginning **1–6** with an appropriate ending **a–e**.

1 Smiling contentedly, Elisa sat **gazing**
2 Once in the street, he could only **stare**
3 She read the last question and **glanced**
4 David lifted the lid a little and **peered**
5 Catherine only **glimpsed** the intruder
6 After receiving the red card he **glared**

a **momentarily,** but his face was familiar.
b **furiously** at the referee and left the pitch.
c **in wonder** at the spectacular scenery.
d **in disbelief** at his burning house.
e **anxiously** up at the exam room clock.
f **inquisitively** into the box.

Reading and Use of English
Part 1

Multiple-choice cloze

For questions **1–8**, read the text below and decide which answer (**A**, **B**, **C** or **D**) best fits each gap. There is an example at the beginning (**0**).

Solving a mystery

A scuba diver has (0) ___ a British family with the photos from a camera they lost on a canoeing (1) ___ on the Dordogne river in France. The camera fell into the water when their canoe hit a bridge and (2) ___ . The father, Andrew Sully, dived down to look for it, but soon (3) ___ up, as the water was too muddy to see clearly.

Soon afterwards, however, French student Kevin Quirin came (4) ___ the camera while exploring the river. (5) ___ the camera was broken, the memory card was still intact, so he downloaded the photos and followed the (6) ___ to trace the owners. He found two humorous photos of Andrew standing next to signs with the word 'Sully' on them and (7) ___ that might be their surname. There were also photos of Andrew taking (8) ___ in a charity bike ride in Paris: searching the Internet, Kevin found an Andrew Sully on the participants list and forwarded the photos to the family in Wales.

	A	B	C	D
0	replaced	encountered	<u>reunited</u>	joined
1	travel	trip	voyage	cruise
2	dropped	divided	overturned	drowned
3	held	put	turned	gave
4	up	towards	across	over
5	Although	Apart	Since	Despite
6	hints	clues	ways	paths
7	assured	guessed	worked	seemed
8	place	prize	pose	part

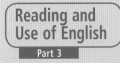

Reading and Use of English
Part 3

Word formation

Read the following story of an unsolved mystery. Use the word given in capitals at the end of some of the lines to form a word that fits in the gap **in the same line**. There is an example at the beginning **(0)**. Write your answers **IN CAPITAL LETTERS**.

A Strange Journey

It was a warm, (0)___SUNNY___October morning in 1593 and in front of
the palace in Mexico City there were the usual bustling crowds of people   **SUN**
moving (1) _____ across the plaza. One soldier stood out from the   **NOISE**
rest. Unlike the (2) _____ grey uniform of the other palace guards,   **TRADITION**
his was bright and (3) _____ and he carried a different kind of   **COLOUR**
gun. The strange soldier said that his orders were to guard the Philippine
governor's palace in Manila. '(4) _____ , I am not in Manila,' he   **EVIDENCE**
said, 'but this is a palace so I am doing my duty.' By now, officers were
(5) _____ of the man and his amazing tale of an overnight journey   **SUSPICION**
from Manila to Mexico City. And when he told them that the governor of
Manila had been killed the night before, he was arrested.

(6) _____ afterwards, a ship arrived from the Philippines, bringing   **SHORT**
news that the governor had been murdered – on the night before the soldier
had appeared. The soldier was (7) _____ released and sent back to   **EVENTUAL**
Manila. To this day his (8) _____ voyage through time and space   **MYSTERY**
remains unexplained.

Reading and Use of English
Part 4

Transformations

For Questions **1–6,** complete the second sentence so that it has a similar meaning to the first sentence, using the word given. **Do not change the word given**. You must use between **two** and **five** words, including the word given.

Write the missing words **IN CAPITAL LETTERS**.

1 The goalkeeper was injured last week, so maybe he isn't playing today.
   MIGHT
   The goalkeeper was injured last week, so he _____ today.

2 I expect you were very pleased to have your book published.
   GIVEN
   It must _____ to have your book published.

3 Tim seems to drink only tea now so perhaps he has stopped drinking coffee altogether.
   MAY
   Tim seems to drink only tea now so he _____ up drinking coffee altogether.

4 You can keep a secret, can't you?
   GIVE
   You wouldn't _____ you?

5 If you don't let me have your homework tomorrow, there'll be trouble!
   BETTER
   You _____ in your essay tomorrow or there'll be trouble!

6 I only glimpsed him briefly, but I'm sure it was David.
   BRIEF
   I only _____ of him, but I'm sure it was David.

Ready for **Listening**

Part 1: Multiple choice ● 2.1–2.8

1 Part 1 contains eight short unrelated extracts with multiple-choice questions. In each extract you will hear either a monologue or a conversation. There are several different types of questions which test your ability to understand, for example, the general idea or main points of the extract, *what* people's opinions are, *how* they feel, *where* they are or *who* they are speaking to.

Here is a typical question from Part 1.

You are on a bus and you overhear a conversation between two women.
What has one of the women just bought?
A a blouse
B a skirt
C a dress

Distractors

2 Simply hearing the same word or phrase which is in one of the alternatives will not guarantee that you have found the right answer. These words could be distractors.

Consider the following with regard to the question above:

<u>I was thinking of getting</u> **a dress** <u>but</u> I decided I couldn't afford it.

<u>If I'd bought that</u> **blouse** I might have regretted it.

<u>Annie bought herself</u> **a skirt** <u>whereas I</u> decided I wanted something more formal.

Read the script for the question above. What is the answer?

Woman 1: That's lovely. Celebrating something, are you?
Woman 2: Yes, well, my nephew's getting married next week, so I needed something a bit special. It's pure silk, you know.
Woman 1: Yes, I can see that. Must have cost a fortune!
Woman 2: Not really. Cheaper than getting a dress, that's for sure, and I'll probably wear it a lot more, too. It'll go really well with a skirt I bought last week. The sleeves are a bit short, but if I wear a jacket over it, no one'll notice.

Which key words and expressions helped you decide on the answer?
Which are used to create distractors?

3 You will hear people talking in eight different situations. For questions **1–8**, choose the best answer (**A**, **B** or **C**).

What to expect in the exam

In Part 1, the introductory sentence is read out before each recording.
For question 1, for example:
- you will hear the sentence, *You hear part of a sports commentary on the radio.*
- you will not hear the question *What sport is it?* or the three options **A–C**.

1 You hear part of a sports commentary on the radio.

What sport is it?

A tennis

B basketball

C football

2 You hear a man talking on his mobile phone.

Who is he speaking to?

A a friend

B his doctor

C his boss

3 Listen to this man and woman speaking.

Where are they?

A in a cinema

B in a restaurant

C at home

4 You hear this woman telling her friend about a restaurant.

What does she say about it?

A The waiters were rude.

B The food was badly cooked.

C It was too formal.

5 You hear this man talking to his friend on the phone about a day trip to London.

What is he going to do at the end of the day?

A stay in a hotel

B stay at his friend's house

C travel back home

6 You hear a woman talking to her husband in a supermarket.

How does she feel?

A confused

B annoyed

C disappointed

7 You hear this man talking.

Who is he?

A a policeman

B a social worker

C a teacher

8 You overhear a man talking to a woman about a flat which is for rent.

Why has the man decided not to rent the flat?

A It is too expensive.

B It is not big enough.

C It is badly located.

Part 2: Sentence completion ◉ 2.9

1 Look at the statements **1–8** about Part 2 of the **Listening** paper and decide which are True and which are False. If a statement is false, give reasons for your answer.

1 You only hear the Part 2 recording once. _____

2 You have 45 seconds to read through the questions. _____

3 You should use this time to predict the type of information which is missing from each space. _____

4 You have to write between three and five words in each space. _____

5 You have to rephrase the words you hear so that they fit into the sentence. _____

6 You do not usually hear the answers in the same order as the questions. _____

7 For difficult questions, keep listening as you'll hear the answer sooner or later. _____

8 You should check the spelling of your answers. _____

2 Now read the following Listening Part 2 question.

You will hear a man talking on the radio about Welsh speakers in Patagonia, Argentina. For questions **1–10**, complete the sentences.

Before you listen, predict the type of information you might hear for questions **1–10**.

Example:
1 This might be a type of building, like a school or a church.

What to expect in the exam

- The words and the sentence structure in the question may not be the same as those in the recording. For question 8 for example, you will hear the following:

  ... every year, as part of a programme administered by the National Assembly for Wales, groups of ... come to Patagonia.

- You can also expect to hear some distractors. For number **2**, for example, you will need to choose between two different numbers that you hear. And for number **4**, several different types of people are mentioned.

A popular place for tourists to visit in Patagonia is a Welsh **(1)** ....

There are estimated to be **(2)** .... speakers of Welsh in Patagonia.

The first settlers wanted to establish a colony in an area which was **(3)** ....

There were very few **(4)** .... among the first Welsh settlers.

The settlers soon became friendly with the **(5)** ....

The name for the Andean region where the Welsh settled means **(6)** '............................'

A Welsh **(7)** .... festival is held each year in Patagonia.

The National Assembly for Wales sends **(8)** .... to Patagonia each year.

The streets and houses of Gaiman are decorated with **(9)** ....

The speaker decides to eat **(10)** .... with his tea.

Part 3: Multiple matching ● 2.10–2.14

1 In Part 3 you will hear five different people speaking for about 30 seconds each on the same topic. You are given eight options **A–H**, five of which you have to match to the correct speakers.

The speakers will not use exactly the same words that appear in options **A–H**. When you read each one, therefore, think of other ways of saying the same thing. Underlining key words may help, but do not choose an answer simply because you hear the key words.

Example:

A I will need a <u>specific qualification</u> to do this job.

I've got to pass some exams/I've been advised to do a college course/I'll have to study for a degree.

Now do the same for options **B–H**.

What to expect in the exam

- You may hear the language which guides you to the correct answer:
  - **a** at the beginning of the extract
  - **b** in the middle of the extract
  - **c** at the end of the extract
  - **d** in more than one part of the extract
- Listen **both times** to **all** of what the speaker says before making your final decision.

2 You will hear five young people talking about the job they would like to do. For questions **1–5**, choose from the list **A–H** what each speaker says. Use the letters only once. There are three extra letters which you do not need to use.

A I will need a specific qualification to do this job.

B I currently combine work with studying.

C I disagree with the careers advice I have been given.

D I heard about this job from someone in my family.

E I do not really mind what job I do.

F I think I have the necessary personal qualities.

G I am not clever enough for the job I would like to do.

H I am studying a relevant subject.

Speaker 1 [___] 1
Speaker 2 [___] 2
Speaker 3 [___] 3
Speaker 4 [___] 4
Speaker 5 [___] 5

Part 4: Multiple choice 2.15

1   In Part 4 you will hear an interview, or a conversation with two or more speakers of approximately three minutes. You have to answer seven multiple-choice questions, each with three options.

2   Now read the following Part 4 instructions.

You will hear an interview with an organizer of the Tall Person's Club conference. For questions 1–7 choose the best answer (**A**, **B** or **C**).

3   Read question 1 and the interviewer's introduction from the recording. Decide on the correct answer, underlining the part or parts of the text which justify your choice.

1 What comment does the presenter make about his height?

   A He is below average height for a British male.

   B He is the tallest person in his profession.

   C He feels tall in comparison to his colleagues.

At one metre eight-four I've always thought of myself as being a little on the tall side, particularly when I stand next to the people I work with here in the Round Britain studio. Rather curiously, most of them are below the national average height of one metre seventy-eight for men and one sixty-two for women. But when I popped in yesterday to the annual conference of the TPC – that's the Tall Person's Club of Great Britain and Ireland – I felt decidedly small.

4   With your partner, explain with reference to the text why the other options are wrong.

5   Now read questions 2–7. Then listen to the recording and choose the best answers.

What to expect in the exam

- You are given one minute to read all seven questions before you hear the recording.
- Although a particular option might be mentioned, it may not be the correct answer to the question you are asked. In question 3 below, for example, **A**, **B** and **C** are all mentioned as problems, but only one answers the question: *What is the biggest problem faced by tall people?*

2 Jenny says that the Tall Person's Club conference

   A is usually held in a countryside hotel.

   B is one of many events they organize.

   C is very different to other club conferences.

3 According to Jenny, what is the biggest problem faced by tall people?

   A buying clothes that fit

   B travelling on public transport

   C sleeping in normal size beds

4 How does Jenny feel about some people's reactions towards her height?

   A irritated

   B amused

   C offended

5 Jenny says that at their first meeting, new club members

   A are encouraged to change their posture.

   B very quickly grow in confidence.

   C have to talk to everyone in the room.

6 According to Jenny, one advantage for tall people is that

   A they are naturally talented at certain sports.

   B they always have a good view at spectator events.

   C they are more suited than others to certain professions.

7 What does Jenny say about membership of the Tall Person's Club of Great Britain and Ireland?

   A It includes membership of the American club.

   B A special committee decides who can join.

   C There is no minimum height requirement.

6   Look at the listening script on page 232 and for questions 2–7 follow the same procedure as in exercises 3 and 4 above.

10 Nothing but the truth

Vocabulary 1: Crime and punishment

1 ⬤ Talk about a crime which has been in the news recently. Say what you know about the facts of the crime and, where relevant, the investigation and the trial.

A Crimes and criminals

1 Match the crimes in the box with each of the people in sentences **1–8**. The first one has been done for you.

burglary	drink-driving	identity fraud	internet piracy
~~mugging~~	shoplifting	trafficking	vandalism

1 A young man attacks another and robs him of his wallet. ___*mugging*___

2 A 78-year-old woman steals a scarf from a department store. _____

3 A 14-year-old sets fire to litter bins and breaks car windows. _____

4 A driver stops to sleep in his car; he has had three glasses of wine. _____

5 A criminal gang earns millions from buying and selling drugs. _____

6 A group of teenagers illegally distributes films online. _____

7 A man has tricked people into emailing him their bank details; he uses this information to take money from their accounts. _____

8 A journalist breaks into the town hall to steal documents that will prove the mayor is guilty of corruption. _____

2 What title would be given to each of the criminals in exercise **1**?

Example:
mugging – mugger

B Punishment

1 Look at the following types of decisions which can be taken by courts. Put them in order from the least to the most severe.

a to sentence someone to life imprisonment

b to order someone to do 200 hours of community service

c to acquit someone of all charges

d to order someone to pay a fine of £2000

e to give someone a two-year prison sentence

Useful language

Giving opinions	Agreeing and disagreeing
In my opinion/view ...	*That's right/true. I think so, too.*
To my mind ...	*I agree (up to a point).*
Personally, I think ...	*I really don't think so.*
I strongly believe ...	*I completely disagree.*

2 ⬤ Decide what punishment, if any, should be given to the person or people in exercise **A1** above. Discuss your ideas using some of the language of agreement and opinion in the Useful language box.

Listening 1
Part 4

Multiple choice 2.16

1   Tell your partner about the last crime novel you read or crime film you saw. Why do you think crime novels and films are so popular?

2   You will hear an interview with a crime writer. For questions **1–7**, choose the best answer (**A, B** or **C**).

1 Why did Justin become a crime writer?
  A His favourite genre as a reader has always been crime.
  B He had previously worked in the police force.
  C He was encouraged to do so by his editor.

2 The setting for Justin's novels helps him create
  A a sense of authenticity.
  B a mood of optimism.
  C a degree of tension.

3 Both the city in which Justin's novels are set and his fictional characters
  A are physically very attractive.
  B have two very different sides.
  C are very unwelcoming.

4 According to Justin, what is his main character's most appealing feature?
  A He is very unpredictable.
  B He is happy with his appearance.
  C He looks like a typical detective.

5 Justin initially set up his website in order to
  A publicize his work.
  B help new crime writers.
  C encourage an exchange of ideas.

6 Justin says writers should carry out their main research by
  A working closely with a detective.
  B consulting criminal documents.
  C observing police professionals.

7 What is Justin not happy about with the film version of his latest book?
  A the actors
  B the script
  C the location

3   If you were writing a crime novel, where would you set it? Why?

Language focus 1: *Too* and *enough*

1 a Read extracts **1–5** from the listening script, then choose the correct alternatives in sentences **a–d**.
  1 There are **too many novels** that lack credibility ...
  2 ... if not, he'd be **too dull**.
  3 It moves **too fast** for my liking.
  4 ... he thinks he's **good enough** as he is ...
  5 ... make sure your detectives have **enough paperwork** to keep them busy.

  a *Too much* and *too many* are used before **nouns/ adjectives** and **adverbs**.
  b *Too* is used before **nouns/adjectives** and **adverbs**.
  c *Enough* is used **before/after nouns**.
  d *Enough* is used **before/after adjectives** and **adverbs**.

  b Which form of the verb is used after *enough* in sentence **5**?

  G Read more about *too* and *enough* in the Grammar reference on page 217.

2 Complete the second sentence so that it has a similar meaning to the first sentence, using the word given. You must use between two and five words, including the word given.
  1 I couldn't hear what they were saying because they were speaking so quietly.
    TOO
    They were speaking _____ hear what they were saying.

2 He couldn't see over the wall because he was so small.
  ENOUGH
  He was _____ see over the wall.

3 We'll need more eggs if we want to make an omelette.
  ENOUGH
  There _____ us to make an omelette.

4 I didn't go into the bar because it was too crowded.
  TOO
  I didn't go into the bar because _____ _____ people.

3 a Write six true sentences using the phrases below.
  Example:
  enough time – I didn't have enough time to finish my homework last night.

enough money	too difficult	strong enough
too much noise	old enough	too many people

  b Ask your partner about his or her sentences.

  Example:
  Why didn't you have enough time to finish the homework?

Multiple choice

1 ⬤ Why might somebody hire a private detective?
What image do you have of private detectives?
What qualities do you think are required to do the job well?

2 Read through the newspaper article and compare your ideas in exercise **1**.

Private investigators investigated

David Lee investigates the world of the private eye – and uncovers some surprising truths

When I walk into the offices of Wright & Wrong Ltd, a predominantly female firm of private investigators, I am a little disappointed. My only previous contact with private detective agencies has been through black and
5 white films from the golden age of Hollywood. So I am half expecting to see a small, dark, smoke-filled room, a single desk with an empty in-tray and a long, scruffy raincoat hanging from a hat stand.

Clearly, my romantic image of the profession needs
10 updating. Wright & Wrong Ltd's offices are light and spacious and there are no ashtrays in sight on any of the dozen or so desks. These are tidy and free of paper, but concentrated faces at large computer screens give the place a busy feel.

15 Jenny Wright, founder of the agency, is not surprised at my error, and with a note of irritation in her voice, points to further misconceptions. 'Cinema and television are mostly to blame for our reputation. Contrary to popular belief, we always work very strictly within the law –
20 there's no violence, no break-ins, and certainly no guns. The laws relating to our activities are very tight, and if we don't stick to them there's a very real danger that the evidence we obtain will not be accepted in court.'

The types of cases her agency deals with are varied
25 but the day-to-day work is often far from stimulating. Wright & Wrong Ltd handles anything from infidelity in a marriage or tracing a missing person to insurance fraud, employee theft and advising companies on security measures. 'Resolving a case is very rewarding,' says
30 Jenny, 'but the actual investigation can be rather dull. When we're not dealing with paperwork or Internet searches, we're usually involved in surveillance. And that normally means just sitting around in cars or cafés for hours, waiting for something to happen.'

35 Not surprisingly, then, patience is an important asset for anyone doing this kind of work. Is that why nine of the twelve investigators in her team are women? 'Obviously, women don't have a monopoly on patience,' replies Jenny, 'but perhaps it's no coincidence that they tend to
40 stay in the job longer than men.'

Jenny tells me that people's perceptions of women make them popular with clients, and also, consequently, with her as an employer. Women are often considered to be more sensitive than men. They're looked upon as less
45 threatening when it comes to making inquiries. 'People open up to women more readily,' she says, 'and are relieved when a woman picks up the phone to speak to them. We're also good at breaking bad news. What may be a victory for the agency – filming someone
50 doing something they shouldn't be doing, for example – tends not to be such a pleasant discovery for the client, and there's a right and wrong way of handling that information.'

Most of Jenny's clients are wealthy. The hourly rate is
55 anything between fifty and eighty pounds, so the cost of a single case will often run into thousands of pounds. Even with the latest hi-tech equipment, such as long-range listening devices, a surveillance campaign can last several days. 'The technology is freely available and most
60 of what we do could be done by the clients,' explains Jenny, 'but they're reluctant to get involved. Finding out the truth is often just too painful to do on your own.'

I ask Jenny, a former night club owner, how she came to be a private detective. Her face turns red, she gives a
65 slight grin and drops her voice to a whisper so as not to be overheard by her staff. 'I used to read a lot of crime novels,' she confides, 'and I started to think "I could do that". I went on a training course and realized I was in the wrong job.' I am about to ask her whether she ever
70 wears a long, scruffy raincoat, when her mobile phone rings and she is called away on business.

3   For questions **1–6**, choose the answer (**A**, **B**, **C** or **D**) which you think fits best according to the text.

1 What does the writer discover on his visit to the offices of Wright & Wrong Ltd?
  A   The firm is not as dynamic as he had been told.
  B   The offices have recently been modernized.
  C   All the private detectives in the firm are women.
  D   He has an old-fashioned idea of private detectives.

2 Jenny Wright is annoyed by
  A   the strict laws controlling private detectives.
  B   the inflexibility of the law courts.
  C   the way her profession is represented in films.
  D   the violence used by other detective agencies.

3 According to Jenny, most of the work of a private detective is
  A   monotonous.
  B   challenging.
  C   exhausting.
  D   enjoyable.

4 Jenny is influenced in her decision to take on women by
  A   women's ability to get results.
  B   the speed at which women work.
  C   women's tendency to speak openly.
  D   the way clients see women.

5 What do we learn about Jenny's clients?
  A   They cannot afford to buy the surveillance equipment.
  B   They do not want to do the detective work themselves.
  C   They object to paying such high prices for the work.
  D   They prefer more than one detective to work on a case.

6 How does Jenny feel about telling her story in the last paragraph?
  A   embarrassed
  B   frightened
  C   proud
  D   angry

Reacting to the text

Do you think you would make a good private detective? Why/Why not?

Vocabulary 2: Paraphrasing and recording

1 a In **1–8** below, complete each gap with **one** word so that the second sentence has the same meaning as the first. The second sentence is taken from the reading text on page 130. There is an example at the beginning (**0**). **Do the exercise without looking at the reading text on page 130.**

   0 I cannot see any ashtrays.
   There are no ashtrays **in** _____*sight*_____ . [11]

   1 Our reputation is mostly the fault of cinema and television.
   Cinema and television **are** mostly **to** _____ **for** our reputation. [18]

   2 The day-to-day work is often not at all stimulating.
   The day-to-day work is often _____ **from stimulating**. [25]

   3 We know how to tell people bad news.
   We're _____ **at breaking bad news.** [48]

   4 We charge anything between fifty and eighty pounds per hour.
   The _____ **rate is** anything between fifty and eighty pounds. [54–55]

   5 A single case will often cost thousands of pounds.
   The cost of a single case will often _____ **into thousands of pounds**. [56]

   6 Everyone can obtain the technology.
   The technology **is freely** _____ . [59]

   7 Finding out the truth is often just too painful to do alone.
   Finding out the truth is often just too painful to do **on your** _____ . [62]

   8 Jenny used to be a night club owner.
   Jenny is a _____ night club owner. [63]

   b Check your answers in the reading text on page 130. The relevant line numbers are given in brackets.

2 Paraphrase the following sentences from the reading text and record both sentences in your vocabulary notebook. You do not need to change every word in the sentence. The first one has been done for you.

   a The desks are free of paper. [12]
      e.g. There is no paper on the desks.

   b Concentrated faces … give the place a busy feel. [13–14]

   c We always work very strictly within the law. [19]

   d Women don't have a monopoly on patience. [38]

   e People open up to a woman more readily. [45–46]

   f Clients are reluctant to get involved. [61]

   g She gives a slight grin. [64–65]

Language focus 2: Passives

1 a Look at the following sentences from the reading text on page 130. In each one underline one example of the passive.

1 *If we don't stick to the laws, there's a very real danger that the evidence we obtain will not be accepted in court.*
2 *Most of what we do could be done by the clients.*
3 *She drops her voice to a whisper so as not to be overheard by her staff.*
4 *Her mobile phone rings and she is called away on business.*

b Complete the following sentence about the passive:

To form the passive, we use an appropriate form of the verb _____ and the _____ participle.

c In sentences with passives, the agents are the people or things who do the action. They appear after the preposition *by*.

Who are the agents in sentences **2** and **3** above?

Why are there no agents in sentences **1** or **4**?

🅖 Read more about passives in A and B on page 217 of the Grammar reference.

2 Complete the gaps in the following texts with an appropriate form of the verb in brackets. Use the words in **bold** to help you make your choices.

A

Antisocial behaviour ____*is defined*____ (define) as conduct that causes or is likely to cause alarm or distress to other people. Different types of anti-social behaviour may _____ (categorize) as follows:

- Disrespect for the community,
  e.g. noisy neighbours

- Acts that target people,
  e.g. threatening behaviour

- Environmental damage,
  e.g. vandalism and graffiti

- Misuse of public places,
  e.g. street drinking

B

Closed Circuit Television Cameras _____ (install) on buses in four major cities **next month**. A spokesman for the government, which _____ (criticize) **in recent weeks** for being 'too soft on crime', said the CCTV cameras would improve passenger safety and help reduce antisocial behaviour such as vandalism.

C

Last month police patrols _____ (increase) in the town's parks and open spaces. Their aim **is** not necessarily to arrest young people who _____ (find) drinking in public places. In most cases **so far**, parents _____ (contact) and asked to come and take their child home. 'Parents **need** _____ (make) aware of their responsibilities,' said a police spokesperson. 'We emphasize to them the importance of knowing where their children go and what they do there.'

D

Noisy neighbours who consistently played loud music in their town-centre flat _____ (fine) £300 **yesterday** and ordered to pay £250 court costs. The court _____ (tell) that students Joe Cave and Irene Burstall _____ (**warn**) on several occasions **previously** that legal action _____ (take) **if** the music _____ (not/turn) down. Both now have criminal records.

E

'**When I got there**, the little one _____ (push) around by the four older boys,' said 70-year-old Mrs Slade. '**They were pushing him quite hard**. I was worried he **might** _____ (attack) more seriously, so I started hitting them with my umbrella. Then I fell over and they ran off.' **After** _____ (treat) in hospital for minor cuts and bruises, Mrs Slade _____ (send) home **last night**.

3 🔘 How serious a problem is antisocial behaviour where you live?

How effective would the above methods, **B–E,** be in dealing with antisocial behaviour in your area?

Article

1 Look at these sentences from the article on page 130.

Clearly, my romantic image of the profession needs updating.

Not surprisingly, patience is an important asset for anyone doing this kind of work.

Obviously, women don't have a monopoly on patience.

Each one begins with an adverb which expresses the writer's attitude to or opinion of what follows. In **1–8** below replace the underlined phrase with an adverb from the box.

Astonishingly	Interestingly	Curiously	Personally
Happily	Sadly	Worryingly	Unfortunately

1 <u>In my opinion, I think that</u> any form of physical punishment is unacceptable.
2 <u>I'm absolutely amazed that</u> he was released after only two years in prison.
3 <u>It is sad that</u> there is a growing trend towards violence in our schools.
4 <u>It is regrettable that</u> many parents just don't communicate with their children.
5 <u>It's strange that</u> some kidnap victims end up sympathizing with their captors.
6 <u>It is of some concern that</u> many drivers still do not wear their seat belts.
7 <u>It's worth noting that</u> most children don't leave home until they get married.
8 <u>I'm pleased to be able to say that</u> this is an exception rather than the rule.

2 ⬤ Read the following Writing Part 2 instructions and discuss with your partner how you might answer the question.

You see this announcement in an international magazine:

> We invite you, our readers, to write an article giving your opinions on:
>
> **DEALING WITH LITTER**
>
> • How serious a problem is litter in your area?
>
> • What can be done to stop people dropping litter in the street?
>
> The best articles answering this question will be published next month.

3 Now read the following article and compare the writer's ideas with those you discussed in exercise **2**.

A load of rubbish

I'm sure the people of Brenton don't drop crisp packets and drink cans on the floor in their own home. So why do so many think it's acceptable to do so on the streets of our town?

A walk in the area around the cathedral reveals how serious the problem has become. Litter lines the pavements outside some of our most picturesque buildings, giving tourists a poor impression of the town and its residents. And incredibly, there are sometimes more plastic bags in our parks and playgrounds than there are people. Clearly, something needs to be done.

More litter bins won't solve the problem – there are already plenty of these, but most people ignore them. What we need is an awareness campaign organized by the council encouraging people to use the bins or take their rubbish home. Also, heavier fines should be imposed on anyone who is caught dropping litter – the current maximum of £100 is not enough.

Unfortunately, the council seem reluctant to act. But surely they, more than anyone, want a town they can be proud of, don't they?

4   Read the model answer again and find examples of the following common features of articles:

   a title
   b interesting beginning
   c Direct questions
   d adverbs which express the writer's attitude or opinion
   e more informal use of linking words
   f leaving the reader something to think about at the end

5   How are the writer's ideas organized in the model answer? What information is contained in each paragraph?

   Paragraph 1: _____
   Paragraph 2: _____
   Paragraph 3: _____
   Paragraph 4: _____

6   Read the following Writing Part 2 instructions.
   You see this announcement in an international magazine:

   > We invite you, our readers, to write an article giving your opinions on:
   >
   > **DEALING WITH GRAFFITI**
   >
   > - How serious a problem is graffiti in your area?
   > - What can be done to stop people covering walls with graffiti?
   >
   > The best articles answering this question will be published next month.

   Write your **article** in **140–190** words.

   ## Don't forget!

   - Give your article a title. It may be better to do this after you have written your answer.
   - Organize your ideas into logical paragraphs.
   - Include the techniques and language features you saw in exercise 4.
   - Do not copy whole phrases from the article in exercise 3.

Speaking Part 2

Talking about photos 2

Why are the children being told off?

1 Look at the photographs, which show children being told off.

Student A Compare photographs **1** and **2** and say why you think the children are being told off.

Student B When your partner has finished, say how you think the adults are feeling.

2 Now change roles. Follow the instructions above using photographs **3** and **4** on page 137.

Listening 2 Part 3

Multiple matching 2.17–2.21

1 Read the text on page 204 and answer the following question.
What reasons are given for children telling lies?

2 Tell your partner about a time when you or someone you know told a lie:

• as a child   • recently

What was the reason for telling the lie? What were the consequences?

3 You will hear five different people talking about a time when they told a lie. For questions **1–5**, choose from the list (**A–H**) what each speaker says. There are three extra letters which you do not need to use.

A I insisted on my innocence.

B I did not want to hurt someone's feelings.

C I disliked the way I had been treated in the past.

D I made some money by telling a lie.

E I lied because I was in a hurry.

F I did not lie intentionally.

G I gave two different versions of my story.

H I should have destroyed the evidence.

Speaker 1	1
Speaker 2	2
Speaker 3	3
Speaker 4	4
Speaker 5	5

4 Have you ever told any similar lies to those of the five speakers?

Vocabulary 3: Phrasal verbs

1 Look at the listening script on page 233 and use the context to help you guess the meanings of the phrasal verbs in bold.

Example:
*... I **owned up** to my dad about lying – I felt so guilty, I had to tell him.*
Own up means to admit or confess that you have done something wrong.

2 Record the phrasal verbs in your notebook. Include the definition and the sentence from the listening script in which the verb appears, as in the example in exercise **1**.

3 Write three sentences, each including one of the phrasal verbs from the listening script. Leave gaps where the phrasal verbs should be. Include enough information in your sentences to illustrate the meanings of the phrasal verbs.

Example:
No one admitted to breaking the window, so the teacher said that if the person responsible did not _____ , the whole class would be punished.

4 Show your sentences from exercise **3** to another student, who will complete the gaps.

Language focus 3: Passive of reporting verbs

1 Infinitive forms (*to do, to be doing, to have done*) can be used after the passive of a number of reporting verbs to talk about beliefs and opinions which are shared by many people.

Example:
*Young children **are known to lie** to avoid punishment.*

This has the same meaning as:

*It is known that young children **lie** to avoid punishment.*

Change the following sentence in the same way.

He **is believed to have made up** the story about being mugged.

It _____ .

Examples of reporting verbs are: *believe, consider, expect, know, say* and *think*.

🔍 Read more about the passive of reporting verbs in **C** on page 217 of the Grammar reference.

2 For questions **1–5**, complete the second sentence so that it has a similar meaning to the first sentence. Be sure to use the correct form of the verbs in **bold**.

  1 It is **believed** that continual nose touching **indicates** that someone is lying.

  Continual nose touching is
  _____ that someone is lying.

2 It is **said** that people who repeatedly cover their mouth **are trying** to hide the truth.

  People who repeatedly cover their mouth
  _____ to hide the truth.

3 It is **considered** that avoiding eye contact **is** a sure sign of deception.

  Avoiding eye contact _____
  a sure sign of deception.

4 People **think** that we **use** fewer hand gestures when telling a lie.

  We _____ fewer hand
  gestures when telling a lie.

5 Everyone **knows** he **lied** because he kept moving about in his chair.

  He _____ because
  he kept moving about in his chair.

3 ⬛ The statements in exercise **2** are believed by some people to be myths, widely held beliefs which are simply not true. What do you think?

Phrasal verbs

The following phrasal verbs have appeared either in this unit or in previous units.

1 Phrasal verbs with *out*

Complete each gap with the correct form of a verb from the box.

> fall   find   get   give   run   sort

1 We _____ **out of drink** at the party and had to go and buy some more.
2 Joe said he felt ill, but he was just trying to _____ **out of doing the housework**.
3 I can't _____ **out your problems** for you; you've got to solve them yourself.
4 Leah hired a detective in an attempt to _____ **out the truth** about her husband.
5 Patsy _____ **out with her best friend** last week after a huge argument.
6 I've corrected your homework. Could I have a volunteer to _____ **out the books**?

2 Phrasal verbs with *up*

Complete each gap with the correct form of an appropriate verb.

1 She never tells the truth; she's always _____ **up stories**.
2 Of course, nobody has _____ **up to stealing** the money, but we think we know who did it.
3 Paul's stopped going to karate classes and _____ **up judo** instead.
4 I'm seriously thinking of _____ **up my career** as a lawyer; I can't _____ **up with the stress** much longer.
5 Being a parent is so hard; there's nothing more difficult than _____ **up a child**.
6 _____ **up**! Don't look so sad.

Reading and Use of English — Part 4

Transformations

For questions **1–6**, complete the second sentence so that it has a similar meaning to the first sentence, using the word given. **Do not change the word given.** You must use between **two** and **five** words, including the word given.

1 You should keep dust off the computer screen.
   FREE
   The computer screen should _____ dust.

2 The orange walls make the living room feel warm.
   GIVEN
   The living room _____ feel by the orange walls.

3 Maia earned five pounds an hour in her last job.
   PAID
   Maia _____ rate of five pounds in her last job.

4 Most cats don't mind it if you leave them at home alone.
   LEFT
   Most cats don't mind _____ own at home.

5 It was unfair that she was sent to prison.
   DESERVE
   She _____ sent to prison.

6 It wasn't Luke's fault that the chair broke.
   BLAME
   Luke was _____ the broken chair.

Reading and Use of English
Part 1

Multiple-choice cloze

For questions **1–8**, read the text below and decide which answer (**A**, **B**, **C** or **D**) best fits each gap. The is an example at the beginning (**0**).

Ex-athlete taken in ... again.

The home of **(0)** _____ athlete Helen Barnett was burgled this weekend and a large number of sporting medals and trophies were **(1)** ____ . Ms Barnett, who now **(2)** ____ a successful sportswear company, is **(3)** ____ to be 'devastated' at the loss.

The burglary took **(4)** ____ on Saturday afternoon when Ms Barnett went to investigate smoke coming from a wooded area in her large two-acre garden. The burglar is thought to have **(5)** ____ fire to undergrowth in order to attract Ms Barnett out of the house. A young man carrying a large bag was seen climbing over the garden wall, before making his **(6)** ___ in a sports car.

The theft comes just ten months after a similar incident in which a man posing as a telephone engineer had **(7)** ____ the ex-athlete into leaving the house while another helped himself to her jewels. The thieves were eventually caught and **(8)** ____ to four years in jail.

0	A earlier	B sooner	C <u>former</u>	D preceding
1	A robbed	B mugged	C lifted	D stolen
2	A runs	B overtakes	C works	D holds
3	A spoken	B said	C felt	D told
4	A part	B hold	C place	D time
5	A made	B given	C set	D put
6	A getaway	B runaway	C hideaway	D takeaway
7	A succeeded	B managed	C tricked	D obtained
8	A imprisoned	B ordered	C given	D sentenced

Writing
Part 1

Essay

In your English class you have been talking about situations in which people might tell lies. Now, your English teacher has asked you to write an essay.

Write an essay using **all** the notes and give reasons for your point of view.

Write your **essay** in **140–190** words.

Essay question

Is it always better to tell the truth than to lie?

Notes

Write about:

1 when the truth might be painful

2 when lying might be harmless

3 .... (your own idea)

Vocabulary 1: Weather

1 ⬤ Describe the typical weather conditions in your area for each season.

2 All the words in each of the groups **1–7** below can be used with one of the nouns in the box to form strong collocations. For each group of words write the noun which can be used in the appropriate space. There is an example at the beginning **(0).**

| sunshine |
| showers |
| ~~sky~~ |
| sea |
| storm |
| clouds |
| rain |
| winds |

0 overcast
clear _sky_
stormy

1 violent
severe _____
electric

2 fine
heavy _____
torrential

3 strong
gale-force _____
light

4 warm
brilliant _____
glorious

5 rough
calm _____
choppy

6 thick
storm _____
angry-looking

7 light
scattered _____
snow

3 Study the words in exercise **1** for two minutes. Then cover up the adjectives and see how many you can remember for each noun.

4 Complete each gap with a two-word adjective + noun collocation from exercise **2**. More than one answer may be possible. The first one has been done for you.

1 There's a lovely____*clear sky*____ tonight so we might see a shooting star.

2 Our garden wall was blown down during the night by _____ .

3 Heavy _____ will fall on high ground tonight, so skiers can look forward to a good day on the slopes tomorrow.

4 It's going to rain – there are some very _____ overhead. Look at them.

5 _____ has caused serious flooding throughout the region.

6 We sailed on a beautiful _____ with not a wave in sight.

5 ⬤ Describe the photos above using as many of the adjective + noun collocations as possible. What types of weather do you prefer? What weather conditions do you least like?

Listening 1
Part 2

Sentence completion 👁 2.22

1 👁 How often do you watch, read or listen to the weather forecast? Why?
How accurate do you think the weather forecasts are for your area?

2 You will hear an Irishman called Michael Gallagher giving a talk about the traditional
methods he uses to forecast the weather. For questions **1–10**, complete the sentences.

Michael Gallagher has been predicting the weather for over **(1)** ....
years.

Michael has gained a lot of his knowledge from local people, especially
(2) ....

The title of the book that Michael has written is *Traditional* **(3)** ....

Michael says that if you see swallows flying **(4)** ...., it means the
weather will improve.

A cat with its back to the fire is a sign that **(5)** .... weather is on its way.

If a storm is coming, cows, horses and **(6)** .... keep their backs to a
hedge while eating.

Michael successfully predicted a warm summer by observing sheep moving towards
the **(7)** .... at the end of spring.

The late growth of **(8)** .... in October helped Michael predict a cold
winter.

One popular saying predicts good weather if there is a **(9)** .... at the
end of the day.

Michael forecasts very **(10)** .... for his area over the next few days.

3 👁 Would you have confidence in Michael's methods? Why/Why not?
Do you know any popular sayings in your country related to the weather?

Language focus 1: *So, neither* and *nor*

1 Read **a** and **b**, then answer the questions below.

a In these sentences from the listening, Michael expresses
similarities in the way some birds and animals behave.

*Swallows flying low are a sign that rain is on its way, and
so are crows if they're flying in groups.*

*Cows don't stay in the middle of a field if they sense a
storm coming, and neither do horses.*

b These sentences express **differences** in the way some
people behave or think.

I'll probably read Michael's book, but I know Rita won't.

*She doesn't think traditional methods are reliable, but I
do.*

What determines whether *so* or *neither* is used when
expressing similarities?

What determines which auxiliary verb is used, for both
similarities and differences?

Ⓖ Check your ideas on pages 217–18 of the Grammar
reference.

2 a Match each statement **1–8** with a reply **a–h**.

1 I'm not very interested in <u>politics</u>.   a So would I.
2 I don't know how to <u>play chess</u>.   b I don't
3 Last night I didn't <u>sleep very well</u>.   c Neither are we.
4 Next week I'm going to   d So is mine.
    <u>start revising for the exams</u>.   e Mark does.
5 I'd like to <u>go for a drink</u> now.   f Nor did I.
6 I've never <u>been windsurfing</u>.   g So are we.
7 I really enjoy <u>going for long walks</u>.   h Neither have I.
8 My favourite colour is <u>green</u>.

b Change the underlined part of each statement **1–8** to
make sentences that are true for you.

c Read out the sentences you wrote in **b**. Respond to your
partner using *so, neither* and *nor*.

Multiple matching

1 ⬤ Which of the following occur in your country?

droughts	floods	avalanches	hurricanes
earthquakes	tornadoes	volcanic eruptions	

Have you experienced any of these? What was it like?

What are the worst weather conditions you have had to endure?

2 ⬤ The film posters on this page and on page 143 all show natural disaster films.

Have you seen any of these films?

If so, did you enjoy it/them? Why/Why not?

If not, do you think you would enjoy any of them? Why/Why not?

3 You are going to read an article about natural disaster films. For questions **1–10**, choose from the films (**A–E**). The films may be chosen more than once.

> ### Don't forget!
>
> Before doing the matching task, underline key words in the statements **1–10**.

I found the film just as absorbing as the book on which it is based. ☐ 1

The level of the acting was the main reason I enjoyed this film. ☐ 2

The plot is predictable. ☐ 3

The ending of the film may come as a surprise. ☐ 4

I had read good reviews of the film before I saw it. ☐ 5

I initially thought that no special effects had been used in the film. ☐ 6

I enjoy seeing this film in certain weather conditions. ☐ 7

The structure of the film differs from that of many other disaster movies. ☐ 8

The film should not be taken too seriously. ☐ 9

There are several scenes which are both memorable and rather unpleasant. ☐ 10

What a disaster!

James Borja reviews five natural disaster movies from his DVD collection

A *Dante's Peak* (1997)

I read the novel, which is based on the script, before watching the film itself. But it was the positive opinions I'd seen online, rather than the book, that persuaded me to buy the DVD. And I was not disappointed. The plot of Dante's
5 Peak, starring Pierce Brosnan and Linda Hamilton, is built around a spectacular volcanic eruption, which brings disaster to a small town in the Cascade Mountains in North America. But what impressed me most about this film was the quality of the lead performances, rather than the volcano and all the
10 visual effects. For once, I really cared about the fate of the main characters. I even wanted their dog to survive!

142

B *Twister* (1996)

Helen Hunt and Bill Paxton star as meteorologists who put their lives at risk by chasing tornadoes, or 'twisters', in order to try out a new piece of technology.
If you watch this film hoping for a complex storyline, you'll be disappointed.
15 It's obvious from the start who will fall victim to a twister, and there are no surprises in the central love story, either. What makes this movie are the special effects. The tornadoes are frighteningly realistic and, unlike in numerous other films of this genre which slowly build up to a dramatic climax, they appear from the very beginning. Watch out for the flying cow and airborne
20 petrol tanker: if they'd made this film in 3D, cinema audiences would have run for the exit at the sight of them.

C *The Perfect Storm* (2000)

I couldn't put the novel down when I was reading it, and the film adaptation gripped me in the same way. First there's the gradual build-up as the film explores the relationships of the crew being put together
25 by Captain Billy Tyne (George Clooney) for one final fishing trip in the season. Then comes the suspense as three storm fronts, including a hurricane, move together while the boat is at sea, eventually colliding to create a 'perfect storm'. The special effects are so well done, my first impression was that I was watching a real storm. And if I hadn't seen
30 the special features on the DVD afterwards, I'd probably still think they hadn't employed any visual tricks.

D *Earthquake* (1974)

If you can put up with the fact that the Sensurround effect, which made cinema seats shake in the seventies, cannot be recreated on the DVD in your lounge, then this all-star classic still has plenty to offer. Computer Generated Imagery
35 (CGI) was yet to be developed, but the special effects are still impressive, creating a number of unforgettable, if slightly disagreeable moments. Deaths are frequent and this is not a cosy family film to put your feet up with on a Sunday afternoon. And the final scene might not be what you're expecting. It certainly didn't turn out the way I thought it would.

E *The Day after Tomorrow* (2004)

40 If you combined all the extreme weather scenes of every natural disaster movie ever made, you would end up with something like this film. It has everything: hurricanes, tornadoes, floods, tidal waves, blizzards and even giant hailstones, all caused by global warming. Pure fantasy, of course, but it's all good fun, and as long as you see it as that and don't look for any
45 deeper message, you should enjoy the film. I always find it works better for me if I watch it during a storm or when it's snowing outside. It adds a touch of realism to the experience!

◐ Reacting to the text

Which of the films above sound the most and least appealing? Why?

How much attention do you pay to reviews when deciding which film to see? Why?

Is it better to read a book before or after watching the film adaptation? Why?

Language focus 2: Conditionals

1 In relation to which of the films in the reading on pages 142 and 143 are each of the following statements made?

Zero conditional
*It **works** better for me if I **watch** it during a storm.*

First conditional
*If you **watch** this film hoping for a complex storyline, you**'ll be** disappointed.*

Second conditional
*If you **combined** all the extreme weather scenes of every natural disaster movie ever made, you **would end up** with something like this film.*

Third conditional
*If they**'d made** this film in 3D, cinema audiences **would have run** for the exit at the sight of them.*

Mixed conditional
*If I **hadn't seen** the special features on the DVD afterwards, I'd probably still **think** they hadn't employed any visual tricks.*

2 Identify the verb forms in **bold** in the sentences in **1**.

3 Conditional sentences consist of two clauses; a main clause and a clause introduced by *if* (or certain other words). Events in the main clause depend on, or are conditional on, events in the *if* clause. Underline the correct alternatives in the following explanations for the sentences in exercise **1**.

Zero conditional: a situation in which one event always occurs as the result of another. *If* in this sentence means *whenever/although*.

First conditional: *a possible/an impossible* situation in the future and its likely result.

Second conditional: a present or *past/future* situation which the speaker considers to be unlikely or impossible.

Third conditional: an imaginary situation in the past, with speculation about its effect on *present/past* events.

Mixed conditional: an imaginary situation in the past, with speculation about its effect on *present/past* events.

4 Modal verbs can be used instead of *will* and *would* in conditional sentences. Explain the difference in meaning between these three sentences.

  a If we leave now, we'll be home by six o'clock.
  b If we leave now, we should be home by six o'clock.
  c If we leave now, we might be home by six o'clock.

5 A number of conjunctions can be used instead of *if* in conditional sentences. Complete each gap with **one** word from the box. You do not need to use all the words.

unless	unlike	promising	providing
far	exclusion	condition	long

  a As _____ as you don't look for any deeper message, you should enjoy the film.
  b I'll let you borrow it, _____ you're careful with it.
  c Her employer will pay for her studies on _____ that she attends every class.
  d We'll have a barbecue in the garden, _____ of course it rains. I hate wet sausages!

  Read more about conditionals on page 218 of the Grammar reference.

6 Each of the following sentences contains a mistake. Find the mistakes and correct them.

  1 If you'd have asked me, I would have lent you the money.
  2 I'll give you a ring if I'll find out what time he's arriving.
  3 What would you have done if she wouldn't have phoned?
  4 If I would drink coffee after six o'clock, I can never sleep.
  5 If they lose this match, I never go to see them play again.

7 Work in pairs.

  Student A: Turn to page 202.
  Student B: Turn to page 204.

Conditionals: Expressing regret

The third conditional can be used to express regrets. For each of the following situations, imagine what the person might be thinking. Write a third conditional sentence for each picture.

0 *If I'd brought my umbrella,*
I wouldn't have got so wet

1 _____

2 _____

3 _____

4 _____

5 _____

Vocabulary 2: *Put*

1 **a** Write **one** word in each gap to complete the phrasal verbs and expressions in **bold** in these extracts from the article on pages 142 and 143. Then check your answers in the article.

   1 … *meteorologists who* **put** *their lives* ____ **risk** *by chasing tornadoes* …(B)

   2 *I couldn't* **put** *the novel* ____ *when I was reading it.* (C)

   3 … *the crew being* **put** ____ *by Captain Billy Tyne for one final fishing trip in the season.* (C)

   4 *If you can* **put up** ____ *the fact that the Sensurround effect …cannot be recreated on the DVD in your lounge* … (D)

   5 … *this is not a cosy family film to* **put your feet** ____ *with on a Sunday afternoon.* (D)

   b Match these meanings to the phrasal verbs and expressions you completed in **a**.

tolerate   endanger   relax   stop reading   assemble

2 Match each sentence beginning **1–9** with an appropriate ending **a–i**.

   1 I've joined an amateur dramatics society: we're going to **put on**

   2 These trousers are far too tight for me now: I must have **put on**

   3 There's nothing on the television this evening: we could **put on**

   4 I'm going to have to move out of my flat. My landlord's **put up**

   5 Don't shout out the answer, Lara. You know you have to **put up**

   6 Robin's coming to London today and I've offered to **put** him **up**

   7 The groom had an accident in the morning so they had to **put off**

   8 It rained every single day and the tent got flooded. It **put** him **off**

   9 She found it hard to study, as several things were **putting** her **off**

   a weight.

   b for the night.

   c camping for life.

   d the radio instead.

   e the rent yet again.

   f the wedding to a later date.

   g a production of *Hamlet* in June.

   h your hand if you want to say something.

   i like the noise of the traffic and the neighbours arguing.

3 The phrasal verbs *put on*, *put up* and *put off*, each have multiple meanings. Use the sentences in exercise **2** to help you match each verb to the following groups of meanings.

   a increase; raise into the air; accommodate   _____

   b postpone; discourage from; distract   _____

   c organize an event; gain; make equipment start working   _____

4 Complete the gaps **1–4** with the words in the box.

money   effort   blame   pressure

   A My parents used to **put** a lot of **(1)**_____ **on** me to study harder. They said I wouldn't get into university if I didn't **put** more **time and (2)** _____ **into** my school work.

   B I'd been **putting** some **(3)** _____ **aside** each week to pay for our holiday, and during the night someone broke in and stole it. The policeman who came had the cheek to **put the (4)**_____ **on** me; he said I shouldn't have left so much cash in the house.

145

Speaking
Part 3

Collaborative task

Before you do the following Speaking Part 3 task, do the exercise in the Useful language box below.

1   Imagine that you belong to an environmental group and you want to inform people of the environmental issues below. Talk with your partner about what ordinary people can do to help solve these issues.

2   Now decide which two issues ordinary people can do most to help solve.

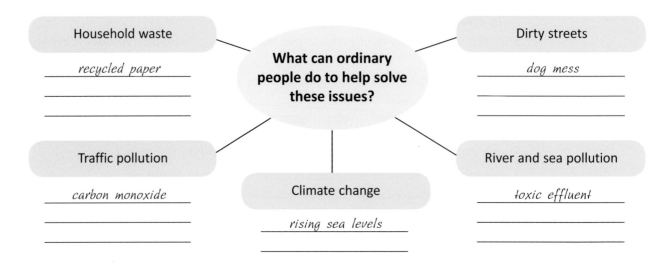

Household waste
recycled paper
_____
_____

What can ordinary people do to help solve these issues?

Dirty streets
dog mess
_____
_____

Traffic pollution
carbon monoxide
_____
_____

Climate change
rising sea levels
_____
_____

River and sea pollution
toxic effluent
_____
_____

Useful language

● One vocabulary item has been given for each of the five issues above. Add two more of the following items to each issue.

bottle bank	biofuel cars	cigarette butts	dropping litter	plastic containers
dumping waste	exhaust fumes	global warming	greenhouse effect	oil slick

● When commenting on your partner's opinions you can use *so, neither* or *nor* and the language you saw on page 128 of Unit 10 for agreeing and disagreeing.

Reading and Use of English 2
Part 6

Gapped text

1   How many items do you have with you now which are made of or contain plastic? What other plastic items can you see in the classroom?

In what ways might your daily life be affected if there was no plastic?

2   Read the base text on page 147 about the North Pacific gyre. Is there any information in the text which surprises you?

3 Six sentences have been removed from the text. Choose from the sentences **A–G** the one which fits each gap (**1–6**). There is one extra sentence which you do not need to use.

The Trash Vortex

The North Pacific gyre is a large area of the Pacific in which the water moves slowly round in a clockwise direction. Winds are light and the currents tend to force any floating material, including plastics and other slow degrading rubbish, into the central area of the gyre, where it remains in huge quantities. This gyre is sometimes called the Trash Vortex or the Pacific Garbage Patch. Some plastics here will not break down in the lifetimes of the grandchildren of the people who threw them away.

Around 100 million tonnes of plastic are produced each year, of which about ten per cent ends up in the sea. Take a walk along any beach anywhere in the world and you will find polythene plastic bags, bottles and containers, plastic drums, polystyrene packing, pieces of polypropylene fishing net, traffic cones, disposable lighters, vehicle tyres and toothbrushes. **1** ☐

These larger items are the visible signs of a much larger problem. They do not degrade like natural materials. **2** ☐ A single one litre bottle could separate into enough tiny pieces to put one on every mile of beach in the entire world.

3 ☐ However, items such as bottle tops, lighters and balloons are consumed by seabirds and other animals which mistake them for food. A turtle found dead in Hawaii had over a thousand pieces of plastic in its stomach and intestines. It has been estimated that plastic kills over a million seabirds and one hundred thousand marine mammals and sea turtles each year.

The North Pacific gyre is only one of five major ocean gyres. **4** ☐ The Sargasso Sea is a well known slow circulation area in the Atlantic, and research there has also demonstrated high concentrations of plastic particles present in the water.

5 ☐ In fact, around 70 per cent of discarded plastic sinks to the bottom. In the North Sea, Dutch scientists have counted around 110 pieces of litter for every square kilometre of the seabed, a staggering 600 000 tonnes in the North Sea alone. These plastics can cover the sea bottom and kill the marine life which is found there.

The issue of plastic waste is one that needs to be urgently addressed. **6** ☐ Obviously though, there is a need to make ship owners and operators, offshore platforms and fishing boat operators more aware of the consequences of irresponsible disposal of plastic items.

With so many threats to the world oceans including pollution, overfishing and climate change we urgently need to rescue marine biodiversity in the most effective way possible.

A At sea and on shore, under the influence of sunlight and the action of waves, they simply break down slowly into increasingly smaller particles.

B We can all contribute by avoiding plastics in the things we buy and by disposing of our waste responsibly.

C It is possible that this Trash Vortex problem is one which is present in other oceans as well.

D Even tiny jellyfish eat the small plastic particles floating in the water.

E They have been casually thrown away on land and at sea and carried ashore by wind and tide.

F Of course, not all plastic floats.

G This perhaps wouldn't be too much of a problem if the plastic had no harmful effects.

4 ⬤ Give examples of ways in which we could 'avoid plastics in the things we buy'.

Open cloze

1 ⬭ You are going to read a text about World Carfree Day. What do you think happens on this day and why?

2 Read through the text quite quickly, ignoring the gaps. Compare what it says with your own ideas in exercise **1**.

World Carfree Day

Each year, **(0)** _on_ 22 September, people in over 1,500 cities in 40 countries celebrate World Carfree Day. **(1)** _____ annual event aims to raise awareness of the problems caused by our dependence on private cars. Streets are closed to traffic and opened instead to street parties, theatre, bicycle demonstrations or outdoor cafés, in **(2)** _____ to show people what their city might look like **(3)** _____ there were fewer or no cars. Over one hundred million people are believed to take **(4)** _____ in the celebrations, although this figure is difficult to verify.

The hope is that the initiative will encourage more environmentally friendly alternatives to the car, **(5)** _____ as walking, cycling and public transport. **(6)** _____ , with increasing global car production and a world which **(7)** _____ grown used to the benefits of private transport, some say the battle is already lost. But even if we are unlikely to see cities **(8)** _____ any cars at all, people may at least begin to change their habits and leave their car at home more often.

3 Read the text again and for questions **1–8**, think of the word which best fits each gap. Use only **one** word in each gap. There is an example at the beginning (**0**). Write your answers **IN CAPITAL LETTERS**.

What to expect in the exam

The Open cloze task focuses mainly on grammar (see page 44). However, occasionally your knowledge of vocabulary may be tested (e.g. question **4** above).

4 ⬭ Do people in your country celebrate World Carfree Day? If so, how successful is it?

How dependent are you and your family on the car?

Essay

In your English class you have been talking about ways in which individuals can help the environment. Now, your English teacher has asked you to write an essay.

Write an essay using **all** the notes and give reasons for your point of view.

Write your **essay** in **140–190** words.

Essay question
There is little that individuals can do to help the environment. Do you agree?

Notes
Write about:
1 pollution
2 household waste
3 .... (your own idea)

How to go about it

Plan what you are going to write and how you are going to express your ideas.

Use the Speaking task and Reading text on pages 146 and 147, as well as the Open cloze text above, to help you with ideas and useful language.

Listening 2
Part 1

Multiple choice 👁 2.23–2.30

You will hear people talking in eight different situations. For Questions **1–8**, choose the best answer, **A**, **B** or **C**.

What to expect in the exam

- In Unit 4, you saw how contrast linkers such as *although*, *whereas* and *but*, as well as other words and expressions, can be used to create distractors in listening exercises.
- Look at question **1** below, together with the script, and choose the best answer.
- Which structure is used to create distractors? Which words help you to choose the answer?

1 You hear a man talking about a new fire station that has just been built.
   Where was it built?
   A in the city centre
   B in the countryside
   C on the outskirts of the city

I really can't understand why they put it all the way out there. They maintained that if they'd built it in the heart of the city there would have been problems getting out to fires in the rural areas. Too far and too much traffic, they said. But that's exactly why it would have made more sense to build it in the centre instead of on the edge. You know, it takes a fire engine nearly 20 minutes to get from that suburb to the other side of the city.

Now do questions **2–8** below. In questions **2**, **3** and **4** you will hear conditional sentences. These are used to create distractors as in question **1** above.

2 You hear a man talking about litter.
   Who is the man?
   A a shopkeeper
   B a town councillor
   C a local resident

3 You hear an environmentalist speaking on the radio about a recent project.
   How does she feel?
   A pessimistic
   B disappointed
   C pleased

4 You overhear this woman talking to her friend about her holiday.
   Why did she enjoy it?
   A She liked the beaches.
   B There wasn't much traffic.
   C There weren't many people.

5 You hear a conversation between two people.
   What is the relationship between them?
   A They are married.
   B They are teachers in the same school.
   C They are neighbours.

6 You are listening to the radio when you hear the following being read.
   What is it?
   A a story
   B a news report
   C a weather forecast

7 You overhear this conversation between a man and his neighbour.
   What is the man doing?
   A asking for help
   B apologizing
   C complaining

8 You hear a man talking about a recent environmental disaster.
   What is he going to do?
   A help clean up
   B take part in a protest demonstration
   C write to his Member of Parliament

Vocabulary

A Weather

1 Match the adjectives **1–3** with the nouns **a–d** to make appropriate adjective + noun collocations. Each adjective may be used with more than one noun.

1 light	**a** storm
2 heavy	**b** winds
3 strong	**c** showers
	d rain

2 Match each sentence beginning **1–8** with an appropriate ending **a–h**.

1 There is a possibility of **scattered**	**a** **breeze** blew into the room.
2 Northern areas suffered **torrential**	**b** **seas** to reach the safety of the port.
3 A tree blown down by **gale-force**	**c** **showers** in the region tomorrow.
4 She opened the door and a **gentle**	**d** **sunshine**, like a scene from a painting.
5 The valley was bathed in **brilliant**	**e** **wave** will follow the earthquake.
6 The boat fought through **rough**	**f** **rain**, which caused heavy flooding.
7 Experts have predicted that a **tidal**	**g** **skies** and occasional showers.
8 It will be a grey day with **overcast**	**h** **winds** blocked the road and held up traffic.

B *Put*

Complete each of the gaps in sentences **1–6** with one of the words from the box. Use each word twice.

off	up	on

1 Put your hand _____ if you want to ask a question.

2 We're putting _____ a concert to raise money for charity.

3 That job I had in the butcher's put me _____ eating meat for life.

4 Could you put the radio _____ ? I want to listen to the news.

5 When I'm next in London, could you put me _____ for the night?

6 Never put _____ until tomorrow what you can do today.

Conditional sentences

1 If the weather _____ (stay) good next weekend, we _____ (probably/go) away somewhere.

2 Why didn't you phone us? If I _____ (know) you were coming, I _____ (could/prepare) something special to eat.

3 I _____ (not/do) a bungee jump even if you _____ (pay) me a million pounds, so stop trying to persuade me.

4 I thought this might happen. If you _____ (take) my advice, you _____ (not/be) in this mess now.

5 Stop being naughty! I _____ (send) you to bed early unless you _____ (start) behaving yourself right now!

6 It was very kind of you. I don't know what I _____ (do) yesterday if you _____ (not/help) me.

7 My printer's getting old now, but it _____ (usually/work) all right if you _____ (feed) the paper in manually.

8 I _____ (go) to the cinema more often if I _____ (have) the time, but unfortunately it's just not possible.

Reading and Use of English
Part 4

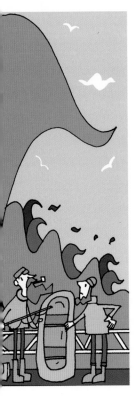

Transformations

Complete the second sentence so that it has a similar meaning to the first sentence, using the word given. **Do not change the word given.** You must use between **two** and **five** words, including the word given.

1 It's a good thing I spoke to you or I would have forgotten her birthday.

   IF

   I would have forgotten her birthday _____ to you.

2 I only wrote the letter because my mother made me do it.

   HAVE

   If my mother hadn't made me do it, _____ the letter.

3 I will help you only if you tidy your room.

   NOT

   I will _____ tidy your room.

4 You can borrow it, but you must return it to me next week.

   LONG

   You can borrow it _____ it back to me next week.

5 The factory fumes are endangering the health of local residents.

   PUT

   The health of local residents _____ risk by the factory fumes.

6 If the sea wasn't so rough, we could go out in the boat today.

   ENOUGH

   The sea _____ us to be able to go out in the boat today.

Writing
Part 2

Write an answer to **one** of the following questions. Write your answer in **140–190** words in an appropriate style.

1   You have received an email from your Irish friend, Liam. Read this part of the email and then write your email to Liam.

> I'm definitely coming in January. Shame you won't be there then, but perhaps you could give me some advice. What's the weather like in your area at that time of year? What sort of clothes should I pack and what can I do there?
> Thanks
> Liam

Write your **email**.

2   You see this announcement in an English-language magazine called *Cinema World*.

> ### Reviews needed
> The themes in next month's issue of our magazine are The Weather and The Environment. Send us a review of a film in which the weather and/or the environment play an important part. Write about what you did and did not like about the film and say whether you would recommend it to others. We will publish the most interesting reviews.

Write your **review**.

(12) Looking after yourself

Vocabulary 1: Food and drink

1 Work out the meanings of the words and expressions in **bold** in the following sentences.

    1 Are you a **fussy eater** or do you tend to eat all types of food?

    2 Do you always **eat** everything **up** or do you sometimes **leave food on your plate**?

    3 Do you **chew** your food several times before you **swallow** it, or do you tend to **bolt** it **down** quickly?

    4 Which drinks, if any, do you usually **sip** slowly? When, if ever, do you **gulp down** your drink quickly?

    5 When buying or ordering a **soft drink**, do you prefer **still drinks** like orange juice or **fizzy drinks** like lemonade?

    6 Do you often **drink straight from a bottle or a can,** or do you usually **drink from a glass**?

2 👁 Discuss the questions in exercise **1** with your partner. Give as much information as possible.

Language focus 1: Countable and uncountable nouns A

1 The word *plate* is usually countable: we can say *a plate, two plates, three plates* and so on.

The word *bread* is usually uncountable: we say *bread* or *some bread*, rather than *a bread* or *two breads*.

Decide which of the following words are countable, and which are uncountable. Some of them can be both countable and uncountable. How does this affect the meaning?

milk	diet	chicken	health	chip
chocolate	meal	pepper	spaghetti	cake

2 The word *bread* can be made countable by saying *a loaf of bread* or *two slices of bread*. Write the following uncountable nouns next to an appropriate phrase to make them countable. Some of the nouns can be used with more than one phrase.

sugar	cheese	jam	milk	toast
cake	spaghetti	salt	chocolate	

1 a piece of _____
2 a slice of _____
3 a plate of _____
4 a teaspoonful of _____
5 a pinch of _____
6 a bar of _____
7 a jar of _____
8 a carton of _____

 See pages 218–19 of the Grammar reference.

Listening 1 Multiple matching 🔘 2.31–2.35

Part 3

1 🔘 How effective do you think diets are? What are the dangers?

2 You will hear five people talking about food and dieting. For questions **1–5**, choose from the list **A–H** what each speaker says. Use the letters only once. There are three extra letters which you do not need to use.

A I never leave anything on my plate.

B I found one form of dieting too expensive.

C I used to feel under pressure to lose weight.

D I have never been on a diet.

E I had to change my eating habits.

F I do not follow all the advice I am given.

G I pay regular visits to my doctor.

H I follow the advice given in books.

Speaker 1 ☐ 1
Speaker 2 ☐ 2
Speaker 3 ☐ 3
Speaker 4 ☐ 4
Speaker 5 ☐ 5

3 🔘 The last woman said: *We are constantly under attack from advertising and the media, who tell us that 'thin is beautiful'.*
To what extent is this the case in your country?

Language focus 2: Countable and uncountable nouns B

1 Why does the woman say 'Just a few' and not 'Just a little'?

2 The following sentences are all from the recording. Complete each of the spaces with one of the words from the box. Some words will be used more than once and more than one answer may be possible for each space.

little	few	much	many	some	any	no
deal	number	piece	lot	plenty	several	

Speaker 1

You drink nothing but lemonade with **a)** _____ salt and pepper for about seven days without **b)** _____ food.

I wasn't earning a great **c)** _____ of money and I simply couldn't afford to keep it up.

Speaker 2

I used to eat a **d)** _____ of junk food.

I ate very **e)** _____ fresh food, and this had a serious effect on my health.

And now if I get hungry between meals, I have a **f)** _____ cheese or **g)** _____ nuts, just to keep me going.

Speaker 3

When I want to treat myself I have a **h)** _____ of cake or a **i)** _____ biscuits.

As long as you eat sweet things after a meal, then there's **j)** _____ problem.

I only ever eat chocolates after lunch or dinner. And never too **k)** _____ of course – just one or two.

Speaker 4

A sensible, balanced diet: **l)** _____ of fresh fruit and vegetables ….. **m)** _____ glasses of water a day – and **n)** _____ snacks between meals.

Speaker 5

A large **o)** _____ of people follow diets, but very **p)** _____ of them are happier as a result.

I don't pay **q)** _____ attention to what others think or say.

3 🔘 2.31–2.35 Now listen to the recording again and compare your answers.

Multiple matching

1 ⬤ What types of things can you cook?
Do you enjoy cooking? Why/Why not?
Are you a vegetarian? If so, why? If not, would you ever consider becoming one?
Why/Why not?

2 **a** You are going to read an article about a certain type of cooking. Read the title of
the article and the introductory sentence and answer this question:

What types of things do you expect to read about in the article?

b Read the article and check your predictions.

3 Read the article again and for questions **1–10**, choose from the paragraphs (**A–E**). The
paragraphs may be chosen more than once.

Which paragraphs mention the following?

using one type of food as a substitute for another	1
the possibility of watching others cook online	2
statistics which give us a reason to worry	3
a lack of awareness caused by everyone doing the same as each other	4
the value of reducing waste, given our current need to spend less money	5
only using that part of the food which is safe to eat	6
doing something without deliberately intending to	7
passing on knowledge to different age groups	8
seeing others do something and deciding not to imitate them	9
the desire to lead by demonstration rather than telling people how to behave	10

Zero-waste vegetarian cooking
Samuel Muston discovers why we should think twice before we throw away those peelings

A

Watch a few cookery shows on TV and you'll see that nearly all of the chefs waste food. Not consciously, but still they do it. When they slice off that bit of fat or throw away those peelings, they are wasting things we probably would have eaten in the past. And the reason we don't notice it is because that's the way we all cook – they simply cook like us, and, indeed, we cook like them. That's what the 26-year-old chef Shane Jordan is telling me
5 over a plate of vegan curry at Arc Café, where he works. 'TV chefs are all chop, chop, chop, put this to the side, throw away this,' says Jordan. 'I used to watch and think "I could make a dish out of what you are throwing away alone."' So that's what he started doing.

B

At Arc he has created a series of dishes that are zero waste, or very nearly. So if he uses one part of a vegetable or fruit, he'll use the rest of it elsewhere, as long as it isn't harmful to health. In fact, his curry is banana-skins
10 curry, the skins filling in for what would normally be meat. 'I make a lot of banana fritters with the flesh, so I'm left with all these skins,' he says. 'And I thought, "what can I do with them?" Then I found an Asian recipe which tells you how to make them edible and I built the dish around that.'

C

Jordan's cooking is inventive, but it also has a backwards-looking feel to it – and that may not be a bad thing, Tom Tanner, of the Sustainable Restaurant Association, says. 'We have become used to fast, quick, disposable
15 food. A return to the culinary values and good housekeeping of our grandparents may help reduce the vast quantity of food we all chuck away.' Certainly the figures on waste are a cause for concern. A recent study into home eating concluded that we waste one-fifth of all the food we buy. It is against this that Jordan is fighting. 'I believe in spreading what knowledge I have of my type of low-waste cooking, I don't want to lecture people,' Jordan says. 'But I do want to try and show people there's another way.'

D

20 To help do this he has created a programme of school visits. In these, he'll teach kids how to cut vegetables and fruit (tight to the flesh) and think about food as something that isn't infinitely available from the fridge – and infinitely disposable. He is also targeting slightly older cooks. 'In the next few months we also plan to set up a webcam to livestream what we do in the kitchen so people can learn exactly what you can and can't eat,' Jordan says. Using peelings from fruit to add flavour to cakes and jams, for example, seems very sensible. The ends of
25 broccoli stalks and leeks, often overlooked, are also great for throwing in stir-frys.

E

This type of creative thinking might just be what we need, according to Tanner. 'We have to face up to the fact we have a waste problem,' he says. 'It costs us money and it's bad for the environment – and to change it we need to change our attitude to the food we eat.' At a time when we are having to tighten our belts, we could all do with cutting down on the throwaway – and Jordan may just be one of the men to help us.

◯ Reacting to the text

'*... we waste one-fifth of all the food we buy.*' How true is this in your household?

What else can be done, in addition to Shane Jordan's idea, to reduce the amount of food wasted?

Language focus 3: Reported speech

1 Look at the following example of direct speech from the text, together with a reported version. What change is made to the tense of the verb when it is reported?

Direct speech: *'I don't want to lecture people.'*

Reported speech: *Jordan said he didn't want to lecture people.*

In this case, the following sentence without the tense change is also possible. Why?

Jordan said he doesn't want to lecture people.

2 Complete the columns below, to show how verb tenses and other words and expressions can change in reported speech. Write either **one or two words** in each space. The first one has been done for you.

Direct speech	Reported speech
a 'We're meeting her tomorrow.'	They said they _were meeting_ her ___the next___ day.
b 'I've seen him twice today.'	She said she _____ him twice _____ day.
c 'She's been living here for years.'	He told me she _____ living _____ for years.
d 'I spoke to her last week.'	He said he _____ to her _____ week.
e 'I was working yesterday.'	He told me he _____ working _____ before.
f 'We'd asked her several times.'	They said they _____ her several times.

3 Name the tense in each sentence in exercise **2**.
Example: a present continuous → past continuous

4 What happens to the modal verbs *will, may, can* and *must* in reported speech?

What happens to *would, might, could, should* and *ought to*?

5 What happens to these time expressions in reported speech?

two days ago   next month   tonight   this morning now

Ⓖ Check your ideas on page 219 of the Grammar reference.

6 **a** Write down at least five things that different people have said recently. Think about the following people:

family and friends	*teachers*	*classmates*
work colleagues	*newsreaders*	*politicians*
sportsmen and women	*other famous people*	*yourself*

Example:
'I think I'll be fit for the match on Saturday.'
(Steve James – *footballer*)

b ◯ Report the different statements to your partner using reported speech.

Example:
Steve James said he thought he would be fit for the match on Saturday.

Reading and Use of English 2
Part 2

Open cloze

1 ◯ For some people, placing your elbows on the table at mealtimes is bad manners. Give examples of what you consider to be good and bad table manners.

2 For questions **1–8**, read the text below and think of the word which best fits each gap. Use only **one** word in each gap. There is an example at the beginning (**0**). Write your answers **IN CAPITAL LETTERS**.

Table manners

Perhaps because many families no longer eat together (**0**) _ON_ a regular basis, very (**1**) ____ attention seems to be paid any more to the teaching of good table manners. It is not at (**2**) ____ uncommon nowadays to see people with their elbows on the table, speaking with their mouth full, or worse, answering their phone or writing an email mid-meal. In one recent UK survey, nearly a quarter of adults and slightly more (**3**) ____ a third of teenagers admitted to using their smartphone during mealtimes.

In an attempt to discourage mobile phone use (**4**) ____ the meal table, blogger Brian Perez invented the Phone Stack game, in (**5**) ____ diners place their phones face down in the middle of the table in a stack, (**6**) ____ on top of the other. The first person (**7**) ____ look at his or her phone has to pay the whole bill; if, however, by the end of the meal, the stack remains untouched and (**8**) ____ phone has been turned over, everyone wins and pays for their own meal.

3 ◯ Do you consider using the phone during meals to be bad manners? Why/Why not? How important do you think table manners are? Why?

Speaking
Part 2
Talking about photos ⊙

How are the people feeling?

1 Look at the photographs, which show people eating in different places.

Student A Compare photographs **1** and **2** and say how you think the people are feeling.

Student B When your partner has finished, say which of these places you would prefer to eat in.

2 Now change roles. Follow the instructions above using photographs **3** and **4**.

Language focus 4: Reporting verbs

1 Look at these different ways of reporting what people say:

a 'I'll get you a drink,' said Jan to Tom.

Jan told Tom she would get him a drink.

Jan **offered to get** Tom a drink.

b 'You should go and see a doctor,' said Tim.

Tim said I should go and see a doctor.

Tim **advised me to go** and see a doctor.

2 Which of the following verbs follow the same pattern as *advise* (verb + object + infinitive with *to*) and which are like *offer* (verb + infinitive with *to*)? Make two columns in your notebook.

order   urge   refuse   threaten

persuade   warn   tell   remind

ask   promise   encourage   recommend

3 Report the following sentences using an appropriate verb from exercise **2**. There is an example at the beginning (**0**).

0 'I'll give you the £5 back tomorrow,' he told her.

He *promised to give her the £5 back the next day.*

1 'I'm not going to clean my room!' she said.

She _____ .

2 'Don't forget to take your sandwiches, John,' said his father.

John's father _____ .

3 'If you don't turn your music down, I'll call the police,' said my neighbour.

My neighbour _____ .

4 'Don't take the car out. The roads are very icy,' said her friend.

Her friend _____ .

5 'Get out of my office immediately!' shouted his boss.

His boss _____ .

6 'You really ought to report the theft to the police' my friend told me.

My friend _____ .

4 Look at the following structures which can follow the verb *recommend*.

The doctor recommended him to do exercise.

The doctor recommended (that) he (should) do exercise.

The doctor recommended doing exercise.

Which structure is **not** possible with the verb *suggest*?

5 ⊙ Work with a partner. You each have various problems and you would like your partner's suggestions and advice. Student A should turn to page 202 and student B to page 205 to find out what your problems are.

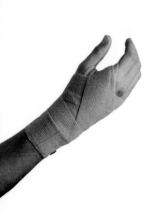

Vocabulary 2: Health matters

1 In parts **A** and **B** below complete the gaps with one of the words from the box.

A

ear	tooth	stomach	~~nose~~	heart	blood

0 If you get a ... *nose* **bleed,**   pinch it with two fingers until it stops.
1 She'll have a ... _____ **attack**   when she sees what you've done!
2 He'll have serious ... _____ **decay**   if he doesn't clean them regularly.
3 Of course he has a ... _____ **ache.**   He ate far too many cream cakes.
4 With such high ... _____ **pressure**   you should eat less salt.
5 She's got a bad ... _____ **infection**   so she can't come swimming.

B

ankle	nose	eye	throat	neck

1 That's a nasty ... **black** _____ .   Did somebody hit you?
2 She's got a very ... **sore** _____ .   She can hardly speak.
3 I've got a ... **stiff** _____ .   It hurts when I turn my head.
4 You've got a ... **runny** _____ .   Would you like a handkerchief?
5 It's just a badly ... **sprained** _____ .   You haven't broken anything.

2 Study the collocations in the shaded boxes in exercise **1** for one minute, then cover up the words on the right in each one. How many can you remember?

3 Choose the correct alternative in each sentence.

  1 My father wrapped a *bandage/band* round my sprained wrist.

  2 You've cut your finger. You should put *a plaster/plaster* on it.

  3 The doctor gave me a *receipt/prescription* for a course of antibiotics.

  4 When I broke my arm, I had it in *a plaster/plaster* for about five weeks.

  5 The nurse gave him an *infusion/injection* in his arm to help him sleep.

4 ⬭ When was the last time you were ill?

Do you often have accidents? What about when you were younger?

Which of the conditions in exercise **1** have you suffered?

Listening 2
Part 4

Multiple choice ⬉ 2.36

1 ⬭ The photograph shows a woman working with a personal trainer. What do you think the job of a personal trainer involves?

2 You'll hear an interview with a personal trainer. For questions **1–7**, choose the best answer (**A**, **B** or **C**).

1 When Naomi takes on a new client, what is the first thing she does?

  A give the client advice on what food to eat

  B ask the client to do some basic exercises

  C find out the client's personal aims

2 Naomi says she has specialist knowledge in helping

  A athletes improve their performance.

  B sportspeople recover from injury.

  C older people control their diet.

3 What quality does Naomi believe a personal trainer should have?

 A a sense of fun

 B a love of hard work

 C an ability to impose discipline

4 How does Naomi's business differ from that of other personal trainers in the area?

 A She operates from her converted garage.

 B She conducts some of her classes outdoors.

 C She has a large number of exercise machines.

5 What did Naomi find frustrating in her job at the gym?

 A The clients changed frequently.

 B There were too many clients.

 C The clients were treated badly.

6 Naomi finally decided to leave her job at the gym when she was asked to

 A work at weekends.

 B wear specific clothes.

 C sell the gym's products.

7 How does Naomi find new clients?

 A Her existing clients recommend her to others.

 B She advertises for clients in the local press.

 C Her previous employer sends her clients.

3 🔵 If you had a personal trainer, what would your aims be?

What do you do to keep fit and healthy?

Word formation: Nouns 2

1 In the following extract from the listening, complete each gap with the correct noun form of the verb in brackets.

I carry out a needs (**1**) _____ (analyse) ... This includes asking them about their diet, their (**2**) _____ (injure) history and any medical (**3**) _____ (complain) or conditions they have, such as high blood (**4**) _____ (press). Then basically, I design exercise routines and give (**5**) _____ (advise) on nutrition in (**6**) _____ (respond) to the information they give me.

Check your answers in the listening script on page 235.

2 In **1–6**, form nouns by adding the same suffix from the box to all four words in each group. You may need to make further spelling changes. There is an example at the beginning (**0**).

-al	-ight	-ing	-ship	-th	-ure	~~-y~~

0	honest	difficult	safe	poor
	honesty	*difficulty*	*safety*	*poverty*
1	say	meet	build	advertise
2	press	depart	please	sign
3	arrive	refuse	survive	approve
4	warm	deep	true	grow
5	fly	see	weigh	high
6	friend	member	champion	partner

3 a Complete each gap with an appropriate noun formed from the word in brackets. The first one has been done for you.

 1 _Laughter_ (laugh) is the best medicine.

 2 Hair _____ (lose) is not a problem, so no _____ (solve) is required.

 3 The secret of _____ (succeed) is hard work.

 4 Too much _____ (choose) is a bad thing.

 5 A little _____ (know) is a dangerous thing.

 6 Protecting freedom of _____ (speak) is more important than protecting people from being offended.

 7 There is no _____ (prove) that alien life exists.

 8 The most important _____ (believe) is self-_____ (believe).

 b 🔵 Discuss each of the statements in **a**.

Language focus 5: Reported questions

1 a Here are two examples of direct questions from the listening on page 158, each followed by its reported version. Compare the two versions then answer the question in **b** below.

1 Direct question: 'What reasons do clients have for coming to see you?'

Reported question: The interviewer asked Naomi what reasons clients had for going to see her.

2 Direct question: 'Are you pleased you became self-employed?'

Reported question: He asked her if she was pleased she had become self-employed.

b What changes are made when we report direct questions? Consider the following:

- auxiliary verbs *do, does, did*
- verb tenses
- word order
- yes/no questions
- punctuation

(G) Check your answers on page 220 of the Grammar reference.

2 Report the following questions, which were asked to a doctor.

1   How long have you been a doctor?

The interviewer asked her _____

_____ .

2   What made you decide to enter the medical profession?

He also asked her _____

_____ .

3   How many patients do you see each day on average?

He wanted to know _____

_____ .

4   Do your friends often ask you for medical advice?

He wondered _____

_____ .

5   Are you planning to retire soon?

He asked her _____

_____ .

Writing
Part 2

Report

1   (○)   Read the following Part 2 instructions. Which places would you recommend in your area? Why?

A group of foreign students is going to be staying in your area for a month this summer. They are keen to keep fit during their stay and the group leader has asked you to write a report giving advice on the best places to go running, swimming and cycling. In your report you should explain why these places will be of interest to the group.

2   Read the following answer, ignoring the gaps. How similar is the area described in the report to the area in which you live?

Introduction

The aim of this report is to describe the best places in this area for your students to go running, cycling and swimming during their stay here.

Running

The town has one of the longest promenades in the country. As **(1)** _____ as being wide and flat, it offers spectacular views out to sea. A run **(2)** _____ just before breakfast is the perfect way for your students to start the day and prepare themselves mentally for their English classes.

Cycling

Cycling is forbidden on the promenade, **(3)** _____ there is a cycle path on the outskirts of town, **(4)** _____ your students can burn a few calories after class. **(5)** _____ takes cyclists through an area of woods and hills, with more superb views of the town and the sea.

Swimming

Swimming in the sea is not recommended, **(6)** _____ the water is not particularly clean. **(7)** _____ , there is a lake just outside the town, **(8)** _____ is pleasant to swim in and less crowded than the town's swimming pool.

Conclusion

This area offers plenty of opportunities to keep fit and your students will be able to do sport and enjoy beautiful scenery at the same time.

3 Linking

a Your answers in the Writing paper in the *First* exam should contain evidence of linking.

Eight words which link ideas in the report have been removed. Complete each gap (**1–8**) with a word from the box.

as	but	here	however	this	well	where	which

b How has the writer of the report created links between

1 the paragraphs on running and cycling?

2 the paragraphs on cycling and swimming?

4 Answering the question

You must address all the points in the question.

Underline those sections of the report where the writer has addressed the point which says: *you should explain why these places will be of interest to the group.*

Example:

<u>Running</u> – *A run here just before breakfast is the perfect way for your students to start the day and prepare themselves mentally for their English classes.*

5 Write an answer to the following Writing Part 2 question:

A group of foreign students is going to be staying in your area for a month. You have been asked to write a report for the group leader giving advice on eating out. Describe the best places to eat cheaply in your area and say why, in addition to the reasons of cost, you think the students will enjoy eating in these places.

Write your **report** in **140–190** words.

Don't forget!

- Plan your answer before you start writing.
- Give each paragraph a heading.
- Make sure you address all the points in the question.
- Invent ideas if you want to.

- Use a variety of linking words and expressions.
- Write in a neutral or formal style.

For more information on writing reports, see pages 54 and 55 in Unit 4, and page 200 in Ready for Writing.

Useful language

The food *is cheap/inexpensive/reasonably priced/affordable.*
The price *is/prices are low/reasonable/competitive/affordable.*
The atmosphere *is pleasant/friendly/relaxed/lively.*
The portions *are generous/huge/(more than) adequate.*
The food *is tasty/delicious/healthy/homemade.*

12 Review

Word formation

For questions **1–8**, read the text below. Use the word given in capitals at the end of some of the lines to form a word that fits in the gap **in the same line**. There is an example at the beginning (**0**).

Freegans

The term 'freegan' is a (**0**) _COMBINATION_ of the words 'free' and 'vegan'   **COMBINE**
and describes a person who looks through rubbish bins to find food which
others have thrown away. Some live (**1**) _____ off the contents of   **WHOLE**
supermarket bins, eating nothing but food which has been thrown out
because its sell-by or best-before date has passed. The food is often in very
good condition and (**2**) _____ such as food poisoning are the   **ILL**
exception rather than the rule amongst freegans.

For many, freeganism is a lifestyle (**3**) _____ rather than a necessity.   **CHOOSE**
They are not homeless or living in (**4**) _____ ; they are simply   **POOR**
adopting an alternative way to meet their daily food needs. Their movement
represents a (**5**) _____ to add to the huge amounts of consumer   **REFUSE**
waste in a world in which (**6**) _____ food prices are causing millions   **RISE**
to go hungry. (**7**) _____ for freegans, however, many of the major   **FORTUNATE**
supermarkets now lock their bins away. Some are even known to have made
food inedible before discarding it, in order to (**8**) _____ freegans.   **COURAGE**

Transformations

For Questions **1–6** complete the second sentence so that it has a similar meaning to the first sentence, using the word given. **Do not change the word given**. You must use between **two** and **five** words, including the word given. Write the missing words **IN CAPITAL LETTERS**.

1 I don't weigh as much as I did when I last saw you.
   LOST
   I _____ I last saw you.

2 'I wouldn't go to that restaurant if I were you, Matt,' I said.
   ADVISED
   I _____ to that restaurant.

3 I'm amazed by how much English he knows.
   OF
   His _____ me.

4 'Can you swim, Sarah?' asked her teacher.
   HOW
   Sarah's teacher asked her _____ to swim.

5 'I'll drive Dawn to the station ,' he said.
   OFFERED
   He _____ a lift to the station.

6 'There'll be very few people at the party,' she told Roger.
   NOT
   She told Roger there _____ people at the party.

Collocation revision: Units 1–12

1 In each of the spaces below write one word which collocates with *all* three of the other words. The question numbers also refer to the relevant units of the book where the words you require first appeared.

1 baggy
scruffy
trendy _____

2 talented
session
rock _____

3 hands-free
landline
mobile _____

4 horror
action
science-fiction _____

5 challenging
monotonous
badly paid _____

6 flowing
shoulder-length _____
spiky

7 prosperous
bustling
run-down _____

8 business
day
weekend _____

9 _____
a piercing scream
a nervous laugh
a broad smile

10 death
life
two-year prison _____

11 strong
gale-force
light _____

12 soft
still
fizzy _____

2 Use other collocations from the first 12 units of the book to create your own exercise. Choose three words or phrases which can all be used with the same verb or noun, as in exercise 1 above. Write four examples like this for another student to complete.

Reading and Use of English
Part 1

Multiple-choice cloze

For questions **1–8**, read the text below and decide which answer (**A, B, C** or **D**) best fits each gap. There is an example at the beginning (**0**).

The dangers of a sedentary lifestyle

Evidence **(0)** ____ that a sedentary lifestyle can have a serious **(1)** ____ on your health. According to the World Heart Foundation, physical inactivity **(2)** ____ the risk of heart disease by 50 per cent.

You should, therefore, **(3)** ____ of spending too long in front of your computer without taking breaks. Sitting for lengthy periods at your desk may cause your shoulders, neck and upper back to become **(4)** ____ , and you are likely to become increasingly unproductive as your concentration begins to wander. In an attempt to remedy this, you may try to keep yourself going with junk food, sweetened coffee or **(5)** ____ drinks, leading to weight gain and perhaps even high blood **(6)** ____ .

If taking time out for vigorous exercise is not a possibility, you should at least get up from your desk at regular **(7)** ____ to do stretching exercises or walk around. Drink **(8)** ____ of water too – it improves concentration, and the resulting trips to the toilet will keep you active.

0 A advises   B warns   C <u>suggests</u>   D persuades
1 A harm   B damage   C effect   D importance
2 A rises   B increases   C gains   D grows
3 A beware   B avoid   C discourage   D care
4 A tough   B hurtful   C stiff   D intense
5 A floppy   B foggy   C furry   D fizzy
6 A tenseness   B movement   C problem   D pressure
7 A intervals   B interruptions   C stops   D delays
8 A much   B full   C plenty   D lot

Introduction

The **Speaking** paper consists of four separate parts and lasts about 14 minutes. You will probably take the test with another candidate, although it is possible to be part of a group of three; in this case, the test lasts about 21 minutes. There are two examiners: the Interlocutor, who conducts the test and asks the questions, and the Assessor, who listens to the test and assesses your performance. The Interlocutor also assesses and contributes to your final mark.

1 Read the descriptions of the four parts of the **Speaking** paper below and match each one to a diagram **a–d**. The arrows (⟷) show who is speaking to whom.

a **INTERLOCUTOR**

CANDIDATE A ⟷ CANDIDATE B

b **INTERLOCUTOR**

CANDIDATE A (⟷) CANDIDATE B

c **INTERLOCUTOR**

CANDIDATE A ⟷ CANDIDATE B

d **INTERLOCUTOR**

CANDIDATE A   CANDIDATE B

Part 1 Interview   Total time: 2 minutes

The Interlocutor asks you questions which require you to give basic personal information about yourself. You may speak with your partner in this part if you want to, although you do not have to.

Part 2 Talking about photographs   Total time: 4 minutes

You have one minute to compare two photographs and add some further comment about them. You also have about 30 seconds to comment on your partner's pictures. You do not talk to your partner in this part.

Part 3 Collaborative task   Total time: 4 minutes

After explaining the task, the interlocutor listens while you and your partner talk about something together for two minutes. The interlocutor then gives you a further minute to try to agree on a decision related to your initial discussion.

Part 4 Further discussion   Total time: 4 minutes

The interlocutor asks further questions related to the topic introduced in Part 3. As well as responding to these questions, you can, or indeed may be asked to, interact with your partner and comment on what he or she says.

2 The following comments were all made by students who had just taken the **Speaking** test of the *First* exam. Look at each one and answer these questions:

Does the student set a good example to follow in the **Speaking** test? Why/why not?

If not, how would you avoid making the same mistake?

Part 1

a 'The examiner asked us some really simple questions at the beginning of the exam. So I just gave some short, simple answers, as I would in my own language.'

b 'Before the exam, I learnt and rehearsed some nice long answers to all the typical questions they ask you about yourself in the exam. I knew exactly what I was going to say.'

c 'I was a bit nervous in this part, but the questions were not difficult so I tried to answer them as fully and as naturally as I could, as if I was talking to someone I knew. It helped me to relax for the rest of the test.'

Part 2

a 'I used some really good vocabulary to describe what everyone in the pictures was wearing, what they were doing, and so on.'

b 'The examiner stopped me after a minute and I hadn't finished what I wanted to say!'

c 'I was concentrating so much on the pictures when the examiner gave them to me that I forget to listen to the instructions! I had to ask her to repeat them.'

Part 3

a 'I did really well in this part of the exam. I had lots of ideas and I couldn't stop talking. My partner was a bit quiet, though.'

b 'We had to talk about five different sports and what was difficult about them. We didn't need the full two minutes – we did it in about half the time. '

c 'We had about a minute to decide on the two most important qualities of a language learner. We agreed on one without too much problem but when the examiner stopped us we were still trying to agree on the second.'

Part 4

a 'The examiner didn't really say very much in this part. We seemed to do most of the talking.'

b 'My partner said that e-readers would eventually replace books. 'Nonsense,' I said, 'you must be mad.' I thought that was really good – an expression of disagreement and a modal verb of deduction in one sentence!'

c 'We had to talk about the environment, which I don't know much about, so I tried to change the topic of conversation to pets; I've got two dogs and a hamster, you see.'

Part 1: Interview Total time: 2 minutes

1 Choose three of the following categories and for each one write three questions you could ask another student.

work and study	sport and keeping fit	family and friends	travel and holidays
future plans	hobbies and interests	TV and Internet	likes and dislikes

Begin your questions with the following words:

> Do/Are/Have/Would you ...?   What ...?   Where ...?   Who ...?
> Why ...?   When ...?   How ...?   How long/often/much/many ...?

If you write a question which only requires a short answer, write another which will encourage the other student to say more.

Example:
Where do you live? What do you like about living there?

2 🗨 Work with another student. Interview each other using the questions you have prepared. Develop your answers, making sure they are relevant to the question.

3 🔘 **2.37** Listen to two students, Christina and Paolo, doing Part 1 of the Speaking test and answer the following questions:

1 Does the interlocutor ask any of the same questions you prepared?

2 Why does the interlocutor interrupt Christina at the beginning?

3 What advice would you give to Paolo to help him improve his performance?

Don't forget!

- Do not learn long pre-prepared answers for this part of the exam. They may not be entirely appropriate to the question you are asked and they will probably not sound very natural.

- Do, however, make sure you know individual items of vocabulary which are relevant to yourself.

  For example:

  Your hobbies and interests

  'I'm really keen on rock climbing.'

  The course you have decided to study

  'I would like to study for a degree in aeronautical engineering.'

  What your parents do

  'My mother's a systems analyst.'

Part 2: Talking about photos Total time: 4 minutes

Useful language

'Fillers' are words or phrases which enable you to think while you are speaking. Look at the following examples and think about the equivalent expressions you would use in your own language.

Buying time

Well ...

Let me see ...

What else (can I say)?

Is there anything else (I can add)?

Gathering your thoughts

I'm not quite sure, but I think ...

I haven't thought about it before, but perhaps ...

I don't really know, but I imagine ...

Don't forget!

Student A

- Do not describe the photographs in detail.
- Use the written prompt above the photographs to help you remember the task.

Student B

- Try to speak for the full 30 seconds.
- Give reasons for your opinions.

1 **Student A**   Look at these two photographs. They show people on holiday in different places. Compare the photographs and say why you think the people have chosen to go on holiday to these different places.

> **Why have the people chosen to go on holiday to these different places?**

Student B   When your partner has finished say which of these places you would prefer to go to on holiday.

Now change roles and do the Part 2 task on page 203.

2 👁 **2.38** Listen to Christina and Paolo doing the Part 2 task and answer the following questions.

1 How well does each person carry out their task when they are Student A?

2 How well do they use the 30 seconds when they are Student B?

Part 3: Collaborative task   Total time: 4 minutes

1 Imagine that the History Museum in your town would like to introduce some new features to attract more visitors. Below are some of the ideas which have been suggested. Talk with your partner for two minutes about what types of people these different ideas would appeal to.

Useful language

This might appeal to (elderly people).
(Younger people) are likely to find this interesting.
This might bring in a lot of (young families).

This would be suitable/ideal/enjoyable/good fun for (children).
This would attract people with an interest in (clothes).

See also the Useful language box on page 71 of Unit 6.

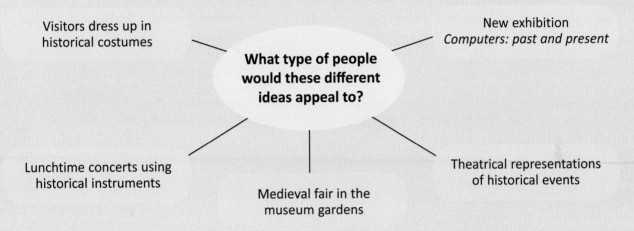

Visitors dress up in historical costumes

New exhibition
Computers: past and present

What type of people would these different ideas appeal to?

Lunchtime concerts using historical instruments

Theatrical representations of historical events

Medieval fair in the museum gardens

2 Now you have about a minute to decide which two ideas would be most successful in attracting new visitors.

The Useful language box on page 120 of Unit 9 contains expressions you could use here for referring back to your discussion in exercise 1.

3 ⦿ 2.39 Listen to Christina and Paolo doing Part 3 and answer the following questions.

1 How does Christina encourage Paolo to talk in the first task in Part 3?
2 Which two activities do Paolo and Christina choose in the second task in Part 3?

Part 4: Further discussion   Total time: 4 minutes

1 Discuss the following questions with your partner.

- What do you think makes a good museum?
- How could the teaching of history in schools be improved?
- Do you agree that learning about the past is important for our future?

- What was the most important moment in the history of the twentieth century?
- What has been the most important moment in your life so far?
- What items from our lives today will be in the history museums of the future?

2 ⦿ 2.40 Listen to Part 4 and answer the following questions.

1 How well do Christina and Paolo interact with each other:
  a in the first half of Part 4?
  b in the second half of Part 4?
2 Who helps the interaction more, Christina or Paolo?

A video of the Speaking test covered in this unit can be found on the Ready for First Practice Online website.

Don't forget!

Develop your answers, justifying your opinions and giving examples if necessary.

Interact with your partner, listening and responding to each other's comments.

Vocabulary 1: The Arts

1 Both words in each of the pairs below can be used in combination with one of the words in the box. Write an appropriate word from the box in each of the spaces. There is an example at the beginning (**0**).

> novel   opera   ~~concert~~   painting   stone   classical   gallery

0 open-air   _concert_   **1** _____   ballet   **4** portrait   _____
jazz   music   art

                                   2 _____   singer   **5** abstract   _____
                                                   house   priceless

                                   3 _____   sculpture   **6** detective   _____
                                                   statue   historical

2 Which people do you associate with each of the following areas of the arts?

> theatre   music   literature   art   opera   ballet   sculpture

Example:
Theatre: *actor, actress, director, cast, playwright, audience*

Check your answers in the Wordlist on page 208.

Reading and Use of English | Part 6

Gapped text

1 ◯ Look at the work of art in the photograph and discuss the following questions.

What type of person might want to own such a work of art?
Where might they put it on display?

2 You are going to read an article about British artist Damien Hirst, who created the work in the photograph. Six sentences have been removed from the article. Choose from the sentences **A–G** the one which fits each gap (**1–6**). There is one extra sentence which you do not need to use.

The most successful living artist

Have you ever thought, 'I wish I could be an artist'? Don't give up hope. Damien Hirst nearly failed his art A Level at school and his work now sells for millions.

Controversial British painter Damien Hirst is generally considered to be the most successful artist alive, thanks to the huge prices paid for his work. Hirst changed the face of contemporary art in the 1990s with his *Natural History* series, in which dead animals are preserved in formaldehyde and displayed in glass cases.

The first of these, his four-metre shark entitled *The Physical Impossibility of Death in the Mind of Someone Living*, fetched an incredible £6.5 million when it was sold to an unnamed American collector. **1** After that came a string of similarly provocative works, which included a pickled lamb in *Away from the Flock*, as well as dissected cows and rotting animal carcasses.

2 Animal rights activists objected strongly to his *Amazing Revelations*, a triangular collage made of thousands of dismembered butterfly wings. In 1994, *Away from the Flock* became the focus of attention when Mark Bridger, an artist from Oxford, poured black ink into the tank containing the dead lamb. However, Bridger claimed he was contributing to the artwork, not protesting against it and he renamed it *Black Sheep*.

The controversy surrounding Hirst's work inevitably raises the question of whether or not it constitutes art. For some, there is absolutely no doubt: he has been described as 'a genius' and 'a pioneer of the British art movement'. Others have a very different view. When Hirst won the prestigious Turner prize in 1995, a Conservative politician writing in *The Sun* newspaper asked: 'Have they gone stark raving mad?' **3**

But there are also many people within the art world who have attacked and ridiculed the artist, accusing him of producing work which is exaggerated and silly. **4** He, too, has used the word 'silly' to describe his spin paintings, a series of works created by dropping paint onto a spinning canvas. 'You do turn round after a few years and look at your stuff and you think it's embarrassing,' he confessed at an exhibition in 2005. 'Certainly everything you make is not a masterpiece.'

He also freely admits to using assistants to do most of his spot-paintings, which consist of rows of randomly coloured dots. Of the 500 or more such works produced, he is said to have painted only five himself. **5** And indeed, there is nothing new about artists getting others to do some of the work for them: Rembrandt, for example, had very large workshops with pupils to help him, and they had to pay for the privilege.

In recent years Hirst has branched out and taken on new challenges. He has made short films, opened a restaurant, set up a publishing company and even recorded a pop music single. **6** But of course, it is his art for which he will be best remembered, and like it or not, it continues to sell.

A Indeed, the tabloid press is one of Hirst's strongest critics.

B Entitled 'Vindaloo', it reached number two in the UK charts in 1998.

C The work caused a sensation when it was first shown in 1992 and quickly became a symbol for the circle known as the Young British Artists, or YBAs.

D In defence of this practice he is quoted as saying, 'Architects don't build their own houses.'

E *Mother and Child Divided*, a cow and calf cut in half, certainly fits this description.

F Predictably, the artist has come in for criticism for his use of real animals.

G Surprisingly enough, though, Hirst seems to agree with some of this criticism.

⬤ Reacting to the text

Do you think Damien Hirst's work constitutes art? Why/Why not?

Why do some people pay vast sums of money for artworks? Would you?

Vocabulary 2: Paraphrasing and recording

1 **a** In **1–8** below, complete each gap with **one** word so that the second sentence has the same meaning as the first. The second sentence is taken from the reading text on page 169. There is an example at the beginning **(0)**. **Do the exercise without looking at the reading text on page 169.**

0 Don't abandon hope.

Don't ___give___ **up hope**. [subheading]

1 [Damien Hirst] gave contemporary art a new look.

[Damien Hirst] _____ **the face of** contemporary art. [4]

2 An unnamed American collector bought his four-metre shark for £6.5 million.

His four-metre shark _____ **£6.5 million** when it was sold to an unnamed American collector. [8–10]

3 The controversy surrounding Damien Hirst's work makes you wonder whether or not it constitutes art.

The controversy surrounding Damien Hirst's work _____ **the question of** whether or not it constitutes art. [23–24]

4 Some people have a very clear opinion.

For some, **there is absolutely no** _____. [25]

5 He doesn't mind admitting that he uses assistants to do most of his spot-paintings.

He _____ **admits to** using assistants to do most of his spot-paintings. [42–43]

6 In recent years Hirst has started doing different things and accepted new challenges.

In recent years Hirst has _____ **out** and _____ **on new challenges**. [51–52]

7 There was a lot of interest and excitement when the work was first shown.

The work **caused a** _____ when it was first shown. [C]

8 People have criticized the artist for his use of real animals.

The artist has _____ **in for criticism** for his use of real animals. [F]

b Check your answers in the reading text on page 169. The numbers in brackets refer to the lines in the text; the letters refer to the missing sentences.

2 Paraphrase the following sentences from the reading text and record both sentences in your vocabulary notebook. You do not need to change every word in the sentence. The first one has been done for you.

0 Damien Hirst is generally considered to be the most successful artist alive. [1–2]

Most people think he is the most successful artist alive.

1 Animal rights activists objected strongly to his *Amazing Revelations*. [15–16]

2 In 1994 *Away from the Flock* became the focus of attention. [17–18]

3 He is said to have painted only five himself. [45]

4 There is nothing new about artists getting others to do some of the work for them. [46–47]

5 It is his art for which he will be best remembered. [55–56]

Language focus 1: Hypothetical situations

A Wishes

1 The reading text began with this sentence:

Have you ever thought, 'I wish I could be an artist'?

We use *wish* (or for more emphasis *if only*) to express how we would like things to be different if we had the power to change them.

2 Look at the following sentences and then complete each of the three rules below with words from the box.

  1 I wish it wasn't/weren't so cold here in winter.
  2 If only I had more time to study.
  3 I wish you'd stop interrupting me!
  4 I wish he wouldn't drive so fast.
  5 I wish I hadn't gone to see that boring play last night.
  6 If only you'd told me earlier.

> *would*   the past perfect   the past simple

  a We use *wish/if only* + _____ to express wishes about present states.
  b We use *wish/if only* + _____ to express irritation at other people's actions or behaviour.
  c We use *wish/if only* + _____ to express wishes and regrets about the past.

3 a The following sentence would sound strange. Reword it to make it sound more natural.

I wish I would give up smoking.

  b What is the difference in meaning between these sentences?

I wish she could come to my party on Saturday.
I hope she can come to my party on Saturday.

Check your ideas in section A on page 220 of the Grammar reference and read more about expressing wishes.

4 In **1–5** below, underline the correct alternative in each sentence.

  1 I wish I *could/would/did* remember where I put my glasses.

2 I wish I *don't/didn't/won't* have to do so much homework. I never have any time to myself.
3 The car has broken down again! I'm beginning to wish we *wouldn't buy/didn't buy/hadn't bought* it.
4 I wish they *didn't/would/had* turn their music down next door. I can't hear myself think.
5 If only *you'll listen/you'd have listened/you'd listened* to me! None of this would have happened.

5 In **1–5** below, complete each gap with the correct form of the verb in brackets.

  1 What glorious sunshine! I bet you wish you _____ (be) on the beach right now, don't you?
  2 I wish you two _____ (stop) shouting! You're driving me mad!
  3 It has rained every day of this holiday. If only we _____ (go) to Greece instead!
  4 I can't afford to buy any new clothes. If only I _____ (have) a job!
  5 One minute you want to come, the next minute you don't. I wish you _____ (make) up your mind!

B *It's time* and *would rather*

1 Choose the correct alternative in the following sentences.

  1 I'd rather you *didn't/wouldn't/don't* bring a mobile phone to school.
  2 It's time you *went/will go/go* to bed now.

Check your ideas in sections B and C of the Grammar reference on page 220 and read more about *it's time* and *would rather*.

2 You have decided to spend the day complaining, telling different people how you would like them to change! The people you are going to speak to are:

- your mother or father
- your brother, sister or cousin
- your best friend
- a neighbour
- the leader of your country
- another person of your choice

Write one sentence for each person beginning with one of the following phrases:

I wish you …

It's time you …

I'd rather you …

Then compare your sentences with those that your partner has written. Are you unhappy about any of the same things?

Multiple choice 2.41

1 ⬤ The following animals can all be kept as pets. Look at the list then discuss the questions below.

- ants
- tarantulas
- snakes
- rats

What dangers might there be in keeping these animals as pets?

What conditions do you think they each need to be kept in?

Why do you think some people prefer these animals to more traditional types of pets?

2 You will hear an interview with a pet shop owner. For questions **1–7**, choose the best answer (**A**, **B** or **C**).

1 According to Sally what is the main reason people buy insects and spiders?
 A Cats and dogs are expensive to look after.
 B Owners want to impress their friends.
 C Insects and spiders require little attention.

2 Sally says that ants can teach us the importance of
 A working together.
 B keeping clean.
 C building relationships.

3 Sally says that some children
 A get bitten by the ants.
 B lose interest in the ants.
 C like playing with the ants.

4 What is the main reason Sally gives for not handling the tarantulas she sells?
 A Their bite is deadly.
 B They can easily be injured.
 C They might try to escape.

5 What warning does she give about snakes to potential owners?
 A They can live for a long time.
 B They are difficult to feed.
 C They are very different to other pets.

6 Sally recommends feeding pre-killed animals to snakes because
 A dead animals are more nutritious.
 B dead animals are cheaper than live ones.
 C live animals can harm snakes.

7 What do we learn from Sally about rats as pets?
 A They are very easy to tame.
 B They are social animals.
 C They are only ever active at night.

3 ⬤ Do you think it's right to keep animals such as those mentioned in the listening as pets? Why/Why not?

Which pets have you owned? What advice would you give to someone thinking of buying the same animal?

If you have never owned a pet, which animal would you most like to have? Why?

Word formation: Suffixes *-ible* and *-able*

1   The suffixes *-ible* and *-able* are used to form a number of adjectives; *-ibly* and *-ably* are used for corresponding adverb forms. Can you remember what the underlined word refers to in each of the following examples from the listening?

   a ... can <u>they</u> be handled?   It's not **advisable.**
   b ...<u>they're</u> very **flexible** creatures.
   c So **inevitably** some children start to grow tired of <u>them</u>.
   d ... <u>which</u> can be bought frozen at **reasonably** little cost from pet stores.

2   Add an appropriate prefix and/or suffix to the part of the word in bold in the sentences below. The completed word may be an adjective, an adverb or a noun. Nouns may be singular or plural. There is an example at the beginning (**0**).

   0 This chair is a little   <u>un</u> **comfort** <u>able</u> . I'm going to sit somewhere else.
   1 The weather here is ____**predict**____ : take an umbrella with you, just in case.
   2 You can't touch your right elbow with your right hand. It's a physical ____**poss**____ .
   3 I wouldn't say I was **incred**____ rich, but I'm certainly **comfort**____ well-off.
   4 The hotel management does not accept **respons**____ for the loss of **valu**____ .
   5 We'll have to walk to the village. It's ____**access**____ to cars.
   6 Her written work has improved **consider**____ since she started the course.

3   ⬤ What for you would be the best and worst *imaginable* way to spend a Sunday? Do any of the following describe your last weekend? What did you do?
   unbelievably boring   *reasonably enjoyable*   *remarkably good*   *unforgettable*

Language focus 2: Prepositions and gerunds

1   In Unit 2, you saw that if a verb follows a preposition, the gerund is used. Complete the gaps in these extracts from the listening with a preposition.

   a *Corn snakes and ball pythons ... can sometimes go for months _____ eating.*
   b *But a bite from the species we sell is rather _____ being stung by a bee.*
   c *... you don't have to worry _____ finding someone to feed them while you're away.*

2   Gerunds are also used after phrasal verbs which end in a preposition.

   *An increasing number of animal-lovers ...have **taken to keeping** them as pets.*

   If the subject of the gerund is different to the subject of the phrasal verb, a noun or an object pronoun is added.

   *I can't **put up with you and Alex arguing** all the time.*

   In **1–5** complete each gap with a preposition.

   1 I'm **looking forward** _____ Sam **coming** tomorrow: she's bringing her new puppy.
   2 I've just been made redundant, so we'll have to **put** _____ **buying** a horse for a while.
   3 Raul isn't ready for a new pet yet: he still hasn't **got** _____ his cat **dying** last year.
   4 We've **given** _____ **trying** to teach our dog to do tricks; she's just not interested.
   5 My sister always manages to **get out** _____ **cleaning** the hamster's cage; I'm usually the one that has to do it.

3   A number of linking words also function as prepositions, and can be followed by gerunds.

__Besides being__ more humane for the mice and rats and so on, it's also safer for the snakes.

*__David got__ to the interview on time, **despite the bus breaking down** on the way.*

   Ⓖ Read more about Prepositions with gerunds on pages 220–1 of the Grammar reference.

4   In **1–4**, complete the second sentence so that it has a similar meaning to the first sentence, using the word given. Use between two and five words, including the word given.

   1 Paul eats lots of fried food, even though he knows it's very bad for his health.
   UNHEALTHY
   Paul eats lots of fried food, despite
   _____ it is for him.

   2 Although I threw away a lot of my old clothes, I still don't have much room in my wardrobe.
   RID
   In spite _____ a lot of my old clothes, I still don't have much room in my wardrobe.

   3 I decided not to drive to work, and went there by bus.
   INSTEAD
   I decided to get the bus to work
   _____ there.

   4 Sven missed the meeting because his flight was delayed by three hours.
   RESULT
   Sven missed the meeting as a
   _____ delayed by three hours.

Vocabulary 3: Animals

1 **a** Complete each of the gaps with the names of animals from the box to complete these well-known similes. The first one has been done for you.

bat	bee	fox	lamb	lion	mouse	~~mule~~	owl	ox	peacock

1 as stubborn as a ___mule___

2 as blind as a _____

3 as busy as a _____

4 as cunning as a _____

5 as brave as a _____

6 as proud as a _____

7 as quiet as a _____

8 as gentle as a _____

9 as strong as an _____

10 as wise as an _____

b Do you know any people who could be described using one or more of the similes above? Give details.

Example:

My brother's as stubborn as a mule. Even when he knows he's wrong, he won't change his mind or do things differently. Last weekend, when I asked him to …

2 Complete these expressions using the names of the animals from the box.

bear	cat	dog	fish	fly	frog	horse

1 She's so kind and gentle. She **wouldn't hurt a** _____ .

2 I'm so hungry I **could eat a** _____ .

3 I know you're upset about splitting up with Gary, but **there are plenty more** _____ **in the sea**.

4 My two kids **fight like** _____ **and** _____ all the time.

5 I was so pleased to see him again, I rushed up and **gave him a big** _____ **hug**.

6 I'm sorry I can't speak any louder. **I've got a** _____ **in my throat**.

3 Match each of these groups of nouns to an animal from the box.

bird	cat	fish	horse

a _____
feathers
beak
wings

b _____
gills
scales
fin

c _____
whiskers
paw
fur

d _____
hooves
tail
mane

4 Discuss the following with your partner, giving reasons for your answers. Which of the animals in exercises **1** and **2**:

- makes the best pet?
- is the most useful to humans?
- makes the most noise?

- is the ugliest?
- is the most attractive?
- is your favourite?

Collaborative task

What to expect in the exam

- In Part 3 of the Speaking test, the examiner explains the first task and gives you 15 seconds of silent preparation time. You then have two minutes to discuss the task with your partner.
- At the end of the two minutes, the examiner explains the second task and gives you a further minute to complete it.
- When you do the following Speaking Part 3 tasks, practise keeping to these time limits.

1 Imagine that a school is organizing its annual Careers Day, on which people from different professions inform school leavers about the jobs they do. The jobs below all involve working with animals. Talk with your partner about what you think are the good and bad points about doing these jobs.

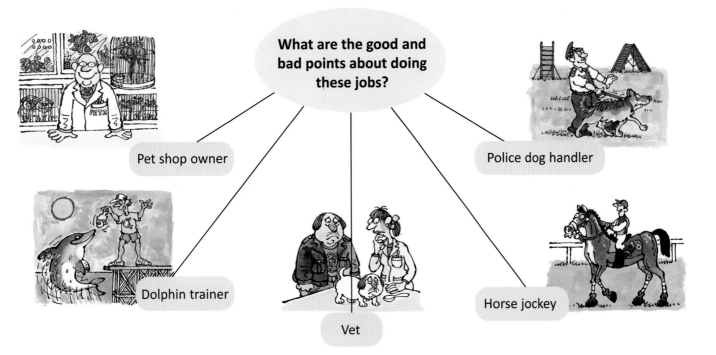

What are the good and bad points about doing these jobs?

Pet shop owner

Police dog handler

Dolphin trainer

Vet

Horse jockey

2 Now decide which two jobs school leavers would be most interested to hear about.

Useful language

One good/bad thing about this job is ...
The best/worst thing about this job is ...
On the plus/positive side, you can/don't have to ...
On the minus/negative side, you can't/have to ...
It must be very rewarding/pleasant/tiring/unpleasant to ...
You have to spend a lot of time grooming/cleaning/working ...

Further discussion

Discuss the following questions with your partner.

- Do you think it's useful to have a Careers Day in schools?
- What else can schools do to prepare young people for the world of work?
- What are the advantages and disadvantages of students having a part-time job while they're still at school?
- What things do you need to think about when choosing a career?
- What can young people in your country do to increase their chances of finding a job?
- Rather than stay in one job after leaving school or college, some people think it's better to try out a number of different jobs. Do you agree?

Listening 2
Part 2

Sentence completion ◉ 2.42

1 ⬭ The photograph shows Ham the chimp, who went into space in 1961. What other animals do you know of that have been into space? Why are they sent there?

2 You will hear part of a radio report about animals in space. For questions **1–10**, complete the sentences.

Animals in space

The first animals to survive a space flight were a pair of **(1)** ....

Able and Baker's spacecraft reached speeds of **(2)** .... miles per hour.

One animal welfare group called for a **(3)** .... every day that Laika was in space.

Pictures of Laika appeared on **(4)** .... in several countries.

The Laika monument shows a dog on a rocket combined with a **(5)** ....

For his 1961 space mission, Ham the chimp received training in **(6)** ....

Ham performed tasks in which he responded to a **(7)** .... by pulling a lever.

Ham's space flight lasted **(8)** .... minutes.

When he was picked up, Ham was given an apple and **(9)** .... as a reward.

Ham answered some letters by sending his **(10)** .... to fans.

3 ⬭ How do you feel about animals being sent into space? Why?

Do you object to animals being used in any of the following situations? Why/Why not?

- medical research
- the cosmetics industry
- zoos
- the entertainment industry (circuses, magic shows, films)

Vocabulary 4: Verbs followed by prepositions

1 Complete each gap in this sentence from the listening with an appropriate preposition.

*Space scientists have been **accused** ____ being cruel to animals and strongly **criticized** ____ carrying out their experiments on defenceless creatures.*

Check your answers in the listening script on page 238.

2 Match each sentence beginning **1–10** on the left with a suitable ending **a–i**. Complete each of the gaps with an appropriate preposition.

Example: 1c

1 I'd like to **thank** you __*for*__   a being late. I'm so sorry to keep you waiting.
2 The cyclist **blamed** me ____   b watching the film. They said it was too violent.
3 I really must **apologize** ____   c sending me those flowers. It was so kind of you.
4 I'm always being **told off** ____   d swearing, try fining them for using bad language.
5 Sue can't **forgive** him ____   e causing the accident, but it was his fault, not mine.
6 My parents **prevented** me ____   f driving me home. 'It's too cold to walk,' she said.
7 To **discourage** children ____   g doing my homework with you singing all the time!
8 We **congratulated** Paul ____   h laughing in class. My teachers are far too serious.
9 My aunt **insisted** ____   i leaving her to bring up the children on her own.
10 I can't **concentrate** ____   j passing all his exams. He deserved to do well.

3 **a** Choose four of the sentence beginnings from exercise **2** and write your own ending for each one.

b Read out your endings to your partner, who will try to guess the beginning of each sentence.

4 ⬭ Talk to your partner about the last time you:

- apologized
- were congratulated
- couldn't concentrate
- thanked someone
- were prevented from doing something
- were told off

Writing
Part 2

Email

1 Read the following Writing Part 2 instructions and the sample answer. Comment on the following features in the sample answer, giving examples to support your opinion:

Range of language	Style of the language	Use of paragraphs and linking words
Accuracy	Relevance	Effect on the target reader

You have received an email from your Australian friend, Anna. Read this part of the email and then write your email to Anna.

> My last exam is in June and then I'm going to spend a month in your country. You know how much I like being in the countryside – can you recommend a couple of areas where I could go walking and also see some interesting wildlife?
> Thanks
> Anna

Write your **email** in **140–190** words.

Hi Anna

You must be mad to want to go walking! When I finished my exams last year I spent about a week at home doing almost nothing. It was great. I stayed in bed all morning, played on the computer all afternoon and then went out in the evening. I got a summer job after that so I could pay for my holiday to Greece, where I spent most of the time sunbathing.

Anyway, here are a couple of places you might want to go to during your month here. Firstly, there are the mountains in the north of the country. Lots of people go there in the summer to get away from the city. Personally, I wouldn't want to, because there's nothing to do in the evenings, so I'd find it a bit boring – but you might like it.

Secondly, there's the path that goes along the coast in the south. There are no beaches and it can get a bit windy, so it's not my favourite place. But there are some good views from the cliffs, if you like that kind of thing.

Bye

David

2 Write your own answer to the task in exercise **1** in **140–190** words. Use some of the ideas in the Useful language box below.

Useful language

Walking
a lovely/popular/spectacular/superb **walking area**
coastal/forest/mountain/riverside/rocky/steep **paths**
challenging/circular/gentle/scenic/strenuous **walks**
breathtaking/magnificent/spectacular/stunning **views**

Wildlife
It's a great place to see (birds).
You might catch sight of (a deer).
The area is known for (bears).
Keep an eye out for (bats).
People come here to observe (seals).

Read more about writing emails on page 197.

 **Review**

Word formation

For questions **1–8** read the text below. Use the word given in capitals at the end of some of the lines to form a word that fits in the space **in the same line**. There is an example at the beginning **(0)**. Write your answers **IN CAPITAL LETTERS**.

A record-breaking fish

The world's **(0)** _oldest_ known captive goldfish, named Tish, died	OLD
(1) _____ at home in his tank in 1999. Tish, who had reached the	PEACE
(2) _____ age of 43, was won by seven-year-old Peter Hand at a	REMARK
fair. He **(3)** _____ shared his bowl with Tosh, who died in 1975;	ORIGIN
he also outlived the family's other pets including dogs, rabbits and	
hamsters. When Peter left home his parents took **(4)** _____ for Tish.	RESPONSIBLE
The pet's **(5)** _____ in the *Guinness Book of Records* came when	APPEAR
he turned 41. The normal procedure of counting the microscopic growth	
rings on a fish's scales could not be used to establish **(6)** _____ of	PROVE
Tish's age. This method was **(7)** _____ because he had been kept	RELY
indoors and was unaffected by seasonal changes, so friends of the	
family had to sign affidavits, written **(8)** _____ supporting the	STATE
owner's claim.	

Vocabulary

A The Arts

Complete the gaps in the following sentences with an appropriate word.
The beginning of each missing word has been given to help you.

1 He had a full-length **po**_____ painted of himself.

2 The museum contains several bronze **sc**_____ of animals.

3 I am reading a great **no**_____ at the moment. The author's Canadian.

4 There'll be sixteen groups playing live the weekend after next at the Bletchley
   op_____-_____ jazz festival.

5 You really can't put a value on this Chinese vase. It's **pr**_____ .

6 Shakespeare is England's best-known **pl**_____ .

7 This piece of music is by a famous eighteenth-century German **co**_____ .

8 We went to a marvellous **ex**_____ of contemporary art at the weekend.

B Animals

1 Which animal is being described below?

> This animal lives in small groups. Its sharp claws and teeth are
> used for killing and eating other animals, both small and large.
> It has light brown fur, whiskers on its face and the male can be
> identified by the beautiful golden mane on its head and neck.

2 Now write descriptions of three other animals, without mentioning the name of the
   animal. Use the Wordlist on page 208 to help you. When you have finished, give your
   descriptions to your partner, who will try to guess which animals you have described.

C Prepositions

Complete each gap with **one** word.

1 My dog has suddenly taken _____ barking at six o'clock in the morning. I've tried to stop him, but he doesn't pay any attention _____ me. I've had to apologize to the neighbours _____ waking them up.

2 Our parrot makes such a noise I find it hard to concentrate _____ anything. I blame my husband _____ teaching him to talk. It's 'Pretty boy' and 'Give us a kiss' all day long – he can go for hours _____ stopping!

3 I kept asking my parents _____ a cat, but they were strongly opposed _____ having a pet in the house. Eventually, though, they gave in, and now they both freely admit _____ being pleased they let me have one; they absolutely adore Tiger.

4 When I tell my dog off _____ doing something she knows she shouldn't, instead _____ looking sad and sorry, she jumps up at me and licks me in the face. It's hard not to forgive her _____ being naughty.

Reading and Use of English
Part 4

Transformations

In **1–6** below, complete the second sentence so that it has a similar meaning to the first sentence, using the word given. **Do not change the word given.** You must use between **two** and **five** words, including the word given.

Write the missing words **IN CAPITAL LETTERS**.

1 It's a pity I don't live nearer the school.
  CLOSER
  I wish _____ the school.

2 I regret telling Anne about my new boyfriend.
  WISH
  I _____ Anne about my new boyfriend.

3 I'd prefer you not to wear those jeans to the wedding.
  RATHER
  I'd _____ those jeans to the wedding.

4 He's a good guitar player, and he also has an excellent singing voice.
  WELL
  In addition _____ , he has an excellent singing voice.

5 Because it was so cold, we didn't have a barbecue.
  PREVENTED
  The cold weather _____ a barbecue.

6 We demanded to see the hotel manager.
  SEEING
  We _____ the hotel manager.

Writing
Part 2

Write an answer to **one** of the following in **140–190** words.

1 You have seen this announcement in an English-language magazine called *Pet World*:

FAMILY PETS

Tell us what you think is the best type of pet for a family of busy working parents and young children, giving reasons for your choice.
We will publish the most interesting articles next month.

Write your **article**.

2 Your school wants to decorate the walls of the building with photographs, posters and/or paintings. Write a report for the Principal, suggesting how the walls should be decorated in **two** of the following areas:

- the classrooms
- the library
- the reception area
- the corridors

In your report you should give reasons for your choices.

Write your **report**.

14 Mind your language

Multiple matching 2.43–2.47

1 ⬭ How important is it to learn a foreign language?

In what ways might English be useful to you in the future?

What problems can occur if you do not know the language of a country you visit?

2 You will hear five different people talking about their experiences of learning another language. For Questions **1–5**, choose from the list (**A–H**) what each speaker says about his or her experience. There are three extra letters which you do not need to use.

A I had problems learning the grammar.

B I sometimes used the language to avoid being understood.

C I made more progress on my second visit.

D Going to the cinema helped me learn.

E Hearing things twice worked for me.

F Progress was very slow at first.

G I focused on learning business language.

H Studying abroad brought success.

Speaker 1 ☐ 1
Speaker 2 ☐ 2
Speaker 3 ☐ 3
Speaker 4 ☐ 4
Speaker 5 ☐ 5

3 ⬭ Summarize your experience of learning English in one sentence. Tell your partner, giving more details.

Vocabulary 1: Phrasal verbs with *turn*

1 What is the meaning of the underlined phrasal verb in the following extract from Speaker 4 of the listening?

All three French-owned companies I applied to <u>turned me down</u> at the interview stage.

2 Match each sentence beginning **1–8** with an appropriate ending **a–h**.

1 Why are you two still awake? **Turn**
2 I can't hear it very well. Can you **turn**
3 He seemed very normal, but it **turned**
4 According to this map we have to **turn**
5 It started at 8.00 but Helen didn't **turn**
6 He left port early but was forced to **turn**
7 This small seed will gradually **turn**
8 The exam starts now. You may **turn**

a **back** by rough seas and strong winds.
b **out** that he was wanted by the police.
c **over** the paper and read the questions.
d **off** the light and go to sleep, please.
e **off** the motorway at the next exit.
f **up** the sound a little, please?
g **up** until much later.
h **into** a beautiful rose.

3 Match the eight phrasal verbs with *turn* from exercise **2** to the meanings **(a–h)** below.

Example: 1f

a become known
b increase the volume
c arrive in a way that was not planned
d turn a page to see the other side

e leave one road to take another
f stop something working
g return instead of continuing
h change or develop into

Language focus 1: Compound adjectives

1 A compound adjective is one with two or more words joined by a hyphen, as in this example from the listening:

*All three **French-owned** companies I applied to turned me down.*

Here are some more examples. What do you notice about nouns used in compound adjectives after a number?

home-made bread   ***Spanish-speaking*** tour guides
a **four-hour** flight   a **three-week-old** baby

🄖 Read more about compound adjectives on page 221 of the Grammar reference.

2 In **1–5**, complete each gap in **b** with a compound adjective which expresses the same idea as the words in bold in **a**. There is an example at the beginning **(0)** from the listening.

0 I signed up for a language course **which lasted two months**.
I signed up for a ____two-month____ language course.

1 a It takes **five minutes** to walk from the language school to the beach.
  b The language school is a _____ walk from the beach.

2 a I want to work in a country **where people speak English**.
  b I want to work in an _____ country.

3 a Police are looking for a teenage girl **with blonde hair** and **blue eyes**.
  b Police are looking for a _____ , _____ teenage girl.

4 a My grandmother, **who was born in Italy**, emigrated when she was three.
  b My _____ grandmother emigrated when she was three.

5 a Teaching children **who behave themselves well** is a pleasure.
  b Teaching _____ children is a pleasure.

3 Use the descriptions to help you complete the compound adjectives. You have already seen these compound adjectives: the numbers in brackets refer to the units in which they appear. There is an example at the beginning **(0)**.

0 clothes which fit closely to your body → **tight-**_fitting_ clothes (1)
1 a phone you do not need to hold → a **hands-**_____ phone (3)
2 work you do for only part of the day → a **part-**_____ job (5)
3 a person who easily becomes angry → a **bad-**_____ person (6)
4 goods marked with the name of the store → **own-**_____ goods (7)
5 a building in very bad condition → a **run-**_____ building (7)
6 a plane journey to the other side of the world → a **long-**_____ flight (8)
7 very strong winds → **gale-**_____ winds (11)
8 a concert which takes place outside → an **open-**_____ concert (13)

4 ⬤ Use compound adjectives to talk about:

• the age of people in your family, *e.g. I've got a seven-year-old sister.*
• the number and duration of lessons each day at your school
• the duration of your last holiday
• the time taken to get from your house to your school/place of work/town centre

Reading and Use of English 1 Part 5

Multiple choice

1 ○ What do you think are the advantages of growing up bilingual? What, if any, are the disadvantages?

2 You are going to read an article on multilingualism. For questions **1–6**, choose the answer (**A**, **B**, **C** or **D**) which you think best fits according to the text.

Don't forget!

Read the text through quite quickly first to get a general idea of the content. As you read, compare your ideas in exercise **1** with those contained in the text.

Two languages good, three languages even better

Naomi is the nine-year-old daughter of Jane and Dug Gray, a translator and stone-mason who live in Finistère, the heart of Celtic Brittany in north-west France. They have opted not to bring up their
5 three children bilingually in French and English, but trilingually, by enrolling them in Brittany's educational system, Diwan, whereby all lessons, bar English and French, are taught in Breton. Around 3000 children in Brittany are educated via this immersion method
10 that has played an important role in the revival of the Breton language.

Jane admits that the decision was controversial: 'Other British parents said: "How dare you do that? Don't your children have enough to take on?"' But
15 she had seen how quickly the girls absorbed French: 'I felt sure they could take in another language.' The girls' father, Dug, admits to being envious of their abilities. 'After 16 years in France, I'm comfortable with the language, but the kids still pick me up on my
20 pronunciation and grammar mistakes,' he says.

It was once thought that forcing a child to learn more than one language could slow academic development but according to Professor Colin Baker, a world expert on bilingualism, the effect is the opposite. The
25 evidence is that bi- and trilingualism actually increases mental capacity and that multilingual children tend to do better at school. 'The latest research shows that in intelligence tests, children with two or more well developed languages have higher scores,' he says.
30 'Bilingual children have two or more words for objects and ideas, so the links between words and concepts are looser, allowing more fluent, flexible and creative thinking.' He adds that children learning languages young also tend to have more confidence and better
35 general communication skills.

Professor Tony Cline is an educational psychologist specializing in language development in children. He says, 'We used to think [the brain] had a limited capacity, like a milk bottle, and that it was impossible
40 to pour two pints of milk into a pint bottle. Now we understand that our brains are capable of making an infinite number of connections; there is no limit to what we can take in.' He concedes that there might be minor disadvantages in having a bi- or trilingual
45 childhood: 'The child sometimes applies the rules of one language to another, and so makes mistakes – but
50 these grammatical 'errors' are soon outgrown, as long as the child is exposed to
55 good models of language.'

It seems that by giving your child the option of becoming multilingual, you are offering
60 them far more than just the acquisition of foreign language. That certainly seems to be the case for the Gray girls. All three are getting top grades at school and are literate in three languages. Naomi has also successfully taken on German, where she is proof that
65 bilingualism increases language-learning aptitude. Says Prof Cline: 'Multilingual children pick up other languages quickly because they have a more flexible approach and are used to handling different forms of syntax, grammar and vocabulary.'

70 Jane thinks her daughters have gained more than just language; they have also gained culturally. In fact, the girls are all enthusiastic about Breton culture: Naomi does extra-curricular Breton step dancing and loves singing in Breton and attending dance evenings
75 known as fest-noz while Nina takes part in the Breton sport of Gouren, a form of Celtic wrestling. Says Prof Baker: 'Multilingual children gain the benefits of multiple sets of literatures, traditions, ideas, ways of thinking and behaving.'

80 And, he stresses, if parents have the opportunity to give their child the gift of another language, they should jump at it. Because in today's global marketplace, on top of all the above, multilinguals are far more employable than monolinguals. 'I find it a great shame
85 that languages don't have a higher place in the classroom in the UK because English is a mainstream language of business but, in the future, that is going to change.'

1 What does the writer say about the school that Naomi attends?

   A All of the lessons are taught in Breton.

   B English and French are not taught.

   C It is helping Breton to regain its popularity.

   D The pupils are all fluent in three languages.

2 Some people criticized the Grays for

   A not encouraging their children to learn French.

   B helping to promote a minority language.

   C not sending their children to a British school.

   D expecting too much of their children.

3 Professor Baker says that, compared to other children, multilingual children

   A work harder at school.

   B tend to do better in examinations.

   C have a less rigid way of thinking.

   D are generally more talkative.

4 Professor Cline uses the example of the milk bottle to illustrate

   A our knowledge that the brain has limitations.

   B how much language can be stored in the brain.

   C the link between brain size and intelligence.

   D a previous way of thinking about the brain.

5 Naomi's experience is presented as evidence that multilingual children

   A enjoy taking part in group activities.

   B are better equipped to learn foreign languages.

   C take advantage of opportunities they are offered.

   D integrate easily into any new cultural environment.

6 What does 'it' refer to in line 82?

   A the opportunity

   B their child

   C the gift

   D another language

⬤ Reacting to the text

In the last line, Professor Baker says 'that is going to change'. What do you think might replace English as the language of business?

How might your life be different now if you had grown up bilingual in your mother tongue and English?

Vocabulary 2: *Make* and *do*

1 Complete the gaps in **1–8** with the correct form of *make* or *do*. Write one or two words in each gap. Here are two examples from the reading.

*Multilingual children tend __to do__ **better** at school.*

*The child sometimes applies the rules of one language to another, and so __makes__ **mistakes**.*

1 I don't always _____ **my homework**; I know I should _____ **more effort**.

2 I think I _____ a lot of **progress** since I started _____ this **course**.

3 I always _____ **sure** I _____ some form of physical **exercise** every day.

4 I'm not very good at _____ **decisions**; it takes me ages _____ **up my mind**.

5 I should _____ some **housework** this weekend; my house **could** _____ **with** a good clean.

6 I'd be very nervous if I was asked _____ **a speech** in public; I'd probably _____ **a mess of** it.

7 I've been _____ **nothing but** work lately; it would _____ **me good to** go out more in the evenings. It certainly wouldn't _____ me any **harm**.

8 I'd love _____ **a job** that **has something** _____ **with** animals; it would be a great way _____ **a living**.

2 ⬤ Discuss how true each of the sentences in exercise **1** is for you.

Language focus 2: Expressing purpose

A *In order to*, *so as to* and *so that*

1 The full infinitive or *in order to* + infinitive can be used to show the purpose of an action.

Professor Cline uses the example of the milk bottle **to illustrate** *a previous way of thinking about the brain.*

She studied another language **in order to make** *herself more employable.*

In order to can also be used in the negative:

I set two alarm clocks **in order not to oversleep**.

So as (not) to + infinitive is another possibility.

He left work early **so as not to miss** *his daughter's birthday.*

2 *So (that)* + a clause is yet another way of expressing purpose. Look at the following examples and decide which verb forms are used after *so (that)* to refer to the future and which verb forms are used to refer to the past.

  1 I turned the light on so I could see what I was doing.
  2 Put your bag by the door so that you don't forget it when you leave.
  3 I'm going to buy a phrase book so I can at least order a coffee in Polish.
  4 I wore my raincoat so that I wouldn't get wet.
  5 I've put an extra blanket on your bed so that you won't get cold again tonight.

  Check your ideas in the Grammar reference on page 221 and read more about expressing purpose.

3 Complete the following sentences in an appropriate way.

  1 We've decided to get my grandmother a computer so that …
  2 We're going to get to the concert two hours before the start in order …
  3 I'm taking the *First* exam so …
  4 I pretended to be ill so …
  5 She moved house in order …
  6 He went up the stairs very quietly so as …
  7 I'm going to do my homework as soon as I get home so …

4 Think of three reasons for each of the following. Use clauses of purpose in your answers.

Why do people:
- go to nightclubs?
- do dangerous sports?
- take exams?
- learn languages?
- get married?
- support football teams?

Example:

People go to nightclubs … **so as to** *meet new people.*
                  in order to *have a good time.*
                  so that *they can dance.*

B *In case*

1 *I'll take my credit card* **in case I run out** *of cash.*

The first action (taking the credit card) is done to prepare for a possible situation or problem in the future (running out of cash). When *in case* is followed by the present simple, it has a future meaning.

To refer to past situations we use *in case* + the past simple.
I wore my raincoat **in case it rained**.

2 Complete the following sentences in an appropriate way.

  1 Take a spare pen into the exam in case …
  2 We decided not to take the car in case …
  3 You should insure the contents of your house in case …
  4 I'm taking a sandwich to work in case …
  5 My mum gave me some extra money in case …
  6 We've left a key with the neighbours in case …

Roleplay: Expressing purpose

1 Work in pairs. Decide who is student A and who is B and follow the relevant instructions.

Student A

You are a rather fussy, over-protective parent whose teenage son/daughter is going away on a one-week camping trip with some friends. It is the first time he/she has been away on holiday without you, and you are going to give advice on what items he/she should take. Write down eight things which you consider to be essential for the trip, together with your reasons. Use the expressions above (*so that*, *in case*, etc). Use the prompts in the box below to help you.

Student B

You are a teenager who is about to go on a one-week camping trip with a group of friends. Your parents always worry too much and one of them is going to give you lots of advice about what to take. You just want to have a good time, so you're not interested in boring details. Write down at least eight items you want to take on the trip, together with your reasons. Use the expressions above (*so that*, *in case*, etc). Use the prompts in the box below to help you.

food	drink	cooking equipment	entertainment
medicines	clothing	emergency provisions	

2 When you have each prepared your list, take it in turns to talk about each of the items, giving your reasons. Try to agree on at least five items which will be taken on the trip.

Who was the most persuasive?

Writing 1
Part 2

Article

Your college magazine has asked you to write an article, giving advice to next year's *First* students about how to prepare for the examination throughout the course.

Write your **article** for the magazine, based on your own experience. Write your answer in **140–190** words in an appropriate style.

How to go about it

When planning your article, consider the following:

- organizing and learning new vocabulary
- studying grammar
- improving reading, listening, writing and speaking skills
- where and when to do homework
- organizing your time
- watching films, reading books, etc

Clauses of purpose might be useful when giving the reasons for your advice.

Examples:

I've read several short stories this year **in order to prepare** for the Reading Paper.

I bought a separate notebook **so that I could** organize new vocabulary.

Don't forget to make reference to your own experience.

Speaking
Part 2

Talking about photos

What to expect in the exam

In Part 2 of the Speaking test, Student A speaks for one minute and Student B has 30 seconds.

When you do the following Speaking Part 2 tasks, practise keeping to these time limits.

1 Look at the photographs below, which show people learning a foreign language.

Student A Compare the photographs and say how difficult you think it is for the people to learn the foreign language.

Student B When your partner has finished, say whether there are any foreign languages, apart from English, that you would like to learn.

> **How difficult is it for the people to learn the foreign language?**

2 Now change roles and do the Part 2 task on page 205.

Multiple choice ⊙ 2.48–2.55

You will hear people talking in eight different situations. For questions **1–8**, choose the best answer (**A**, **B** or **C**).

1 You hear a man talking about the language school he owns.

What does he say is the main reason for the school's success?

A the quality of the teaching

B the cost of the classes

C the location of the school

2 You overhear a young woman talking to a friend about going abroad.

What is the woman concerned about?

A not being fluent in the language

B not finding work straight away

C not knowing anybody

3 You hear a man giving part of a speech.
Who is he?

A a politician

B a sportsman

C the manager of a sports centre

4 You hear a woman talking to her friend about going rock climbing.

How does she feel about it?

A She thinks she'll enjoy it.

B She does not want to do it.

C She is nervous about it.

5 You hear a man talking on the radio.
Who is the man?

A an explorer

B a lorry driver

C an inventor

6 You hear a woman talking to a friend about her husband's work situation.

How does the woman feel?

A annoyed

B worried

C relieved

7 You overhear a man talking to his wife about a friend.

What does the man say about their friend's success?

A He was lucky.

B He worked hard for it.

C He didn't deserve it.

8 Listen to this woman talking to her son on the phone.

What is she doing?

A giving him advice

B criticizing him

C congratulating him

Word formation: Suffixes -*ful* and -*less*

1 Look at the following sentences from sections **6** and **7** of the listening. Complete each gap with the appropriate adjective or adverb form of the word in brackets.

a I wasn't happy about him losing his job. We had a few _____ (sleep) nights.

b _____ (thank) , it all worked out in the end.

c Dave's been very _____ (success), hasn't he? He's done well for himself.

d Fortune always smiled on him - he seemed to pass exams _____ (effort).

Check your answers on page 239.

2 Sometimes both -*ful* and -*less* can be used to form adjectives from the same word.
*You are making too many **careless** mistakes. You need to be more **careful**.*

Sometimes only one of the suffixes may be used.
*I'm going to bed; I feel a little **sleepy**. (**not** sleepful)*
*He made several **unsuccessful** attempts to stop biting his nails. (**not** successless)*

Which of the suffixes -*ful* and -*less* can be used to form adjectives from the nouns in the box? If neither of them can be used, is there an alternative?
Example: event → *eventful* → *uneventful* (**not** eventless)

| event | home | power | skill | pain | point |
| delight | end | harm | peace | stress | thought |

3 Now do the exercise on page 204.

Language focus 3: Ability

1 Look at the following extract from section **8** of the listening on page 186. Complete each gap with the correct form of the verb in brackets. Write either one or two words.

We're very pleased **you** actually **managed (1)** _____ (phone) us. At least **you've succeeded in (2)** _____ (do) something right. ... If **you aren't capable of (3)** _____ (keep) promises then you shouldn't make them ... No, **we can't (4)** _____ (come) and pick you up. You're old enough **to be able (5)** _____ (solve) your own problems now.

2 Sentences **a–e** are all incorrect. Explain why, and correct them by changing the underlined words. You may need to write more than one word.

  a I'd love to <u>can</u> play the piano.
  b Rebecca has never <u>could</u> sing very well.
  c After hours of searching, I <u>could</u> find my glasses; they were in the car.
  d Police have so far been <u>unabled</u> to recover the stolen jewels.
  e Jess seems to be <u>uncapable</u> of keeping her bedroom tidy.

   Check your ideas on page 221 of the Grammar reference.

3 Complete the second sentence so that it has a similar meaning to the first sentence, using the word given. **Do not change the word given**. You must use between **two** and **five** words, including the word given.

  1 The camel can go for long periods without water.
  CAPABLE
  The camel _____ for long periods without water.

2 Management failed to convince the workers to end their strike.
  SUCCEED
  Management _____ the workers to end their strike.

3 Although he can't play any instruments, Steve wants to form a rock band.
  UNABLE
  Despite _____ any instruments, Steve wants to form a rock band.

4 It's a pity I couldn't go to the concert with Leslie.
  ABLE
  I wish I _____ go to the concert with Leslie.

5 He just cannot seem to get to meetings on time.
  INCAPABLE
  He seems completely _____ up to meetings on time.

6 I'm afraid I wasn't able to buy the brand of dog food you asked for.
  MANAGE
  I'm afraid I _____ the brand of dog food you asked for.

4   Tell your partner about something:
  • you could do when you were younger but can't do now
  • you couldn't do when you were younger but can do now
  • you managed to do last weekend
  • you would like to be able to do
  • you don't think you'll ever succeed in doing

Reading and
Use of English 2
Part 2

Open cloze

1 For questions **1–8**, read the text below and think of the word which best fits each gap. Use only **one** word in each gap. There is an example at the beginning (**0**).

Write your answers **in CAPITAL LETTERS**.

> **Don't forget!**
>
> Read through the whole text first, before you begin to complete the gaps.

A happy landing

'This is going to hurt,' thought Adam Potter, as (**0**) _HE_ fell off the side of a Scottish mountain. The climber, (**1**) _____ amazed his rescuers by (**2**) _____ both alive and able to stand up after falling 300 metres, spoke yesterday of his ordeal.

Mr Potter was standing next to his girlfriend when he slipped (**3**) _____ fell over a precipice close (**4**) _____ the peak of Sgurr Choinnich Mor. He tried desperately to slow his fall, grasping at the snow and ice with his hands, and kicking out his feet as he tumbled down, but (**5**) _____ any effect.

The rescue team were astonished to find him standing up at the bottom consulting his map, trying to work (**6**) _____ how to get back to his car. Mr Potter was airlifted to hospital, where he (**7**) _____ found to have three fractured vertebrae and multiple bruises, as (**8**) _____ as having lost several layers of skin from his face. Speaking from his hospital bed, he said: 'I feel extremely, extremely lucky to have survived.'

2 Tell the class about any other survival stories that you know.

Writing 2
Part 2

Letter of application

1 Read the newspaper advertisement below and the letter of application on page 189 and answer the following questions.

Who is the target reader for the letter?

What effect do you think the letter would have on that person?

STUDY GRANTS in the UK

St George's House is offering grants to students wishing to study English in one of their three UK centres this summer. Grants cover:

- two months' tuition fees
- full board and accommodation
- help towards travel costs

Write to the address below, stating why you are applying and how you would expect to benefit from the grant.

The Director
St George's House
13 Southdown Road
York, YO12 4XJ

Dear Sir or Madam

I saw your advertisement in this week's edition of 'Education International' and I would like to apply for a grant to study English in one of your schools this summer.

It would be better for me if it was in your Manchester school as I have a cousin living there, who I have never met. Furthermore, the night life in Manchester is said to be excellent and I would be able to go clubbing every night after class. Manchester would also be a good base for travelling, and I could visit Wales, the Lake District and the birthplace of The Beatles, Liverpool.

I would be grateful if you could put me in a class of no more than six students as it is difficult to learn if the class size is larger. I would particularly like to have help with idiomatic expressions in order to sound more like a native English speaker.

I know you offer free wi-fi Internet access and that would be very useful to me, too. I hope you will consider my application.

Yours faithfully

Ausra Zeronys

2   You are going to write your own application for one of the advertised grants at St George's House. Here is a possible paragraph plan.

   Paragraph 1:   A short opening paragraph stating your reasons for writing.

   Paragraphs 2 and 3:   Give relevant information about yourself, explaining why the grant would be useful and how you would benefit from studying English in the UK.

   Paragraph 4:   A suitable, brief closing paragraph, re-stating your interest in obtaining the grant.

3   Here are four reasons to support your application. Can you add at least four more?

   • You could not afford to study in the UK without the grant.
   • A period of study in the UK would help you to get a job in your own country.
   • A recent illness has caused you to fall behind in your studies.
   • You are interested in learning about British culture and the British way of life.

   What further details could you add to each of the reasons?

   Example:
   You could not afford to study in the UK without a grant.

   Although I have saved up enough money to pay the travel costs, both of my parents are unemployed and would be unable to pay for tuition or accommodation.

4   Now you are ready to write your **letter of application**. Write **140–190** words.

Don't forget!

   • Use formal language throughout the letter.
   • Provide relevant personal information together with an explanation of the different ways in which you will benefit from the grant.
   • The information you give does not need to be true.

189

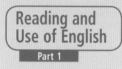

Multiple-choice cloze

For questions **1–8**, read the text below and decide which answer (**A**, **B**, **C** or **D**) best fits each gap. There is an example at the beginning (**0**).

Homestay

When studying a foreign language abroad, a (**0**) _____ majority of students choose 'homestay' accommodation, living with a host family while they (**1**) _____ classes in a language school. Very (**2**) _____, however, once lessons have finished, students speak their mother tongue with other class members of the (**3**) _____ nationality. On a *Homestay Language International* study trip, we ensure total immersion in the target language environment by arranging accommodation and one-to-one tuition in your teacher's home, (**4**) _____ you are surrounded by the language at all times.

As you are the (**5**) _____ student, you learn at your own pace, and lessons are tailor-made to (**6**) _____ your individual interests and objectives. You will also have the chance to (**7**) _____ fully in your host teacher's family and social life, including trips to places of interest in the local area. All our teachers have a university (**8**) _____ and a relevant teaching qualification, and most have spent time abroad so understand the needs and concerns of their student guests.

0	**A** broad	**B** <u>large</u>	**C** grand	**D** high
1	**A** assist	**B** present	**C** attend	**D** go
2	**A** more	**B** often	**C** much	**D** well
3	**A** same	**B** own	**C** personal	**D** equal
4	**A** because of	**B** in case	**C** in order	**D** so that
5	**A** only	**B** alone	**C** unique	**D** lonely
6	**A** agree	**B** adapt	**C** suit	**D** adjust
7	**A** enjoy	**B** involve	**C** participate	**D** include
8	**A** title	**B** degree	**C** career	**D** grade

Compound adjectives

Use the descriptions on the left to help you complete each gap on the right with an appropriate compound adjective. There is an example at the beginning (**0**).

0 a holiday which lasts a fortnight   a ___*two-week*___ holiday

1 a bank note worth twenty pounds   a _____ note

2 a journey which takes three hours   a _____ journey

3 a shirt with short sleeves   a _____ shirt

4 a job which starts at 9 am and ends at 5 pm   a _____ job

5 a train which travels at high speeds   a _____ train

6 a meal with a starter, main course and dessert   a _____ meal

7 a baby girl born the day before yesterday   a _____ baby girl

8 a business which makes money   a _____ business

Transformations

For questions **1–6**, complete the second sentence so that it has a similar meaning to the first sentence, using the word given. **Do not change the word given**. You must use between **two** and **five** words, including the word given.

Write the missing words **IN CAPITAL LETTERS**.

1 You should put an extra jumper on so that you don't get cold.
   ORDER
   You should put an extra jumper on _____ cold.

2 He left early because he didn't want to miss the last bus.
   AS
   He left early _____ the last bus.

3 I've kept the receipt for the shirt because it may not fit you.
   CASE
   I've kept the receipt for the shirt _____ fit you.

4 The workers were offered a three per cent pay increase but they didn't accept it.
   TURNED
   The workers _____ of a three per cent pay increase.

5 You really ought to complain to the manager about the service.
   MAKE
   You really should _____ to the manager about the service.

6 Have you decided where you're going on holiday this year?
   MIND
   Have you _____ where you're going on holiday this year?

Word formation

For questions **1–8**, read the text below. Use the word given in capitals at the end of some of the lines to form a word that fits in the space **in the same line**. There is an example at the beginning (**0**). Write your answers **IN CAPITAL LETTERS**.

The Liet International Song Contest

(**0**) _KNOWN_ to many as 'the alternative Eurovision Song Contest', Liet — **KNOW**
International is an annual festival for (**1**) _____ who sing in any — **PERFORM**
of Europe's 82 minority languages, defined as those which are
(**2**) _____ spoken within a European nation but used today by — **TRADITION**
less than half of its population. The (**3**) _____ , which was first — **COMPETE**
held in 2002 in Friesland, Holland ('liet' is Frisian for 'song'), has proved
very (**4**) _____ , with the twelve finalists now selected from over — **SUCCEED**
60 initial entries. These have included songs in Frioulian, Occitanian,
Romansh, Ladin, Basque, Sami and even Votian, a language spoken in just
two Russian villages and which is now close to (**5**) _____ . Liet — **EXTINCT**
International is clearly a (**6**) _____ vehicle for encouraging artists — **USE**
who sing in minority languages, but also for raising awareness of the
linguistic diversity in Europe and contributing to its (**7**) _____ . — **SURVIVE**
The event does not enjoy the same (**8**) _____ as Eurovision, but it — **POPULAR**
still attracts an estimated television audience of around six million viewers.

Ready for **Writing**

Introduction

For the **Writing** paper you have to complete two different writing tasks in 1 hour 20 minutes: the compulsory Part 1 task and then another from a choice of three in Part 2. For each task you write between **140** and **190** words.

Part 1

For Part 1 you have to write an (**1**) essay on a particular topic. You are given the title of the essay, together with some notes to guide your writing.

Part 2

For Part 2 you write one from a choice of three tasks. The possible task types are

(**2**) an article   (**5**) an email or letter, which could be either

(**3**) a report   **a** formal or

(**4**) a review   **b** informal

Extracts

Decide which writing task type (**1–5**) each extract (**A–F**) is taken from.

A And remember, we can always put you up for the night if you want – just let us know when you're thinking of coming.

B Some people are strongly opposed to keeping animals in cages. Others, however, argue that zoos have many important benefits.

C It is full of action and adventure and the acting is very convincing, but I have to admit, I found the plot rather too predictable.

D I have gained a considerable amount of relevant experience in this field, and consequently feel I would be well suited to the position.

E Have you ever wondered what it would be like to live without a mobile phone for a month? I have, and I'm really not sure I'd be able to survive that long.

F A visit to the Museum of Modern Art is an option worth considering. However, queues can be long, so it is advisable to buy your tickets online before you go.

Register

1   The following comments were made about extracts similar to those above. Circle the appropriate alternative and match each sentence to the feature of language which is being commented on.

    1 The use of 'can't' and 'isn't' show that the letter is *formal/informal*.   **a** phrasal verbs

    2 'Furthermore' is a very *formal/informal* word.   **b** question forms

    3 'Own up' is a more *formal/informal* way of saying 'confess'.   **c** punctuation

    4 An exclamation mark would not be used in *formal/informal* writing.   **d** contractions

    5 'Could you possibly tell me what time it starts?' sounds quite *formal/informal* to me.   **e** linking words

2   Now look at extracts **A–F** again and decide whether the register in each one is formal, informal or neutral. Give reasons for your decisions, commenting on the language used.

Example:

Extract A is informal. There is a contraction and a phrasal verb, 'put up', is used. Starting a sentence with 'And' is informal, and so is the use of the dash.

Marking

When marking answers for the **Writing** paper, examiners consider the features in the box. Match each feature to the general advice and information in **a–f** below. The first one has been done for you.

> Content   Register   Accuracy   ~~Range~~   Organization and cohesion

1 _Range_

a Use a variety of grammatical structures and vocabulary appropriate to the task.

2 _____

b Check that your answer addresses all the points in the task.

3 _____

c Write in clear paragraphs of a suitable length.

d Ensure the content is logically ordered and ideas are connected using appropriate linking words and expressions.

4 _____

e Consider the task and the target reader, and decide whether the language of your answer should be formal, neutral or informal.

5 _____

f Avoid making too many mistakes, particularly basic ones or ones which prevent understanding.

Planning and checking

The sentences below show the stages to follow when planning and checking your written work. Match each stage **1–6** below to the piece of general advice in **a–f** above to which it corresponds.

Example: **1 b**

1 Read the task at least twice, underlining key information and requirements.
2 Pay particular attention to the person or people for whom your piece of writing is intended.
3 Make a list of ideas for your answer, then select the best ones and arrange them into logical groupings. This is your basic plan.
4 Note down words and expressions which might be suitable for linking your ideas.
5 Write down relevant words, collocations and structures which you might be able to include in your answer.
6 When you have written your answer, check spelling, punctuation and grammar.

Part 1: Essay

Type one

In the model answer below, **both sides of the argument are considered**, before a conclusion is reached in the final paragraph.

In your English class you have been discussing the role of technology in the home.

Now, your teacher has asked you to write an essay.

Write an essay using **all** the notes and give reasons for your point of view.

Write your **essay** in **140–190** words.

Model answer

Essay question

Do you agree that modern domestic appliances have improved the quality of our lives?

Notes

Write about:

1 effect on household chores

2 time saved for other activities

3 .... (your own idea)

---

a general introduction

{ Have domestic appliances improved the quality of our lives? Nowadays, many people have a wide range of appliances and devices in their home, all of which are designed to make life easier. However, they also have some disadvantages.

positive aspects (point 1 of Notes)

{ On the one hand, they have reduced the amount of time required to complete domestic chores. Cleaning and ironing, for example, can be done far more quickly and efficiently than fifty years ago. In addition, some inventions have meant that certain tasks no longer have to be performed. Washing up is almost extinct in households with a dishwasher, and thanks to the microwave, cooking is no more than pushing a button.

negative aspects (points 2 & 3 of Notes)

{ On the other hand, some modern technology has made our lives less interesting than before. Food which has been taken from the freezer and heated in a microwave is not as tasty as fresh food cooked in a conventional oven. Moreover, the reason many people buy these labour-saving devices is to enable them to spend more time working, which does not necessarily make them happier.

conclusion, summarizing opinion

{ To sum up, although technology has made life easier in the home, it has not improved the overall quality of our lives.

appropriat formal styl

use of link words and phrases

Essay question

Some people think that school does not prepare students adequately for real life. Do you agree?

Notes

Write about:

1 the content of lessons

2 social relationships

3 .... (your own idea)

Task

In your English class you have been talking about education in schools in your country.

Now, your English teacher has asked you to write an essay.

Write an essay using **all** the notes and give reasons for your point of view.

Write your **essay** in **140–190** words.

Useful language

Saying what people thin

Some/Many people feel that .
Others argue that ...
Another point of view is that
It is sometimes said/claimed t...
It is widely believed that ...
It is generally agreed that ...

Part 1: Essay

Type two

In the model answer below, **only one point of view is considered**. This is clearly stated in the first paragraph and supported with reasons in the subsequent paragraphs.

In your English class you have been talking about relationships with family and friends.

Now, your English teacher has asked you to write an essay.

Write an essay using **all** the notes and give reasons for your point of view.

Write your **essay** in **140–190** words.

Model answer

Essay question

Is it better to go on holiday with family or friends?

Notes

Write about:

1 which is cheaper

2 which is more fun

3 .... (your own idea)

---

introduction, ...ting opinion

> Is it better to go on holiday with family or friends?
> Provided there are reasonably strong and healthy relationships between parents and children, it is my opinion that a family holiday has more advantages than one with friends.

first reason ...t 1 of Notes)

> To begin with, it is much more economical to spend your holiday with your family, particularly if you are a teenager. Parents are happy to pay for most almost everything, enabling their children to do things they would not be able to afford to if they were with friends.

...econd reason ...t 2 of Notes)

> Secondly, even though the two types of holiday are very different, you can have just as much fun with your family as with your friends. Parents and children may not always agree on what to do each day, but this is also true between friends.

third reason ...t 3 of Notes)

> Finally, an important advantage of having fun with your family is that it helps to strengthen relationships between the different members. In their busy lives, they have little time to spend with each other; a holiday helps bring everyone together in a relaxed situation.

conclusion, ...ating opinion

> In conclusion, whilst time spent away with friends can be very enjoyable, a holiday spent with the family has a much more beneficial effect.

appropriately formal style

use of linking words and phrases

Task

In your English class you have been talking about the effects of fame.

Now, your English teacher has asked you to write an essay.

Write an essay using **all** the notes and give reasons for your point of view.

Write your **essay** in **140–190** words.

Essay question

Is it better to be famous or unknown?

Notes

Write about:

1 money

2 friends

3 .... (your own idea)

...ays

...ressing your opinion

...sonally feel that ...

...nly believe that ...

...tly/fully agree that ...

...y opinion ...

...personal view is that ...

...page 39 of Unit 3 for linking
...ces.

Part 2: Article

You see this announcement in an international magazine.

MY IDEAL JOB

We're interested to know what jobs people would most like to do. Write us an article telling us what your ideal job would be and why.

The best articles will be published in next month's magazine.

Write your **article** in **140–190** words.

Model answer

interesting title to attract reader's attention

opening sente relevant to titl

<u>Working with wildlife – naturally!</u>

<u>What else would a zoology student and keen nature photographer possibly want to do?</u> Office jobs are dull, sales jobs are stressful and industry is out of the question. The ideal job for me is that of a warden on a nature reserve.

direct question and statement addressed to t reader

a lively informal style throughout the article

<u>Can you imagine being outside all day, surrounded by nature and wildlife?</u> You would hear the sound of birdsong rather than the noise of traffic, smell flowers and trees instead of exhaust fumes and cigarettes, and see peaceful rivers, not busy roads. <u>You have to admit</u>, those are wonderful working conditions.

Importantly, with a job like this, I would be doing something I believe in, helping to preserve the environment for future generations. <u>And</u> although I'd be far from built-up areas and large populations, I would still have contact with people, teaching visitors to the reserve about nature conservation.

informal linking devices

Of course, it's not the best-paid job in the world. <u>But</u> I'd probably be able to afford to rent a small cottage with a cosy fireplace and a vegetable garden. It's not everybody's idea of luxury, but <u>personally, I couldn't imagine anything better</u>.

a closing comment

Task

Either: **a** write your own answer to the task above in **140–190** words;

or **b** answer the following question.

You see this announcement in your school's English-language magazine.

Write your **article** in **140–190** words.

MY IDEAL EVENING OUT

We'd like to hear about your ideal evening out. Where would you go, who would you go with and what would you do?

Write us an article answering these questions and giving your reasons. We'll print the three most interesting articles in next month's magazine.

Useful language for articles

Involving the reader	Attitude adverbs	
Can you imagine ...?	*Naturally, ...*	*Importantly, ...*
Have you ever ...?	*Personally, ...*	*(Not) surprisingly, ...*
How would you feel if ...?	*Interestingly, ...*	*Worryingly, ...*
Did you know that ...?	*(Un)fortunately, ...*	
Just think ...		
You have to admit ...		

Part 2: Email and letter

This is part of an email you receive from your English friend, Emma.

> It was a brilliant holiday, but my health and fitness have suffered. Too many ice creams and not enough exercise! You're the healthiest person I know – can you give me some advice on how to get fit and healthy again?
> Thanks
> Emma

Write your **email** in **140–190** words.

Model answer

brief, relevant opening paragraph

Hi Emma

Thanks for your email. It sounds as if you had a good time on your holiday – perhaps a little too good! You definitely need to change some of those bad habits you picked up.

language for giving advice

Firstly, <u>you should</u> do some regular physical exercise. <u>If I were you, I'd</u> go jogging at least three or four times a week. You live in a beautiful area with lots of lovely country paths, <u>so</u> there's no excuse for not getting out and going for a run. It's <u>also</u> a good idea to leave the car in the garage and walk to the shops <u>instead</u>. They're not far from your house, and you'll be surprised how much better you'll feel as a result.

use of linking words

And as I'm sure you realize, you should also change your diet. Try <u>cutting down on</u> fried food, butter, cheese and fatty meat — and <u>cut out</u> ice creams completely! Getting fit and healthy takes time, so be consistent and don't <u>give up</u> after just a couple of weeks.

use of phrasal verbs

appropriately informal style

I hope that's useful. Good luck and let me know how you get on.

All the best

David

appropriate ending

Useful language for informal emails and letters

Beginning the email/letter

Thanks for your email/letter.

It was great/lovely to hear from you.

(The holiday) sounds wonderful/terrible.

Giving advice and making suggestions

If I were you, I'd/I wouldn't (take some board games).

Make sure you (take a pack of cards).

You could/should try (eating more fruit).

It's (not) a good idea to (go on your own).

It's best (not) to (do too much).

Ending the email/letter

I hope that's useful/helpful.

Let me know (what happens).

Hope to see you/hear from you soon.

Closing phrases

All the best   Best wishes

Bye for now   (Lots of) love

Task

This is part of an email you receive from your English friend, Simon.

> I won't be here next week, as I've rented a holiday cottage with some friends near the coast. Unfortunately, it looks as if it's going to rain a lot, so we want to take some games with us to play in the house. Can you suggest any? How do you play them?
> Thanks
> Simon

Write your **email** in **140–190** words.

Part 2: Letter of application

You have seen this advertisement in an international magazine.

Write your **letter of application** in **140–190** words.

UK SUMMER CAMPS

Helpers required to work on one of our UK Summer Camps. Applicants should be hard-working, energetic and able to organize activities for young children in these areas:

- workshops
- sports
- outdoor pursuits
- indoor and outdoor games

Write to the director, Mrs Simpson, giving your reasons for applying and saying why you would be suitable for the job.

Model answer

introduction

Dear Mrs Simpson
I would like to apply for the job of Camp Helper as advertised in this month's issue of 'International Student'.

reasons for applying

I like being with children very much and I would certainly enjoy the challenge of working with them on one of your camps. <u>Moreover,</u> I have just finished school and in October I will be starting a degree course in English. I am <u>therefore</u> very keen to improve my language skills in an English-speaking country <u>before</u> I go to university.

use of link words

relevant skills and experience

There are a number of activities I could organize for the children. My interests include basketball, tennis and orienteering, and I also play the guitar and compose my own songs. For the past seven years I have attended summer camps in my country with the scouts, and last year I helped to run a number of events, including an orienteering competition and a kite-making workshop.

appropriate formal style

personal qualities and suitability for the job

I feel I have the necessary patience and energy to make a positive and enthusiastic contribution to your camps and I hope you will consider my application favourably.

<u>I look forward to hearing from you.</u>
<u>Yours sincerely,</u>

appropriate ending

Costas Sergis

Useful language for letters of application

Beginnings and endings

Dear Sir or Madam and *Yours faithfully*

Dear Ms Bentley and *Yours sincerely*

Reason for writing

I saw/have seen your advertisement in ...

I am writing to apply for the job/position of (a shop assistant) ...

I would like to apply for a grant to study/for ...

I would like to volunteer to work with (the elderly) ...

Describing skills and experience

I have (a great deal of/some) experience of (looking after animals).

I spent (two months) working as (a kitchen assistant).

I have excellent communication/computer/ organizational skills.

I have a good knowledge of (first aid/French/ website development).

Personal qualities and suitability

I have a/an friendly/sensitive/easy-going/ enthusiastic nature.

I feel I have the necessary (patience) and (energy) for the job.

I am confident I would be well suited to the job.

I believe I am an ideal candidate for a grant/the job.

Closing remarks

I hope you will consider my application.

I look forward to your reply/hearing from you.

Task

You have seen this advertisement in an international magazine.

Coastal Campsites require

- Reception Assistants
- Bar and Restaurant Staff
- Swimming Pool Attendants
- Entertainers

to work in the UK on our busy, five-star campsites this summer. Applicants must have a reasonable command of English and be willing to work long hours.

Write to the director, Mr Peabody, and explain why you would be suitable for the job.

Write your **letter of application** in **140–190** words.

Part 2: Report

A group of elderly tourists will be spending a morning in your town as part of a ten-day tour of the region. The local tourist office has asked you to write a report for the group leader, suggesting ways in which the tourists might spend the morning. You should give advice on sightseeing and shopping, as well as information on where they could have lunch.

Write your **report** in **140–190** words.

Model answer

a suitable heading for each section of the report

a range of language for giving advice

conclude with summarizing comment and/or final recommendation

Introduction

The aim of this report is to give suggestions to a group of elderly tourists on how to make the most of their morning in Roxburgh.

Sightseeing

The group might like to begin the morning with a visit to the sixteenth century church, with its impressive stained-glassed windows. Within easy walking distance of the church is the Roxburgh Folk Museum, containing numerous exhibits which show what life was like in the town in former centuries.

Shopping

For those who would like to go shopping, the farmers' market in the main square is an option worth considering. A wide choice of fresh, organic produce is on sale, together with locally made cheeses, bread and wine. The square also contains a number of interesting pottery shops, some of which offer discounts to senior citizens.

Lunch

After a busy morning, lunch in one of the reasonably priced restaurants on the seafront is to be recommended. Non-vegetarians should try one of the many fresh fish dishes for which Roxburgh is famous.

Conclusion

Although the group is only in Roxburgh for a short time, everyone is guaranteed a warm welcome and a memorable morning.

summarize the aim of the report without copying the wording of the question

a variety of words and phrases to describe amounts and quantities

a consistent style, in this case formal

Task

A group of foreign teenage students on an exchange programme in your region is planning to visit your town for an afternoon and evening. You have been asked to write a report for the leader of the group, suggesting ways in which the students might spend their time in your town. You should give advice on places to go for shopping and entertainment, explaining why you recommend these places.

Write your **report** in **140–190** words.

Useful language for reports

Giving advice and making suggestions

I would recommend/advise them to (go to the shopping centre).

I suggest you/they (shop for clothes at 'RHN').

The best place for (music) is ('Spins').

You/They should/really must/are advised to (go to 'Aquaworld').

(A visit to the zoo) is an option worth considering.

(A boat trip) is a must/to be recommended.

It is advisable/a good idea to (book in advance).

Describing amounts or quantities

a wide range/selection/variety of (clothes shops)

a large number of (restaurants)

a great deal/large amount of (litter)

plenty of/several/many/numerous (parks and gardens)

Talking about facilities

The shopping/sports/cultural/leisure/ restaurant etc facilities are ...

... excellent/outstanding/second to none.

... adequate/reasonable.

... poor/inadequate/basic.

Part 2: Review

You have seen this notice in an English-language magazine called *Stageshow*.

> Have you been to see a musical, a concert, a circus, a comedian or any other kind of live show recently? If so, write us a review, telling us what you did and did not enjoy about the show and whether you would recommend it to other people.

Write your **review** in **140–190** words.

Model answer

Wizard Warren Whizzbang

I had a truly magical evening when I went to see Warren Whizzbang with my ten-year-old nephew last month. It was the first live magic show I had been to, and it won't be my last. *(introduction, including a general opinion)*

Warren started the show with a few of the typical tricks you often see on television, but it was so much more <u>impressive</u> to see them performed live. The audience watched <u>open-mouthed</u> as he made a variety of objects disappear, turned rabbits into birds and seemed to cut his assistant in half. *(a range of adjectives)*

The most <u>entertaining</u> part of the show came when he invited members of the audience onto the stage. We couldn't stop laughing as he produced pencils from people's ears and mice from their pockets. It was absolutely hilarious. *(positive points about the show)*

The card tricks were a little disappointing, <u>mainly because</u> it wasn't always easy to see what was happening. My nephew and I both lost interest at this point, <u>although</u> fortunately, this section of the show was quite short. *(negative point about the show / use of linking words and phrases)*

Whatever your age, Warren Whizzbang is definitely worth going to see, even if you are unimpressed by magic on the television. The live experience is simply unforgettable. *(recommendation)*

Useful language for reviews

Giving information about a film, TV series, play or book

It is set in (Wales) in (the 1990s).

It tells the story of (a family in crisis).

The main character is (Owen, a miner).

It stars (Paul Fairburn) as (Owen).

Giving an opinion

One of its strengths/weaknesses is …

It is full of humour/action/suspense.

The (acting) is outstanding/disappointing.

The best/worst part of the (play) is when …

Making a recommendation

It is definitely worth seeing.

I would recommend it to teenagers.

It will appeal to (anyone interested in sport).

(Young children) are sure to enjoy it.

Task

Either: **a** write your own answer to the task above in **140–190** words;

or **b** answer the following question.

You have seen this notice in your school's English-language magazine.

> **Television reviews needed**
>
> We'd like to hear about a television series you watch regularly. Write us a review, telling us what you enjoy about the series and whether there is anything you don't like about it. Don't forget to say who you would recommend it to.

Write your **review** in **140–190** words.

Additional material

Unit 2
Writing 1: Part 2 Letter of application, page 21

> **How to go about it**
>
> - Write a plan for your letter.
>   *Decide how you are going to answer each of the three questions in the advertisement and make notes. Consider also why you would be suitable as a volunteer. Remember that you can invent information.*
> - Organize your ideas into logical paragraphs.
>   *In addition to an introductory paragraph, you could write one paragraph for each of the three questions in the advertisement.*
> - Write your letter in a formal style.
>   *Some of the formal language in Sandra Agar's letter in exercise 1 on page 21 might be useful.*
> - Check your work for grammar and spelling mistakes.
>
> Read more about writing letters of application on pages 198 and 199.

Unit 2
Writing 2: Part 2 Article, page 27

1 Read this model answer to the writing question on page 27 and answer the questions below.

> *A strange way to enjoy yourself*
>
> *(1) Have you ever seen a smile on the face of a long-distance runner? Running 10 kilometres or more certainly doesn't sound much fun, but this sport is a powerful addiction and once you've started, you'll find it difficult to give it up.*
>
> *(2) So what is the attraction of running? For me, whether I'm working or studying, there is no better way of getting rid of stress. I can think my problems through and at the end of the race I have the answers. And simply completing a half or full marathon increases my confidence and makes me feel on top of the world.*
>
> *(3) If you're thinking of taking it up yourself, don't try to do too much at the beginning. You should set yourself realistic targets and always do warm-up exercises before you run. Also, make sure you buy a good pair of running shoes to protect your knees and back from injury.*
>
> *(4) And don't be put off by the expressions on the faces of the runners – they're enjoying every minute, and so will you!*

2 Match each of these summaries to a paragraph in the article.
   a Benefits of the sport and reasons for liking it.
   b Closing comment.
   c What the sport is and what is special about it.
   d Advice to people who want to do this sport.

3 Who is the article written for (the target reader)?

4 Is it written in a more formal or informal style? Find examples of the following:
   a contractions: e.g. *she's, won't*
   b informal linking words: e.g. *but*
   c direct questions
   d phrasal verbs

5 Match each of the features **1–3** with its purpose **a–c**.
   1 The title   **a** to involve the reader
   2 Direct questions   **b** to encourage the reader to take up the sport
   3 The final sentence **c** to attract the reader's attention

6 Now write your own answer to the question on page 27. Read the How to go about it box on the same page before you begin to write.

Unit 11
Language focus 2: Conditionals, page 144
Student A

1 In **1–4** below you are given the second half of four sentences. For each one write three possible beginnings.

Example:

a *If I could speak English fluently,*
b *If I went to live in the capital,*
c *If my dad asked the right people,*

I'd probably get a good job.

   1 ... I'd probably be extremely popular.
   2 ... the world would be a happier place.
   3 ... I'll never speak to you again.
   4 ... he starts to cry.

2 Read out the sentence halves you have written and your partner will try to guess the sentence halves you were given.

Unit 12
Language focus 4: Reporting verbs, page 157
Student A

1 Tell each other your problems (see below) and give each other suggestions and advice. Use the following structures:

You should ...   *Why don't you ...?*
If I were you, I'd ...   *Try + gerund*

   - I'm finding it difficult to sleep at night.
   - I eat a lot of junk food, because I'm so busy.
   - I'm addicted to the Internet. I spend six hours a day on it.
   - I think someone in this class is stealing things.
   - I get very nervous when I take exams.

2 Change partners and report your conversations using the verbs *suggest, recommend* and *advise*.

Example:

I told Ana I was finding it difficult to sleep at night, and she suggested I should stop eating cheese in the evening.

Unit 3

Listening 2: Part 3 Multiple matching, page 38
Expressions with *as ... as*

1 Complete these sentences from the listening using a word from the box.

far	long	many	soon	well

1 As _____ as having absolutely no interpersonal skills, he has a habit of making changes without bothering to find out what anyone else thinks first. (Speaker 1)

2 I teach maths to as _____ as two hundred students in one year. (Speaker 3)

3 As _____ as it's carefully written, it's fine. (Speaker 3)

4 It's a waste of time as _____ as I'm concerned. (Speaker 3)

5 As _____ as the work's finished, I'm moving straight back to my old room. (Speaker 5)

2 Match each of the completed expressions in **bold** in exercise **1** to a word or expression with a similar meaning from the box.

in my opinion	in addition to	immediately
provided	the surprisingly large number of	

Unit 3

Writing: Part 1 Essay, page 39

Read the following Writing Part 1 instructions and the advice in the How to go about it box.

Your English class has been discussing the role of the Internet in today's world. Now your English teacher has asked you to write an essay.

Write an essay using **all** the notes and give reasons for your point of view.

Essay question
Do we need the Internet to enjoy life to the full?
Notes
Write about:
1 friendships
2 entertainment
3 .... (your own idea)

Write your **essay** in 140–190 words.

How to go about it

- List ways we can enjoy **friendships** with and without the Internet.
  With the Internet, e.g. *social networking sites ...*
  Without the Internet, e.g. *going out with friends ...*
- Now do the same for **entertainment** and one more category (**your own idea**).

- From your lists, select the points you want to include in your essay. Make notes, developing your ideas.
- Decide how you will introduce and conclude your essay.
- Write your essay. Make sure you:
  a organize your ideas and opinions using paragraphs and linking devices.
  b include a range of vocabulary and grammatical structures and avoid repetition wherever possible.
  c write in a consistently formal or neutral style.
- Check your work for grammar, vocabulary, spelling and punctuation errors.

Ready for Speaking
Speaking: Part 2 Talking about photos, page 166

Student A: Look at these two photographs. They show people doing exercise in different places. Compare the photographs and say what you think the people are enjoying about doing exercise in these different places.

Student B: When your partner has finished, say which of these places you would prefer to do exercise in.

What are the people enjoying about doing exercise in these different places?

Unit 8

Vocabulary 1: Sleep, page 101

1 Underline the correct alternative.

1 Do you usually find it easy to *get/fall* **to sleep**?

2 Are you **a light sleeper** or do you **sleep like a** *dog/log*?

3 Do you **sleep** *in/off* at weekends and get up late?

4 Do you ever *take/give* **an afternoon nap**?

5 When do you **find it difficult to** *hold/stay* **awake**?

2 Discuss the questions in **1** above.

Unit 9

Speaking: Part 4 Further discussion, page 120

Following on from your discussion in the Part 3 task on page 120, discuss these questions with your partner.

- What other types of places, institutions or organizations should be considered for a donation? Why?
- Some people say that money can't buy happiness. What do you think?
- How important is it to save money?
- Which types of workers in your country do you think deserve to earn more money? Why?
- Do you think sports stars earn too much money? Why/ Why not?
- Some people think that all students should work part time to earn money. What do you think?

Unit 14

Word formation: Suffixes *-ful* and *-less*, page 186

For questions **1–10** use the word given in capitals at the end of each sentence to form a word that fits in the space in the same sentence. (You may need to form a noun, an adjective or an adverb).

1 This charming cottage has been _____ and lovingly restored. **SKILL**

2 Many accidents are caused by drivers' _____ at the wheel. **CARE**

3 Thank you so much! That's very _____ of you. **THOUGHT**

4 Before I met Erica, my life had been dull and _____. **EVENT**

5 Her doctor reassured her that the operation would be _____. **PAIN**

6 Her most attractive quality is her constant _____. **CHEER**

7 He won't change his mind. It's _____ arguing with him. **POINT**

8 The Government intends to tackle the problem of _____. **HOME**

9 Thousands demonstrated _____ against the education cuts. **PEACE**

10 My dog won't bite; he's perfectly _____. **HARM**

Unit 9

Reading and Use of English 2: Part 2 Open cloze, page 117

- Wind-surfer Nick Dempsey won't wear anything green when he competes.
- Boxer James DeGale puts his left sock and shoe on first before climbing in the ring.
- Hockey player Helen Richardson has to be the last person onto the pitch when the British team goes out to play a match.
- Canoeist Helen Reeves always listens to the same three songs in the same order before competing.

Unit 10

Listening 2: Part 3 Multiple matching, page 136

When children first begin lying, they lie to avoid punishment, and because of that, they lie indiscriminately – whenever punishment seems to be a possibility. A three-year-old will say, 'I didn't hit my sister,' even though a parent witnessed the child hit her sibling. A six-year-old won't make that mistake – she'll lie only about a punch that occurred when the parent was out of the room.

By the time a child reaches school age, the reasons for lying are more complex. Punishment is a primary catalyst for lying, but as kids develop empathy and become more aware of social relations, they start to consider others when they lie. They may lie to spare a friend's feelings. Secret keeping becomes an important part of friendship – and so lying may be a part of that. Lying also becomes a way to increase a child's power and sense of control – by bragging* to assert his status, and by learning that he can fool his parents.

*talking about achievements or possessions in a proud way that annoys people

Unit 11

Language focus 2: Conditionals page 144

Student B

1 In **1–4** below you are given the first half of four sentences. For each one write three possible continuations.

Example:

If I were 10 years older,   *a* *I'd probably be married.*
b *I wouldn't have to go to school.*
c *I'd be able to vote.*

1 If I lived in Britain, …

2 If I wanted to make new friends, …

3 If you help me with my homework, …

4 If it rains this weekend, …

2 Read out the sentence halves you have written and your partner will try to guess the sentence halves you were given.

Unit 14

Speaking: Part 2 Talking about photos, page 185

The following photographs show people who have achieved success in something.

Student A: Compare the photographs and say how much help you think the people needed to achieve their success.

Student B: When your partner has finished, say who you think will remember their success longer.

> How much help did the people need to achieve their success?

Unit 12

Language focus 4: Reporting verbs, page 157

Student B

1 Tell each other your problems (see below) and give each other suggestions and advice. Use the following structures:

You should …   *Why don't you …?*
If I were you, I'd …   *Try + gerund*

- I've got a bad cold.
- I don't like meat, but I'm bored of vegetarian food.
- I need to lose weight fast, but I don't know the best way.
- No one phones me on my mobile phone.
- I want to go to a concert, but I have to go to a wedding.

2 Change partners and report your conversations using the verbs *suggest, recommend* and *advise*.

Example:

I told Diego I had a bad cold, and he suggested I should drink lots of water.

Wordlist

Unit 1

Adjectives for lifestyles
alternative
busy
chaotic
comfortable
exciting
(un)healthy
luxurious
quiet
relaxing
sedentary
simple
stressful

Other lifestyle expressions
American/modern/
   traditional way of
   life
change your lifestyle
lead an active social
   life
private life

Items of clothing
belt
blazer
blouse
boots
bow-tie
(baseball) cap
cardigan
dinner jacket

dress
dressing gown
dungarees
evening dress
fancy dress
(top) hat
helmet
high-heeled shoes
(sports) jacket
jeans
jumper/pullover/
   sweater
overcoat
raincoat
scarf
shirt
shoes
shorts
skirt

slippers
socks
suit
sweatshirt
swimming costume
swimming trunks
T-shirt
tie
tights
top
tracksuit
trainers
trousers
waistcoat

Jewellery
bracelet
brooch
earrings

necklace
pendant
ring

Adjectives: The pattern of clothes
checked
flowery
patterned
plain
spotted
striped

Other adjectives for clothes
baggy
casual
colourful
designer

Wordlist

formal
long-sleeved
loose-fitting
pleated
scruffy
second-hand
shabby
short-sleeved
sleeveless
smart
tasteful
tight-fitting
trendy
(un)fashionable
waterproof
worn out

Materials for clothes
cotton
denim
leather
silk
suede
woollen

Verbs for clothing
dress up as sb/sth
fit
get (un)dressed
go with
match
put on
suit
take off
wear

People
audience
bride
candidate
competitor
doctor
groom
guest
host
invigilator
opponent
patient
performer
spectator
star
witness

Unit 2
Musical instruments
accordion
cello
clarinet
double bass
drum(s)
flute
guitar
harp
keyboards
organ
electric/grand piano
saxophone
tambourine

trombone
trumpet
violin
wind/stringed/
    percussion
    instrument

Music: people
backing vocalist
concert audience
lead singer/guitarist/
    vocalist
rock/folk/rap etc band/
    singer/star
session musician

Playing and performing
a live album/concert/
    gig/performance
a music/rock festival
be in tune
give a concert
have a record in the
    charts
on tour/on stage/on
    the radio
play a tune/a record/a
    track
sing/perform/mime a
    song

Sports
do...
aerobics
athletics
gymnastics

go...
cycling
diving
horse-riding
jogging
running
sailing
skiing
snowboarding
swimming
(wind)surfing

play...
badminton
baseball
basketball
football
golf
handball
hockey
rugby
tennis
volleyball

People
athlete
badminton/baseball/
    basketball *etc* player
competitor
cyclist
diver

gymnast
horse-rider
jogger
runner
skier
snowboarder
swimmer
(wind)surfer

competitor
opponent
participant
peloton
referee (basketball/
    football/rugby)
runner-up
spectator
supporter
team
umpire (badminton/
    tennis/volleyball)
winner

Places
athletics track
athletics/football/
    sports stadium
basketball/tennis/
    volleyball court
fairway
football/hockey/rugby
    pitch
golf course
green
gym
ice-skating rink
lane
motor-racing circuit
ski run/slope
swimming pool

Events
play/take part/compete
    in ...
a football match
a golf/tennis
    tournament
a sporting event
a surfing/swimming
    competition
an athletics meeting
the national/world
    championship

Equipment
badminton/tennis
    racket
baseball/table tennis
    bat
football/rugby boots
goal posts
golf clubs
hockey stick
net
safety helmet
shuttlecock
skiing/swimming
    goggles
skis and ski sticks

Verbs
beat an opponent/
    opposing team
break/hold a record
commit a foul
compete in a sporting
    event
do/play a sport
draw a match/game
go in for a sport
hit/kick/pass the ball
lose a game/match
practise a shot
score a goal/point
take a corner
take place
take up a new sport
win a medal/match/
    competition/game

Unit 3
Technology
charger
compass
device
discman/walkman
digital camera
DVD player
(external) hard drive
landline phone
laptop
hand-held/hands-free
    mobile phone
headset
MP3/MP4 player
netbook
notebook
personal computer
radar
remote control
robot
smartphone
space blanket
tablet
video recorder

Verbs
browse
click on (an icon)
download
email
log in to/out of an
    email account
log on to/off the
    Internet
multitask
plug in/unplug
post (a picture/status
    update)
print out
scan
surf
switch on/off
text
upload

Internet and mobile phones
app/application
browser
chat room
email
instant messaging
    (IM)
operating system (OS)
short message service
    (SMS)
social networking sites
text
textspeak
webpage
website

Expressions with *as ... as*
as far as (I'm
    concerned/I know)
as long as
as many/much as
as soon as
as well as

Unit 4
Types of film
action film
animated film
cartoon
comedy
historical drama
horror film
remake
romance
science fiction film
thriller
western

People and elements of a film
acting
action/opening scene
actor/actress
animation
cast
director
film/movie star
main character
make-up
photography
plot
producer
screenplay
script
soundtrack
special effects
stuntman/woman
supporting role

Other vocabulary
a box office hit
a dubbed/subtitled
    film
a film critic
a good/bad review

give a good/bad
    performance
go to an audition
have a part in a film
the film is set in

Unit 5
Jobs
accountant
air traffic controller
architect
baker
butcher
chef
childminder
civil servant
company director
cook
dustman
electrician
engineer
firefighter
flight attendant
hairdresser
journalist
judge
lawyer
librarian
nurse
photographer
plumber
police officer
politician
receptionist
scientist
secretary
shop assistant
surgeon
teacher
vet
waiter/waitress

Career
apply for a job
get a job
go for an interview for
    a job
look for a job

change career
give up your career
devote yourself to a
    career
start a career

be dismissed/sacked
be made redundant
be out of work/out of
    a job
resign from a job

Earn
earn a good living
earn a high/low salary
earn a lot of money
earn a weekly wage

Work
work as a nurse
work flexitime
work for yourself
work hard

work long hours
work overtime
work part/full time
work shifts

Work: skills
artistic skills
computer skills
language skills
organisational skills
telephone skills

Adjectives to describe jobs
badly paid
challenging
monotonous
responsible
satisfying
stressful
tiring
unpleasant
well-paid

Work: other vocabulary
form a new company
go into business
join a company
run a business
set up a company

a colleague
a recruit
be on/take sick leave
be one's own boss
be promoted
be/go on strike
be self-employed
a temporary job
retire
take time off (work)
working hours

Unit 6
Adjectives for personality
adventurous
affectionate
ambitious
bad-tempered
bossy
brave
calm
caring
cheerful
clumsy
confident
creative
decisive
determined
dull
easy-going

energetic
enthusiastic
even-tempered
fair
foolish
fussy
generous
hardworking
honest
kind
lazy
lively
loyal
mature
mean
miserable
moody
nervous
outgoing
patient
polite
practical
reliable
reserved
responsible
rude
selfish
selfless
sensible
sensitive
shy
silly
sincere
sociable
stubborn
sweet-tempered
talkative
tolerant

Adjectives for hair
curly/dyed/flowing/
    shoulder-length/
    spiky/straight/
    thinning/untidy/
    wavy

be bald/balding
have a beard/
    moustache

Adjectives for eyes
almond-shaped/hazel/
piercing/sparkling

Adjectives for faces
expressive/freckled/
    round/smiling/
    tanned/thin/
    wrinkled

Adjectives for complexion
dark/healthy/pale/
    smooth/spotty

Adjectives for build
fat/overweight/plump
thin/slim/skinny
stocky/well-built

Unit 7
Shops
baker's
bookshop
butcher's
chemist's
clothes shop
department store
florist's
gift shop
greengrocer's
grocer's
hardware shop
jeweller's
local corner shop
newsagent
sports shop
supermarket/
    hypermarket

In a supermarket
aisle
cashier
cash register/till
counter
checkout
end-of-aisle area
receipt
shelf/shelves
shopping basket
shopping trolley

Goods on sale
alcoholic drinks
bakery
confectionery
dairy products
foodstuffs
freezer goods
fresh fruit/vegetables/
    meat/fish
household goods
own-brand products
pre-packed meat
soft drinks
tinned/frozen
    convenience food
toiletries
well-known brands

Shopping: other vocabulary
a bargain
a discount
a (money-back)
    guarantee
a special offer/be on
    offer
ask for a refund
be faulty
be good value for
    money
be nearing/past its sell-
    by date
be on order
buy sth in the sales
buy sth on impulse
charge sb £10
have sth in stock
make a purchase

Places
apartment block
block of flats
building site
caravan site
conservation area
historic site
housing estate
industrial estate
in the city/town centre
leisure centre
local amenities
office block
one-way street
on the outskirts
pedestrian street
rented
    accommodation
residential area
rural area
indoor/out-of-town
    shopping centre/
    mall/street
shopping/sports
    facilities
skyscraper
tower block
within easy walking
    distance

Adjectives for towns and villages
bustling
depressing
dull
leafy
lively
picturesque
pleasant
prosperous
quaint
run-down
shabby
vibrant

Unit 8
Sleep
be a light sleeper
fall asleep
get to sleep
nod off
sleep in
sleep like a log
snooze
stay awake
take an afternoon nap

Travel
to go on a/an ...
cruise
excursion
(long-haul) flight
(bus/car/train) journey
package holiday
(guided) tour
(business/day) trip
voyage
be crowded (with)
be full (of)

Wordlist

be good/great fun
enjoy oneself
go camping
go sightseeing
have a good/great time
pack one's suitcase
relax
stay on a campsite/in a hotel

a brochure
a good/spectacular view
a holiday/ski resort
a souvenir

Unit 9
Ways of looking: verbs
catch a (brief) glimpse of
gaze (dreamily)
glance (quickly)
glare (angrily)
glimpse (briefly)
peer (cautiously)
stare (wide-eyed/open-mouthed)

Unit 10
Crimes and criminals
arson/arsonist
assassination/assassin
blackmail/blackmailer
burglary/burglar
drink-driving/drink-driver
drug trafficking/drug trafficker
espionage/spy
hijack(ing)/hijacker
identity fraud/identity fraudster
Internet piracy/Internet pirate
kidnap(ping)/kidnapper
mugging/mugger
murder/murderer
pickpocketing/pickpocket
robbery/robber
shoplifting/shoplifter
smuggling/smuggler
theft/thief
vandalism/vandal

Crime: verbs
accuse sb of a crime
acquit sb (of all charges)
arrest sb for a crime
burgle a house/an office
deter sb from committing a crime
find sb (not) guilty of a crime
give sb a (two-year) prison sentence
order sb to do community service
order sb to pay a fine
rob a person/bank (of £2000)
sentence sb to two years in prison/life imprisonment/death
steal money/jewellery (from a person/a shop)

Unit 11
Weather
angry-looking/storm/ thick clouds
brilliant/glorious/ warm sunshine
calm/choppy/rough sea
clear/overcast/stormy sky/skies
electric/severe/violent storm
fine/heavy/torrential rain
gale-force/light/strong winds
light/scattered/snow showers

Weather: other vocabulary
be struck by lightning
flash of lightning
gale
gentle breeze
gust of wind
hailstones/raindrops/ snowflakes
it's pouring with rain
thunderclaps
weather forecast

Natural disasters
avalanche
drought
earthquake
flood
hurricane
tidal wave
tornado
volcanic eruption

The environment
air/river/sea pollution
biofuel cars
bottle bank
carbon dioxide/ monoxide
cigarette butts
climate change
conservation area
dog mess
drop litter
dump waste
endangered species
exhaust fumes
face extinction
global warming
greenhouse effect
household waste
natural habitat
nature reserve
nuclear power station
oil slick
ozone layer
plastic containers
preserve wildlife
raise awareness
recycled paper
rising sea levels
toxic effluent
traffic pollution
unleaded petrol

Unit 12
Food and drink
bolt food down
chew food
drink (straight) from a bottle/glass
eat everything up
fizzy/soft/still drink
fussy eater
gulp a drink down
leave food on one's plate
sip a drink
swallow food/drink

Adjectives for food
bitter
bland
creamy
crunchy
greasy
heavy
hot
rich
salty
savoury
sickly
sour
spicy
stodgy
sweet
tasteless
tasty

Illnesses and injuries
black eye
chest pain
cough
earache
ear infection
flu
headache
heart attack
high/low blood pressure
nose bleed
runny nose
sore throat
sprained ankle/wrist
stiff neck
stomach ache
toothache
tooth decay

Health: verbs
bleed
catch a cold
cure sb of an illness
feel sick
give sb a prescription
give sb an injection
have one's arm/leg in plaster
have a temperature
have an operation on a part of one's body
heal
hurt
injure
keep fit and healthy
put a plaster on sth
put sb on antibiotics
recover
take some medicine / painkillers/a pill
take sb's temperature
treat sb for an illness/ injury
wound
wrap a bandage round part of one's body

Unit 13
Art
abstract painting
art collector
art/portrait gallery
artist
exhibition
landscape
painter
portrait
portrait gallery
priceless painting

Ballet
ballerina
ballet dancer
choreographer
classical/modern ballet

Literature
author
(auto)biography
detective/historical/ romantic etc novel
novelist
publisher
short story
writer

Music
cellist/pianist/violinist
classical music
composer
conductor
concert hall
musician
open-air concert
orchestra

Opera
cast
director
opera house
opera singer
soprano
tenor

Sculpture
sculptor
stone/bronze sculpture/statue

Theatre
Act I Scene II
actor/actress
audience
cast
director
performance
play
playwright
rehearsal
stage

Animals
Birds: owl/peacock/ pigeon/sparrow
Farm animals: cow/ goat/lamb/mule/pig/ sheep/ox
Fish: cod/shark/trout
Pets: budgerigar/ cat/dog/goldfish/ hamster/parrot
Insects: ant/bee/beetle/ fly/wasp
Other animals: bat/ bear/fox/frog/lion/ mouse/rat/snake

Parts of animals
Fish: fin/gills/scales/ tail
Bird: beak/feathers/ tail/wings
Cat: claws/fur/paws/ tail/whiskers
Horse: hooves/mane/ tail

Unit 14
The vocabulary for this unit (*turn, make* and *do*) appears in the Workbook in the Lexical phrase list and the Phrasal verb list.

Grammar reference

Unit 1
Habitual behaviour in the present

A The present simple is used for habitual actions or permanent situations in the present.

*I **go** for a run twice a week. She **lives** near the park.*

B Frequency adverbs are used to indicate how often an action occurs. They are usually placed:

1 before the main verb.

*I **always** go to bed before midnight.*

2 after the verb to be or an auxiliary verb.

*She is **very often** late for work.*

*They have **rarely** been seen together.*

3 *Usually, normally, frequently, sometimes, (very/quite) often* and *occasionally* can also be placed at the beginning of the sentence or clause.

***Occasionally** we go out to the cinema, but **usually** we stay in and watch a DVD.*

NB *always, rarely, seldom, hardly ever* and *never* cannot be used in the same way.

4 *Sometimes* and *quite/not very often* can be placed at the end of the sentence or clause.

*Farm vets have to do some pretty unpleasant things **sometimes**.*

*I don't go to the cinema **very often**.*

5 Adverb phrases such as *now and again, from time to time, twice a week* and *every day* are placed at the beginning or end of a clause or sentence, but not between the subject and the verb.

*I see Paul at work **every day** and **from time to time** we have lunch together.*

Alternatives

1 The present continuous + *always* is used to talk about things which occur frequently and which the speaker finds annoying.

*He's **always complaining** about something!*

2 Adjectives can be used as an alternative to *rarely, normally* and *(not) usually*.

*It's **rare/normal/(un)usual** for him to eat meat.*

3 *Tend to* + infinitive is used to make general statements about the habitual actions and situations of groups of people or individuals.

*British people **tend to drink** tea rather than coffee.*

*I **tend not to get up** very early on Sundays.*

4 *Will* + infinitive is used to talk about habitual behaviour. Frequency adverbs can also be added.

*She'**ll sometimes spend** the whole day reading.*

5 *It's not like someone to do something* is used to suggest that the way a person has behaved is not typical of their character.

*I'm surprised Graham didn't send me a card. **It's not like him to forget** my birthday. (He doesn't usually forget it)*

Habitual behaviour in the past

A The past simple is used for regular actions or habitual behaviour in the past, often with a frequency adverb.

*I **hardly ever went away** on holiday when I was young.*

B *Used to* + infinitive is used to refer to past habits and situations which no longer occur or exist now. Frequency adverbs can be used for emphasis and are placed before *used to*.

*We **used to have** a cat, but he died last year.*

*I **always used to walk** to work until I bought a car.*

Note the negative and question forms:

*I **didn't use to like** cheese. Where **did you use to live**?*

NB *use to* cannot express present habitual behaviour.

I usually (not use to) play tennis twice a week.

C *Would* + infinitive is used to refer to past habits, but not past situations. Frequency adverbs are placed after *would*.

Habit: *My father **would often** read to me when I was a young boy.*

Situation: *I used to (not would) have a bicycle.*

Stative verbs such as *have* (possession), *be, live, like, believe, think* (= have an opinion), *understand* and *know* are not used with *would* to refer to the past.

Be used to/get used to + noun or gerund

Be used to + noun/gerund means 'to be accustomed to'.

*She's a nurse so she's **used to seeing** sick people.*

Get used to + noun/gerund means 'become accustomed to'.

*I want to leave Athens; I can't **get used to the heat**.*

Unit 2
Indirect ways of asking questions

A number of expressions can be used to ask questions in a more indirect way. Indirect questions can sound more polite than direct ones.

***Could you tell me what** time it is?*

***Would you mind telling me where** he works?*

***We'd like to know when** you first started singing.*

When asking indirect questions the same word order is used as when we make statements. The auxiliary verbs, *do, does* and *did*, are omitted.

If or *whether* is used if there is no question word such as *where, what, why, when, who* and *how*.

***Could you tell us if/whether** you are married?*

Gerunds and infinitives

A The gerund is used in the following cases:

1 as the subject/object/complement of a clause or sentence:

Subject: ***Reading** in the car makes me feel sick.*

Object: *I find **shopping** for clothes really boring.*

Complement: *My favourite sport is **swimming**.*

2 after prepositions

*I'm not very **good at making** things.*

3 after certain verbs

*Peter **suggested going** for a picnic.*

B The infinitive with *to* is used:

1 to express purpose

*I'm learning English **to help** me get a better job.*

2 after many adjectives, e.g. *delighted, disappointed, easy, happy, important, lucky, necessary, normal, possible, surprised*

I was **surprised to hear** she had failed the exam.

3 after certain verbs

He **offered to give** her a lift, but she **decided to walk**.

C The infinitive without *to* is used:

1 after modal verbs.

You **can look** at it, but you **mustn't touch** it.

2 after *help, let, make, would rather, had better*

I'd better go – it's late. **I'd rather stay** here, though.

To is optional if an infinitive is used after *help*.

Classical music **helps** me **(to) relax**.

D Gerunds and infinitives after verbs

1 Verb + gerund:

Have you **finished cleaning** your room?

The following verbs, like *finish*, are normally followed by the gerund:

a certain verbs expressing likes and dislikes: *adore, detest, dislike, enjoy, don't mind, can't stand*

b other verbs: *admit, avoid, can't help, consider, delay, deny, feel like, forgive, give up, imagine, involve, keep, mind, miss, postpone, put off, practise, prevent, regret, resist, risk, suggest*

2 Verb + infinitive with *to*:

He **promised not to tell** anyone what she had said.

a The following verbs, like *promise*, are normally followed by the infinitive with *to*: *(can't) afford, agree, appear, arrange, ask, attempt, choose, decide, deserve, expect, fail, hesitate, hope, learn, manage, offer, prepare, pretend, refuse, seem.*

b With these verbs, a direct object is needed:

advise, allow, enable, encourage, force, invite, order, persuade, recommend, remind, teach, tell, warn.

My job **enables me to use** my language skills.

c The infinitive with *to* is also used after:

would like, would love, would hate, would prefer.

3 Verb + gerund or infinitive with *to*:

a *like, love, hate* and *prefer* are usually followed by the gerund. However, the infinitive with *to* is also possible with little, if any, difference in meaning.

I **love going/to go** for long walks in the hills.

The infinitive with *to* is common after *hate* for specific situations, and after *like* when it means *be in the habit of*.

I **hate to interrupt**, but we really must be going.

I **like to have a shower** when I get home from work.

b *begin, start, continue* and *intend* can be followed by the gerund or infinitive with no change in meaning.

She fell over and **started crying/to cry**.

c *forget, remember, go on, mean, need, stop* and *try* can be followed by the gerund or the infinitive with *to*, but with a change in meaning.

• *remember* + gerund = recall a previous action

I **remember coming** here when I was young.

forget + gerund is not often used to talk about an action you do not recall. Instead, *not remember* is used.

I **don't remember seeing** Jim at the party.

remember/forget + infinitive = (not) remember what you have to do

We **must remember to feed** the cat before we go.

Don't **forget to phone** me if you need any help.

• *go on* + gerund = continue with the same activity

Some footballers **go on playing** professionally until they're nearly 40.

go on + infinitive = change to a different activity

After a successful career as a football player, Johan Cruyff **went on to become** a respected manager.

• *mean* + gerund = involve

Dieting usually **means giving up** things you enjoy.

mean + infinitive = intend

I **meant to phone** the electrician but I forgot.

• *need* + gerund = (passive meaning)

This house **needs painting**. (= needs to be painted)

need + infinitive = (active meaning)

I **need to get** some new shoes.

• *stop* + gerund = no longer do something

I've **stopped smoking**: it's too expensive.

stop + infinitive = interrupt one activity in order to do another

Let's **stop to buy** some sweets on the way home.

• *try* + gerund = experiment in order to see what will happen

Try resting for a while: you might feel better then.

try + infinitive = attempt to do something

Alan **tried to stop** the thief as he ran away.

Unit 3

Comparisons

A Forms

1 Regular one-syllable adjectives:

a add *-er* and *-est* to the adjective.

Adjective	Comparative	Superlative
cheap	cheap**er**	the cheap**est**

Other examples: *clean, dark, light, short, tall, slow*

b add *-r* and *-st* to adjectives ending in *-e*.

late	late**r**	the lat**est**

Other examples: *large, loose, safe, strange, wise*

c double the consonant of adjectives ending in a short vowel and a consonant, and add *-er* and *-est*.

thin	thin**ner**	the thin**nest**

Other examples: *fat, sad, wet, red, big, hot, fit*

2 Regular adjectives with more than one syllable:

a use *more* and *most* (or *less* and *least*) in front of the adjective.

sincere	**more** sincere	the **most** sincere

Other examples: *boring, careful, modern, comfortable*

b change *-y* to *-i* and add *-er* and *-est* to adjectives ending in *-y* after a consonant.

happy	happ**ier**	the happ**iest**

Other examples: *dirty, friendly, funny, noisy, silly, tidy*

c a limited number of two-syllable adjectives can form the comparative and superlative in two ways.

stupid	stupid**er**	the stupid**est**
	more stupid	the **most** stupid

Other examples: *clever, common, friendly, gentle, narrow, pleasant, polite, quiet, simple*

3 Adverbs:

a use *more* and *most* in front of most adverbs.

quietly   **more** quietly   the **most** quietly

b A limited number of adverbs have comparative and superlative forms with *-er* (or *-r*) and *-est* (or *-st*).

fast   fast**er**   the fast**est**

Other examples: *hard, late, long, soon*

4 Irregular forms:

Some adjectives and adverbs have irregular comparative and superlative forms.

good/well	better	the best
bad/badly	worse	the worst
far	further/farther	the furthest/farthest

B Use

1 Comparatives and superlatives:

To talk about people or things that are different in some way we use:

a comparative forms of adjectives/adverbs + *than*.

*I think listening is **more difficult than** reading.*

For small differences, use a *bit, a little, slightly*.

*You need to work **a little harder**.*

For big differences, use *much, (quite) a lot, far, significantly*.

*My new car's **much faster than** my old one.*

b superlative forms of adjectives/adverbs.

*That's the **nicest** thing you've said to me all day.*

To emphasize the difference between one person or thing from all the others, use *by far* or *easily*.

*This is **by far the best** book I've ever read.*

Use *in* before a noun when specifying the group.

*Steven's the **naughtiest** boy **in the class.***

c *less* and *the least*.

Less and *least* are the opposites of *more* and *most*.

*Rugby is **less popular** than football here.*

*That's my **least favourite** track on the album.*

Like *more* and *most*, they can be used as adverbs.

*You should eat **less** and exercise **more**.*

Use *less/least* with uncountable nouns, and *fewer/fewest* with plural countable nouns. Use *more/most* with all nouns.

*I'm eating **less chocolate** and **fewer sweets**, and drinking **more water**.*

2 *As … as*:

a For people or things that are the same in some way, we use *as* + adjective/adverb + *as*.

*She's **as intelligent as** her sister.*

Use *almost, nearly, just* to qualify the comparisons.

*It's **almost as hot** today **as** it was yesterday.*

b *So* can replace the first *as* in negative sentences.

*It's **not so difficult as** I thought it would be.*

To describe small differences, use *not quite*.

*He's **not quite so impatient as** his brother.*

(= He's a little more patient than his brother.)

To describe big differences, use *not nearly*.

*Her new film **isn't nearly as bad as** her last one.*

(= Her new film is much better than her last one.)

c Use *as much* with uncountable nouns, and *as many* with countable nouns.

*I haven't got **as many chips as** Sally.*

*It's not **as much fun** without Joe here.*

d *The same* + noun + *as*

*My mum's **the same age as** my dad.*

3 *The* + comparative, *the* + comparative:

Use this structure for changes which occur together; the second is often the result of the first.

***The more money** I have, the **faster** I spend it.*

4 *little/no/(not) a lot of/(not) much difference between*:

*There **isn't much difference between** my job and yours.*

(= My job is similar to yours.)

Articles

A The definite article (*the*) is most commonly used:

1 when there is only one of something, either in existence or in a particular context.

*I'd like to speak to **the manager**, please.*

2 when something is mentioned again.

'I've read three novels and two plays by Camus.'

*'What did you think of **the plays**?'*

3 when both listener and speaker know what is being referred to.

*Hurry up! **The film** starts in 10 minutes.*

4 when talking about a specific aspect or part of something, where the noun is followed by *of*.

*We're studying **the history of** architecture.*

*Hand in your books at **the end of** the lesson.*

5 to speak generally about certain groups of singular countable nouns.

  a Inventions: ***The mobile phone** is thought to pose a serious threat to health.*

  b Animal species: ***The whale** is still hunted by countries such as Japan.*

6 with adjectives referring to general classes of people,

e.g. *the homeless, the blind, the deaf, the rich, the poor, the old, the young, the French, the Spanish*.

*Not enough is being done to help **the homeless**.*

7 with superlatives.

*Who is **the greatest footballer** in the world?*

8 with musical instruments.

*I'd love to learn to play **the piano**.*

9 with types of transport which have a fixed timetable.

*Shall we get **the bus** or take **a taxi**?*

10 with some countries, e.g. *the USA, the UK*.

11 with oceans, mountain ranges, deserts, rivers etc, e.g. *the Atlantic, the Pyrenees, the Sahara, the Thames*.

12 with some geographical areas.

*We're going to **the mountains** rather than **the coast**.*

B The indefinite article (*a/an*) is most commonly used:

1 when a singular countable noun is mentioned for the first time.

***A man** went into **a bar** with **a fish**.*

2 when referring to any one of several things.

*It's quiet in here. Shall I put **a record** on?*

3 when talking about a person's job.

*My father is **a nuclear scientist**.*

4 with some numbers, e.g. **a hundred** and one Dalmatians, **a thousand** people, **a million** pounds.

5 when it means *per* in some expressions, e.g. *twice **a day**, 50 miles **an hour**, £80 **a month**.*

Grammar reference

C No article is used:

1 when referring to nouns in a general sense.
   a Plural countable nouns:
   *Do you think **computers** will replace **teachers**?*
   b Abstract nouns:
   *We sang songs of **love** and **peace**.*
   c Other uncountable nouns:
   *Alan won't eat **cheese** or **meat**.*

2 with most streets, towns, cities and countries.
   *I went to **Bond Street** when I was in **London**.*

3 when a town's name is used with a building, e.g. **Luton Airport, Oxford University**.

4 in many common expressions, e.g. *to go home, to go to work/school/university/prison/hospital/ church/bed, to go on holiday, to be at home/work/ school/university, to be in hospital/church/bed/prison, to go by car/bus/coach/train/plane, to have breakfast/ lunch/dinner* (but *have **a** meal*), *at night* (but *in **the** morning/afternoon/evening*).

Unit 4

Past tenses

A The past simple is used to refer to:

1 completed actions which happened at a specific time.
   *I **went** to the cinema last night.*

2 completed actions and situations which happened over a specific period of time.
   *I **lived** and **worked** in Germany for three years.*

3 habitual actions or behaviour in the past.
   *We **played** football in the street when I was a child.*

4 a series of consecutive events in the past.
   *He **kissed** her, **said** goodbye and **closed** the door.*

B The past continuous is used to refer to:

1 temporary activities or situations in progress at a particular moment in the past.
   *This time last week **we were sitting** on the beach.*

2 a past activity or situation which was already in progress when another action occurred (the activity or situation in progress may or may not continue).
   *I **was reading** to my son when the lights went out.*

3 activities or situations occurring at the same time.
   *Ann **was cutting** the grass while I was cooking.*

4 the background events in a narrative.
   *It **was snowing** heavily and a cold wind **was blowing**. My brother and I **were reading** in front of the fire. Suddenly there was a knock at the door.*

C The past perfect is used to:

1 show that a past action or situation occurred before another past action or situation.
   *When I saw Tim, **he had** just **passed** his driving test.*

2 We use the continuous form to emphasize the duration of the first past action or situation.
   *She **had been waiting** for over two hours when he phoned to say he couldn't come.*

D Time linkers

1 The past perfect is often used with time linkers e.g. *after, before, by the time, as soon as, once, when, until.*
   *I couldn't go out **until** I had done my homework.*

2 The past simple can be used if the order of events is clear.
   *He sold his house **before** he left the country.*
   Or if the second event occurred as a result of the first.
   ***When** I realized what time it was, I ran outside.*

3 After/afterwards
   After is used to show the order of two or more events in the same sentence.
   ***After** he'd cleaned the house, he went shopping.*
   Afterwards means *after that* and can go at the beginning or the end of a clause.
   *We had lunch and **afterwards** we went for a walk.*
   *They played tennis and had a coffee **afterwards**.*
   NB *after* would not be correct in these two sentences.

4 At last/in the end/at the end
   At last suggests that something good happens after a long period of time or more than one attempt.
   *I've passed the First exam **at last**! I failed twice before!*
   In the end has a similar meaning and may also suggest there have been one or more changes or problems. The result may be good or bad.
   *The car broke down several times on the way but we got there **in the end**.*
   NB *eventually* can also be used in this sentence.
   At the end means at the point when something finishes.
   *Hand in your books **at the end** of the lesson.*

5 When/as/while
   These can all be used with the past continuous to introduce an action which was already in progress when another action occurred.
   ***As/when/while** I was running, I saw a rabbit.*

6 During/in/for
   These are all used as prepositions when referring to time, and are followed by a noun. *During* and *in* are used to say *when* something happened.
   *It rained a lot **during/in** the night.*
   For is used to say *how long* something took or lasted.
   *We went to Spain **for** two weeks **during** the summer.*

So and such

These intensifiers are used to give emphasis.

1 *So* is used before:
   a adjectives and adverbs without nouns.
   *I'm **so tired**. I'll have to go to bed.*
   b much, many, little, few.
   *You shouldn't eat **so much**, Ian.*
   *I didn't expect there to be **so many people** at the concert.*

2 *Such* is used with or without an adjective before:
   a singular countable nouns (the indefinite article *a/an* is also needed).
   *I can't stand him. He's **such an idiot**.*
   *I'd never heard **such a wonderful voice** before.*
   b uncountable nouns and plural countable nouns (the article is not needed).
   *I haven't eaten **such good food** for a long time.*
   *Our neighbours are **such friendly people**.*

3 *So* and *such* can both be used with a *that* clause to talk about the results or consequences.
   *It was **such a boring place that** we decided to leave.*
   *It was raining **so hard** we had to stop the car.*

Unit 5

Obligation and necessity

A *Must/Mustn't* + infinitive without *to*

1 *Must* is used:

  a for strong obligations imposed by the speaker. The speaker uses *must* to express his/her authority.
    *You **must be** here by 8 am.* (manager to employee)

  b to give strong advice.
    *It's a great film. You really **must go** and see it.*

  c to tell oneself what is necessary.
    *I **must remember** to phone Roger.*

  d in signs and notices indicating rules and laws.
    *Competition entries **must be submitted** by email.*

2 *Must not* or *mustn't* is used:

  a to talk about something that is not permitted.
    *Passengers **must not smoke** on the aircraft.*
    *You **mustn't drive** without your seatbelt on in Britain.*

  b to give strong advice.
    *You **mustn't work** too hard. You'll make yourself ill.*

3 Past form

  Must does not have a past form. *Had to* is therefore used to refer to the past.
  *We **had to write** a formal email in the exam.*

4 Question form

  Must is possible in questions forms
  ***Must you wear** that horrible dress?*
  although *have to* is more common
  *What do we **have to do** for homework?*

B *Have to/Don't have to*

  Have to is used to refer to strong obligations imposed by another person rather than by the speaker.
  *I **have to be** at work by 8 o'clock. The boss will get angry if I'm late.* (employee to a friend)
  Don't have to expresses a lack of obligation.
  *I'm glad I **don't have to** wear a suit. It's so hot today.*

C *Need to/don't need to/needn't*

  Need to is used to express necessity.
  *Can we go to the baker's next. I **need to get** some bread.*
  Don't need to/needn't express a lack of necessity.
  *We **don't need to/needn't** leave yet. It's only 2 o'clock.*

D *Should/Shouldn't* + infinitive without *to*

  Should and *shouldn't* are used to express obligation or give advice. *Ought to* can also be used with the same meaning as *should*.
  *You **ought to/should see** a doctor about your backache.*
  *If you're on a diet you **shouldn't drink** beer.*

E *Be supposed to/Had better*

  Be supposed to is used to talk about what should be done because of a rule or because it is expected.
  *Come on, it's 10 o'clock. You**'re supposed to be** in bed!*
  Had better + infinitive without *to* often implies a warning of possible negative consequences if the advice or precaution is not taken. The negative is *had better not*.
  *We**'d better not eat** it – it might be poisonous.*
  *You**'d better wear** a hat. I don't want you to get a cold.*

Permission

To express permission it is possible to use *can, may* (more formal) or *be allowed to*.

In the negative these express lack of permission, or prohibition.

*You **can have** a drink but you **can't have** any crisps.*

*We **aren't allowed to wear** trainers to school.*

Could and *was/were allowed to* are possible for general permission in the past.

*In my last job we had flexitime, so we **could arrive** more or less when we wanted to.*

Could is not used when referring to a particular situation in the past. Only *was/were allowed to* is possible.

*I **was allowed to stay** up late last night.*

Let and *make*

Both these verbs are followed by the infinitive without *to*.

Let is used to express permission

*My dad doesn't/won't **let me watch** that programme.*

Let is not normally used in the passive. *Be allowed* to is used instead.

*I **wasn't allowed to go** to the party on my own.*

Make is used to express obligation.

*The teacher **made her do** some extra homework.*

In the passive, *make* is followed by the infinitive with *to*.

*He **was made to pay** for the window he had broken.*

Noun phrases

A Noun + noun can be used:

1 in a large number of commonly accepted compound nouns. The two nouns together describe a single idea.
  Some compound nouns are usually written as two words:
  a post office   a hand towel   a mouse mat
  Others are written as one word:
  a postman   a handbag   a mousetrap

2 for containers.
  a tea cup   a water bottle   an ice bucket

3 for things that occur or appear regularly.
  the evening flight   the weekend edition the January sales

B *Noun + of + noun* can be used:

1 where no commonly accepted compound noun exists.
  the time of the year   the sound of laughter a lack of money

2 with words like *top, bottom, side, edge, back, front, beginning, middle* and end to indicate a part of something.
  the bottom of the stairs   the back of an envelope the front of the book
  Sometimes other types of noun phrase are also possible with these words:
  the water's edge   the mountainside   the sea bottom

3 for containers and their contents.
  a cup of tea   a box of tissues   a bucket of water

C *Noun + 's/s' + noun* can be used:

1 when talking about possession by a person or animal.
  Lara's pen   the woman's house   my dog's basket

2 for things that occur or appear at a specific time.
  last night's match   Tuesday's storm next week's edition

3 to show duration.

an hour's delay   two weeks' holiday
five minutes' rest

Compound adjectives can sometimes be used to express the same ideas. [See Unit 14]

Unit 6

Relative clauses

Relative clauses give information about something or someone in the main clause.

A Defining relative clauses

Defining relative clauses contain information which is essential for our understanding of the whole sentence.

*The man **who normally comes to clean our windows** is on holiday this month.*

*There's only one clock **that works properly in this flat!***

*A widow is a woman **whose husband has died**.*

In each case, the relative clause identifies which person or thing is being talked about.

Features of defining relative clauses

- No commas are required either at the beginning or the end of the relative clause.
- *That* can be used instead of *who* for people and *which* for things, particularly in spoken English.

	For people	For things
Subject:	*who/that*	*which/that*
Object:	*who/that/whom**	*which/that*
Possessive:	*whose*	*whose*

**whom* is more formal than *who*

- The relative pronoun can be omitted if it is the object of the verb in the relative clause.

*I'm enjoying the book (**which/that**) you lent me.*

- The relative pronoun cannot be omitted if it is the subject of the verb in the relative clause.

*That's the shop assistant **who/that** served me the last time I came here.*

B Non-defining relative clauses

Non-defining relative clauses contain information which is not essential for our understanding of the sentence. We can identify which person or thing is being talked about without the information in the relative clause.

*Their new house, **which has five bedrooms and a games room**, is much larger than their previous one.*

*At the party she spoke to Mr Peterson, **whose father owned the company she worked for**.*

Features of non-defining relative clauses

- Commas are required both at the beginning and the end of the relative clause (except when the end of the relative clause is also the end of the sentence).
- *That* cannot be used in place of *who* or *which*.

	For people	For things
Subject:	*who*	*which*
Object:	*who/whom*	*which*
Possessive:	*whose*	*whose*

- Relative pronouns cannot be omitted from non-defining relative clauses.

*Her maths teacher, **who/whom** everyone in the class adored, announced that he was leaving the school.*

- Non-defining relative clauses are more common in written English.
- *Which* can be used in non-defining relative clauses to refer to the whole of the main clause.

*No one phoned him on his birthday, **which** made him feel rather depressed.*

C Relative clauses and prepositions

1 Prepositions usually come at the end of defining and non-defining relative clauses.

In defining relative clauses the relative pronoun is usually omitted.

*The town I grew up **in** has changed a lot since I left.*

In non-defining relative clauses the relative pronoun is never omitted.

*Keith Rolf, **who** I used to work **with**, lives in Paris now.*

2 In more formal English, prepositions often come before the relative pronouns *whom* for people and *which* for things (in which case the pronoun cannot be omitted).

*We shall be visiting the room **in which** Turner painted some of his greatest works.*

*The head waiter, **to whom** we addressed our complaint, was not particularly helpful.*

D Relative adverbs: *where, when* and *why*

Where, when and *why* can be used in relative clauses after nouns which refer to a place (*where*), a time (*when*) or a reason (*why*).

1 *Where* has the meaning 'in/at which'.

Defining: *They've booked a week in the campsite **where** we stayed last year.*

Non-defining: *She's in Southlands Hospital, **where** you were born.*

2 *When* has the meaning 'on/in which' and can be omitted or replaced by *that* in defining relative clauses.

Defining: *Do you remember the day (**when/that**) we went to Rhyl and it snowed.*

Non-defining: *We're going on holiday in September, **when** most people are back at work.*

3 *Why* has the meaning 'for which' and can be omitted or replaced by *that* in defining relative clauses.

Defining: *The reason (**why/that**) I'm phoning is to ask you for Tina's address.*

Causative passive with *have* and *get*

1 The structure *have/get* + object + past participle to indicate that the action is done for the subject by someone else and not by the subject. The subject causes the action to be done.

Compare the following:

I repainted the windows.   (= I did it myself)

I had the windows repainted. (= someone did it for me)

Get can be used instead of *have* in this structure. It is slightly more informal.

*Where **did** you **get** your photos **developed**?*

All tenses of *have* and *get* are possible.

*We've just **had** our washing machine **repaired**.*

*I'm **getting** my hair **done** tomorrow.*

2 The same structure can also be used for events (usually unpleasant) which are outside of the speaker's control.

John had his car stolen last week.

Unit 7

The present perfect

The present perfect links **past** events and situations with the **present**.

A The present perfect is used:

1 to give news of recent **past** events which have some relevance to the **present**.

Lisa has had an accident: she's in hospital but she's OK.

2 to describe something that started in the **past** and continues to the **present**.

We have lived in the same house ever since we got married.

3 to describe events which occurred at some time between the **past** and the **present**. Exactly when they happened is not known or not important.

I've been to Poland three or four times.

4 to talk about something which occurred in the **past**, but in a time period which includes the **present**.

Judy's boyfriend has phoned her three times this morning – and it's not even 11 o'clock!

5 after the expression *it/this/that is the first/second/third, etc time*.

This is the first time I've seen this programme.

B Time expressions

1 The present perfect is commonly used with *ever, never, just, recently, so far, still, yet* and *already* when referring to a time period up to now.

They haven't booked their holiday yet.

I've had three cups of coffee so far this morning.

2 *For* is used with periods of time to show how long something has lasted.

I've known Eric for twenty years.

Since is used with points in time to show when something started.

I've had this watch since 1984.

C The present perfect continuous can be used:

1 to emphasize the **duration** of a situation or activity.

It's been snowing all day.

2 to suggest that a situation or activity is temporary.

My mum's not well, so I've been looking after her.

3 to suggest a situation or activity is incomplete.

I've been painting the house – that's why it's in a mess.

4 to focus on the repetition of a situation or activity.

He's been getting into trouble at school a lot recently.

D The present perfect simple and continuous

1 Both simple and continuous forms of the present perfect can be used to talk about the effects in the present of a past event.

Your new shoes are ruined! You've been playing football in them, haven't you? (an activity)

I can't do any sport for a few weeks; I've broken my arm. (a single action)

2 The continuous form is not used if we talk about the number of things that have been completed or the number of times a thing has been done.

She's been eating chocolate biscuits.

She's eaten six chocolate biscuits.

c Stative verbs such as *have* (to possess/own), *think* (to have an opinion), *be, like, believe, understand* and *know* are not normally used in the continuous form.

We've known each other for a long time. ✓
We've been knowing each other for a long time. ✗

Expressing preferences

A *Prefer*

1 *Prefer* + gerund + *to* + gerund is usually used to talk about general preferences.

I prefer playing basketball to watching it.

2 *Would prefer* + infinitive with *to* + *rather than* + infinitive without *to* is normally used to talk about preferences on a specific occasion.

I'd prefer to walk to school today rather than go by bus.

B *Would (much) rather*

would rather + infinitive without *to* + *than* + infinitive without *to* has the same meaning as *would prefer to*.

I'd rather not talk about it at the moment.

I'd much rather do nothing all day than go to school.

Unit 8

The future

1 *Will* + infinitive without *to* can be used to talk about:

a hopes, expectations and predictions. These can be introduced by verbs such as *believe, expect, hope* and *think*. Adverbs such as *definitely, (almost) certainly* and *probably* may also be used; they come after *will* and before *won't*.

United will probably win the league again this year.

'Where's Anne?' 'I expect she'll be here soon.'

She definitely won't pass her exams; she's too lazy.

b decisions made at the moment of speaking, including offers.

We'll babysit for you if you want to go out.

c future facts; events which the speaker knows or believes are certain to happen.

Summer will be here soon.

2 *Be going* + infinitive with *to* can be used to talk about:

a personal intentions and plans formulated before the moment of speaking.

I'm going to stay in tonight and read my book.

The infinitive *to go* can be omitted.

Do you know where you're going (to go) on holiday yet?

b predictions, as an alternative to *will*.

I don't think I'm going to do/'ll do very well in the exam.

If there is evidence now that something is certain to happen, we usually use *going to*.

Stand back! The building's going to collapse!

3 Modal verbs express degrees of possibility when talking about:

a intentions.

I may/might go swimming tomorrow. (possibility)

b predictions.

It may/might/could well rain tomorrow. (probability)

If we leave now, we should be home by six. (probability)

We may not/might not have time to see everything in the museum. (possibility)

4 The present continuous can be used to talk about future arrangements which have already been made, usually with other people or organizations.

215

Grammar reference

*Sue and Alan **are getting** married in June.*

*We**'re having** lunch out tomorrow. I've booked a table.*

5 The present simple can be used:

  a to talk about timetabled or scheduled events.

    *The film **starts** at 9.15, just after the news.*

    *What time **does** your bus **leave**?*

  b to refer to the future after time linkers such as *when, before, after, until, by the time, as soon as.*

    *Give me a call **as soon as you arrive**.*

    The present perfect can also be used in this way.

    *You can't go out **until you've tidied** your room.*

6 The future continuous, *will + be + -ing*, is used to talk about actions or events which will be in progress at a certain time in the future.

*This time tomorrow I**'ll be flying** over France.*

7 The future perfect simple, *will + have + past participle*, is used to talk about actions and events that will be completed by a certain time in the future.

*By the end of today we**'ll have driven** over 500km.*

8 The future perfect continuous, *will + have + been + -ing*, is used to talk about actions and events which continue to a certain time in the future.

*On 21 May I**'ll have been living** here for exactly 10 years.*

9 *Be about to + infinitive/be on the point of + gerund* can be used to talk about the immediate future.

*Can I phone you back? I**'m** just **about to have** lunch.*

*The police are said **to be on the point of solving** the crime.*

10 *Be (un)likely + infinitive with to* expresses probability.

*They've got a map with them so they**'re unlikely (not likely) to get** lost.* (= they probably won't get lost)

11 *Shall I/we + infinitive without to* is used to ask for suggestions, advice and instructions.

*Where **shall we** go tomorrow night?*

***Shall I phone** Les? What **shall I say**?*

12 A number of other verbs can be used to talk about future hopes, plans, intentions and expectations.

*We **hope/expect to win** tomorrow.*

*Are you **planning to go/on going out** tonight?*

*We're **thinking of moving** abroad.*

Unit 9

Modal verbs for speculation and deduction

A Certainty

If we are fairly certain about something, *must, can't* and *couldn't* can be used to express this.

1 For present situations the modal verbs *must, can't* and *couldn't* are followed by the infinitive without *to*.

*'I haven't slept for two days.' 'You **must be** exhausted!'*

*I can hear singing, so we **can't be** far from the stadium.*

The continuous infinitive can also be used.

*Why is he wearing his uniform? He **couldn't be going** to school – it's Saturday today.*

2 For past situations we use the same modal verbs + *have* + past participle (the perfect infinitive without *to*).

*I can't find my book. I **must have left** it at school.*

*This essay is poor. You **can't have spent** long on it.*

The continuous form can also be used.

*The road's wet – it **must have been raining**.*

NB *mustn't* is not normally used when making deductions about present or past situations.

B Possibility

If we are not certain about something but think it is possible, we use *may (not), might (not)* or *could* (but not *could not*).

1 For present situations these modal verbs are followed by the infinitive without *to*. The continuous infinitive is also possible.

*'Ed's not answering my emails.' 'He **might be** on holiday.'*

*He **could be telling** the truth, but it's hard to believe.*

2 For past situations we use the same modal verbs + *have* + past participle (the perfect infinitive without *to*). The continuous form is also possible.

*I think we **may have taken** the wrong road. This doesn't look familiar.*

*Sean looked sad. He **might not have been feeling** well.*

NB It is not possible to use *can* when speculating about present or past situations.

Question tags

A Form

Question tags are formed using either a modal verb, an auxiliary verb or the verb *to be* + subject pronoun. A negative tag is normally used with a positive statement, and a positive tag with a negative statement.

1 If the verb *to be* appears in the statement, it is repeated in the question tag.

*He **isn't** married, **is he**?*

*I'm late again, **aren't I**?* (not **amn't I**?)

2 If an auxiliary verb or a modal verb appears in the statement, it is repeated in the question tag.

*You**'ve been** to Warsaw before, **haven't you**?*

*You**'d rather** stay in tonight, **wouldn't you**?*

3 If the verb in the statement is a full verb (i.e. there is no modal verb or auxiliary verb), an appropriate form of the auxiliary verb *do* is required in the question tag.

*You **bought** it last year, **didn't you**?*

4 *Will you?* and *can you?* are used with imperatives. *Would you?* and *could you?* are more formal alternatives.

***Open** the window, **will/can/would/could** you?*

Will you? is used after a negative imperative.

***Don't forget** to write, **will you**?*

5 If *let's* appears in the statement, the question tag *shall we?* is used.

***Let's** go home, **shall we**?*

6 If the statement contains negative words such as *nothing* or *nobody*, the question tag is positive.

***Nothing** frightens you, **does it**?*

NB The pronoun *they* is used with *nobody/no one, somebody/someone* and *everybody/everyone*.

***Nobody** was watching, **were they**?*

B Use and intonation

We can use question tags to ask a real question if we are unsure if the statement is true or not. In this case we say the question tag with rising intonation.

I've met you before, haven't I?

We can also use question tags when we expect someone to agree with a statement. In this case we say the question tag with falling intonation.

She can't sing very well, can she?

Contrast linkers

1 *But* contrasts two ideas in the same sentence.

*The weather was bad **but** she enjoyed the trip.*

In informal writing, *but* is often used at the beginning of the sentence.

*John's got the flu. **But** the rest of us are fine.*

2 *Although* and *though* (informal) are also used to contrast ideas in the same sentence. They can go at the beginning of the sentence or in the middle.

***Although** the weather was bad, she enjoyed the trip.*

*I liked the book, **although** I wouldn't recommend it.*

Even used before *though* emphasizes the contrast.

*He still wears his ring, **even though** he's divorced.*

3 *However* contrasts ideas in two different sentences. It often goes at the beginning of the second sentence and is followed by a comma.

*The hotel was expensive. **However,** the others were full, so she had to book it.*

It can also go in the middle of a sentence or at the end.

*Tim hated York. He did not, **however,** want to move.*

*Amy often tells lies. She would never steal, **however**.*

4 *Nevertheless* is a more formal alternative to *however*.

*It was snowing. **Nevertheless,** the game went ahead.*

5 *In spite of* and *despite* are both followed by a gerund or a noun. They can go at the beginning of a sentence or in the middle.

*We enjoyed the meal **in spite of the poor service**.*

***Despite feeling** terrible, she still went to work.*

If the subject of the gerund is different to the subject of the main verb, a noun, an object pronoun or possessive adjective is added. [See Unit 13 for more on this use of the gerund.]

***She** paid for the meal **despite me/my** telling her not to.*

The words *the fact that* are added before a verb clause.

*Chloe invited Steve to her party, **despite the fact that he had treated** her so badly.*

6 *Whereas*, *while* and *whilst* (formal) are used to contrast two things, people or situations in the same sentence.

*Jake likes heavy metal **whereas/while** I prefer rap.*

Unit 10

Too and enough

A *Too* means 'more than is necessary or desirable'.

1 *Too* + adjective/adverb

*This jumper's **too big**.   Don't work **too hard**!*

2 *Too much/Too many* (+ noun)

*I can't eat this. There's **too much salt** in it.*

*There are **too many people** here. Let's go somewhere else.*

*I feel terrible! I've eaten **too much**.*

3 *Too* + adverb/adjective (+ *for* + object) + infinitive with *to*

*It's **too cold to play** tennis today.*

*He spoke **too quickly for me to understand** him.*

B *Enough* means 'as much as is necessary'.

1 Adjective/Adverb + *enough*

*Are you **warm enough** or shall I turn the heating on?*

*You haven't done your homework **carefully enough**.*

2 *Enough* (+ noun)

*We'll have to stand because there aren't **enough chairs**.*

*I'll buy some more bread. We haven't got **enough**.*

3 *Enough* (+ *for* + object) + infinitive with *to*

*The floor is **clean enough for you to sit** on.*

*I haven't got **enough time to see** you today.*

The passive

A Form

The verb *to be* + past participle

Present simple:	*Goods worth £750 million **are stolen** from shops each year.*
Present continuous:	*A man **is being questioned** in connection with the robbery.*
Present perfect:	*Photos of the suspects **have been put** up around the town.*
Past simple:	*He **was taken** away in a police van.*
Past continuous:	*The burglar didn't realize he **was being filmed**.*
Past perfect:	*Two people **had been mugged** there on the previous day.*
Future simple:	*All football supporters **will be searched** at the airport.*
Infinitive:	*He is hoping **to be released** from prison next week.*
Gerund:	*I can't remember **being hit** on the head.*
Modal verbs:	*He **should be sentenced** to life imprisonment.*

B Use

The passive is used to focus attention on the person or thing affected by the action, rather than on the agent (the 'doer' of the action). If we are interested in the agent, we use the preposition *by*:

*Sue and Mark were brought up **by their grandparents**.*

When we talk about the instrument used by the agent to do the action, we use the preposition *with*:

*He was hit on the head **with a vase**.*

The agent is not usually included:

1 when it is clear from the context who the agent is.

Colin was arrested for dangerous driving. (by the police)

2 when we don't know the agent/the agent is unimportant.

My car was stolen yesterday afternoon.

This castle was built in the Middle Ages.

3 in official notices to avoid using *you*.

Food may not be consumed on the premises.

4 when the agent is people in general.

Texas is known as The Lone Star State.

C Passive of reporting verbs

The infinitive can be used after the passive of reporting verbs to talk about widely held beliefs or opinions. Examples of reporting verbs are *believe, consider, expect, know, say* and *think*.

*The President is expected **to arrive** at 9.30 am.*

*The man is believed **to be carrying** a weapon.*

The perfect infinitive (*have* + past participle) is used to refer to the past.

*Fifteen people are known **to have died** in the accident.*

Unit 11

So, neither and nor

A Use

To indicate that we have the same feelings, behaviour or abilities as others, we can use *so* (positive statements), and *neither* or *nor* (negative statements).

Grammar reference

B Form

so/neither/nor + (modal) auxiliary verb or the verb *to be* + subject noun or pronoun

The rules for deciding which verb is used after *so*, *neither* or *nor* are the same as those for question tags [Unit 9]. The verb is always positive. The clause with *so*, *neither* or *nor* can appear in the same sentence as the main clause or it can be said by a different speaker:

*She can't play a musical instrument and **neither can I**.*

'I'll phone him tonight.' **'So will I'**

'My mum isn't working tomorrow.' **'Neither is mine.'**

C If our feelings, behaviour or abilities are different from those of others, we use the following structure:

subject + (modal) auxiliary verb or the verb *to be*.

He doesn't eat meat but I do.

'We're allowed to wear jeans to school.' *'We aren't.'*

Conditionals

Conditional sentences contain a conditional clause (introduced by words such as *if*, *as long as* and *unless*) and a main clause.

If the conditional clause comes first, a comma usually separates it from the main clause (as in this sentence).

A comma is not needed if the conditional clause comes after the main clause (as in this sentence).

A Zero conditional

if + present simple, present simple

We use the zero conditional to talk about situations which are always true. *If* has the same meaning as *when*, *whenever* or *every time* in such sentences.

My eyes start to hurt if I spend too long on the computer.

If you mix blue and yellow, you get green.

B First conditional

if + present simple, *will* + infinitive without *to*

We use the first conditional to talk about possible situations and their likely results in the future.

She'll be very happy if you phone her.

It can be used for warnings, promises and threats.

I'll send you to bed if you don't behave yourself.

If you pass your driving test, I'll take you out for a meal.

Other future forms and imperatives are possible in the main clause.

We're going to the cinema if my dad gets home in time.

If you see Alan, give him my regards.

Modal verbs can also be used in the main clause. *May*, *might* and *could* express possibility or uncertainty about the outcome. *Should* expresses probability.

If I finish my homework early, I might watch the film.

If you post it today, it should get there by Friday.

C Second conditional

if + past simple, *would* + infinitive without *to*

We use the second conditional to talk about imaginary, unlikely or impossible situations in the present or future.

If I knew the answer to number six, I would tell you.

If I had wings, I'd fly south in winter.

Note the difference between these two sentences:

First conditional:

If they give me a pay rise, I'll buy a new car. (I feel there is a real possibility that they will give me a pay rise.)

Second conditional:

If they gave me a pay rise, I'd buy a new car. (I feel it is less likely that they will give me a pay rise.)

The second conditional can also be used to give advice.

If I were you, I'd complain to the manager.

Both *was* and *were* are possible in the conditional clause after the subject pronouns *I/he/she/it*. *Was* is more common in spoken English.

If he were a little taller, he'd be an excellent goalkeeper.

Might and *could* can be used in the main clause to express possibility or uncertainty about the outcome.

If you worked a bit harder, you might have more success.

D Third conditional

if + past perfect, *would/might/could have* + past participle

We use the third conditional to talk about imaginary situations in the past and to speculate about their effects on past events or situations.

If we hadn't taken a map, we would have got lost. (But we took a map, so we didn't get lost.)

E Mixed conditional

if + past perfect, *would/might/could* + infinitive without *to*

Mixed conditionals are a combination of a second and a third conditional. They can express an imaginary past event and a possible or probable present result.

If you'd listened to my advice, you might/would not be in this situation now.

F Alternative words for *if*

As long as, *provided (that)*, *providing (that)* and *on condition (that)* can be used in place of *if* to emphasize the condition.

I'll lend you £10 as long as you give it back tomorrow.

We'll take the boat out provided the sea isn't too rough.

Unit 12

Countable and uncountable nouns

A Countable nouns are nouns which can be counted.

one plate   two cats   five chairs

B Uncountable nouns cannot be counted. They are not used with the indefinite article (*a/an*), they do not have a plural and they are used with a singular verb form.

*Can you get **some bread**?*

***A lot of damage** was done to the building.*

The following nouns are usually uncountable: *accommodation, advice, damage, English, furniture, graffiti, health, homework, information, knowledge, luggage, news, progress, research, spaghetti, travel, weather, work.*

This spaghetti isn't cooked properly.

The news is very depressing today.

C Some nouns are both countable and uncountable.

1 Many words for food and drink can be used both countably and uncountably.

I've made a chocolate cake. (**C**)

Could I have some more cake? (**U**)

Would you like another coffee? (**C**) (= cup of coffee)

I don't like coffee. (**U**)

2 A word used countably may have a very different meaning from its uncountable version.

*I'd like a double **room** for one night.* (**C**) (= hotel room)

*There's no more **room** on this bus.* (**U**) (= space)

D Making uncountable nouns countable

1 Some uncountable nouns have countable equivalents with similar meanings.

*There isn't much **work** in this town.* (**U**)

*There aren't many **jobs** in this town.* (**C**)

*My job involves a lot of business **travel**.* (**U**)

*I have to make a lot of business **trips**.* (**C**)

2 Some other uncountable nouns can be made countable by using *piece(s) of* or *item(s) of*.

*Let me give you **a piece of advice**.*

***Two items of news** caught my attention.*

3 Certain other expressions are used with words for food and drink: *a plate of spaghetti, a pinch of salt, a loaf of bread, a slice of cake/toast, a spoonful of sugar, a bar of chocolate, a carton of milk, a jar of jam.*

E Words used with nouns

1 Words used with countable nouns: *a/an, few, a few, many, a large number of, each, every, several.*

2 Words used with uncountable nouns: *little, a little, much, a great deal of, a large amount of.*

3 Words used with countable and uncountable nouns: *some, any, no, a lot of, lots of, all, plenty of, most.*

4 *Little* and *few*

These two words have more negative meanings. They mean 'not much/many' or 'not as much/many as desired or expected'.

*Sue has made **little progress** since the beginning of term.*

*There were **very few people** at the concert.*

5 *A little* and *a few*

These have more positive meanings. They mean 'some' or 'more than expected'.

*I've managed to save **a little money** to buy Al a present.*

*I've still got **a few eggs** – enough to make an omelette.*

6 *Plenty of*

This means 'a lot of' or 'more than enough'.

*Don't hurry – we've got **plenty of time**.*

Direct and reported speech

When reporting what someone has said or written, we can use either direct speech or reported speech.

When we use direct speech we report the exact words which someone has used.

'I'm staying here tomorrow,' said Heather.

When we use reported speech, changes may have to be made to verb tenses, pronouns and certain words indicating place and time.

*Heather said **she was** staying **there the next day**.*

A Reporting statements

1 The following changes are usually made to verbs. In each case the verb 'moves back' one tense.

Direct speech	→	Reported speech
Present simple	→	Past simple
'I work in an office,' he said.		*He said he worked in an office.*
Present continuous	→	Past continuous
'We aren't going away on holiday,' she said.		*She said they weren't going away on holiday.*
Present perfect	→	Past perfect
'I've known her for a long time,' he said.		*He said he'd known her for a long time.*
Present perfect continuous	→	Past perfect continuous
'He's been playing tennis,' she said.		*She said he'd been playing tennis.*
Past simple	→	Past perfect
'I saw Nigel in town,' he said.		*He said he'd seen Nigel in town.*
Past continuous	→	Past perfect continuous
'We were trying to help him,' she said.		*She said they'd been trying to help him.*

2 No changes are made in the verb tense:

a if the verb in the direct speech is in the past perfect.

'He had never spoken about it before,' she said.

She said he had never spoken about it before.

b if the direct speech contains one of the following modal verbs: *would, might, could, should, ought to.*

'You should go to the doctor's,' he said.

He said I should go to the doctor's.

c if the statement being reported is still true. The tense change is optional.

'I like fish,' she said. She said she likes/liked fish.

d if the reporting verb is in the present.

'It's 40° in Athens at the moment.' (Jeremy to his mother on the phone)

Jeremy says it's 40° in Athens at the moment. (Jeremy's mother to her husband)

3 Pronouns in direct speech may have to change when we use reported speech.

*'I'll see **you** soon,' said Peter.*

*Peter said **he** would see **me** soon.*

4 The following changes may also need to be made to words indicating place and time.

Direct speech	→	Reported speech
now	→	then
today	→	that day
this morning	→	that morning
tomorrow	→	the next/following day
next week	→	the next/following week
yesterday	→	the day before, the previous day
two days ago	→	two days before/earlier
last week	→	the week before, the previous week
here	→	there
come	→	go

5 *This, that, these* and *those* may change to *the*.

*'**That** book you lent me is really boring,' he said.*

*He said **the** book I had lent him was really boring.*

B Reporting verbs for statements

1 *Tell* is used with a direct object.

He told me (that) he was getting married.

2 *Say* and *explain* are used without a direct object.

She said (that) she was ill. (not *She said me ...*)

They can, however, be used with an indirect object.

I explained to them (that) I'd left my passport at home. (not *I explained them ...*)

3 Some reporting verbs can be used with an infinitive.

a verb + object noun/pronoun + infinitive with *to*

advise, ask, encourage, invite, order, persuade, recommend, remind, tell, warn

'Don't forget to phone Jim,' he told her.

He reminded her to phone Jim.

219

b verb + infinitive with *to*

offer, promise, refuse, threaten

'I'll help you mend the car if you like.'

He offered to help me mend the car.

4 The following patterns can be used after both *recommend* and *suggest*:

He recommended/suggested (that) I (should) eat less.

She recommended/suggested joining a youth club.

The infinitive with *to* can only be used after *recommend*.

He suggested me to go to the chemist's. ✗

C Reporting questions

When we report questions we make the same changes to verb tenses, pronouns and words indicating place and time as we do when we report statements. The following changes are also made:

Auxiliary verbs:	Auxiliary verbs *do, does* and *did* are omitted.
Word order:	The word order is the same as that of a statement.
Punctuation:	Question marks are not used.

'What do you want to do?' he asked me.

He asked me what I wanted to do.

'Where have you been?' she asked him.

She asked him where he had been.

Yes/No questions:	If there is no question word (*what, where, who,* etc) in the direct question, we use *if* or *whether*.

'Does she know Joe?'

He asked if/whether she knew Joe.

D Ask and *tell*

Each of these verbs can be used in two different ways in reported speech.

1 *Ask*

a Requests (*ask* + object + infinitive with *to*)

'Can you help me, please?'

He asked me to help him.

b Questions

'Can you ride a horse?'

She asked me if I could ride a horse.

2 *Tell*

a Commands (*tell* + object + infinitive with *to*)

'Put your coat on.'

She told him to put his coat on.

b Statements

'I can't find my coat.'

He told her (that) he couldn't find his coat.

Unit 13

Hypothetical situations

A *Wish* and *if only*

Wish or *if only* can express how we would like things to be different if we had the power to change them.

1 Present states

We use *wish/if only* + past simple to express wishes about present states. Stative verbs such as *be, have, know* and *understand* are used.

I wish I was/were taller.

If only I knew how to play the guitar.

2 Present actions

We use *wish/if only* + *would* when we want something to happen or someone to do something. Active verbs (verbs describing actions) are used.

I wish you would turn your music down.

If only this wind would stop blowing.

Wish/if only + *would* is used if we want to express irritation at other peoples' actions or behaviour.

I wish you would stop tapping your foot.

Wish/if only + past simple can also be used if the action occurs habitually.

I wish you didn't (or wouldn't) smoke so much.

3 Present ability

Wish/if only + *would* is used for events which are outside of our control. Consequently, we do not normally say 'I wish I would …'. Instead, we use 'I wish I could …' to indicate our inability to change things.

I wish I could remember where I put my keys.

4 Wishes for the future

Wish/if only + *would* or *could* can be used to express wishes for the future. This use of *wish* suggests that the action will probably not happen.

I wish I could go on holiday with you in summer. (I know that I can't go with you.)

If there is more possibility that the action will happen, we use *hope*.

I hope I can go on holiday with you in summer. (I don't know if I can or not.)

5 Past situations

We use *wish/if only* + past perfect to express wishes and regrets about the past.

I wish I hadn't left school when I was 16.

The following structures can also be used to express wishes and regrets about the past.

a Third and mixed conditionals [see Unit 11]

If I hadn't been so tired, this wouldn't have happened.

b *should have* + past participle

We should have got the train. This traffic's terrible.

B *Would rather*

We use *would rather* + past simple when we want someone else to do something in the present or future.

I'd rather you went to get some bread now.

He said he'd rather we didn't arrive too early tomorrow.

If the subject of *would rather* and the following verb is the same, we usually use the infinitive without *to*.

We'd rather sit in the garden than go to the beach.

C *It's time*

We use *it's (high/about) time* + past simple when we want something to happen or be done now. It implies that the action should have been done already.

It's time you went to bed. You've got school tomorrow.

It's high time you stopped talking and did some work.

Prepositions and gerunds

1 Verbs which come immediately after prepositions must be in the gerund form.

He was fined **for parking** on a yellow line.

If the subject of the gerund is different to the subject of the main verb, we add a noun, object pronoun or possessive adjective.

We're not happy about **James** riding a motorbike.

They insisted on **me/my** showing them the photos.

2 These noun + preposition combinations are commonly followed by gerunds:

(be no/little) point in, (have) difficulty in, (be/have a good/not much) chance of, (be in) favour of

*There's no **point in inviting** her; she won't come.*

*Is there any **chance of you playing** tennis later?*

3 Gerunds are used after a number of phrasal verbs containing prepositions, such as *get out of, get over, give up, look forward to, put off, put up with, take to.*

*He **gave up phoning** her and **took to texting** her poems.*

4 These linking words and expressions can also be used as prepositions and followed by a gerund: *after, apart from, as a result of, as well as, before, besides, despite, in addition to, in spite of, instead of.*

***Apart from tasting** great, it's also very good for you.*

*She opened the window, **despite me asking** her not to.*

Unit 14

Compound adjectives

Compound adjectives consist of two or more words joined by a hyphen.

A Many compound adjectives include a participle.

1 Past participles can be combined with:
- nouns, e.g. *home-made, air-conditioned, tree-lined*
- adjectives, e.g. *open-mouthed, French-born*
- adverbs, e.g. *well-paid, brightly-coloured, fully-grown*
- particles, e.g. *a made-up story, a broken-down car*

2 Present participles can be combined with:
- nouns, e.g. *German-speaking, time-saving*
- adjectives, e.g. *good-looking, sweet-smelling*
- adverbs, e.g. *hard-working, fast-moving, long-lasting*

B Many other compound adjectives do not include a participle, e.g. *cycle-friendly, full-time, high-speed, shoulder-length, twentieth-century, world-famous, out-of-town, up-to-date, nine-to-five, top-of-the-range.*

C When a noun is used with a number to form a compound adjective, the singular form of the noun is used, e.g. *a ten-kilometre walk, a sixty-page report, a fifty-pound note, a three-hour journey, a five-year-old child.*

Expressing purpose

There are several different ways of expressing purpose (saying why people do things).

1 Infinitive with *to*

*I'm writing **to thank** you for the lovely present you sent.*

The negative infinitive, *not to do something,* cannot be used to express purpose.

2 *In order (not) to* + infinitive

*She wore dark glasses **in order not to be recognized.***

3 *So as (not) to* + infinitive

*We set off early **so as to** avoid the traffic.*

4 *So (that)* + clause
  a Future meaning: *so (that)* + *can/will*/present simple
  *Let's move to the front **so we can see** better.*
  *I'll take an umbrella **so that I don't/won't get** wet.*
  b Past meaning: *so (that)* + *could/would*
  *He shut the door **so that no one would** disturb him.*

5 *In case* + clause

If we do something to prepare for a possible situation or problem we use *in case* + present simple/past simple.

  a Future meaning: *in case* + present simple
  *Here are some crisps **in case you get** hungry later on.*
  b Past meaning: *in case* + past simple
  *He made a copy **in case he lost** the original.*

6 *In case* and *if*

Note the difference in meaning between *in case* and *if*:

I'll take my umbrella if it rains. (= I'll take my umbrella only if it is raining when I leave the house.)

I'll take my umbrella in case it rains. (= I'll take it as a precaution, even if it isn't raining when I leave the house.)

Expressing ability

A *Can* and *be able to*

Can and *be able to* are both used to express ability. However, *can* only has present tense (*can*) and past tense (*could*) forms. If another form of the verb is required, *be able to* is used.

Present:	*She can/is able to speak French.*
Past:	*She could/was able to read when she was two.*
Infinitive:	*I'd like to be able to ski.*
Present perfect:	*He's never been able to save money.*
Will future:	*She'll be able to buy a car soon.*

B Present ability

1 We use *can* or *be able to* to talk about present ability. *Be able to* is more formal than *can*.

I can run faster than you.

He is able to speak without moving his lips.

2 The negative form of *can* is *can't* or *cannot*. To form the negative of *be able to, not* is used before *able*. You can also use *be unable to.*

I cannot understand why she married him.

We regret we are unable/not able to accept credit cards.

3 *Be capable of* + gerund can also be used to express ability. It means to have the ability, capacity or potential to do something.

This team is capable of winning the championship.

4 The negative form *be incapable of* + gerund can be used, or *not* can be placed before *capable.*

She is incapable/isn't capable of looking after herself.

C Past ability

1 When we talk about general ability in the past, both *could* and *was/were able to* are possible.

My grandfather could play the trumpet until he was 90.

As a child I was never able to beat my father at chess.

2 *Be capable of* can also be used in the past.

Joe wasn't capable of making toast without burning it.

3 When we talk about ability to do something on one occasion in the past, *could* is not possible. Instead, *was/were able to, managed to* + infinitive or *succeeded in* + gerund have to be used.

I managed to/was able to speak to Frank last night.

Firefighters succeeded in controlling the flames.

However, *could* can be used for ability on one occasion when it is used with verbs of the senses: *see, smell, hear, feel, sense, taste.*

I knew my wife had arrived; I could smell her perfume.

4 When we talk about inability to do something on one occasion in the past, *couldn't, weren't/wasn't able to, was/were unable to, didn't manage to* and *didn't succeed in* are all possible.

I couldn't do the homework; it was too difficult.

I didn't manage to/wasn't able to repair the fridge.

Listening scripts

Unit 1 🔘 1.1–1.5

Part 3: Multiple matching

Speaker 1
After we got the invitation, my mum and I kept having huge rows about what I was going to wear for the big event. She's always criticizing me for my taste in clothes and she'd bought me this long, bright red dress to wear on the day. Of course, I refused. I went instead in a short black skirt, trainers and a sports top, thinking I'd look really cool and trendy. But of course, when we got to the church and I saw all the other guests in their smart new clothes and expensive hats, I just felt really, really stupid and embarrassed. The bride and groom looked quite surprised when they saw me, so I spent most of the time at the reception trying to avoid them.

Speaker 2
We really had no other option but to send her home to get changed, dye her hair back and take out the nose stud. We have rules and the rules are there to prepare young people for the reality of the world of work. I don't know of many jobs where you could turn up with scruffy old clothes, green hair and a pierced nose. We insist on uniform from the first day until the last, and that includes when sitting exams. It's unfair on other candidates who respect the regulations, and distracting for them at a time when they need maximum concentration.

Speaker 3
… Indeed attitudes were already beginning to change in the first half of the century. In 1919, the young French star Suzanne Lenglen caused a sensation at the British championships by wearing a calf-length, sleeveless dress. Her unconventional, yet practical clothing shocked spectators, who were used to seeing women play in the long heavy dresses which were typical of that period. As a result, Lenglen attracted the kind of attention from the world's press which was normally reserved for the stars of the silent movies. She silenced her critics, however, by beating her opponents and going on to win several major titles.

Speaker 4
He clearly has ability. You only have to look at his examination results to see that. And he used to live in France, which means he probably wouldn't mind changing countries, if we needed him to. No, what concerns me is his appearance. If he's prepared to turn up for something as important as this, wearing what can only be described as casual clothes, what would he be like with our clients? If he really is a serious candidate and we decide to take him on, then he will have to get used to wearing something a little more formal.

Speaker 5
They had to have their little joke, didn't they. 'Jane's having a little celebration at her house for her "coming of age" and she wants everyone to go in fancy dress.' That's what they said. So I thought about it for ages, what I was going to go as and everything. I spent more time thinking about my costume than about what present I was going to get for Jane. Of course, when I turned up at the house dressed as Coco the Clown and everybody else was wearing normal clothes, I don't know who was more surprised, me or Jane.

Unit 1 🔘 1.6–1.13

Part 1: Multiple choice

1 You hear two people talking about a friend of theirs.

M = Man   W = Woman

M: How many houses has Mike got now?

W: Four I think. This one here, the flat in Brighton, the country cottage, and …

M: … and the villa in Spain.

W: That's right.

M: Hmm. Easy for some, isn't it?

W: I'm not so sure. I get the impression he's a bit fed up with it all – always moving around. I wouldn't be surprised if he got rid of everything over here and lived in Spain permanently.

M: Is that what he's said he'll do?

W: Well, you know Mike. It's not like him to talk much about his plans. But he did say he might settle down one day – stay in one place. And you know how much he likes Spain.

2 You overhear a man talking to a friend on his mobile phone.

I'm stressed out, to be honest, what with work and the problems with the house and everything. I need to do something to help me relax … Well, I wanted to do yoga, but the class is on Friday and I play squash then. And then I saw they do Pilates on Tuesdays and Thursdays, which would be ideal for me … I know. You did it for a couple of years, didn't you? … So anyway, I was wondering if you could tell me what it was like, what sort of things you did. I had a look on the Internet, but it's always better to talk to someone with first-hand experience.

3 You hear a woman talking about her family's financial situation.

We just about get by, but it's always a struggle to get to the end of the month. Frank – my husband – hasn't had a job for over a year and I've got the two children to look after. Frank said he'll look after the kids and I can go out and look for work. Trouble is, he's useless around the house and he can't cook to save his life. But there's no alternative, really. Both our mums aren't very well these days, so we can't get either of them to come and help out. And we haven't got any family jewels we can sell. So, this weekend I'll be teaching Frank to cook and writing a few application letters.

4 You overhear a man and a woman talking about their morning routine.

W = Woman   M = Man

W: Don't you just hate it when the alarm goes off in the morning?

M: I usually wake up before the alarm goes off. I'm an early riser.

W: That sounds worse. Aren't you tired for the rest of the day?

M: No, I just don't need to sleep so much. I take the dog out for a walk, talk to him about this and that …

W: You talk to your dog?

M: Sure. Much easier than talking to people – he doesn't answer back or ask questions, like people do. I find that much harder to cope with first thing in the morning. I'm the same in the car – most people can't stand the journey to work, but I have a good old chat with myself.

W: Weird.

5 You hear a woman on the radio talking about her experiences in a foreign country.

On my travels, I've got used to eating all sorts of weird and wonderful things, so I was prepared for things like fried insects and scorpions. I don't particularly like them, but I'll eat them if I have to. And it's very hot and humid there, so I was also ready for the rather slow pace of life and relaxed way they go about doing things, like work, for example. What I wasn't expecting was the way they dress out there. In my experience it's unusual for people in that part of the world to take so much care over what they wear. Colour, style, fashion – it all mattered to them. I was positively scruffy by comparison.

6 You turn on the radio and hear the following.

The world today is faster and more dynamic than when our great-grandparents were alive, but as a result, life is often more stressful and unhealthy. Self-help books offer people the hope of finding a solution to their problems, improving their health and well-being, and generally making their lives better. The author of *Back to basics* says his book will help you achieve all these things in a matter of weeks. He's lying – the only thing it's good for is sending you to sleep, and you'd be wasting your money if you bought it, and your time if you read it.

7 You hear two people talking about the village they both live in.

M = Man   W = Woman

M: Are you enjoying it here in the village?

W: Yes, I am. I think I know nearly everyone now. When I came here last year everyone went out of their way to introduce themselves and make me feel welcome.

M: That's good. So you feel comfortable here, then?

W: Yes, I do. And the children have settled in well, too. I just get a bit nervous about the traffic sometimes.

M: What, on the main road?

W: Yes, and a couple of other spots as well. There are certain places I won't let the children go without me. Some drivers just don't slow down for them.

8 You hear a man talking about his job.

I don't get to wear a uniform – you know, with a cap and all, like they do at some of the other hotels, but I do wear a suit. A decent one – tailor made – not just any old suit. Inside, at the front desk – in reception – they reckon I look smarter than the boss. I'm not so sure about that, but I do like to look good for the guests – I'm the first person they see before they go into the hotel. And I've got this long black overcoat, as well – it can get pretty cold standing outside on the steps in winter, I can tell you.

Unit 2 👁 1.14

Part 2: Sentence completion

Hello, Jim Dunne here, with a look at what's on in the area this coming week. And I'm delighted to be able to tell you that *Pagagnini* is in town, with its own special mix of music and comedy. It's great fun and I can guarantee the whole family will enjoy watching these four guys. They play all those bits of classical music that everyone knows, but sometimes can't put a name to – and they have a laugh at the same time. *Pagagnini* is actually based in Madrid, but the show tours a lot and I was lucky enough to see it last year with my wife and our two girls when we were in Mexico. They're a really versatile bunch of musicians. At one point, they start using their violins and cellos as guitars, mandolins and even percussion instruments. And they move away from classical into rock, blues and country and western. Very impressive and we're all looking forward to seeing them again. They're on stage for about ninety minutes, but it's a very intense hour and a half, I can tell you. It's exhausting just watching them, and they don't stop for an interval, either.

Now, for those of you who like Irish dancing there's *Rhythm of the Dance* at the Apollo Theatre. Most of you will know about *Riverdance*, which began way back in 1994 – at the Eurovision Song Contest in Dublin, curiously enough. But *Rhythm of the Dance* goes back a long way too. It started out just five years later in 1999 in Norway. It's a similar kind of thing: the traditional music, the step dancing and so on, but there's a theme running through it. It's a kind of history of the Irish Celts. I haven't seen it yet, but I certainly will do – they're clearly very popular. It says here in the publicity that *Rhythm of the Dance* has played to live audiences totalling well over four million in no fewer than forty-four countries. And if you want to find out more about the show, go to their website. There isn't any Reviews section to look at there, but if you click on where it says 'Photo gallery' you get a pretty good idea of what to expect.

Now, the circus is back in town. Not just any circus, but the hugely talented Cirque Éloize from Canada. They're at the Regent Theatre again. The show's called *iD* and it promises to be every bit as good as the one they put on the first time they were there. That one was called *Rain* – as in, the wet stuff that falls from the sky. And there was plenty of water on stage, as you'll remember if you went to see it.

Now I've been looking at the video for *iD* on the show's website and I can tell you it has a totally urban setting. There's hip-hop and breakdance, electronic music and rock, and some of the artists moving around the stage on bikes and Rollerblades™. There are no animals, and no clowns, either. It's not your traditional kind of circus. And judging from the press reviews, it's well worth going to see. One that I have here in front of me says that it's an excellent show, full of originality, energy and excitement.

And if you want even more energy, then those Australian tap dancers, the Tap Dogs are on their way. They'll be at the Orion from Wednesday …

Unit 2 👁 1.15

Part 4: Multiple choice

M = Mike Taylor   I = Interviewer

I: Octopushing, elephant polo, ice racing or cheese rolling. Our sports correspondent, Mike Taylor, has been finding out about some of the world's strangest sports. Which is the most unusual one for you, Mike?

M: Well, I think it has to be chess boxing, because it's such a bizarre combination. A match starts off with a four-minute round of speed chess, followed by a three-minute round of boxing. There can be up to six rounds of chess and five of boxing before a **winner** is decided. Now you may think this is just a bit of fun, but when I watched two men competing in a match on German television last year, I was amazed by their level of skill in each of these two very different disciplines. After all, boxing is such

an aggressive, violent sport – it's about using the body, whereas chess is all about using the brain. You don't expect a **boxer** to be good at chess, or a chess **player** to be good in the ring.

I: Have you found any other unusual combinations like that?

M: No, but at the beginning you mentioned octopushing, which is underwater hockey – so it's an unusual setting for a familiar game. I haven't seen it played, but I've read that it's a very exciting **spectator** sport – major tournaments have TV screens which show the images captured by underwater cameras. I've also read that you don't have to be very fit to play. But I'm not convinced, to be honest – it seems physically very demanding to me. The good thing, though, is that because it's a team sport, no individual player has to stay underwater for long periods at a time. People like me who can't hold their breath for very long can keep coming up for air.

I: Hmm, not one for me, though, I'm afraid. What else have you got?

M: Well, there's wife carrying. That's where **competitors** race over a 250-metre course with a woman on their back. The female **participant** has to weigh more than 49 kilos, but she doesn't actually have to be the man's wife. So it would be more accurate to call it 'woman carrying', I suppose. Anyway, if she isn't heavy enough she has to wear a rucksack with some kind of weight in it. The regulations are surprisingly strict.

I: Now that sounds alright. Fancy carrying me, Mike?

M: Er … no. Bad back, I'm afraid. Actually, there are quite a few sports like this one that rather irritate me.

I: Why's that?

M: Well, they're a bit ridiculous, to be honest. Wife carrying, retro running, pea shooting, egg throwing … they all seem very childish to me. I'm sorry if that upsets **listeners**, but they're just not sports I'd want to do or even watch.

I: So which one is the silliest?

M: Well, it has to be toe wrestling, where you have to force your opponent's foot to the ground. It's fine for kids, and a toe wrestling competition is the kind of thing you might expect them to organize in the school playground. But for grown men and women to hold a World Championship every year, and then for **organizers** to apply for toe wrestling to become an Olympic sport – well, it's too daft for words. I'm just pleased the application wasn't accepted.

I: Alright. But you seem to like chess boxing and octopushing. Are there any more that impress you?

M: Well, how about the Man Versus Horse Marathon, which takes place every July in Wales? Human **runners**

223

race cross-country against **riders** on horseback for twenty-two miles – that's around thirty-five kilometres – and on two occasions in the last thirty years, a human **contestant** has won. Now that's not as astonishing as it might seem – horses are fast in short races but not so good over long distances. But it does seem a little unfair that the human victories are not mentioned in the same breath as some of the world's more famous sporting achievements. These people are heroes, but they're virtually unknown outside Wales.

I: Yes, it's the first time I've heard of the race. You're a runner, aren't you, Mike?

M: I was, but I damaged my knee when I was skiing and had to stop. I was a real enthusiast – used to run for a couple of hours after work every evening – but even then, I wouldn't have beaten a horse, that's for sure.

I: There's no shame in that! Right, thanks Mike. Time now for …

Unit 3 1.16

Part 4: Multiple choice

P = Presenter   K = Keith Wells

P: My guest today is robot scientist Keith Wells. Keith's company, ELA Robotics, hit the news a few years ago with their Home Help robot, the first of its kind to be able to perform more than one domestic task. What are you working on these days, Keith?

K: I can't really tell you that, I'm afraid. It's not that I don't want to, it's just that we've all been given our instructions and signed an agreement not to give anything away until it actually comes onto the market. I don't quite know when that will be, but probably some time early next year.

P: OK, well we'll look forward to that. In the meantime, perhaps you could tell us what you think are the most important applications of robots in our lives. Why are they useful?

K: Well, they help us to do what we call 'the three Ds'. That's anything which is dull, dirty or dangerous. They can be used in the home or in the car manufacturing industry, to do dull or monotonous work; they're used for doing dirty jobs like mining or cleaning toxic waste; and then they have applications in the military or in the dangerous business of space travel. Of course, that's not an exhaustive list, but it gives you an idea of the range of different uses they have – and also of the variety involved in my line of work.

P: Yes, indeed. Let's talk if we may about one area in particular, though, the more humanoid robots, the ones with a recognizable human form. What are the latest developments there?

K: Hmm, yes, the ones being built now are able to see, hear, touch and even smell and taste. Others can show a range of emotional states, such as sadness, joy, anger and even comical surprise. They can even recognize emotions in humans, by interpreting people's body-language – the postures they adopt, the gestures they make. The hope is that people will be more willing to welcome robots like these into their homes, and they could act as companions and home helps for the sick or the elderly.

P: Amazing. But isn't all this a little bit worrying – robots with emotions? Isn't there a danger of science fiction becoming science fact, with robots taking over?

K: Yes, unfortunately, robots do get rather a bad press sometimes, don't they? Particularly in films and video games where they're either objects of humour and ridicule which we laugh at or else they're menacing characters which threaten to destroy the whole human race. But no, there is actually an ethical code which sets out what we can and can't do in robot design – and one thing we won't do is allow ourselves to lose control over our creations.

P: Don't you think, though, that robots will make us lazy, that we'll no longer want to do anything that requires any effort?

K: I think the car's already done that to us. It's made us physically very lazy. We don't walk so much as we used to and our bodies have suffered as a result. I think robots could well have the same effect on our brains. If we let intelligent robots do all of our thinking for us, there is a danger we won't be able to make any of our own decisions, that we'll become mentally lazy. And that, I think, is just as worrying.

P: Do you really think that the day will come when most homes have their own robot?

K: If you think back to just thirty years or so ago, few of us then would have predicted that we'd soon have a personal computer in our home, be logging onto the Internet and downloading hundreds of songs and videos onto a thing called an MP4 player. So why shouldn't we all have robots? We've been talking about them for nearly a century now and certainly, their initial development wasn't quite as fast as we thought it would be. But now, with advanced computer technology available, very rapid changes are taking place in robot design.

P: Yes, I remember those rather clumsy-looking machines at the end of the 1990s.

K: That's right. The first humanoid robots could do very little, then later models learnt to sit down and stand up, then talk, walk around, dance and so on. It's rather like watching a child grow. Through television and other media, the public is slowly growing accustomed to the idea of robots as a reality, and when they eventually become widely available, people will be ready for them.

P: Thank you, Keith. It's been fascinating having you on the programme.

Unit 3 1.17–1.21

Part 3: Multiple matching

Speaker 1
Apparently, teenagers need more sleep than the rest of us, so next year we're starting lessons at 10, rather than 9 every day. The head says the kids will be more awake, more receptive during class if they come in an hour later. It's a fairly radical idea and it's attracting a lot of attention from the press. The head's given three newspaper interviews already – all of which goes to confirm my belief that she has her own interests in mind rather than those of the kids. It's just another of her schemes to get publicity for herself. Perhaps I should have spoken out at the consultation meeting, but she's got the support of the whole teaching staff, and they don't care that her motives are all wrong.

Speaker 2
I'm really fed up with our head of department. We all are. As well as having absolutely no interpersonal skills, he has a habit of making changes without bothering to find out what anyone else thinks first. He told us in a meeting last week that we're going to be using a different coursebook for Year 8 next term, and he's ordered three class sets already. Now, I'm not saying that a change wasn't necessary – I think we're all a bit tired of the book we're using at the moment – but I do think he could have let us have some say in the matter before going ahead. It's no way to run a department.

Speaker 3
I teach maths to as many as two hundred students in one year, so I'm not at all pleased about the changes to report writing. Until now, a student's end-of-term report consisted of a mark for each subject, and then the class tutor made a summarizing comment at the end. With the new system, each subject teacher has to write a comment as well. It'll take ages! The head says the tutor's comment isn't enough to give parents a full picture of how their child's getting on, but as long as it's carefully written, it's fine. Most parents won't read the comments anyway – they're just interested in the marks. It's a waste of time as far as I'm concerned, and I know the majority of my colleagues feel the same.

Speaker 4
The situation in Year 10 is not much better than it was before. Mixing up the classes like that – splitting up the

troublemakers – is a step in the right direction but it doesn't go far enough. They're still there, and they're still causing disruption to lessons. The head should have asked the parents to come in and got the kids to make certain guarantees in front of them, made them promise to improve their behaviour and so on. Then if the promises aren't kept, expel them from the school. We told her that, but she said expelling them would just create problems for other schools. She needs to be much tougher.

Speaker 5
There's some building work going on outside the music room, so you can imagine how difficult it is to teach in there. The windows are double glazed, but they're not enough to keep out the noise, so I've been moved – along with my piano – to a room on the other side of the school. Now I've changed rooms many times before, but never to one as bad as this. The ceiling's enormously high and the acoustics are terrible for the piano. Plus I practically have to shout to make myself heard, so my throat is suffering. And then the sun streams in during the afternoon and sends the kids to sleep. I'm telling you, as soon as the work's finished, I'm moving straight back to my old room.

Unit 4 👁 1.22–1.29

Part 1: Multiple choice

1   Listen to this woman talking about an actor.

I used to think he was so good looking – those sparkling blue eyes and that sexy smile – but now of course the wrinkles have taken over and he's lost it completely. Call me old-fashioned, but I really don't think that somebody of his age should be wearing tight trousers and flowery shirts. It's obscene. And the way he talks to the press! I mean, 'politeness' is just not a word he understands. I'm not surprised they get upset and give him bad reviews.

2   You overhear this conversation between two friends.

M = Man   W = Woman
M: So, have you decided which film we're going to see, then?

W: Well, I really wanted to see the new Fiona Miller film which everyone is raving about.

M: Oh, please, no! I couldn't stand another costume drama.

W: No, this one's very different from her others. She plays the part of an out-of-work spy who decides to turn to crime and begin a life as a jewel thief. But anyway, Katie says it's not her cup of tea, so I'm afraid it's 'get your handkerchief ready for another tear-jerker'. You know the plot already: boy meets girl, girl meets another boy, first boy gets upset – all that kind of nonsense.

3   You hear a man telling a woman about a storytelling course he attended.

W = Woman   M = Man
W: So what made you decide to do a storytelling course?

M: Well, a friend of mine who did it last year recommended it to me. She thought I might enjoy it – and she was right. It was great fun, really laid-back and everyone was very supportive. It gave me the courage I needed – and the self-belief – to be able to stand up and speak in front of a group of people.

W: So are you going to be leaving us to take up a career as a storyteller, then?

M: No, I like working here too much.

W: Ha-ha! That's a good story.

4   You hear an actress talking about her performance in a play.

Drained, darling, absolutely drained. And have you read what the critics wrote about it? I don't know how anyone could say it was 'disappointing'. I mean, OK, so it's not the most exciting part I've ever had to play but I gave it my all, absolutely everything. One look at my face will tell you just how utterly exhausted I am. I could sleep for a week.

5   You overhear this man talking on the telephone.

What do you think we should get him? … An atlas! That's not very much … I know he's interested in geography, but he's been with the company for nearly 25 years. I really don't think an atlas would express our appreciation for all he's done for the firm. He's been like a father to us all … I don't know, something that will remind him of us in his retirement, something he can use on a regular basis. How about an e-book reader or a decent video camera – that kind of thing?

6   You hear a young woman talking to her friend about a film.

M = Man   W = Woman
M: What was it like?

W: Oh, don't ask. I certainly wouldn't recommend it to anyone.

M: Too violent for you, was it?

W: Hmm … Quite the opposite. I mean, at first there was the usual dose of gratuitous violence – basically what you'd expect from that type of film, and partly why I went to see it. After that, though, not a great deal happened. From what I can remember – when I wasn't falling asleep, that is – the script seemed to focus on an analysis of the protagonist's inner self.

M: A kind of 'non-action film', then.

W: Exactly.

7   You hear a woman telephoning a bookshop.

Hello, yes, it's about a book I bought in your shop last week. A Katharine Adams novel. I just wanted to point out that there were one or two pages missing … No, no, there's really no need to apologize. I mean it's not as if it was the last page or anything. And I got the gist of what was happening without the pages. I just thought you ought to know so you can check the rest of your stock, or talk to the publishers or something … That's OK … Yes, pages 60 to 64 …

8   You hear this young man talking on the phone.

Well, we were born in the same month, but I'm a Leo, as you know, whereas her birthday's at the beginning of July, which makes her a Cancer. I don't know if that's good or bad. We certainly seem to laugh at the same things; the same jokes, the same comedy programmes … Sorry? … Oh, next Friday. We're going to a jazz concert, although I can't say it's my favourite type of music. She's really into it, and she wanted me to go, so …

Unit 5 👁 1.30

Part 4: Multiple choice

D = Deborah Chilton
I = Interviewer
I: Few of us would admit to actually enjoying doing the housework, so getting our teenage children to do their fair share is no easy task. Deborah Chilton, the author of a new parenting book, *The Stress Free Guide to Bringing up Teenagers*, is here to give us a few pointers. Deborah, where do we start?

D: Well, as you say, it's not easy, but if we're aware of what we're trying to achieve and why, then the battle is half won. Getting teenagers to contribute to housework has so many benefits. It's an ideal way of teaching them what it means to belong to a family and a community. They also learn to take on more responsibility as they approach adulthood, and they pick up some useful skills on the way, too. Knowing all this gives parents the strength they need to see their goals through.

I: Right. And at what age should teenagers begin helping out with the housework?

D: Long before they reach adolescence. Teenagers are naturally resistant to being told what to do, and suddenly asking them at fourteen or fifteen to take on chores when they've never done anything to help before – well, let's just say it doesn't meet with a very positive reaction. Parents often fail to take advantage of the fact that young children are quite happy to make their bed, tidy their room, lay the table or wash the dishes. So get them started early and you'll find it easier later on.

Listening scripts

I: And what sort of things can teenagers do?

D: Cleaning, washing, ironing. Anything, really. Planning and cooking a meal each week is excellent training, and teaches teenagers how much time and effort goes into putting food on the table. Whatever they do, just be sure to explain to them carefully how to do it first. My son once almost tried to wash the toaster in the sink while it was still plugged in!

I: Oh dear!

D: Yes. Teenagers will make mistakes, and that's part of the learning process. But it's best to try and avoid them before they actually happen.

I: Indeed. And what if your teenage son or daughter decides not to do a chore? What then?

D: Well, it's a good idea to make their contribution something that's important to them as well. That way, if it's not done, they're the ones to suffer. So for example, if they don't do the washing, they won't have clean clothes for a party; if they don't do the shopping, they can't eat. They'll get the idea eventually.

I: So you wouldn't consider handing out punishments?

D: Only as a last resort. They tend to cause bad feeling and resentment. If things don't get better, sit down together and remind them of their duty to other family members and the need to work as a team. And for the same reasons, don't give financial rewards for completing chores. Housework is an obligation, rather than a choice, and no one gets paid for doing it.

I: Hmm. If only we did! So, housework has to be done, and that's it.

D: Yes, but there's still room for some negotiation. Understandably, teenagers like to feel they have at least some say in the matter. So whilst the chore itself is not negotiable, when it is carried out might be. In fact, rather than say to your teenage child 'could you load the dishwasher?' – to which they could answer 'no' – ask them instead 'would you like to load the dishwasher before or after the film?' That way there's an element of choice, and the job gets done sooner or later.

I: Very clever. I like that.

D: Yes. And I would just like to say, that although domestic duties can be a pain, they can also be a welcome distraction. Teenagers generally have a lot on their minds, whether it's schoolwork, friendship problems or boyfriend/girlfriend issues. Vacuuming the carpet, cutting the grass or cleaning the car provides an alternative focus and helps take a teenager's mind off his or her daily concerns.

I: Certainly. And that's a very positive note to finish on. Deborah, thank you for coming in …

Unit 5 👁 1.31

Part 2: Sentence completion

Right, let's start by talking about the selection procedure. What do you have to do in order to become a firefighter? Well, it's a fairly rigorous process, with a range of different tests. We don't insist on any academic qualifications, but potential recruits do have to take a short educational test. Now this test is aimed at assessing basic literacy and numeracy, or in other words, reading, writing and arithmetic. But we also look at a candidate's people skills, because community work, dealing with the public, is such an important part of the job nowadays. And I'll say a bit more about that later.

Now you may be surprised to hear that firefighters no longer have to be a minimum height. Instead, they do a series of physical tests, which are designed to measure things like how tightly they can grip things, or whether their back and legs are strong enough. If they **get through** this stage they **go on to** the next one, the practical awareness day, which involves fitness tests, checks to see if claustrophobia is a problem and practical tasks such as ladder climbing.

Of course, both sexes are accepted into the force, though I have to say, women are still very much in the minority. In case you're wondering, we've had up to five women working with us at Hove Fire Station at any one time in the past. At the moment, though, there are just three on the workforce.

OK, what's next? Well, as you know, firefighters are on call 24 hours a day, so let me just say a little bit about how the shift system works. At Hove we operate an eight-day rota. That means a firefighter works two nine-hour day shifts, followed by two fifteen-hour night shifts. And then we get four days off before starting again. It's a continuous cycle.

Er, a typical shift begins with the Watch Parade, which is where one shift **hands over** to the next. Now this is a fairly formal affair and it's compulsory for everyone to wear full uniform. After that – if it's a day shift – mornings are **taken up with** training and equipment checks. We have to make sure that vital equipment such as our breathing apparatus is in perfect working order. And our fire engines, of course, have to be checked from top to bottom, too. Er, afternoons are usually **given over to** community safety work, which is what I mentioned at the beginning. So, for example, we do a lot of home safety visits, where we give advice to vulnerable people, such as the elderly and disabled, on how to keep their homes safe. And we'll fit smoke alarms if they haven't got them installed already.

One question I often get asked at these talks is 'What is your busiest time?' Well, we tend to get **called out** more in the evening, rather than during the day.

That's the time when shops and other business premises are left unattended, and also when most people are at home, cooking and so on. As you might expect, the majority of fires are domestic ones. The fires themselves often take only minutes to **put out**, but **clearing up** afterwards can take several hours. We have to do everything we can to prevent the danger of a fire re-igniting, so that means taking all the floors up, getting flammable things like carpets out of the building, and so on.

So what's it like being a firefighter? Well, obviously it's dangerous work and any firefighter who said that he had never felt frightened would be fooling himself and you. But it's all a matter of control. It's what we've been trained for and we learn to control feelings such as fear. But quite apart from the danger and the drama of the job, it's obviously very satisfying being out on the street, knowing that you're helping the public, doing something useful. I certainly don't think I'd be able to do any other job.

Unit 6 👁 1.32–1.36

Part 3: Multiple matching

Speaker 1
Before Paul started school, he used to come round to us every morning while his mother, Lynda – my daughter-in-law – was at work. He was a lovely child but, like most boys, he had almost limitless energy and at times he was rather difficult to control. We only had to look after him for four hours each day, but it completely wore us out. His mother would tell us off for letting him watch too much television – she said Paul needed to work his energy off in the park or on long walks. Easy for her to say, but we weren't getting any younger and watching television was a useful survival strategy. I remember arguing with Lynda on more than one occasion about this.

Speaker 2
I shared a flat once with someone who used to get annoyed about the silliest of things. He seemed quite pleasant at first, and we got on fine for a while. But that's because we hardly saw each other – he had an evening job in a bar and I worked during the day in a supermarket. When I got to know him better, though, I realized just how difficult he could be. Things had to be done his way and his way alone. He was obsessive about tidiness and he couldn't bear it if I left anything lying on the floor. He'd also tell me off for cooking food that made the house smell or for singing in the shower. I had to move out in the end. I couldn't stand it.

Speaker 3
Julie was a friend as well as a colleague. I looked up to her and admired her self-belief and quiet determination. It came as no surprise when she was promoted to senior manager and I wasn't. I didn't think it was unfair or anything. She deserved it. Of course I was disappointed, but I got over it quickly

enough. But Julie was now my boss and it soon became clear that she wasn't good at managing people. She bullied and shouted, and upset most people in the department, including me. To her credit, she realized she wasn't suited to the job and she asked for a transfer. But I haven't spoken to her since she left.

Speaker 4

My brother, Mike, and I often don't see eye to eye with each other, but it's never really affected our relationship. We've always got on very well, despite having very different ideas and opinions about things. Recently, though, something's come between us that's changed all that. The money we inherited from our grandmother wasn't divided equally between us. She left me more because I'm married with two children and Mike's single. At least that's what she said in her will. Understandably, I suppose, Mike thinks it's a bit unfair and feels hard done by. We haven't exactly fallen out with each other, but there's certainly a tension between us that wasn't there before.

Speaker 5

We split up around about this time last year, just before he went off to India. I'd always been very tolerant and understanding – I knew how much John's work meant to him and I'd put up with the situation for as long as I could. But we both realized these long periods of separation weren't good for the relationship. Not being able to make any plans for the future inevitably caused friction, so we decided to end it. We still see each other from time to time, and it's good because there's not the same tension between us that there used to be.

Unit 6 👁 1.37–1.44

Part 1: Multiple choice

1 You hear a woman on the radio talking about her father.

I always got on very well with my mother. I felt I could turn to her for advice, share confidences with her, because she understood my problems. With my father it was different. I found it difficult to talk to him, and when we did speak, you could feel the tension between us. I think it was partly because I take after him so much – I inherited my lack of confidence from him for one thing – and I blamed him for my own weaknesses.

2 You overhear a man talking about a former teacher.

After the first lesson we all thought he was a bit mad. But he was just different. Most of the other teachers in the school were really serious and uninspiring. They'd speak, we'd take notes and that was about it. It was deadly dull. But Hilton-Dennis would jump around the room, waving his arms about and jabbering away in Italian at us. He seemed to really enjoy what he was doing, and I took

to him almost straight away. He managed to communicate his passion for the subject and he got a lot of people interested in learning the language.

3 You hear a woman complaining about one of her employees.

W = Woman   M = Man

W: I'm going to have to have a word with Simon again. If it's not one thing, it's another.

M: Is Simon the scruffy one?

W: Yes, he is. That's not what worries me, though. He doesn't have any contact with the public, so I don't mind what he looks like.

M: So has he been rude again?

W: No, we managed to sort that one out. I took him aside just before Christmas and had a long talk with him. He's been quite pleasant since then. But I need reliable people who turn up on time and he's been late for work three times this last fortnight. I'm beginning to regret taking him on.

4 You hear part of a radio programme in which a man is giving advice.

Unfortunately, there's not always a direct relationship between hard work and good performance at school. Think how demotivating it must be for a young person to spend hours on homework and then get low marks for their trouble. Something like that can seriously affect their self-esteem and their confidence. So they may look for other ways to feel good about themselves. Let's imagine they come to you and say they want to have their nose pierced or get a tattoo done. Would you let them? Maybe not, but perhaps you should at least consider their motives for wanting to do so.

5 You overhear a woman talking on the phone about some clothes.

We're getting rid of anything we don't need before we move. We've got so much rubbish in our house, and there's not a lot of room in the new flat … Well, there are Hannah's old baby clothes, for a start. I've held on to them for years, just in case Hannah started a family of her own. But it doesn't look as if that's going to happen now … No, I haven't got the heart to put them in the bin, and I can't imagine anyone wanting to buy them. Can you? … Well, I'll probably take them round to Marina's. She knows lots of young mothers – I'm sure one of them will be delighted to have them.

6 You hear a man and a woman talking about a person in a photograph.

W = Woman   M = Man

W: It's a lovely photo. She looks so relaxed and cheerful – as if she's really enjoying it all.

M: Yeah, it's my mum's favourite. She's had it framed and it's up on the wall in her living room. She was starting to think she might never see her

daughter in a wedding dress, so it's got pride of place above the telly. Lucy doesn't like it though.

W: Why not?

M: She says you can see all her wrinkles. She's a bit sensitive about her age.

W: Oh dear. So, anyway, do you think there'll be a photo of you above your mum's telly one day? Little brother in a wedding suit?

M: Don't you start!

7 You hear an elderly woman talking to a man about her new neighbours.

M = Man   W = Woman

M: So how are the new neighbours?

F: Well, I must say I'm quite pleased so far. It's early days, of course – they've only been there for a couple of weeks. But they do seem better than the last ones. All those weekend parties. Such an unpleasant family.

M: Have you invited them round yet?

F: Well, no, I haven't had a chance. You see, they've asked me to go to their house on two occasions already – and one of those was for lunch.

M: That's very sociable of them.

F: Yes, it is, isn't it? As I say, I'm rather pleased. They've even offered to come and cut my grass for me.

8 You hear a man talking on the radio about a musician who influenced him.

People are surprised when I mention him as an influence. He played Blues Rock and my music's always in the New Age section. I suppose if he'd moved into Progressive Rock, there might have been some similarity. But he hated all that stuff, and probably would have hated what I do, too. And OK, I have the same kind of knee-length hair, but his was a fashion statement – mine's there because I can't be bothered to get it cut. No, it's the atmosphere he created on stage that I'm referring to – moody, some people call it. Soulful. No moving around – just let the guitar do the talking.

Unit 7 👁 1.45

Part 2: Sentence completion

Right, well, the layout of most major supermarkets is roughly the same, and for more or less the same reasons. You'll notice that the entrance, for example, is usually situated to one side of the building. This is to ensure, of course, that shoppers walk down as many aisles as possible before they leave the store. If we had it in the middle, then they might visit only one half of the supermarket and as a result only buy half as much. The first thing you often see as you come through the entrance is the fruit and vegetable area. As well as being pleasant to the eye, this also gives customers the impression they're coming into an outdoor market. Fresh, colourful products are far more attractive than tins of convenience food so the customer is put in a good buying mood, from the start.

And next to the fruit and vegetable area is the confectionery; er, crisps, chocolates, sweets and so on. Parents often come shopping with their children and we need to ensure that they are kept happy and interested so that they don't disturb mum and dad from the business of spending money. Then at the back of the supermarket in the corner, you'll probably find the fresh meat counter. This is partly to make sure that as little room as possible is taken away from the main display areas by the staff who are serving. But it's also there so as not to distract customers when we have deliveries. They really don't want to see us bringing big carcasses of meat through the store, so, er, it's brought in through the back door. And very close to the fresh meat you can expect to see the pre-packed meat. People who are put off by the sight of blood and um – dead animals – prefer to buy their meat in the form of convenience food to prevent them having to make the connection between the product and the animal. They buy a lamb chop, but they don't think of a baby lamb in the field. The freezer goods are nearby. There's a limited amount of space so the smaller suppliers often find it difficult to get room for their products. That's why you only tend to see the well-known brands here.

Er, moving on to the areas at the ends of the aisles – how do we decide what to put there? Well, these are key selling sites, and sales of goods at these points can be as much as five times higher than other areas. So we generally move goods to the end-of-aisle areas when we want to sell them quickly: goods which have not been selling well, and especially those which are nearing their sell-by date. Bread, too, needs to be sold quickly, but we put the bakery section in the far corner, as far away from the entrance as possible, next to other basic foodstuffs such as milk. This is so that customers have to walk past hundreds of products to reach it. Er, it's expensive to run a bakery but it increases sales of other products. The smell, too, is an important factor as it helps to create a warm, homely atmosphere in the store.

And finally, alcoholic drinks. They're often at the far end too, very near the exit. Er, by this time the shopper is beginning to enjoy the shopping experience, so he or she will buy more alcohol if it's here than if it's by the entrance. Er, the same is true for those products we put at the checkouts; er, more sweets and chocolates, usually. The kind of things people buy on impulse as they wait to pay – er, a reward they give themselves for doing the shopping.

Unit 7 👁 1.46

Part 4: Multiple choice

**I = Interviewer   R = Rebecca
G = Greg**

I: Rebecca, you've been living in a village for nearly five years now. What made you move to the countryside?

R: I suppose my priorities had changed with age. When I first went to London, I used to love the hustle and bustle of the place. But then I gradually became more aware of the planes roaring overhead, car horns beeping all the time, music blaring out at strange hours. I needed a break.

I: Greg, I can see you're smiling.

G: Yes. I remember when I first moved out with my family, we all found it a little too quiet. But we quickly got used to it, and now we prefer living with less noise. We also like the fact that you don't have to worry about the kids so much if they go off on their own.

R: Hmm, I'm not so sure. Some people drive like maniacs on these narrow roads. I have to keep a really close eye on my two young kids and make sure they don't wander off too far.

G: Well, we're lucky enough to have very good neighbours in the village. Everyone looks out for everyone else, and someone will soon tell you if your kids are in danger, or doing something they shouldn't be doing.

R: Yes, you can't do anything in a village without your neighbours knowing about it. But that's good, though. It's like having a big extended family.

I: What about the amenities where you live?

G: The basics are within walking distance from us; the school, the shops, even a couple of tennis courts.

R: I can't say the same, unfortunately. Being able to pop out to the shops when you need something is one of the things I miss about living in the city. We have to get the car out just to go and buy a loaf of bread. And you really do need to be able to drive to live where we do. Everyone in the village relies on their car; the bus service is just too infrequent.

G: It's better than not having one at all. We're actually trying to get the local authorities to put on at least one bus a day, particularly for the older residents who don't have a car and who sometimes need to go into town.

R: Yes, and I'm actually wondering how my two are going to find it when they become teenagers. They'll want to go into town, too. They'll probably complain of boredom and want us to go and live in the city again.

G: And who can blame them? I know at that age I would have been bored out of my mind! No cinemas, no decent shops, no cafés to sit in, no discos to go to …

I: Do you think either of you will ever go and live in the city again?

G: Naturally, I'd prefer to stay in the village and work at home rather than do a nine-to-five job in an office. I have my computer, email and the phone and a wonderful working environment. However, anything can happen and we'd be prepared to move back to London if we felt it was to our advantage.

I: Rebecca, how about you?

R: I'll be going back to work just as soon as my youngest child starts school. September of next year, in fact. Obviously I've thought about it a lot, and the fact that living where I do now will mean spending two hours driving to and from work every day. But I'd rather do that than go back to living in the city.

I: Well, thank you for both coming all that way to speak to us today. We'll have a break for music now and then …

Unit 8 👁 1.47–1.54

Part 1: Multiple choice

1 You overhear this man talking about the hotel where he is staying.

We really didn't expect this. We thought it'd be the typical economy type hotel. You know, nothing special, just a bed, a wardrobe and a shower in the room if you're lucky. Well, we were absolutely amazed by the en suite bathroom, I can tell you. It's twice the size of ours at home. And as for the view from the balcony, it's unbelievable. We really can't complain.

2 Listen to this woman talking about a job she has applied for.

… and I think that although my experience running a restaurant may not seem very relevant, it's still a people-orientated job. I am definitely a people person. I like dealing with the public. So whether it's listening to customers and giving them advice on the best places to go, or talking on the phone to tour operators and trying to get the best deal, I think I'd be well suited to the job. I have good people skills and I think that's an important strength.

3 You hear a woman talking to a tour guide.

T = Tour guide   W = Woman

T: Are you sure you had it when you left the hotel?

W: Positive. I didn't want to bring it but my husband made me put it in my bag. He said you should never leave your money or your passport in your room. And then when we were having a drink and I went to pay, it had gone. Someone must have pulled it out of my bag when I wasn't looking. It had my credit cards in it and everything.

T: It's a good job your passport wasn't in it, too. We'll have to report it straight away.

4 You overhear a man talking about a place he tried to visit on holiday.

We went there because we wanted to see the stained glass windows. They say they're among the finest in Europe and the colours are supposed to be incredible when the sun shines through them. Unfortunately, we couldn't go in because we weren't properly dressed – they won't let you in if you're wearing short trousers. And the next morning when we went back it was Easter Sunday. So of course, we couldn't get to the part where the windows are because there was a special service.

5 Listen to this conversation between a man and a teenage boy.

M = Man   B = Boy

M: Yes, your skin is quite badly burnt. How long were you out in the sun for?

B: About an hour, maybe. It was after lunch and I fell asleep on the beach.

M: Do you have any other symptoms – dizziness, a temperature?

B: No, it just really hurts.

M: Well, it doesn't sound like sunstroke. This cream should take away the sting, but if you start to feel sick or dizzy, get yourself to a doctor straight away.

B: Thanks. How much do I owe you?

M: I'll just check. One second.

6 You hear a local resident talking about tourists in her town.

I shouldn't complain really. I mean, the whole economy of this town is based on tourism and if they stopped coming, then a lot of people would be out of work and on the dole. But I do wish they'd show a little more respect. There are a lot of them who have music blaring out of their cars during the day, and then at night you get big groups coming into the centre for the pubs and clubs. And they don't seem to care that we can't sleep with them making such a racket. Most of them drunk, I shouldn't wonder.

7 You hear this boy talking to his mother.

B = Boy   M = Mother

B: Where are we going?

M: Well, we picked up a leaflet for a nature park just outside the town. They've got all sorts of wild animals and you can drive through and see them in their natural habitat. It looks very good.

B: But you said we were going to the Aqua Park.

M: We can't go in this weather. And besides, your father and I want to do something different.

B: But that's not fair. You can't just change your mind like that.

M: Don't be selfish, Steven. It's our turn today.

8 You hear a man talking about a beach he recently visited.

Now, normally I prefer a beach with fine sand, you know, so it's not painful to walk on. This one, though, had small stones – well, more like pebbles, actually – and I don't remember the brochure saying anything about that. But anyway, we bought ourselves a pair of flip-flops each at one of the shops next to the beach, so that didn't matter too much. And then we spent most of our time there lying about in the water. It was just like being in a warm bath. I could have stayed there all day.

Unit 8 👁 1.55–1.59

Part 3: Multiple matching

Speaker 1
There's a cycle path that goes right round the city, and various shorter ones within it. Now these paths are up on the pavement rather than in the road, so it's pedestrians, not motorists, that have to be careful they don't wander onto them. People have got used to the circular path and they generally keep off it when they're walking along. But it's the ones in the city centre that cause most problems, and it's here the authorities could do more to inform pedestrians, to make them aware of how it works. Every day I cycle to work and every day I get shouted at by people who still haven't caught on that it's me that has right of way, not them.

Speaker 2
Mine's a folding bike, so I get off the train, put on my helmet and head for the office. I could take the bus or the underground, but there's no pleasure in that – they both get so crowded. On the bike I feel the wind in my face and a sense that the city's mine – I can go where I want, when I want. I can even get up on the pavement and jump traffic lights or go the wrong way down one-way streets. And of course, cycling is just so healthy – I've never felt fitter. Some say it's risky too, but I find motorists tend to go more carefully when cyclists are around.

Speaker 3
A year or two ago, someone in the town hall came up with a nice idea to promote cycling in the city. On the first Sunday in every month, a number of the main streets in the centre are closed to traffic for two hours and given over to bicycles. It's gradually grown in popularity, and there's a real festival atmosphere now, with thousands of cyclists of all ages turning out every month. It's a start, and it's certainly helped to get people out on their bikes. But there's still a long way to go. We need a whole series of additional measures to make our roads more cycle-friendly.

Speaker 4
Sometimes you come across some really nasty drivers in the city. I can be cycling along, minding my own business, when some car or van comes right up close to me, almost touching my back wheel. It's really dangerous – sometimes I lose my balance and nearly fall off. It seems to be worse in the evening. I've got my bike lights, my luminous cycling jacket, my reflective cycle clips – so they can see me all right. But they seem to resent the fact that I'm there. They think they own the road and they get impatient if they have to slow down for me. I get beeped and shouted at all the time – it's very unpleasant.

Speaker 5
Cycling here is more a recreational activity than a means of transport. People don't generally use a bike to get about the city. There isn't that culture. They'll maybe rent one in one of the big central parks, or go on the cycle path that runs alongside the river. But they won't use a bike to get from A to B or to go to and from work. It's not an attractive option, really, given the quality of the air here. We're in the middle of a huge industrial area, and many pedestrians wear face masks. So people are hardly likely to expose themselves to more danger by cycling in amongst the traffic.

Unit 9 👁 1.60

Part 4: Multiple choice

A = Alan Stanford
I = Interviewer

I: In the *Talkabout* studio today we have a ghost walk guide. Local man Alan Stanford takes groups of people round the town on guided tours, telling ghost stories about the historic buildings which are said to be haunted. Sounds like an interesting job, Alan.

A: Oh, it is, it's fascinating. I've been a tour guide before but mostly abroad and never here in my own home town. I wouldn't call myself an expert, but I've learnt quite a lot about our local history since I started doing this a couple of years ago. Plus, of course, I get to dress up and tell lots of ghost stories. Acting and storytelling have always been in my blood, so I'm really just doing what comes naturally to me. I have a great time.

I: And how about those who actually go on the tours? Do they get frightened?

A: Well, obviously these are ghost walks, so it wouldn't be much fun if there wasn't a bit of fear involved. Not too much, of course – we often have children in the groups, so we have to be careful. But people expect to be scared, and they'd be disappointed if they weren't, so we aim at least to give them goose bumps, and perhaps even a little fright – after which **they all laugh nervously** and enjoy the release of tension.

Listening scripts

I: And how do you achieve that, giving them a fright?

A: Well, the mark of a good storyteller is the ability to hold an audience's attention, and that's not too hard to do when the subject is ghosts. You take the listeners into your confidence, create the right mood, make them feel safe with you. Then, just at the right moment, when they're least expecting it, you change the tone, give a shout or let out a scream. And they nearly jump out of their skin!

I: Right, yes. And does it work every time?

A: Well, it does with most audiences, people who've been thinking about the ghost walk all day, maybe all week, wondering what's going to happen. **These people usually respond extremely well**. Some of the groups we get, though, come along as part of a surprise event. People like these haven't had time to reflect on what they're coming to, they haven't been given the chance to look forward to it, and the effect isn't the same. They don't normally have such a good time, unfortunately.

I: You mentioned dressing up before. Do you do the ghost walks in character?

A: Yes, I do. And I have different costumes for different characters – there's Lord Warwick, a wealthy noble, the old sea dog Jake Redburn, John Simpkins, who's a servant … none of them real, of course – they're all fictitious. The choice of character I play often depends on the route we take and the stories to be told, or also perhaps how I'm feeling that night and the type of audience I'm expecting. As with all acting, it adds a sense of truth to the whole thing, makes it more credible. So the audience becomes engaged in the tour and responds in a more positive, sometimes more frightened way.

I: One question, I have to ask you, Alan. Do you believe in ghosts?

A: **Regrettably, I have to say that I haven't seen any on the walks**, or had any other paranormal experiences to impress you with. Some people in my audiences say they have, and so have some of my friends, and I wouldn't dare dispute that or suggest they're imagining things. Ghosts are real for those people who say they've seen them, and who am I to suggest they haven't? The most I can say is that I have no personal evidence they exist.

I: And of the stories that you tell on your ghost walks, do you have a favourite?

A: Well, I particularly like stories which involve smells that some buildings are said to give off when ghosts are around. I don't want to give away too much here on the programme, but the one I enjoy telling most of all is about an old woman called Sally Hardcastle, who haunts the town hall. When she appears every now and again, the place absolutely stinks. Now at first, some people thought it was a problem with the rubbish, but if you want to find out the real reason, you'll have to come along on the ghost walk.

I: Oh! We're curious now, Alan. And, if you are interested in going on a ghost walk with Alan …

Unit 9 👁 1.61

Part 2: Sentence completion

Hi, I'm Sally Hurst and I've just got back from Arizona, where I spent two weeks in the Superstition Mountain Range, near Phoenix. It's an area known to many people for its luxury golf courses, and those who can afford it go there to play golf in a desert setting. But it also attracts enthusiasts of more energetic outdoor activities like rock climbing or mountain biking. And I was lucky enough to go hiking when I was there. There are miles of paths and the scenery is absolutely spectacular.

'It's a bit hot there, though, isn't it?', some of my friends have asked. Well, it depends when you go. It's early spring now, of course, and that's fine. Winter and autumn are also OK, but I certainly wouldn't advise going there in summer – whatever the reason for your visit. Temperatures can reach up to 45 degrees or more – and that's far too hot for me.

The main reason I went there was to research some of the legends and mysteries of the area for a forthcoming radio documentary. The very origin of the name, Superstition Mountains is itself a bit of a mystery. One theory says they were given their name by sixteenth-century Spanish settlers, some of whom inexplicably vanished when they went exploring there. But the more likely explanation is that it came about in the nineteenth century, when it was discovered that the local Pima Indians were frightened of the mountains. Farmers in the area attributed this fear to superstition, and they decided to give that name first to one mountain, and then the whole range.

Perhaps the most talked-about mystery in the area is that of the so-called Lost Dutchman's Mine, which is supposedly somewhere in the Superstition Mountains. Far from being Dutch, the owner of the gold mine in question, Jacob Waltz, was actually German, or Deutsch in his native language. Waltz arrived in the United States in November 1839, and spent virtually all his life there prospecting for gold, firstly in North Carolina, then Georgia, California and finally Arizona. When he passed away in October 1891 he took the secret of his mine with him to his grave.

You see, apparently Waltz had found what was believed by some to be the richest gold mine in the world. But he didn't tell anyone where it was, and it's a mystery which remains unsolved to this day. According to one estimate in 1977, up to eight thousand people a year tried to locate the mine. And even today, despite the ban on mineral prospecting in 1983, many people still head for the region to see if they can find it.

Waltz left a few clues, but they weren't particularly helpful. In one of them, for example, he says, 'The rays of the setting sun shine into the entrance of my mine', but that could be just about anywhere.

I did a lot of my research for the documentary in a museum: The Superstition Mountain Museum. It's full of information on the Lost Dutchman's Mine, including a whole collection of maps which are thought to show its location – not that that's been of any use to anyone! So far, anyway.

And I saw another exhibit on the mine in a museum in nearby Goldfield. Now Goldfield was a prosperous mining town at the end of the nineteenth century, but when the gold ran out, everyone left and now it's a ghost town. It's become a popular tourist attraction as well, of course, with museums, rides and shows, but it's still quite impressive, nevertheless.

Now you may have seen a film that was made in 1949 about the Lost Dutchman's Mine entitled *Lust for Gold*, starring Glenn Ford in the role of Jacob Waltz. But here's another piece of trivia for you: in 1960, actor Walter Brennan recorded a song on the subject called *Dutchman's Gold*. Now I bet you didn't know that, did you?

Well you do now, and we're going to play it to you right after the news. To be honest, Walter Brennan talks his way through it rather than …

Unit 9 👁 1.62

Language focus 2: Question tags

2
It's a bit hot there, though, isn't it?
Now I bet you didn't know that, did you?

3
1 You don't believe him, do you?
2 You won't let me down, will you?
3 You went away for the weekend, didn't you?
4 He's not playing very well, is he?
5 He's already passed the *First* exam, hasn't he?
6 I'm right about that, aren't I?
7 You can play chess, can't you?
8 Let's phone Paul, shall we?

Ready for Listening
👁 2.1–2.8

Part 1: Multiple choice

1 You hear part of a sports commentary on the radio.

These two sides are very well matched. You'll remember they both met in the semi-finals last year, when the game ended in a draw. This year we've had some heavy showers in the last few days and one or two of the players are finding the playing conditions on the pitch more than a little difficult. But it's a throw-in now. Briggs takes it and passes to Duckham. Duckham tries a shot … and it goes just wide of the post.

2 You hear a man talking on his mobile phone.

I thought at first it was some kind of virus, but now I'm wondering if it might be something more serious … No, it's annoying. I simply can't do any work on it at the moment … Yes, I phoned them, but they said they'd need to have it for three days before they could give me an answer … Well, I was wondering if you wouldn't mind having a look at it for me … Could you come round after work? … No, that's great; the sooner the better as far as I'm concerned, as long as your boss doesn't mind.

3 Listen to this man and woman speaking.

M = Man   W = Woman

M: Lots of room for the legs, that's nice.

W: Mm, and so comfortable. It's like my favourite armchair. I could go to sleep here and now.

M: Yes, we should've had a coffee after the meal to keep us awake.

W: We'd never have got a ticket to see this if we had.

M: That's true. The queue was enormous.

W: Anyway, wake me up when it starts, won't you.

4 You hear this woman telling her friend about a restaurant.

You can't fault the food, really. Even my husband was impressed and he's always the first to complain if it's not cooked properly. No, I just felt a little uncomfortable; silver cutlery, antique furniture and everyone dressed as if it was a wedding, including the waiters. And the way they spoke to us! It was 'Sir' and 'Madam' every sentence. I suppose I'm just not used to it, that's all.

5 You hear this man talking to his friend on the phone about a day trip to London.

The play finishes at about 11… Well, I had at first thought of coming back on the train straight afterwards, but the last one's at 11.05, so I probably wouldn't make it … Are you sure you don't mind? … I could always stay in a hotel. There are plenty of cheap ones in that part of town … OK, well, if you're going to put me up for the night, then you'll have to let me take you out for a meal … No, I insist.

6 You hear a woman talking to her husband in a supermarket.

W = Woman   M = Man

W: Just look at that. It's incredible.

M: What do you mean?

W: Well, there must be about twenty different types of butter in this section. Low-fat, high-fat, Irish, Dutch, Australian – you name it, they've got it.

M: Confusing, isn't it?

W: That's not the point. I'm sure a lot of people will be disappointed there aren't twenty types of carrots and sixty different varieties of cheese. I just don't see why we need them all. And when you think of the transport costs and the fuel needed to import all this stuff and the effect this has on the environment. Oh! It makes my blood boil.

7 You hear this man talking.

We all know juvenile crime's on the increase. The police do all they can with very limited resources and then it's up to people like ourselves to sort the problem out. In this school alone we have more than twenty youngsters with a criminal record and we get virtually no support from the parents. Social services come in occasionally to give us advice on how to deal with them, but once they've gone and we close the classroom door, we're very much on our own.

8 You overhear a man talking to a woman about a flat which is for rent.

W = Woman   M = Man

W: Did you go and see that flat you were interested in?

M: Yeah, I did. It's not for me, though.

W: Why's that? Too expensive for you?

M: Well, no, I could afford it all right. It's on the edge of town near the industrial estate, and rents out there aren't as high as in the centre.

W: Hmm, that's too far out for me. I like it where I am, near the shopping centre.

M: Well, it's not as if there aren't any shops out there – there are plenty of amenities. It's just that I need space for all my computer equipment, and the lounge and the bedroom are smaller than where I'm living at the moment.

Ready for Listening
⊙ 2.9

Part 2: Sentence completion

Argentina is a country known internationally for the tango, gaucho cowboys and premium quality beef. To many people, therefore, it comes as some surprise to discover that in certain parts of Patagonia, in the south of the country, one of the 'musts' for any tourist is a visit to a Welsh tea house, a place where you can sip tea and enjoy delicious cakes, baked according to traditional Welsh recipes. Perhaps even

more surprising, though, is the fact that some of the locals can actually be heard speaking in Welsh. Exactly how many native Welsh speakers there are in the region is not known, but most estimates put the figure at several hundred, a relatively high number, given that there are just under 600000 speakers of the language in Wales itself.

But how did these Welsh speakers come to be there? The first wave of settlers arrived from Wales in 1865. Unhappy with conditions at home, they were looking for an isolated area to set up a colony, a place where their language and identity would be preserved intact and not assimilated into the dominant culture, as had already happened in the United States. The 153 colonists who landed on the east coast of Argentina included carpenters, tailors and miners, but no real doctors and just one or two farmers. This was rather worrying, since the Chubut valley where they settled was virtually a desert, and what was needed most of all were agricultural skills.

Against all the odds, though, they survived, overcoming droughts, floods and a succession of crop failures. They were also quick to establish friendly relations with the local Indians, who helped the Welsh through the hard times and taught them some of their ways, how to ride and how to hunt. Twenty years after their arrival, some of the settlers moved up into a green fertile region of the Andes mountains, an area which they named Cwm Hyfryd, meaning 'beautiful valley'. Indeed, quite a number of places in Patagonia still bear Welsh names: Bryn Gwyn which means 'white hill', Trevelin, meaning 'milltown' and Trelew or 'Lewistown', named after Lewis Jones, one of the founders.

The Welsh have left their mark in other ways, too. Their windmills and chapels can be found throughout the region and there are a number of cultural activities, such as poetry readings, male voice choirs and the annual Welsh song and dance festival, a smaller version of the International Eisteddfod held in Wales each year. All of this helps to keep the language and traditions alive in a small corner of the world, 8000 miles from the homeland. And so too does the fact that every year, as part of a programme administered by the National Assembly for Wales, groups of teachers come to Patagonia to teach the language to the growing number of people who are interested in learning it.

And then, of course, there are the Welsh teas. For my afternoon treat, I visit *Nain Ceri*, reputed to be one of the best tea houses in Gaiman, where the streets and houses are adorned with Welsh flags, a reminder to visitors that they are in the self-proclaimed Patagonian-Welsh capital of Chubut. Inside, *Nain Ceri* is decorated with prints and paintings of Wales and the music playing is that of a traditional all-male choir. I sit next to the fireplace and my mouth begins to water as I look at the various cakes on offer. I am about to order the cream-topped apple pie to accompany my tea, when I catch sight of an irresistible-looking chocolate cake and choose that instead. I am not disappointed – it is absolutely delicious. Afterwards, I chat at length to the owner, Ceri Morgan – in Spanish, as she speaks no English and I speak no Welsh. She tells me a little more about the history of …

Ready for Listening

 2.10–2.14

Part 3: Multiple matching

Speaker 1

I've been writing for as long as I can remember, and it's something I want to continue to do for a living when I've finished university. I say 'continue' because I've already had one collection of short stories published and I've just started another. I write mostly late at night and at weekends, always after I've finished my coursework. I'm doing a maths degree, which has little to do with writing, but I believe in keeping my options open, just in case my creativity runs out.

Speaker 2

For some strange reason I want to be a tattoo artist; you know, paint people's bodies. I'm doing a course in graphic design at art college, which I've been told will be useful. The brother of a friend of mine has a studio and he lets me go and watch him work when I'm not studying at the college. It's the only way to learn, as there are no official courses and no specific qualifications for tattoo artists. At least, not as far as I know.

Speaker 3

As soon as I leave school I'm going to join the Army. I tried to do it when I was 10 but they told me to go back when I was older – so I will! You can learn a trade and do almost any job you want to, and they let you study while you're working. I'd like to work as a physical training instructor, and then maybe later try and get an engineering qualification or something like that. My granddad's an ex-soldier and he always told such good stories that I knew that was what I wanted to do. My parents just think I'm crazy.

Speaker 4

I hope one day to be a speech therapist. I'll have to get a degree in speech therapy first, and to be able to do that in a decent university I'll need to get good grades next year. It's a job which involves helping people who have difficulty communicating, and I've always known I wanted to work in one of the 'caring professions'. My uncle's a speech therapist, but I learnt all about it from a TV documentary I saw a few years ago. And that's when I thought; 'I want to do that'. Then last year I did some voluntary work while I was studying for my exams, and I was hooked.

Speaker 5

I haven't made up my mind yet, but I'd quite like to go into teaching. Naturally I've had lots of advice from teachers at school about how to go about it and how hard I'll have to work for my exams. But to be honest my decision is based not so much on my academic abilities but rather on the fact that I just feel I'd be right for the job. The teachers I look up to at school are all dynamic, outgoing people and that's precisely how I like to see myself.

Ready for Listening

2.15

Part 4: Multiple choice

P = Presenter   J = Jenny Parfitt

P: Do you consider yourself to be tall, medium or short? At one metre eighty-four, I've always thought of myself as being a little on the tall side, particularly when I stand next to the people I work with here in the *Round Britain* studio. Rather curiously, most of them are below the national average height of one metre seventy-eight for men and one sixty-two for women. But when I popped in yesterday to the annual conference of the TPC – that's the Tall Person's Club of Great Britain and Ireland – I felt decidedly small. I asked one of the organizers, Jenny Parfitt, to tell me about the conference.

J: Well, this is the main event in the club's very busy social calendar. Throughout the year we put on a whole number of activities for members in their local area, like barbecues, theatre excursions, walks and so on. And this conference is the highlight of that year. It's a three-day event that gives tall people from all over the country the chance to meet in the comfort of a hotel, where they can chat, eat, dance and go sightseeing with others who are also above average height.

P: But there's also a serious side to it as well, I gather.

J: That's right, it's not all partying! We discuss a lot of important issues, too. One of the aims of the TPC is to promote the interests of tall people, to change current attitudes. We live in a heightist world, where tall people are discriminated against. Beds in hotels are usually too short for us, and we often have to sleep with our feet hanging off the end. Travelling by bus, train or plane is a major problem too – there's very little leg room and it can feel very cramped. The main difficulty, though, is finding shops that sell long enough trousers or big enough shoes. That can be a real headache.

P: I imagine too that the attitudes of other people can be a problem.

J: Yes, people do tend to stare at us when we walk into the room, treat us like circus freaks. And some actually laugh out loud, as if something funny has just happened. I think if I weren't so used to it now, I might take offence – I know many fellow TPC members do. But to be honest, I find it a little bit annoying. You get tired of it all, particularly when the fifteenth person in a day says something like 'What's the weather like up there?' And they think it's so funny.

P: Yes, not very original, is it? Does the club offer help to tall people who come across attitudes like these?

J: Yes, we regularly give advice to victims of insults and bullying at school or in the workplace. But perhaps the greatest benefit of the club is the opportunity to see that as a tall person you are not alone. When people come to their first meeting and walk into a room full of tall people, they start standing up straighter. They lose their shyness and very soon begin to feel less awkward, more comfortable about their height. It's a remarkable transformation.

P: You've mentioned some of the negative aspects of being taller than average. But surely there must be some advantages, too?

J: Oh yes, there are plenty of them. Er, for example, you can always see over everyone's head if you're watching something in a crowd or an audience, and if you're in a supermarket you can get things off the top shelf that most other people have a job to reach. And then also, you automatically become first choice for sports like basketball, volleyball or rowing. I've never been very good at volleyball, but I always got picked for the university team when I was a student.

P: Now, one thing of course we've failed to mention, Jenny, is your height. How tall are you?

J: One metre eighty-eight. And actually, I'm one of the smaller members at this conference. The tallest woman here is exactly two metres and the tallest man two metres thirty, that's an incredible seven foot six inches.

P: Goodness me!

J: Yes, impressive, isn't it? Incidentally, though, you don't need to be above a certain height to qualify as a member of the Tall Person's Club. Unlike some clubs in the USA, which can be difficult to join because of their restrictions, we are very inclusive over here. We believe that people know for themselves whether they are tall or not and it's up to them to decide if they should join.

P: Jenny, it's been fascinating talking to you …

Unit 10 👁 2.16

Part 4: Multiple choice

I: Interviewer   **J: Justin Blakelock**

I: With us today is local crime writer, Justin Blakelock. Justin, perhaps I should begin by asking you why you decided to write crime fiction rather than any other genre?

J: Whenever I'm asked that question, people think I'm going to say it's because I've always loved reading crime novels. Well, I have, but I'm actually much more of a science fiction fan than anything else, and that's the kind of thing I was writing when I first started out as an author. But then my editor – an ex-policewoman curiously enough – saw elements of crime writing in my work and she gently pushed me in that direction.

I: And was it her idea to set your novels here in Brighton?

J: No, that was mine. Firstly, because I love the place so much and, despite the crime theme, I do try to show it in a positive light. But also, even though I'm writing fiction, I want my stories to be as real and accurate as possible. And because I grew up in this area, because I know it so well, it makes sense for me to set them here. There are too many novels that lack credibility because they're set in fictional places, or they're set in real places which are not accurately described.

I: You show two versions of Brighton in your books, don't you?

J: That's right. To the visitor, Brighton seems a very peaceful city. It has this gentle, calm exterior – the very solid seafront buildings and pleasant shopping streets. But like many other cities it has its darker, more criminal places – the rundown buildings and areas that the tourist rarely sees. And that's also true of many of the characters I create. At first, they seem to be very gentle, very pleasant people, but there's something darker, more criminal hiding below the surface.

I: And how about your protagonist, Detective Inspector George Trent? He's a little more straightforward, isn't he?

J: Yes, yes he is. He does have the occasional moment when he surprises everyone – if not, he'd be too dull. But essentially, what you see is what you get with George. He's very scruffy, slightly overweight, and completely disorganized. He doesn't worry about things like dressing up or combing his hair – he thinks he's good enough as he is, he's very comfortable with the way he looks. And that's really what makes him such a likeable character, I think.

I: Yes, he's not attractive, but he's very human, isn't he? Now, Justin, you have a very popular website. Can you tell us about that?

J: Yes, sure. Well, the original idea behind the site was to get my name out there more and promote my books. But it gradually evolved into a blog – usually articles aimed at crime writers who were just getting started. And then other established authors began reading and commenting on my posts, and now it's effectively become a forum, a kind of debating club.

I: Can you give us an example of the kind of advice you give?

J: Well, I've just posted a list of things you should remember to include in a crime novel. So for example, make sure your detectives have enough paperwork to keep them busy. Real detectives have loads to do, so your fictional ones should be doing their fair share too. To be honest, it's the kind of thing writers ought to pick up themselves by watching what goes on in a police station. There's absolutely no substitute for that. But it's good to compare notes and for every ten pieces of advice I give, you can read twenty more in the comments from other writers who've done their own research. It's a support service, a secondary source.

I: And a very useful one. Now Justin, your last book, *Western Road*, is currently being made into a film. You must be delighted.

J: Yes, I am. More or less. The American producers wanted to move the action to Chicago, but I made it a condition that it had to be filmed in Brighton with British actors. I only wish I'd insisted on having more control over the script. It moves too fast for my liking. But that's the film world for you – what can you do?

I: Not much, I guess. Justin, thank you for coming in. Good luck with …

Unit 10 👁 2.17–2.21

Part 3: Multiple matching

Speaker 1
I was supposed to check all the windows were closed before we left the house for my swimming class, but I was rushing to get ready and I forgot. When we were in the car, my dad asked me if I'd remembered to do it. I didn't want to be late, so I lied and said I had. That morning we were burgled – lost all our TVs and computers. As soon as I heard what had happened, I **owned up** to my dad about lying – I felt so guilty, I had to tell him. Plus it was pretty obvious they'd got in through an open window – there was no sign of a forced entry anywhere.

Speaker 2
When I was about five or six, I took a pair of scissors out of a kitchen drawer and cut off a big chunk of my hair in front of my friends. I'm not sure why – maybe I was just **showing off**, trying to make myself look big. I kept being asked the same question: 'Have you cut some of your hair off?' My mum, my dad, the hairdresser … And I kept saying 'no'. I said it so many times, I almost believed it in the end. I thought I'd **got away with it**, but my mum told me recently she'd always known what had happened.

Speaker 3
I once typed out a note to my teacher and forged my mum's signature, so I could **get out of** doing sport. I think I said I had a stomach ache or something. My mum **found out** and went mad. Like an idiot I'd created a file with the name 'sick note' on our main computer and she spotted it a week or so later. Why I didn't delete it, I have no idea – it was a stupid mistake. My mum was really upset. She said I'd used her to lie to my teacher, which was true, of course. I didn't have to do sport that day, though.

Speaker 4
My mum gave me a hundred pounds in cash to pay for a school trip to France. When I went to give the money to the French teacher, I couldn't find it anywhere. I knew my mum would be angry with me, so I **made up** something about being mugged on the way to school. She phoned the head and they called the police. They realized fairly quickly I was lying, because the second time I described what had happened I got confused and it came out all wrong – not all the details were the same. I've never been in trouble with so many people in one day.

Speaker 5
I remember when my neighbour **came over** a year or so ago. She knocked on my door and said she'd **run out of** flour and asked if she could borrow some. It was a Sunday afternoon and the shop on the corner was closed and she wanted to bake a sponge cake for her kids. Well, I did have some, and under normal circumstances, I'd have been more than happy to lend it to a neighbour in need. But she'd never done me any favours, and in fact, she'd been positively unfriendly to me on occasions. So I said I was sorry, but no I didn't have any flour, and if she hurried she might catch the shop down in the town before it closed.

Unit 11 👁 2.22

Part 2: Sentence completion

Hello, my name's Michael Gallagher, and I've come to talk to you about one of my great passions: the weather. Now for the past forty years I've worked as a postman in an area which includes some of the more remote parts of County Donegal. And for more than twenty-five of those years I've been using traditional methods to make predictions about the weather.

Now, as a postman, I've had the privilege of meeting many people from the surrounding towns and villages, particularly farmers, who've taught me a great deal about how to interpret what goes on in the natural world – the behaviour of the animals, birds, insects and plants that are all around us. These people have had to struggle with the elements to make a living from the land, and over the centuries they've built up a vast store of knowledge and folklore to help them read the signs which are present in nature, signs which can help us predict the weather.

You can read more about these in my book, which is called *Traditional Weather Signs*, but I'll give you a few examples now of what's in it. Let's start with birds. Birds are very sensitive to changes in the weather, and we can learn a lot from them. For example, swallows flying low are a sign that rain is on its way, and so are crows if they're flying in groups. But swallows flying high tell us that the weather's going to get better.

Cats, too, can help us predict the weather, particularly if they're sitting by the fire. A cat washing its face there is a sure sign of wet weather. But if it's sitting with its back to the fire, then you know that frosty weather is coming. Farm animals are good indicators, too. Cows, horses, goats, sheep – you just have to watch the way they behave. Cows, for instance, they don't stay in the middle of a field if they sense a storm approaching, and neither do horses or donkeys. If you see them grazing with their backs to a hedge, you know the weather's going to turn bad.

Now some of you will know me from my longer-range forecasts, which are reported in the media from time to time. Last year, for example, I got it right when I said we were going to have a warm summer in Ireland. Now I knew that, because the sheep on the low ground started heading back to the hills in late spring to graze, and that's always an indication that the harsh winter and spring are over and good weather is on the way.

And then I predicted that cold snap we had two winters ago, and I got that from a combination of events. The sheep were hungry, so they started coming off the mountains at the beginning of December to look for food. Then there was the fact that grass started growing as late as October on the lowland, and also the way the sun was shining on the mountains – it was giving off an orange glow.

The sun, the moon, the stars – they've all been used to make predictions for centuries in rural Ireland. Many of us are familiar with the saying 'red sky at night, shepherd's delight', meaning that the weather will be fine tomorrow if the sky is red at the end of today. But there's a whole lot more that can be predicted from what's up there above us. And you can read more about that in my book.

Now I'm sure some of you would like to know what the weather's going to be like in the week ahead. Well, where I live we can expect some very heavy rain for the next three or four days. I noticed the frogs were coming out of the mud this morning and they weren't their usual bright green colour. They were much darker. Now that's a bad sign. As for this part of the world …

Unit 11 👁 2.23–2.30

Part 1: Multiple choice

1 You hear a man talking about a new fire station that has just been built.

I really can't understand why they put it all the way out there. They maintained that if they'd built it in the heart of the city, there would have been problems getting out to fires in the rural areas. Too far and too much traffic, they said. But that's exactly why it would have made more sense to build it in the centre instead of on the edge. You know, it takes a fire engine nearly twenty minutes to get from that suburb to the other side of the city.

2 You hear a man talking about litter.

If I was a member of the Council, I'd make sure something was done about the mess on the streets. It's an absolute disgrace. Local people need more help to keep them clean, and that help has to come from the authorities. There aren't enough litter bins, for one thing, so the pavements outside my premises are covered with paper, drink cans and cigarette butts. Before I open up in the morning I have to spend about ten minutes sweeping it all up. I wouldn't sell anything if I didn't.

3 You hear an environmentalist speaking on the radio about a recent project.

You have to remember that some species of plants were facing extinction in the area. People would come out to the countryside for a picnic, see all these beautiful flowers and pick them, without realizing the effect this was having. If we hadn't made this a conservation area and limited the number of people coming in, then we'd have no flowers at all, and people would be really upset. As it is, we can congratulate ourselves on the action we took and look forward to a brighter future for this patch of countryside.

4 You overhear this woman talking to her friend about her holiday.

M = Man   W = Woman

M: So what was it like?

W: Marvellous. Just what we were looking for.

M: And what was that?

W: Well, if we'd gone to one of the other islands, we'd have had to put up with busy roads and crowded beaches.

M: So weren't there many tourists where you went?

W: Oh plenty. More than we expected really. But it didn't seem to matter, because with the vehicle restrictions there was almost a total lack of exhaust fumes, no congestion and very little noise. And because the island's so small, you could walk everywhere, anyway.

5 You hear a conversation between two people.

M = Man   W = Woman

M: I think we should all get together and decide what we're going to do. I can't put up with it any more.

W: Neither can we. The noise of that boy's music makes the whole house shake. My husband says it's just like being in an earthquake, only worse.

M: Of course it's the parents' fault, but it's no good talking to them. They're no better than he is.

W: And his teachers can't control him, either. Apparently, he's as rude to them as he is to all of us.

M: So, let's have a meeting of all the residents in the street and we'll decide how to deal with him.

6 You are listening to the radio when you hear the following being read.

Violent storms swept across the south coast today, causing widespread damage to property. Torrential rain and gale-force winds lashed seaside towns and several people had to be evacuated from their flooded homes by rescue services. One man in Bognor narrowly escaped death as the car he was driving was crushed by a falling tree, which had been struck by lightning.

7 You overhear this conversation between a man and his neighbour.

W = Woman   M = Man

W: What's the problem, John?

M: Well, we lost a lot of our plants last night.

W: It wasn't our cat, was it?

M: No, the wind. Pulled up all the roses, it did. Blew down a few bushes, too.

W: I'm sorry to hear that.

M: Oh, not to worry. I'd be grateful if you'd give me a hand to clear up the mess, though.

W: I'd be pleased to.

8 You hear a man talking about a recent environmental disaster.

Something's got to be done. These massive petrol tankers should just not be allowed to sail so close to our shores. The oil slick has already killed thousands of birds and the beaches are a disaster area. Demonstrating is all very well, but it's not going to clean up the mess, is it? We can't leave it in the hands of the politicians, so we've just got to get down to the coast and get our hands dirty with the rest of the volunteers. You coming?

Unit 12 ◉ 2.31–2.35

Part 3: Multiple matching

Speaker 1
I tried crash diets, such as one where you just eat cabbage soup, and another where you drink nothing but lemonade with some salt and pepper for about seven days without any food. They worked temporarily, but after a while I put the weight back on. Then I was introduced to these diet pills and my weight went down to 65 kilos. But I wasn't earning a great deal of money and I simply couldn't afford to keep it up. That's when I decided to save my money and join a gym.

Speaker 2
I used to eat a lot of junk food. It was quick, inexpensive and it satisfied my hunger immediately. The problem was, I ate very little fresh food, and this had a serious effect on my health. I became overweight and suffered all sorts of illnesses. The doctor strongly advised me to rethink my attitude to food. If not, he said, the consequences could be very serious. Well, you can't ignore advice like that, can you? So I started to eat more healthily. And now if I get hungry between meals, I have a little cheese or some nuts, just to keep me going.

Speaker 3
I'm under no real pressure to lose weight, but I take care over what I eat, simply because it makes me feel better. When I want to treat myself, I have a piece of cake or a few biscuits. I read a lot about dieting, and most nutritionists seem to agree that as long as you eat sweet things after a meal, then there's no problem. So, for example, I only ever eat chocolates after lunch or dinner. And never too many of course – just one or two.

Speaker 4
I like eating and I'm not at all interested in dieting. But I do go to see a nutritionist, who helps me maintain a sensible, balanced diet: plenty of fresh fruit and vegetables, er, meat and fish, carbohydrates such as rice and pasta, several glasses of water a day – and no snacks between meals. She told me to give up cheese, but I ignored her. I enjoy good food and I don't want to deprive myself of the things I love.

Speaker 5
A large number of people follow diets, but very few of them are happier as a result. We are constantly under attack from advertising and the media, who tell us that 'thin is beautiful'. I used to believe this and think that I wouldn't find a boyfriend unless I was really skinny, that I had to weigh under 60 kilos for boys to like me. But of course, now I realize there's more to it than that. Just being yourself is what counts and I don't pay much attention to what others think or say.

Unit 12 ◉ 2.36

Part 4: Multiple choice

I = Interviewer   N = Naomi Price

I: On *Health Matters* today we have personal trainer Naomi Price. Naomi, what exactly does a personal trainer do?

N: Well, in my case I try to improve people's quality of life and overall health, by helping them develop their fitness, strength and posture – and working on their diet, as well. These are the general goals, but of course, each client has their own specific, individual goals, so before we do anything, I carry out a needs analysis in order to establish exactly what it is a person wants to achieve. This includes asking them about their diet, their injury history and any medical complaints or conditions they have, such as high blood pressure. Then basically, I design exercise routines and give advice on nutrition in response to the information they give me.

I: And what reasons do clients have for coming to see you?

N: Oh, there's a wide range. I get a lot of clients, especially older ones, who simply want to lose a bit of weight or lower their cholesterol levels. I also have a large number of younger clients who've been injured while doing sport and want to get back to full fitness – that's my area of expertise, it's what I specialize in. I also help one or two people train for marathons and triathlons, but mostly it's people who just want to improve their all-round fitness and as a result, their general self-confidence.

I: And I imagine it's important to build up a good relationship with your clients.

N: Yes, it is. I'm not one of those fitness instructors you sometimes see in films shouting orders at people to do fifty press-ups or run ten times round the park. Certainly, clients have to be dedicated and prepared to work hard when they're with me, but I also want them to enjoy exercising as well. So it's important, I think, for a trainer to bring an element of fun into the sessions, and I always make sure my clients have a good laugh when they come to me.

I: Now your workplace is your garage, isn't it, Naomi?

N: Well, yes, what used to be my garage. I don't park my car there any more – it's full of equipment. There's a rowing machine, two treadmills, two exercise bikes and loads of weights and things. I've also got a massage table, but that's in my lounge, where it's warmer. And then with some people, I go to the park or a nearby wood to run or simply to add a bit of variety to the classes. Clients appreciate that – they've told me that

other local trainers they've been with always hold their sessions inside.

I: You haven't always been your own boss have you?

N: No, I used to work in a gym. The good thing about that was I learnt a lot from watching the other gym instructors and their interaction with the clients – both good and bad examples. I also got experience of working with a lot of different clients, but the trouble was, I rarely had the chance to build up long lasting relationships with them. The client list was different every month – someone would join the gym in April, say, and by June they'd be gone.

I: And is that why you left?

N: It wasn't the only reason. I was getting tired of working on Saturdays, for one thing – I'd only had two or three Saturdays free in over a year. But it was the whole sales thing that I was least happy about. When they told me I had to persuade people to buy things with the gym's logo on it, that's when I made the decision to resign. I just didn't feel comfortable pushing T-shirts and baseball caps, as well as things like protein supplements people maybe didn't need. It's not my style.

I: Are you pleased you became self-employed?

N: Oh, yes, I've got so much more freedom, and so far, touch wood, things are going really well. I thought I might have to put adverts in the local newspaper to get business but those clients I brought with me from the gym tell all their family and friends about me and those people tell all their friends … and so it goes on. The power of word of mouth.

I: Let's hope your success continues, Naomi. Thank you for coming in to the studio.

Ready for Speaking
◉ 2.37

Part 1: Interview

**I = Interlocutor   C = Christina
P = Paolo**

I: Good morning. My name is Kate Benton and this is my colleague Paul Flint. And your names are?

C: Christina.

P: My name is Paolo.

I: Can I have your marksheets, please? Thank you. Where are you from, Paolo?

P: From a small town near Ravenna. In Italy.

I: And you Christina?

C: I'm from Corinth, in Greece. I have lived there all my life. I live there with my three sisters and my parents. I'm in my last year at school. My mother works in …

Listening scripts

I: Thank you, Christina. First we'd like to know something about you. Paolo, what kind of sports are you interested in?

P: Er, I play football, tennis, and I go swimming.

I: How often do you play football?

P: Once a week. Yeah, every Saturday. In a team.

I: And you Christina, do you have any hobbies?

C: Well, not really hobbies, but in my free time I like to go to the cinema, read, going out with my friends, er, things like that.

I: What sort of films do you like to watch?

C: Oh, I like action films. I like films where happen many things. I don't like romantic or historical films. They are very slow sometimes, they are not very interesting for me.

I: Paolo, do you work or are you a student?

P: I work in my uncle's computer business.

I: And how important is English for your work?

P: Well, yes, it's very important. I have to read a lot of things about computers in English. Everything is … well … most things are written in English nowadays.

I: Christina, what do you hope to do in the next few years?

C: Well, I want to go to the university and study business studies first. Then, if it is possible, I'll work in a big company, as accountant or something like that. Maybe, in the future I can use my English and find a job in another country. That would be very exciting.

I: What kind of job do you hope to be doing in ten years' time, Paolo.

P: Well, ten years is a long time, so I'm not sure what will happen. First, I want to help my uncle expanding his business and then perhaps in the future, I could set up my own business.

I: Thank you.

Ready for Speaking
👁 2.38

Part 2: Talking about photos

  I = Interlocutor   C = Christina
  P = Paolo

I: In this part of the test, I'm going to give each of you two photographs. I'd like you to talk about your photographs on your own for about a minute, and also to answer a question about your partner's photographs. Christina, it's your turn first. Here are your photographs. They show people on holiday in different places. I'd like you to compare the photographs and say why you think the people have chosen to go on holiday to these different places. All right?

C: Yes, well, er, in the first picture I can see a small beach, a pretty beach, with several people and in the background a small town or village with mountains behind, and, er, in … whereas in the other picture there are only four people, a family, and they are probably in a camping, a campsite. Er, what else … yes, and er, in both pictures the people are having a relaxing time but are doing different things. In the first picture they are taking the sun or swimming in the sea, whereas in this one they are just … well, sitting down. Er, what else … yes, and, well … people go to these types of places because they want to get out of the towns or the cities where they live. They want to, er, change their routine … er, be in, er … the open air. Yes. And, er, some people prefer to go to the beach, like in this picture, where they can be lazy all day. And other people prefer to be in the nature, in the, the countryside, where it's very quiet … and peaceful, and they can do lots of things like maybe go walking or cycling, and the children can play and have lots of fun … er …

I: Thank you. Paolo, which of these places would you prefer to go to on holiday?

P: Er, I would rather go camping. I don't like going to the beach on holiday. There are too many people.

I: Thank you. Now, Paolo, here are your photographs. They show people doing exercise in different places. I'd like you to compare the photographs, and say what you think the people are enjoying about doing exercise in these different places. All right?

P: OK. In the first picture I can see two men who are jogging, in a park or a forest maybe. Er, one man is middle-aged and the other is younger. They must be enjoying themselves because they are both smiling, perhaps because of something one of them has just said. In the other picture it looks as if they are in a class doing some step exercises. The woman at the front is probably a teacher, in the yellow top. I can see a speaker on the wall, so they might be listening to some music while they are doing their exercise. What are they enjoying? Er … in the first picture they are enjoying being together. Jogging is not good fun on your own – it is much better to do with a friend, having a chat. And they are outside all the time, and that's enjoyable. In the other picture, too, in the gym, they are probably enjoying being with other people, and they might make new friends there. They are probably enjoying having a teacher as well – if the teacher is good, they can feel like they are doing progress … making progress.

I: Thank you. Christina, which of these places would you prefer to do exercise in?

C: Well, I think it is much better to be in a class with other people, like in this photo. Jogging is not very interesting for me, even if I do it with a friend. You run and that's it. But in this type of class you do many things – it is, er, it is more variety – yes, and you can meet new people and make new friends, like Paolo said. Definitely I would prefer to do exercise in a gym.

I: Thank you.

Ready for Speaking
👁 2.39

Part 3: Collaborative task

  I = Interlocutor
  C = Christina   P = Paolo

I: Now, I'd like you to talk about something together for about two minutes. I'd like you to imagine that the History Museum in your town would like to introduce some new features to attract more visitors. Here are some of the ideas which have been suggested and a question for you to discuss. First you have some time to look at the task. Now, talk to each other about what types of people these different ideas would appeal to.

C: Which one shall we start with?

P: Let's talk about the computer exhibition first. I think it would appeal to all different types of people, because computers are so important today. Young people especially would be interested to see what they were like twenty or thirty years ago, before they were born.

C: Yes, and older people, like our parents or even our grandparents would be interested to remember what computers were like when they were younger. OK, let's move on to the medieval fair. I think it would also attract people of all ages. It could be good fun, don't you think?

P: Yes, I do. Er … visitors could take part in different activities and games and eat medieval food. And if the organizers dressed up in costumes, then that would make history very colourful and realistic. I think it would bring in lots of families with young children.

C: Yes, I agree. Now, what do you think about the concerts? This would be ideal for people who work near the museum. They could come during their lunch break and have a relaxing moment.

P: That's true, but I don't think many people would be able to go, especially if the museum is in this city – everyone is busy all day. But retired people would probably appreciate it and have more time to enjoy it.

C: Yes, I suppose you're right. It would be very pleasant for them. Now, let's move on to the theatrical representations. I think it depends if they are serious or funny. If they are serious and formal, then I think they'd probably be more suitable for adults, or people who go to the theatre a lot. But if they are funny, if they make people laugh, then I think nearly everyone would find them enjoyable, including the children. Do you agree?

P: Yes, definitely. I think if the museum wants to attract more visitors, then they have to make sure that they appeal to as many different types of people as possible.

C: Exactly. And I think this will be true for the dressing up in costumes. I think nearly everyone will like this, don't you?

P: Well, I'm not so sure. Er … it wouldn't appeal to me for example. I don't like dressing up or attracting attention to myself. Families with children would enjoy doing this and taking photos of each other, but I don't think couples or people on their own would be very interested.

I: Thank you. Now you have about a minute to decide which two ideas would be most successful in attracting new visitors.

C: Right. Well, I think Paolo made a good point earlier that the museum must appeal to as many different types of people as possible. And I think we both agreed that the medieval fair would attract people of all ages, so, Paolo, do you agree that that might be one of the best two choices?

P: Yes, I do. I think it is – it doesn't matter if you are on your own, in a couple, with friends, in a family – everyone would enjoy it and I am sure it would bring in many … many visitors to the museum. I think this is also true for the computer exhibition, but you don't agree, I think.

C: No, I'm sorry. I know you like computers, but I would be bored! People have enough of computers at work. As I said before, I think nearly everyone will like the dressing up – not you, maybe, but if the museum wants to attract more visitors, it needs to have more fun activities, not more exhibitions.

P: OK, so we don't agree on that. But, we did both agree before that if the theatrical representations were funny and not serious, then that would be very successful.

C: Yes, that's true. I think that …

I: Thank you.

Ready for Speaking
 2.40

Part 4: Further discussion

**I = Interlocutor   C = Christina
P = Paolo**

I: Christina, what do you think makes a good museum?

C: Well … in general I think the museums are a little boring. You only look at objects which are in … er, how do you say? Er, like boxes? Er … glass boxes, er, cupboards? Er, there is nothing to do. But, er, I think if you could touch things in an exhibition, or do fun things like dressing up, that would make it more interesting … more enjoyable experience.

I: Uh huh. Paolo?

P: I think ideas like the medieval fair are good because they help you to have a better idea of life in the past. The last year I went to a museum where people in costumes explained how different things were used. Er, even they cooked with some old saucepans and things. Er … perhaps they weren't real, but it doesn't matter. The important is that you can imagine how people lived before.

I: How could the teaching of history in schools be improved?

C: Well, er, I'm not really sure, er … in school we sit and listen the teachers … listen to the teachers, and write what they say. In Greece there are so many ancient monuments that, er, perhaps we could visit them more and not just read and write about them all the time.

I: What do you think, Paolo?

P: Er, when I was in school we just listened to the teachers. I think history was the worst subject for many people. I think we need better teachers who are good at making a subject more interesting for pupils. I don't know, I think it depends on the teacher.

I: What was the most important moment in the history of the twentieth century?

C: Well, I haven't really thought about it before, but, er, perhaps it was … yes … I think it was when the first man landed on the Moon. I have seen pictures of this, and I think it must have been something quite incredible at that time. Now, travelling to space is quite normal, but that moment was very different. What do you think, Paolo?

P: Well, I think the landing on the Moon was important, but travel in space would not be possible if we did not have computers. The invention of the computer, for me, was the most important moment. It changed the way we live …

C: You only say that because you like computers!

P: No, but everything we do needs computers nowadays. Er … industries, banks, companies, hospitals – everything depends on computers. Er, and if the computers break down, then people cannot do their jobs properly. We cannot survive without computers.

C: Maybe, but I think there are more important things that happened in the last century. Things with people and not machines. For example, when people started to think more about the environment. The planet is in bad condition, and if organizations like Greenpeace didn't exist, then, er, it would be much worse. Don't you agree?

P: Yes, you're right, but even organizations like Greenpeace need computers to do their work!

I: Paolo, what items from our lives today will be in the history museums of the future?

P: Well, in addition to computers … er, possibly, some domestic ap-, ap-, domestic applications? No, it doesn't matter … er, domestic machines that we use for cooking or other jobs, things like the cooker, the vacuum cleaner or the iron. Many of these things will be replaced by robots which do not need people to operate them.

C: Do you really think a robot could do all of our ironing for us?

P: Sure. We already have robot vacuum cleaners to clean our floors, so why not robot irons?

C: Well, I think one thing in the museums of the future will be the money. I think the credit cards and smartphones will be the only things we use. Already, some people never pay for things with cash. Er, … in only a few years I think they will stop making the money.

I: Thank you. That is the end of the test.

Unit 13 2.41

Part 4: Multiple choice

P = Presenter   S = Sally Jefferson

P: Ants, spiders, snakes and rats may not sound like ideal house companions, but as Sally Jefferson can confirm, an increasing number of animal lovers in the Radio Carston area have taken to keeping them as pets. Sally is the owner of Animal Crackers, a large pet shop in the centre of Carston. Sally, why the move away from cats and dogs?

S: Well, primarily, I think the trend reflects changing lifestyles. Cats and dogs need a lot of looking after, whereas insects and spiders, for example, are very low-maintenance – they more or less take care of

Listening scripts

themselves. And that's perfect for busy working couples who are out of the home most of the day and can't afford to spend a great deal of time on the more traditional kinds of pets. And, er, and then of course, there's the so-called educational pet, ants in particular.

P: Yes, I was surprised to hear that you sell a lot of them in your shop.

S: That's right, leaf-cutter ants mostly. You can create your own colony in an ant farm – that's a glass box like a big fish tank filled with clean sand or soil. You can watch them in their nest, digging tunnels and cutting leaves, all collaborating to achieve a common goal. It's a great lesson in the benefits of teamwork, especially for children. And for that reason a lot of parents come in and buy them.

P: And do the kids like them?

S: Yes, most do – after all, ants are fascinating creatures to watch close up. But of course, they're not furry or cuddly, and children can't interact with them in the same way that they can with a cat or a dog. If you pick them up or try to play with them, they can give you quite a nasty bite. So inevitably some children start to grow tired of them, pay less attention to them.

P: Right. And how about spiders? You were telling me before the programme that you sell tarantulas – can they be handled?

S: It's not advisable, but in this case it's more because of the risk involved to the tarantula than to the owner. They do bite, of course, and as we've seen in films, sometimes with fatal results. But a bite from the species we sell is rather like being stung by a bee. No, the main problem is that they are fragile creatures and if they run around when they're on your hand or arm, there's a danger they'll fall off and hurt themselves very badly. So best not to get them out of their cage too often.

P: No, indeed. Now let's move on to another type of pet that seems to be in fashion these days – snakes. Do they need a lot of care and attention?

S: That really depends on the species you buy – different species have different requirements. What's common to the corn snakes and ball pythons that we sell is that they can sometimes go for months without eating. So, if you're going on holiday you don't have to worry about finding someone to feed them while you're away. However, it's important to realize that many snakes have a lifespan of more than twenty years – so you need to be aware that you are making a long-term commitment when you buy one.

P: And what sort of things do they eat?

S: Mice, mainly, and perhaps rats or even rabbits for some of the larger species. It's better to give them pre-killed animals, which can be bought frozen at reasonably little cost from pet stores. Besides being more humane for the mice and rats and so on, it's also safer for the snakes. A rat can seriously wound a snake when it's acting in self-defence.

P: Interesting that you mention rats, because of course, they too are kept as pets nowadays, aren't they?

S: That's right. They make very good pets and they don't bite quite as readily as most people think. You need to bear in mind, though, that they like being with other rats, so they really need to be kept in pairs or even groups, and in a large cage, too. Technically, of course, they're nocturnal animals but they're very flexible creatures – they will adapt to their owners' schedules and are happy to come out and play when people are around during the day.

P: You don't feed them to the snakes, do you, Sally?

S: No, don't worry, we never do that …

Unit 13 👁 2.42

Part 2: Sentence completion

Dogs, cats, chimps, monkeys – even frogs and fish; they've all been up into space at some time in the last fifty years or more. The first living creature in space, of course, was Laika, the dog, who was launched aboard Sputnik 2 on 3 November 1957 by the Soviet Union. Laika, unfortunately, died just a few hours into the flight, and the first animals to actually survive a space mission were two monkeys called Able and Baker. That was in May 1959, when they were fired 300 miles into space from Cape Canaveral in Florida. The pair were weightless for nine minutes and monitored for their heart beat, muscular reaction, body temperature and breathing. They travelled at incredible speeds – up to ten thousand miles an hour – before coming down safely in the South Atlantic near Puerto Rico, 1500 miles away.

Not surprisingly, the use of animals for space research has been unpopular with animal welfare groups ever since it began. Back in 1957, for example, every day that Laika was in space, the National Canine Defence League in Britain asked all dog lovers to observe a one-minute silence. Space scientists have been accused of being cruel to animals and strongly criticized for carrying out their experiments on defenceless creatures. In the meantime, many of the animals themselves have become celebrities. Laika's space flight attracted a huge amount of attention from the world's press, and the dog's image appeared on stamps in a number of countries, including Romania, Poland and Albania. And in 2008, over fifty years after her historic flight, a monument was erected in honour of Laika in Moscow. It features a dog standing on the combination of a rocket and a human hand.

Another animal to achieve celebrity status was Ham, a three-year-old chimp who was sent into orbit in January 1961 to find out whether humans would be able to survive in space. Originally from Cameroon in Africa, Ham was bought by the United States Air Force and sent to New Mexico, where he was trained for the tasks he would carry out during his space flight. For unlike previous animal astronauts, Ham would be more than just a passive passenger. He was taught, for example, to pull a lever in response to a flashing light; if he did so within five seconds of seeing the light flash, he would receive a reward of food. The purpose was to see how well tasks could be performed in space. During the mission, Ham was weightless for over six minutes. His capsule suffered a drop in oxygen levels but he was safe inside his space suit and sixteen minutes after launching from Cape Canaveral, he splashed down in the Atlantic with nothing more than a bruised nose. When the rescue helicopters eventually got to him, he was rewarded with an apple and half an orange. He had beaten the first man into space, the Russian Yuri Gagarin, by over two months. Afterwards, Ham retired to the US National Zoo in Washington DC, where he was well looked after and enjoyed a celebrity lifestyle. His picture appeared on the cover of Life magazine and he even received fan mail, some of which he replied to by sending admirers his fingerprint. In 1980, a very overweight Ham moved to North Carolina Zoo, where he died three years later.

Unit 14 👁 2.43–2.47

Part 3: Multiple matching

Speaker 1
I never had time to go to the German classes my company arranged for us at work, so I used to put CDs on in the car on the way in every morning and just let the language wash over me. I was completely immersed in it for the whole journey. Then I'd play the same section on the way home and that was enough to ensure I learnt what I'd listened to in the morning. When I go to Germany on sales trips now I have very few problems understanding people. Business seems to be improving too.

Speaker 2
I went to Spain, twice, when I was studying languages at university; once on holiday and the next year to work in a bar. The holiday was a disaster in terms of language learning. I spent most of the time with my English friends and hardly learnt a thing. When I went back there to work, though, I spoke Spanish all day and my speaking and understanding really improved. That experience working abroad helped me pass my final exams just as much as studying, I'm

convinced. Oh, and I'm getting married this year to my Spanish girlfriend.

Speaker 3
I spent three years teaching English in Poland with my boyfriend back in the late nineties. It took us both quite a long time to learn any Polish in the beginning, partly because of laziness, but mostly because we were working long hours teaching and speaking English all day. Things got better, though, once we eventually got to know a few Polish people and we had more chance to speak the language. We weren't quite confident enough to go and see films in Polish at the cinema, but we certainly felt more integrated.

Speaker 4
When I left university I desperately wanted to work abroad, but all three French-owned companies I applied to turned me down at the interview stage. I'd only ever learnt grammar when I studied French at school. I had no difficulty at all with that, but when I actually had to speak the language in the interview it was a real problem and I'm sure the interviewers couldn't understand a word of what I was saying. So I signed up for a two-month general language course in Paris and thanks to that, when I came back, I got the first job I applied for.

Speaker 5
Here in Wales everyone can speak English, but it's compulsory for all students to learn Welsh up to the age of sixteen. My mum and dad both came to Wales from England, so I only ever spoke in English till I started school. But all my lessons there were in Welsh – right from day one – and I picked it up really quickly. So then I had the two languages – English with my parents and Welsh with my friends. I sometimes spoke Welsh at home, too, with my brother. It was great, 'cause we could talk about things in front of my mum and dad and they had no idea what we were saying – it was really useful sometimes!

Unit 14 👁 2.48–2.55

Part 1: Multiple choice

1 You hear a man talking about the language school he owns.

We've benefited enormously from being so close to a number of large companies. We're right on their doorstep, so they can either have classes on their premises or else send their workers round to us – usually before or after office hours, but sometimes even during their lunch break. We don't exactly offer the cheapest courses in town, and there are other schools in the area whose teachers are more qualified, more experienced than ours. But we try to make up for that with youthful enthusiasm and, as I say, the key to our survival – and growth – has been the fact that we're so conveniently situated.

2 You overhear a young woman talking to a friend about going abroad.

M = Man   W = Woman

M: Are you nervous about going to France?

W: Excited mostly, but yeah, a bit nervous too I suppose.

M: You don't speak much French, do you?

W: No, but that's not the problem. I know enough to get by and it'll be fun trying it out on people in the shops and asking for directions and so on. It's more about not knowing how long it'll take me to get a job. It needs to be fairly soon, otherwise I'll run out of money.

M: Ah, you'll be all right. If you can't survive, then I don't know who can.

3 You hear a man giving part of a speech.

I'd like to say how flattered I feel to have been invited to open this magnificent sports centre. And I'm particularly proud of the fact that you voted unanimously for my name to be given to the centre. If I think back to all my sporting successes, the medals I've won and records I've broken, none of them ever gave me as much pleasure as this moment today. As a child growing up in this area, I never dreamed I would one day be standing here …

4 You hear a woman talking to her friend about going rock climbing.

M = Man   W = Woman

M: Looking forward to going rock climbing, Sally?

W: Well, to tell you the truth, I haven't made my mind up about it. Everyone tells me it's great fun, especially when you realize that you're quite safe, with all the ropes and everything. But what if you get stuck and can't go on? That's what worries me. I can't see I'm going to enjoy myself, clinging to a rock for survival, waiting for someone to come and pull me off. Still, I won't know if I don't try, will I?

5 You hear a man talking on the radio.

What I like about it is that you're doing things that nobody else has done before, discovering things about yourself as well as the world you live in. I've been to places I never knew existed until I got there, and I've travelled enormous distances without seeing another living soul. It's not whether it's the highest, the hottest or the coldest that matters to me, but being the first person to set foot there … and surviving to tell the tale.

6 You hear a woman talking to a friend about her husband's work situation.

Of course, I wasn't happy about him losing his job. We had a few **sleepless** nights, I can tell you, what with the mortgage to pay and two hungry kids to feed. But no one was to blame for what happened, and **thankfully**, it all

worked out in the end. I'm just glad it's all over now. I don't know how we'd have managed to survive if he hadn't been taken on at the power station.

7 You overhear a man talking to his wife about a friend.

W = Woman   M = Man

W: Dave's been very **successful**, hasn't he? He's done well for himself.

M: Yes, well, it's hardly surprising, is it?

W: Why do you say that?

M: Well, it was the same thing at school. Fortune always smiled on him – he seemed to pass exams **effortlessly** and now he's making money in the same way. He makes a few good decisions, invests in the right companies and bingo! Suddenly he's a millionaire. Still, it couldn't happen to a nicer guy. No one deserves it more than him.

8 Listen to this woman talking to her son on the phone.

Yes, well, we're very pleased you actually managed to phone us. At least you've succeeded in doing something right. You may have noticed, however, that it is now two o'clock in the morning … Yes, but you said you would be home by twelve. If you aren't capable of keeping promises then you shouldn't make them … No, we can't come and pick you up. You're old enough to be able to solve your own problems now.

Answer key

Unit 1 Lifestyle

Reading and Use of English: Multiple matching Page 8

How to go about it

Question **4** is answered by the underlined parts in Text A.

Questions **1** and **7** are the other questions answered in Text A. See key below.

1 A *at home there are usually scripts lying all over the place. It's a bit of a mess, I'm ashamed to say.*

2 D *… I can't see myself in any other profession. There's nothing else I'd rather do.*

3 C *I love my job, especially the variety and not knowing what you'll be doing from one day to the next.*

4 A *I'll sometimes go for a run after I get up, though it's not really my idea of fun. I'm not a fitness fan …*

5 B *I have to get up early and my morning routine is dull and conventional, the same one that's played out in millions of households.*

6 D *My flat overlooks the port, so it's just a short walk to the Ellie May.*

7 A *I always fall asleep as soon as my head hits the pillow.*

8 B *Working at home was a solitary business and I hated the fact that I would often go for days without speaking to anyone.*

9 C *But being a vet – any type of vet – is not what people think it is. It's not all cuddly lambs and cute little pigs. We have to do some pretty unpleasant things sometimes …*

10 B *I often get to bed later than I would like.*

Language focus 1: Habitual behaviour
Page 10

A General tendencies

1

use to be

B Frequency adverbs

1

a immediately before the main verb; after the auxiliary verb and the verb *to be*

b *always* and *never* are incorrectly placed

2

1 correct

2 I usually have my dinner in front of the television.

3 I never spend more than ten minutes doing my English homework.

4 correct

5 I hardly ever play computer games – I prefer reading.

6 correct

C *Used to* and *would*

1 *would* + infinitive can refer to past habits, but not states. It is not used with stative verbs such as *have* to refer to the past.

2

| **1** b | **2** a | **3** a | **4** a | **5** b | **6** c | **7** b |
| **8** c | **9** c | **10** a | | | | |

Vocabulary 2: *Get*   Page 11

1a

b the actor   **c** the farm vet   **d** the fisherman
e the potter   **f** the actor   **g** the fisherman   **h** the potter

b

b get up, go out of bed   **c** do exercise
d become/grow lonely   **e** catch the train
f arrive at/reach the theatre   **g** makes us do
h receive requests/am asked

2

1 touch   **2** chance   **3** paid   **4** ready   **5** trouble
6 over   **7** by   **8** on

Vocabulary 3: Clothes   Page 12

1 hat, top hat, suit, jacket, tie, shirt, jeans, trainers, dress

Listening 1: Multiple matching   Pages 12–13
1–2

Possible answers

A a wedding: guest, witness, priest, best man, in a church, in a registry office

B a birthday party: guest, host, at home, in a disco

C a classical ballet: audience, ballerina, dancer, director, in a concert hall, in an opera house

D a sporting event: spectator, competitor, star, opponent, in a stadium, at a sports centre

E a film premiere: star, audience, director, producer, at a cinema

F an examination: candidate, invigilator, in an examination hall

G a job interview: candidate, interviewer, panel, in an office or other place of work

H a special family meal: guest, host, relative, relations, in-laws, at home, in a restaurant

3

There are many possible answers.

Listening task

1 A   **2** F   **3** D   **4** G   **5** B   C, E and H not used

Answer key

Language focus 2: *Be used to, get used to* and *used to*   Page 13

1

1 a   2 b   3 a

2

Be used to + *-ing*/noun in the affirmative describes the state in which one no longer finds situations new or strange, e.g. *I am used to the heat* means it is no problem for me now.

Get used to + *-ing*/noun in the affirmative describes the process of reaching normality with a new or strange situation, e.g. *I am getting used to the heat* means it is less of a problem for me now than before.

3

the gerund

5c

1 get, having   2 –, cook   3 is, eating   4 –, write

5 get, being   6 be, driving   7 get, driving

Writing: Informal letter   Pages 14–15

1

Mark wants to know how I am settling in to the new house. He wants to know if I can help him in the summer.

2

Paragraph 2: to describe how he spends a typical day

Paragraph 3: to give news and invite you to visit

Paragraph 4: to finish and ask for a reply

3

2 a   3 no, because this expression is too formal
4 c   5 g   6 no, too formal   7 no, too formal
8 d   9 b   10 f

4

1 while   2 as   3 and/so, as well   4 but   5 so

5

> ### Sample answer
> ....
>
> Dear Mark,
>
> I'm writing to you to tell you that I'm not going to go to your farm in summer because of my new work. However, I'll try to see you as soon as possible.
>
> As you know, I moved to a new house six months ago and since then I've met new people.
>
> I think that living there is better than I thought and with regard to my new surroundings I must say that they are excellent. I usually get up at half past seven and I went to work. Then I have a breakfast with my friends and I go to improve my English spoken in the afternoon in a specific classe. In the evening, I'm used to going to the cinema because here it's cheaper.
>
> After all, I think is good have a new experience in your life and this is an example to explain it. As far as I'm concerned, I don't know if I'll have to return to my city, but it doesn't matter so much in these moments.

> I hope you write me as you did.
>
> All the best,
>
> Luis
>
> 186 words

Examiner's comment

Content: Adequate coverage of points.

Communicative achievement: Register is awkward at times – *with regard to my new surroundings* (too formal for the context), and some confusion is evident in the use of *After all* and *As far as I'm concerned*. The overall effect on the target reader would be reasonably positive: the information asked for has been provided and the tone, although inconsistent at times, would not cause problems.

Organization: An abrupt beginning but the letter is organized into paragraphs. Successful use of simple sequencing in the third paragraph – *then, in the afternoon/evening*.

Language: Errors do not obscure communication, but they may distract the reader – *I'm used to going to the cinema* is not appropriate here, the use of *went* instead of *go* in the third paragraph, the omission of the subject in *I think is good* are some examples of inaccuracies. Vocabulary is generally appropriate except for *a breakfast, a specific classe*. Tenses are generally correct – *since then I've met new people*.

Mark: Good pass

Listening 2: Multiple choice   Page 15

1 C   2 B   3 B   4 C   5 A   6 A   7 B   8 A

Review 1   Pages 16–17

Reading and Use of English: Transformations

1 getting rid of   2 got used to wearing
3 always borrowing my things without
4 is/'s unusual for Simon to   5 unlike/not/n't like Helen to be
6 looking forward to seeing

Vocabulary

A Adjectives

2 high-heeled   3 tight-fitting   4 sleeveless   5 baggy
6 long-sleeved

B Expressions crossword

Expressions for use in informal letters

Across 1 thanks   **5** forward   **8** way   **9** love   **12** taken

Down 2 know   **7** better   **11** hear

Expressions with *get*

Across 3 rid   **4** on   **10** touch   **13** paid

Down 1 trouble   **3** ready   **6** dressed

C People

1 e   2 f   3 a   4 b   5 d   6 c

1 competitor, spectators   2 host, guests   3 bride, groom

4 audience, performers   5 doctor, patient
6 candidates, invigilator

Unit 2   High energy

Vocabulary 1: Music   Page 18

1a violin, cello, drums

b

1 lead   **2** a song   **3** musician   **4** on   **5** play   **6** live*
7 in   **8** instrument

*pronunciation /laɪv/

Listening 1: Sentence completion   Page 19

1c

1 whole family   **2** Mexico   **3** country and western
4 interval/interlude   **5** 1999   **6** four/4 million
7 Photo/photo gallery   **8** Rain/rain **9** bikes/bicycles
10 excitement

Language focus 1: Indirect ways of asking questions   Page 20

1

1 When did *Rhythm of the Dance* start performing?

2 Why do you call the show *iD*?

3 Are the Tap Dogs planning to come here?

2

a The auxiliary verbs *did* and *do* are not used in the indirect question form. *Start* changes to *started*; *call* does not change, as the second person present simple form is the same as the infinitive form.

b In the direct question form, the auxiliary verb comes before the subject (*Are the Tap Dogs planning …?*).

In the indirect form, the subject comes first, as in the normal word order for a statement (*the Tap Dogs are planning*).

c *If* (or *whether*) has to be added.

3

Possible answers

a Could you explain why you are called 'Pagagnini'?

b I'd be interested to know when you started performing together.

c Could you tell me if/whether you have ever toured outside of Europe?

d Would you mind telling us what type of music you prefer playing?

e I was wondering if you could tell me how many hours you practise your instrument each day.

f We'd like to know if/whether you clown around when you're off stage as well.

Writing 1: Letter of application   Pages 20–21

2

2 I have seen   **3** I would like to apply
4 I have also been attending   **5** I have no experience

6 a number   **7** I feel   **8** well-suited to   **9** I would love to have the opportunity to   **10** I look forward to hearing

3

Although, In addition, as

4

Paragraph 2: relevant skills

Paragraph 3: relevant experience

Paragraph 4: suitability for the job

5

> **Sample answer**
>
> Dear Mr Groves,
>
> I have seen your advertisement in the last edition of 'English News' and I would like to apply for the post of volunteer at the pop and rock festival.
>
> After reading the advertisement, I think I have the relevent experience to work at the festival. I am in my first year in the university where, I study music. I play guitar, violin and drums and I am also a member of a rock band that last year my friends and I created.
>
> Furthermore, I have some experience to work with people because I used to have a job as waitress in a busy music café. I enjoyed meeting different people and helping the public in general, and I learned a lot in this position.
>
> I would love to have the opportunity to volunteer at the pop and rock festival. I feel I would be well-suited in this role and I would like to help other people enjoy music as I do. Finally, I believe I would learn a lot from hearing different bands stiles and this would benefit my study.
>
> I look forward to hearing from you.
>
> Yours sincerely,
>
> Claudine Diallo
>
> 194 words

Examiner's comment

Content: All points covered and the writer builds on the information given, e.g. *I am also a member of a rock group, I used to have a job as a waitress, I would like to help other people enjoy music.*

Communicative achievement: Register is appropriately formal for a letter of application, and the writer would have a positive effect on the target reader.

Organization: The letter is well-organized with suitable paragraphs and the writer uses linking devices, e.g. *After reading, Furthermore, finally.*

Language: Generally accurate. Grammatical errors do not obscure meaning, e.g. *I have some experience to work (of working) with people, work as (a) waitress, my study (studies).* Punctuation and minor spelling mistakes do not distract the reader e.g. *where, I study, relevent, stiles.* There is a good range of appropriate expressions and vocabulary for the task:

Answer key

would like to apply for the post of, I used to have a job, opportunity to volunteer, I look forward to hearing, Yours sincerely, apply, drums, busy, well-suited.

Mark: Very good pass

Reading and Use of English: Gapped text
Pages 22–23

3

1 C   **2** F   **3** D   **4** A   **5** G   **6** E   B not used

Language focus 2: Gerunds and infinitives
Page 24

1

a *to score: the infinitive with to is used after certain adjectives, in this case,* hard(er)

Note the structure: adjective + for someone to do something

b *be done: an infinitive without to because it follows a modal verb, in this case,* can

  throwing: a gerund is used after a preposition, in this case, by

c *passing: a gerund is used after certain verbs, in this case,* keep.

d *to look: an infinitive with to is used after certain verbs, in this case,* need

2

1 going, to meet   **2** smiling, to hit   **3** to enjoy, buying
4 to take, studying   **5** to let, asking

3

1 to rain, raining   **2** to have   **3** to play, playing
4 run, to run   **5** to drink   **6** using

4

detest, hate, can't stand, don't like, don't mind, quite like, really enjoy, love, absolutely adore

5

interested *in*

fond *of*

good/bad *at*

bored *with*

excited *about*

Vocabulary 2: Sport   Page 25

1

a kick, posts   **b** score   **c** passed   **d** pieces   **d** pitch

2

do   gymnastics

go   skiing, cycling, swimming

play   volleyball, tennis, basketball, football, golf

3a

2 footbally   **3** golf   **4** skiing   **5** athletics   **6** cycling

b

red card – football

fairway – golf

gears – cycling

lift – skiing

service – tennis

triple jump – athletics

4a

1 take   **2** beat   **3** win   **4** hit   **5** take   **6** draw

b

1 ice hockey, figure skating, curling

2 Spain

3 silver

4 tennis, badminton, squash

5 five

6 none

Listening 2: Multiple choice   Page 26

2

1 A   **2** B   **3** B   **4** C   **5** C   **6** B   **7** A

Word formation: Affixes   Page 27

1

boxer, player, spectator, competitor, participant, listener, organizer, runner, rider, contestant

2

employee/trainee, electrician/politician, novelist/scientist, mountaineer/engineer

3

1 *un*   **2** in   **3** il   **4** im   **5** im   **6** ir   **7** dis

4

under	too little/not enough
over	too much/excessive(ly)
pre	before
post	after
hyper	very big
micro	very small
mis	wrongly
re	again
ex	former
extra	outside or beyond

Writing 2: Article   Page 27
Additional material Page 202

2

Paragraph 1 c   **Paragraph 2** a

Paragraph 3 d   **Paragraph 4** b

3

It is written for readers of *International Sports Weekly* magazine.

4

The style is informal.

a Contractions: *doesn't, you've, you'll, I'm, you're, don't, they're*

b Informal linkers: *So, And, Also*

c Direct questions: *Have you ever seen a smile on the face of a long distance runner? So what is the attraction of running?*

d Phrasal verbs: *give up, take up, put off*

5

1 c   **2** a   **3** b

6

> **Sample answer**
>
> In the world, as I know, there are a lot of sports that are very interesting and everyone can occupy with them like, for example, football, basketball, volleyball and so on. But in my opinion, the most famous and the most interesting, in the world, is football. Firstly, I extremely fond of this kind of entertainment (I say this because for me and my friends, football is the same thing with the entertainment). We play football everyday and everywhere. We love it and anything else apart from football is boring for us. Once again I love it. Secondly, football has many particularities. Special equipment and special clothes are usuful. Although the professionals teams play in big football courts, the children play football everywhere. If you want to become a good and a famous football player you must go into training everyday with many efforts but because of the injuries you must be careful.
>
> For all these reasons, I have the impression that this particular sport is lovely and I believe that there is nobody who watch this sport.
>
> By Loukas Geronikolaou
>
> 178 words

Examiner's comment

Content: Adequate coverage of points 1 and 3 but point 2 (*why do you like it?*) not really dealt with. The question incites a personal response but the information given is mostly rather general again.

Communicative achievement: Consistently neutral register in an acceptable article format. The message would not be entirely clear to the target reader; certainly some enthusiasm conveyed, but why does the writer like football so much? Some awkwardness of expressions may distract target reader, and the final sentence is obscure.

Organization: Four paragraphs including an introduction and conclusion. Conventional paragraph links (*Firstly, Secondly*). Some sentence links (*although, if, because of*).

Language: Reasonably accurate. One missing verb (*I extremely fond of* – a slip?), one spelling mistake (*usuful*) one false agreement (*professionals teams*). The problem is awkwardness rather than pure inaccuracy (positive error). Final sentence doesn't communicate. Doesn't have all the vocabulary (*occupy with them, many particularities,*

big football courts) though makes good attempts (*fond of, anything else apart from football, go into training, because of the injuries*). Some variety of structures, some complex sentences.

Mark: Pass

Review 2   Pages 28–29
Word formation

1

1 undersleep   **2** overlittle   **3** oversing   **4** missucceed
5 dislove   **6** unglad

2

1 undercharged   **2** overgrown   **3** overslept
4 misspelt/misspelled   **5** disappearance   **6** uncommon

Reading and Use of English: Word formation

1 spectators   **2** distance   **3** participants
4 walker   **5** extraordinary   **6** performance
7 unlikely   **8** physically

Gerunds and infinitives

1 to write   **2** getting   **3** tapping   **4** to have   **5** talking
6 to study   **7** to open   **8** putting

Vocabulary

A Sport

1 course, hole
2 referee, pitch
3 hit/get, racket/racquet
4 lift, slope(s)/run(s)
5 part, place
6 beat, draw

B Music

1 on the radio   **2** play a tune   **3** in the charts
4 session musicians   **5** in tune   **6** mime a song
7 on tour   **8** play a track

Unit 3   A change for the better?

Vocabulary: Technology   Page 30

2

2 bye   **3** out   **4** by   **5** know   **6** in my opinion
7 happy birthday   **8** for your information   **9** on
10 I see what you mean

Reading and Use of English: Multiple choice
Pages 30–32

2

The effects are mentioned in paragraphs 4–6.

3

1 B   **2** D   **3** A   **4** C   **5** B   **6** D

Answer key

Language focus 1: Comparisons   Page 33

1 more, less   **2** longer, more complex   **3** more, than, more efficiently, more quickly   **4** most militant, youngest   **5** least, most

A Comparative and superlative forms

1

The comparative of adjectives with one syllable, like *long* and *young*, is formed by adding the suffix *-er* (*longer, younger*).

The comparative of most adjectives with two or more syllables is formed by preceding the adjective with the word *more* (*more complex, more militant*).

2

cleaner, the cleanest

hotter, the hottest

stranger, the strangest

happier, the happiest

more clever, the most clever *or* cleverer, the cleverest

better, the best

worse, the worst

farther, the farthest *or* further, the furthest

3

The comparative of adverbs like *quickly* or *efficiently* are usually formed by preceding the adverb with the word *more*, not by adding the suffix *-er*.

4

big differences: *much, significantly, a lot*

small differences: *a bit, a little, slightly*

B Other comparative structures

1

1 c   **2** a   **3** e   **4** b   **5** f   **6** d

2

1 was far worse than

2 the least enjoyable holiday

3 are not as many

4 you work now, the less

5 is/'s the same height as

6 quite as much experience as

Word formation: Nouns 1   Page 34

1

1 consciousness, curiosity

2 entertainment

3 attention, conversations

4 evidence

2

1 enjoyment, treatment, government, argument

2 originality, popularity, majority, ability

3 appearance, performance, annoyance, tolerance

4 sadness, weakness, carelessness, loneliness

5 information, resignation, presentation, explanation

6 difference, existence, dependence, obedience

3

1 amusement, collection, similarities, thickness

2 activities, payment, permission

3 generosity, decisions, disappointment

4 dissatisfaction, differences, description, occurrence

Listening 1: Multiple choice   Page 35

How to go about it

Possible answers

2 How does Keith <u>describe his work</u>?

3 What is the <u>possible result</u> of having <u>robots</u> that can <u>display and detect emotions</u>?

4 What does Keith say about <u>robots in films</u>?

5 Keith expresses <u>concern</u> that <u>robots</u> might <u>cause</u> us

6 Keith says that <u>progress</u> in the <u>robotics industry</u>

7 What does Keith say about <u>humanoid robots</u>?

2

1 B   **2** C   **3** A   **4** A   **5** C   **6** B   **7** C

Language focus 2: Articles   Page 37

1

Travel and transport and Communication

2

1 –   **2** The   **3** –   **4** the   **5** the   **6** the   **7** the
8 A   **9** –   **10** a

11 –   **12** the   **13** an   **14** –   **15** –   **16** a   **17** the
18 the   **19** a   **20** the

3

Question	Grammar reference section
The definite article	
2, 20	A1
4	A4
6, 17	A5a
5	A5b
7	A7
18	A10
12	A12
The indefinite article	
19	B2
8, 16	B4
10, 13	B5
No article	
1, 11	C1a
3, 9, 14	C1b
15	C4

Listening 2: Multiple matching   Page 38
How to go about it
Possible answers

B Too many changes

C insufficient

D We should have been consulted

E for selfish reasons

F Most parents support

G unexpected benefits

H Most teachers, unnecessary

1

1 E   2 D   3 H   4 C   5 A   B, F and G not used

2

Possible answers

1 … *she has her own interests in mind rather than those of the kids. It's just another of her schemes to get publicity for herself.*

2 … *he has a habit of making changes without bothering to find out what anyone else thinks first…he could have let us have some say in the matter before going ahead.*

3 *Most parents won't read the comments anyway – they're just interested in the marks. It's a waste of time as far as I'm concerned, and I know the majority of my colleagues feel the same.*

4 *Mixing up the classes like that – splitting up the troublemakers – is a step in the right direction, but it doesn't go far enough.*

5 *The ceiling's enormously high and the acoustics are terrible for the piano. Plus I practically have to shout to make myself heard, so my throat is suffering. And then the sun streams in during the afternoon and sends the kids to sleep.*

3

Possible answers

2 *Now I'm not saying that a change wasn't necessary …*

3 *The head says the tutor's comment isn't enough to give parents a full picture of how their child's getting on …*

4 … *she said expelling them would just create problems for other schools.*

5 *Now I've changed rooms many times before …*

Additional material Page 203
1

1 well   2 many   3 long   4 far   5 soon

2

1 in addition to   2 the surprisingly large number of
3 provided   4 in my opinion   5 immediately

Writing: Essay   Pages 38–39
2

The safety aspects

3

Paragraph 2: advantages/positive aspects of change

Paragraph 3: disadvantages/negative aspects of change

Paragraph 4: conclusion

4a

on the negative side   on the positive side

on the one hand   on the other hand

b

Adding information	Expressing result	Concluding
In addition (to this)	Consequently	On balance
What is more	As a result	To sum up
Furthermore		In conclusion
Moreover		
Firstly/Secondly/Finally		

Additional material Page 203

Sample answer

The Internet is part of our lives and many people could not imagine how would be the world without it. However, it is not sure that we must have it to enjoy the life completely.

Firstly, in my opinion it is much better to speak with your friends personally and don't get in touch with them online all the time. The only way to keep your friends and have a good relationship with them is see them regularly, rather than chating on networking sites. Similarly, I prefer to go to the shops to buy instead of do it online. There is no sustitute for the personal treat which you can find when you are in a real shop or a market.

In addition, it can be a little sad to spend all your day to play online games or watch films which you download. It is something special when you go to the cinema or sit with your family playing a table game.

To sum up, the best way to enjoy the life is without the Internet, since a computer cannot give you the good relations you have when you speak, shop and play with another people.

Maria Sanz

197 words

Examiner's comment

Content: Adequate coverage of points 1 and 2. However, the candidate's own idea is not completely clear.

Communicative achievement: Language is generally appropriately formal, and despite frequent errors, the message is generally clear and well organized, so the target reader would be sufficiently informed.

Organization: Linking devices used effectively, e.g. *However, firstly, similarly, in addition, to sum up.* Well organized, but the second and third paragraphs could be combined.

Language: In general, the frequent errors do not obscure meaning; however, they do distract the reader: *how would be the world* (what the world would be like), misuse of definite article *enjoy the life*, problems with infinitives and gerunds *don't* (not to) *get in touch, is* (to) *see them regularly, the shops to buy instead of do* (doing) *it online,* misuse of determiners

Answer key

another (other) people. At times, vocabulary errors lead to confusion, e.g. *the personal treat which you can find, playing a table game.* There are also two spelling mistakes, but these do not distract the reader, *substitute, chating.* There is an adequate range of vocabulary for the task, e.g. *get in touch, relationships, networking sites, download.* Some use of more complex language, e.g. *The only way to keep your friends, rather than chating on networking sites.* However, frequent errors with more basic structures.

Mark: Pass

Review 3   Pages 40–41

Vocabulary: Technology

2 laptop   **3** headset   **4** landline   **5** download
6 netbook   **7** multitasking

Expressions with *as … as*

1 long   **2** soon   **3** far   **4** well   **5** many

Comparisons

1

1 the   **2** most   **3** in   **4** many   **5** much   **6** nearly
7 lot   **8** so   **9** by   **10** less

Articles

2

3 in **the** home
4 spend ~~the~~ more
5 killed **the** art
6 write ~~the~~ emails
7 **the** less
8 **the** mobile phone
9 put in **a**
10 on **the** train
11 watched **a** young couple
12 not just **the** young
13 **a** high percentage
14 into ~~the~~ your phone
15 I'm **the** one
16 to **the** mountains

Reading and Use of English: Word formation

1 earliest   **2** inventor   **3** researchers   **4** existence
5 equipment   **6** collection   **7** assistant   **8** responsibilities

Ready for Use of English

What do you know about the Use of English tasks?   Page 42

1 False All except Part 4 (Transformations) for which the six questions are unrelated.

2 True Students should read for gist first. Looking first at the title and predicting the content of the text will help their overall understanding.

3 False There is one mark for each correct answer except in Part 4 (Transformations): in this part, two marks are given for a completely correct answer, one mark if it is partly correct.

4 True

5 True

6 True Unfortunately, some students do this in the exam. If they write the answer to the example where the answer to the first question should go, all their answers will be in the wrong space.

7 False Marks are not deducted for incorrect answers. If students are unsure, they should eliminate any alternatives they consider to be clearly wrong and then, if they still cannot decide on the correct answer, make a sensible guess.

8 False Only one word. Note that contractions (e.g. *can't, won't, I've*) and hyphenated words (e.g. *one-way* count as two words).

9 True No half marks are given in this paper (although one mark out of a possible two can be given in Part 4 – see 3 above).

10 True

Part 1: Multiple-choice cloze   Page 42

What to expect in the exam

1 A   **2** C   **3a** D   **3b** C   **4** B   **5** D

Multiple-choice cloze task

1 A   **2** B   **3** D   **4** A   **5** C   **6** C   **7** D   **8** B

Part 2: Open cloze   Page 44

What to expect in the exam

Type of word	Number and example
Articles	3 a
Auxiliary verbs	8 are
Linking words	6 although
Negative words	2 not
Possessive adjectives (*my, your, his* etc)	1 their
Prepositions	7 to
Relative pronouns	4 which
Words in comparisons	5 than

3

1 where   **2** a   **3** have   **4** What   **5** the   **6** At   **7** to
8 by

Part 3: Word formation   Page 45

1

1 humorous   **2** employees   **3** tighten   **4** increasingly
5 uncomfortable   **6** heat   **7** saucepan   **8** extraordinary

2

1 adjective; spelling change required (the 'u' in 'humour' is dropped)   2 noun in the plural   3 verb   4 adverb
5 negative adjective   6 noun; spelling change required
7 compound noun   8 adjective

4

1 magicians   2 interested   3 ability   4 independent
5 strength   6 easily   7 careless   8 disastrous

Unit 4   A good story

Vocabulary 1: Films   Pages 46–47

1

A science fiction film, action film

B historical drama

C comedy

D fantasy film

2

A 1 terrific   2 terrifying   3 terrible

B 1 review   2 critic   3 criticism

4

1 set   2 cast   3 stars   4 role   5 performance   6 plot
7 main characters   8 special effects

Language focus 1: *So* and *such*   Page 47

1

a Both words intensify the adjective or (adjective +) noun that follow.

b *so* + adjective (or adverb)

such + (indefinite article +) adjective + noun

2

1 were so good that

2 was such bad weather

3 was such an absorbing

4 were so many people

Word formation: Adjectives ending in *-ing* and *-ed*   Page 48

1

Examples of adjectives/adverbs in review of *The Matrix*

To describe how we feel about something or someone

…you will not feel <u>disappointed</u>.

Also: *The plot is <u>complicated</u>.*

To describe the thing or person that produces the feeling

…one of the most <u>entertaining</u> science fiction films I have seen.

The plot … is … at times <u>confusing</u>.

…the special effects are <u>stunning</u>.

Adverbs formed from present participle adjectives

<u>surprisingly</u> competent

<u>convincingly</u> choreographed

2

/d/	/t/	/id/
annoyed	astonished	frustrated
tired	impressed	disappointed
terrified	relaxed	disgusted
amused		fascinated
bored		
frightened		

3

impress – impressive (adj)

4

Suggested answers

1 tiring   2 amused   3 annoying   4 disappointingly
5 fascinating   6 disgusting   7 Astonishingly

Writing 1: Review   Page 48

How to go about it

1 c   2 a   3 d   4 b

Sample answer

The last film I've seen on DVD was 'The Holiday' and it was alright. It is supposed it is a romantic comedy with Cameron Diaz, Kate Winslet, Jude Law and Jack Black and it is nice to watch but it is not a type of film that it makes you to laugh a lot.

The film is about two women very different. They are Iris, who is playing by Kate Winslet and Amanda (Cameron Diaz) and they decide to change houses for a holiday. Iris's house is a small one in England and Amanda's is enormous in Hollywood. Amanda falls in love to Iris's brother, who is widower, and Iris falls in love to Amanda's neighbour, who is componist. Kate Winslet is a bit disappointed in the role of Iris because she is normally very good actress. I like very much the photography and the music.

I would recommend the film to people who they are tires and they do not want to watch a complicate film. It is also very good for a rainy afternoon on Sunday of winter.

By David Benoa

180 words

Examiner's comment

Content: Reasonable realization of the task, though rather a large section of the review is devoted to a simplistic summary of the plot.

Communicative achievement: Both register and format are appropriate to the task. The target reader may have some difficulty following the review due to the number of errors.

Organization: Adequate paragraphing. Some sentences poorly organized, e.g. second sentence of first paragraph.

Answer key

Language: A large number of distracting errors, e.g. *it is supposed it is a romantic comedy, two women very different, who is playing by Kate Winslet* and use of relative clauses. *Disappointed* is used incorrectly (disappointing), and it is not clear what is meant by *componist* (composer?). A very limited range of structures and vocabulary, particularly when expressing opinions, e.g. *very good* (twice) and *nice to watch*.

Mark: Borderline

Preparing for listening: Focus on distractors
Page 50

1

2 d   3 a   4 e   5 b

2

1 B   2 B   3 A   4 B   5 B

Listening: Multiple choice   Page 50

1 C   2 B   3 C   4 A   5 B   6 A   7 B   8 C

Vocabulary 2: *Take*   Page 51

A Phrasal verbs with *take*

1

start (a new job or activity)

2

c

3

a resemble   b start doing   c start to like   d gain control
e move away from other people to talk   f accept as true
g start to become successful   h employ

B Expressions with *take*

1

2 take   3 taking/having taken   4 to take   5 took
6 had taken/had been taking   7 takes   8 are taking/have taken

2

2 take (me) to school   3 taking (his) advice   4 take (any of) the blame   5 took (more) interest in (the children)
6 taken pity on (it)   7 takes (a great deal of) courage
8 taking so long to (do this exercise)

3

1 D   2 A   3 C   4 B

4

to take pride in something C (3)

to be taken to hospital A (2)

to take a joke B (4)

to take the infinitive D (1)

Reading and Use of English: Gapped text
Pages 52–53

1

1 C   2 E   3 A   4 H   5 B   6 F   7 D   8 G

2

1 It is an extract from a crime novel.

2 The narrator is angry because she had been trying to forget her father and now he has 'come back into her life'.

3 She wants to know why no one has been punished for the murder of her father.

3

1 F   2 C   3 E   4 A   5 B   6 G

Language focus 2: Past tenses   Pages 53–54

1

1 past continuous   2 past perfect   3 past continuous + past simple   4 past simple (x3)   5 past perfect continuous

2

1 d   2 b   3 e   4 a   5 c

3

1a He read the newspaper *during* his breakfast. (past continuous)

b He read the newspaper *after* his breakfast. (past perfect)

2a I heard about it *while* I was listening to the news on the radio. (past continuous)

b I heard about it, and *as a result* I listened to the news on the radio. (past simple)

3a I no longer live in Oxford. (past simple)

b I had been living in Oxford for six years *when* ... (past perfect continuous – the speaker may or may not live in Oxford now)

4

While can be used in place of *when* in **1a** and **2a**. It emphasizes that the two things happened at the same time, but does not change the meaning. *As soon as* can be used in place of *when* in **1b** and **2b**. It emphasizes that the action in the main clause happened immediately after the action in the clause introduced by *as soon as*.

5

a at the end   b in the end   c at last

In sentence **b**, *eventually* can be used instead of *in the end*.

6

1 A   2 C   3 B   4 C   5 B   6 C

7

Bus blush
1 was travelling   2 were having   3 saw   4 was sitting
5 ran   6 sat   7 had never seen   8 smiled
9 didn't/did not stop   10 (had) got

Face paint
11 had been asking   12 agreed   13 were playing
14 fell   15 had arranged   16 kept   17 saw   18 burst
19 discovered   20 had drawn

Writing 2: Report   Pages 54–55

2

1 ways   2 aim   3 aims   4 terms   5 contains
6 provide   7 make   8 order

3

The report is for the local mayor and is written in an appropriately formal style.

4

Cinemas: The condition of the cinemas *create[s] a bad impression on anyone visiting our town.*

Theatres and concert halls: These *offer both resident and tourist a wide variety of plays and concerts* but many *overseas visitors* do not attend shows because of *the high prices of tickets.*

Recommendations: One suggestion is for some original version films to be shown *particularly for the benefit of English-speaking tourists.* The other recommends *discounts on theatre and concert tickets for the many young people who come here to study.*

5a

recommend + should + infinitive without to

suggest + gerund

b

Possible answers

create a bad impression on

anyone visiting our town

there is not much choice in terms of

we are fortunate enough to have

offer … a wide variety of

visitors comment on

particularly for the benefit of

6

Sample answer

Report about parks and gardens

Introduction

The aim of this report is to describe what our town offers visitors in terms of parks and gardens. It also makes recommendations for improving these facilities in order to encourage more people to visit the town.

Parks

This town has an excess of 70,000 habitants, but there are only two quite large parks where people can run and play. In addition, only one of the parks 'The Queen's Park', has sports facilities, for example football pitch or tennis court. Moreover, both parks, 'The Queen's Park' and 'The North's Park', are both in the north of the town, the south only has a small park.

Gardens

There are some small parks with flowers and trees that they are good for sitting and eating lunch if you are a worker. However, there is nothing in the town centre, where many people are, including business people and tourists.

Recommendations

I suggest puting sports facilities in 'The North's Park' and make another park in the south. I also recommend to have a garden with flowers in the town centre where the people could enjoy and eat their lunch.

Richard

191 words

Examiner's comment

Content: The report starts well with a clear introduction. However, there is little mention made of visitors. The candidate aims the report at people in general, workers and only briefly mentions tourists.

Communicative achievement: Appropriately formal with clear headings. Despite some inadequacies of content, the reader would be sufficiently informed.

Organization: The report is clearly divided into appropriate sections. Linking devices are used effectively, e.g. *in order to, in addition, moreover, however.*

Language: Some awkward use of language, e.g. *there are only two quite small parks, both parks … are both.* There are also some basic errors, e.g. misuse of possessive 's', *the North's Park,* problems with gerunds *I suggest make (making), recommend to have (having),* omission of reflexive pronoun *people could enjoy (themselves),* use of double subject, *that they are good.* Some errors with word formation and spelling, but these do not distract the reader, e.g. *habitants, putting.* Suitable use of vocabulary for the task, e.g. *aim, facilities, football pitch, tennis court.* Some use of more complex structures, e.g. *also makes recommendations for improving, in order to encourage more people to visit, suggest putting,* but in general the language is very simple.

Mark: Pass

Review 4   Pages 56–57

Reading and Use of English: Transformations

1 soon as the meeting had
2 the time we got to
3 leave until he (had) put
4 not to take him on
5 not take/have/show much interest in
6 never read such a funny

Correcting mistakes

2 part, As for ~~as~~
3 much, the
4 ~~had~~ came, was
5 took ~~to~~ your advice, a

Vocabulary: Cinema

1 cast   2 role   3 critics, reviews   4 plot   5 scene

Reading and Use of English: Word formation

1

to attract new students to the *Storytime School of Storytelling*

2

1 interested   2 librarians   3 confidence   4 creativity
5 fascinating   6 performances   7 surprisingly
8 unlimited/limitless

Unit 5   Doing what you have to

Reading and Use of English 1: Multiple matching   Pages 58–59

2

1 **C** *According to the headteacher, in a busy school piercings present 'a very real risk of accidents'. I can't see why …*

2 **A** *They didn't let us drink water in the classroom either…* [to the end of the paragraph].

Answer key

3 D *... all rules, whatever they are, help to ... get children ready for the real world.*

4 B *David doesn't have to wear a tie if he doesn't want to, even though it's part of the uniform. That's just silly.*

5 C *It seems I agreed to all this when I signed the school rules document at the beginning of last term, but I honestly wasn't aware of any ban on tiny metal objects in the nose.*

6 B *It's very confusing ... Everything was black and white in those days ...*

7 A *... and sometimes this got in the way of learning.*

8 D *Discipline there has gone downhill in the last few years and the kids seem to do what they want.*

9 C *I was still furious when they made her take it out and sent her home for the day: they humiliated her in front of her classmates ...*

10 B *I almost wrote to the school about it, but my son advised me against it.*

Language focus 1: Obligation, necessity and permission   Page 60

1

a 1 *could (do)*   5 *can (be used)*

b 1 *couldn't do*   3 *didn't let us drink*   5 *cannot be used*
7 *isn't allowed to wear*   9 *weren't allowed to have*

c 2 *had to wear*   4 *have to drink*   8 *made her take*

d 6 *doesn't have to wear*   10 *don't need to be convinced*

2

a a teacher (to students)

b one student to another

- *Must* expresses the authority of the speaker, i.e. the obligation comes from the teacher and it is the teacher who is imposing the obligation (the speaker's internal obligation).

- *Have to* is used to show that the authority does not come from the speaker but from someone else, i.e. the teacher (external obligation).

3

1   I don't have to/don't need to tidy ...

2   Do you have to ...?/Must you ...?

3   Last week I had to go ...

4   Were you allowed to watch ...?

5   Now I have to start ...

6   But you don't have to ...

7   You need to prepare ...

8   You really should go/You really must go ...

4a

1   allowed to drink (*let* is not possible in the passive)

2   made to take

b

1 allowed   2 let   3 makes/made

5

1 should   2 mustn't   3 need   4 don't have to
5 ought   6 supposed to   7 have to   8 better

Word formation: *-en* suffix   Page 61

1a

weaken   sweeten   deafen   fatten   brighten   widen
worsen   sadden

b

Adjective	Noun	Verb
strong	strength	strengthen
long	length	lengthen
high	height	heighten

2

2 brighten   3 sweeten   4 deafening
5 worsened   6 strengths   7 lengthen
8 heights

Reading and Use of English 2: Open cloze   Page 62

5

1 so   2 on   3 to   4 Although/Though   5 what/which
6 not   7 in   8 made

Listening 1: Multiple choice   Page 63

2

1 A   2 C   3 B   4 C   5 A   6 B   7 B

Vocabulary: The world of work   Page 64

1a

1 be out of a job   2 look for a job   3 apply for a job
4 go for an interview for a job   5 get a job

b

1 made redundant   2 resigned   3 sacked

2a

study a career   is **not** possible

b

earn a competition   is **not** possible

3

1a *to work part time* – when you are contracted to work fewer hours than the entire time appropriate, e.g. 21 hours per week (a part-time job)

b *to work full time* – when you are contracted to work the entire time appropriate to that job, e.g. 35 hours per week (a full-time job)

2a *to work overtime* – to work supplementary hours for which you are paid extra

b *to work long hours* – to work for many hours each day

3a *to work flexitime* – to work with a flexible timetable: within limits you decide when you start and when you finish, as long as you work the required total number of hours each month

b *to work shifts* – to work for a set period (e.g. 12 am to 8 am) before other workers replace you for the next set period (e.g. 8 am to 4 pm)

5
chef, hairdresser, surgeon, dustman, hotel receptionist

Listening 2: Sentence completion   Page 65

Don't forget!

- You *don't need to* write more than three words for each answer.
- You *should* write a word or phrase that you actually hear. You *don't need to* rephrase.
- Minor spelling errors *can* be made, but the words you write *need to* be recognizable, so you *should* check your spelling.
- You *can* expect to hear the answers in the same order as the questions.

2
1 academic qualifications
2 people
3 back *and* legs
4 three
5 four days
6 wear full uniform
7 elderly *and* disabled
8 evening
9 several hours
10 satisfying

3

get through:	pass a test or stage of something
go on to:	do something after you have finished doing something else
take up with:	[*always passive*] be busy doing something
give over to:	[*usually passive*] use something for a particular purpose
call out:	ask a person or organization that provides a service to come and deal with something for you
put out:	make something stop burning, extinguish
clear up:	make a place tidy

Language focus 2: Noun phrases   Page 66

1
1 workforce   2 a series of tests   3 the top of the ladder
4 a candidate's back and legs   5 a Sunday newspaper
6 next Friday's meeting   7 four weeks' work
8 wine bottle

2
1 start of the day, cups of coffee
2 holiday job, leisure time
3 night shift, month's holiday
4 world of work, waste of time

5 job opportunities, young person's chances
6 work experience, workplace

Writing: Essay   Page 66–67

2

a The writer has dedicated most of the essay to the first point: *contact with people*. Little has been said about *working hours* and in the last paragraph, the writer has misinterpreted what is meant by *your own idea*: the third point in Part 1 Writing questions invites students to write about a third aspect of the essay question.

b The language is repetitive, with the result that some of the writer's ideas are not expressed very coherently. In the second paragraph alone, *talk to* is used four times; there are two more examples in the third paragraph, where *work(ing) all the time* is also repeated.

c The style is too informal, too conversational for an essay. As well as contractions (*I'd, can't, it's*, etc) there are a number of informal words such as *OK, really, loads of, a bit* (*lonely*) and *pretty* (*boring*). Short sentences such as *No one else* and *I think so, anyway* are also very conversational and an example of poor organization of ideas.

d There is evidence of linking, but again this is often informal and limited to *if* (four times), *so* (three times), *but* (twice), *anyway* (twice) and even *OK*.

3

ofice	office
their's only you	there's only you
helthy	healthy
oppinions	opinions
lonley	lonely
your at home	you're at home
poeple	people
intresting	interesting
realy	really
brakes	breaks

4b

> **Sample answer**
>
> Often our parents and grandparents say that the life was more difficult before than now. Personally, I think this is true for some things but not for everything.
>
> For example, on one side the health of people is better now becuase there are more medicins and hospitals and doctors can get better the people easier. In the past the old people could die from illness which today are not very hard. As well, more children goes to school now – before, children started to work with twelve or younger. In some countrys old people cannot read or write very well becuase they left the school early. On another side, the work is still a problem like it was before. Perhaps it is worse now, becuase the unemployment is high and the young people have problems to find a job.

Answer key

In conclusion, I think life is better for young people now, not harder, becuase they have a better health, they go to the school and if they can become a job then they do not have to work many hours.

Mario Prim

178 words

Examiner's comment

Content: Adequate coverage of 1 and 2, and candidate has added their own idea.

Communicative achievement: There is appropriately formal register and format. Although the target reader would be sufficiently informed, the frequent inaccuracies would create a negative effect.

Organization: Has introduction and conclusion, but starts the second paragraph with an example and gives their personal opinion in the introduction. Misuse of linking devices, e.g. *on another side, as well.*

Language: Frequent errors distract the reader, e.g. misuse of definite article *the life, the school, the work, on one side*, false agreement *children goes to school*, confusion with gerunds and infinitives *problems to find a job*, problems with uncountable nouns *a better health*. At times errors lead to confusion, e.g. *doctors can get better the people easier, if they can become a job, very hard (serious).* There are three spelling mistakes, but these do not obscure meaning, *becuase, medicins, countrys.* Limited use of vocabulary and cohesive devices. Language is simple and contains frequent inaccuracies.

Mark: Borderline

Review 5   Pages 68–69

Modal verbs

1 C   2 B   3 B   4 C   5 A   6 B   7 A   8 C

Reading and Use of English: Word formation

1 surprisingly   2 supporters   3 responsibility
4 decisions   5 independence   6 development
7 strengthen   8 heightens

Reading and Use of English: Multiple-choice cloze

1 B   2 A   3 C   4 A   5 B   6 C   7 D   8 D

Reading and Use of English: Transformations

1 wouldn't/didn't let me watch   2 was made to
3 aren't we allowed to   4 don't need to hand
5 had/'d better see   6 are supposed to do

Unit 6   Relative relationships

Vocabulary 1: Phrasal verbs   Page 70

A Romance

1

2 e   3 a   4 b   5 f   6 d

2

1 to fall out with somebody   2 to split up with somebody
3 to be going out with somebody   4 to get on with somebody
5 to fall for somebody   6 to get over somebody

B Family

1

1 to take care of a child until he or she becomes an adult

2 to change from being a baby or young child to being an older child or adult

3 to tolerate or accept unpleasant behaviour by someone without complaining

4 to criticize someone angrily for doing something wrong

5 to admire and respect someone

6 to make someone disappointed

2

1 to bring somebody up   2 to grow up
3 to put up with something   4 to tell somebody off
5 to look up to somebody   6 to let somebody down

Listening 1: Multiple matching   Page 71

1

1 C   2 B   3 F   4 H   5 E   A, D and G not used

Language focus 1: Defining relative clauses
Page 72

1

in the first sentence – *that*

in the second sentence – *which*

They cannot be omitted because they are the subject of the verb in the relative clause.

2

The money (that/which) **we** *inherited* from our grandmother wasn't divided equally between us.

Note: In this sentence, the subject of the verb in *italics* in the relative clause is **we**: the underlined relative pronouns are the object of the verb in the relative clause. They can be omitted.

3

The first sentence is more formal. The relative pronoun can be omitted in the second sentence.

4

a where   b why   c when   d whose

5

1 where/in which (formal)   2 that/which   3 whose
4 that /which/ –   5 who/that   6 that/which
7 that/which/ –   8 when/that/in which/ –

Reading and Use of English 1: Multiple-choice cloze   Page 73

1 B   2 D   3 A   4 D   5 C   6 A   7 B   8 D

Reading and Use of English 2: Multiple choice   Pages 74–75

2

1 A   2 B   3 C   4 D   5 A   6 B

Language focus 2: Non-defining relative clauses   Page 76

2

a cannot

b cannot

c are

3

1 We spent the weekend in York, where my mother was born.

2 My best friend, who always said she wanted to stay single, has just got married.

3 My oldest sister, whose husband is German, lives in Munich.

4 The best time to visit Iceland is in summer, when the average temperature is around ten degrees.

5 He has to work on Saturdays, which he isn't very happy about.

Open cloze: Relative clauses   Page 76

1 which/that/ –   2 which/that   3 who/that   4 who
5 which/that   6 where   7 whose   8 which   9 who/that
10 when

Vocabulary 2: Describing people   Page 77

A Personality

1

Positive: sociable, reliable, sincere, cheerful, polite, tolerant, patient, decisive, mature, sensible, adventurous, practical, sensitive

Negative: bad-tempered, lazy, selfish, moody, mean

2

un-: unsociable, unadventurous, unselfish, unreliable

in-: intolerant, insincere, indecisive, insensitive

im-: impatient, impolite, impractical, immature

different word: mean/generous, cheerful/miserable, sensible/silly *or* foolish, bad-tempered/sweet-tempered *or* calm, lazy/hard-working, selfish/selfless, moody/even-tempered

B Appearance

1

1 *bald   2 pierced   3 thinning   4 well-built

* We can say *he is bald* but not *he has bald hair*.

2a

All the adjectives describe weighing too much.

Fat has negative connotations in many parts of the world.

Plump is more positive and can mean either weighing a little too much or can be used as a 'polite' way of describing someone who is fat.

Overweight is descriptive and of the three, is the most neutral.

b

Thin means having little fat on the body; it is descriptive and neutral.

Slim means being attractively thin and has positive connotations.

Skinny means being unattractively thin and has negative connotations.

Listening 2: Multiple choice   Page 78

1 B   2 C   3 B   4 A   5 B   6 A   7 B   8 C

Language focus 3: Causative passive with *have* and *get*   Page 78

1a

Extract 4: pierced, done

Extract 6: framed

b

the past participle

c

1a   =   He repaired the car himself.

b   =   Someone/A mechanic repaired it for him.

1a   =   He cut his own hair.

b   =   Someone/A hairdresser cut it for him.

2

2 having, shaved

3 have, taken

4 had, filled

5 having, restyled

6 has had, broken

Writing: Article   Page 79

2

The third illustration

3

Paragraph 1: says to me/tells me (says me), in the end (at the end)

Paragraph 2: fallen (fell), problems don't (problems they don't), in a better mood (in better mood)

Paragraph 3: She is always cheerful (Always she is cheerful)

Paragraph 4: so small (such small), look up to (look up at)

4

a The first sentence follows on directly from a catchy title. The use of direct speech also adds colour.

b The writer plays with the meaning of *live up to* and ends by comparing her small size and big influence.

5

a *She has a straight back and a determined look on her face. She's always cheerful and I've never seen her in a bad temper... she's nearly half my size and so small that she sometimes wears children's clothes*

b *turn out, fallen out with, sort ... out, look up to*

c *And, So, And although, But despite this, So even though*

Review 6   Pages 80–81

Relative clauses

1 Lady Gaga, whose real name is Stefani Joanne Angelina Germanotta, was born on March 28 1986.

   Non-defining (the name itself defines the person)

2 What's the name of the village where you got married?

   Defining – *where* cannot be omitted

3 He hasn't given me back the book that I lent him.

   Defining – *that* can be omitted

4 She told me that Vasilis had failed his driving test, which didn't surprise me at all.

   Non-defining – *which* refers to the whole clause

5 That song always reminds me of the time when I was working in Brazil.

   Defining – *when* can be omitted

6 He's the only person in this class whose first name begins with 'Z'.

   Defining – *whose* cannot be omitted

7 Emma received a phone call from her Managing Director, who had been impressed by her sales performance.

   Non-defining – she has, we assume, only one Managing Director

8 Few written records have survived so it is a period of history about which we know very little.

   Defining – *which* cannot be omitted as it follows a preposition. The sentence could be changed to: *Few written records have survived so it is a period of history **which** we know very little **about**.*

   In this case, *which* could be omitted.

Vocabulary

A Describing people

Across

1 unsociable   3 green   6 generous   8 ear   9 in
10 selfish   11 skinny   12 bad   14 pale

Down

1 un   2 cheerful   4 hair   5 mean   7 sensible
10 slim   11 shy   13 dis

B Phrasal verbs

1 let down   2 told off   3 brought up   4 looked up
5 get on   6 fell for   7 falling out   8 got over

Reading and Use of English: Transformations

1 to put up with

2 whose example you should

3 of the most sincere

4 are having the roof repaired

5 had his tonsils taken out

6 to have it done by

Ready for Reading

Part 5: Multiple choice   Pages 82–83

1

The purpose of the text is to give advice to people who go walking in hot weather. You might find it in a specialist magazine for walkers or people who like outdoor activities. It could also come from the travel section of a newspaper.

2

pump (verb) – move liquid or gas in a particular direction, e.g. blood around the body

intake (noun) – the amount you eat or drink

raging (adjective) – very strong or severe

swig (noun) – a quick drink of a liquid

palatable (adjective) – having a pleasant or acceptable taste

3

swell (verb) – to become bigger

blister (noun) – a swelling on the surface of the skin, which contains a clear liquid.

leak (verb) – (in this case) the water gets or enters into your boots

rash (noun) – lots of red spots on your skin

breeze (noun) – a light wind

deceptive (adjective) – from the verb 'deceive'; something which tricks you, which makes you believe something which is not true

4

1 A Not stated. The writer says that *The majority of mountain rescue statistics are made up from summer walkers suffering heart attacks* but this does not mean that heat is the main cause of heart attacks in general.

   B Not stated. The writer implies merely that if you are not fit you will suffer the effects of heat even more.

   C Correct answer. *The answer is to keep up your water intake* and *keep taking regular swigs from your water bottle.*

   D Not stated.

2 A Not stated.

   B No. It replaces the body salts lost through sweating, but it doesn't prevent their loss.

   C No. It is a treatment for diarrhoea, not a prevention.

   D Correct answer – *Dioralyte will do the job just as well.*

3 A Correct answer – *Extra sweating makes the skin softer and increases the chance of blisters forming, in the same way as when water leaks into your boots and gets to your feet.*

   B No. ... *cool water ... reduces swelling and helps ... comfort.*

C No. Your boots feel tight because the heat makes your feet swell. It does not mean they are the wrong size.

D Not stated.

4 A Not stated. *The answer, if this does develop, is to try and stay cool* is a distractor.

B The writer says walkers should ideally wear *lightweight and loose-fitting* clothing. He does not suggest that loose-fitting clothing is usually very light.

C Not stated.

D Correct answer. *Tight clothing ... may even lead to the formation of an irritating rash known as 'prickly heat' on your skin.*

5 B Correct answer. *It's understandable to want to remove any extraneous clothing when it's extremely hot...*

6 A Not stated. *... a good strong sun cream should therefore be applied* is a distractor.

B Correct answer. *... deceptive. It might not feel so hot, so you probably won't notice the damage being done.*

C Not stated. *harmless* and *damage* are distractors.

D *breeze* is not a strong wind. *an apparently harmless breeze.*

Part 6: Gapped text   Pages 84–85

4

1 C   **2** G   **3** A   **4** E   **5** F   **6** D

Part 7: Multiple matching   Pages 86–87

How to go about it

Possible underlinings

5 I read the <u>original version</u> of this story <u>as a child</u>.

6 It shows <u>a way of life</u> which <u>unfortunately</u> does <u>not exist now</u>.

7 It <u>reminds</u> me of <u>a certain period</u> of my life.

8 The story proved to be very <u>educational</u>.

9 Children will find it <u>easier to read</u> than the other books in this selection.

10 The <u>beginning</u> of the book <u>gave me ideas</u> for the <u>start of my latest work</u>.

3

1 A *I ordered it on the Internet with the audiobook / The CD arrived first / In the end I didn't bother with the book*

2 D *Stevenson writes with a good deal of humour anyway, something which many aren't expecting when they read the book for the first time.*

3 B *... the great affection with which Mark Twain writes about his protagonists, Tom and his friend Huckleberry Finn, who both come across as cheeky, but likeable rogues.*

4 A

5 C *Of all the books here that I read when I was growing up, this was the only one which wasn't adapted or abridged in any way.*

6 B *... it's sad to think that young children can no longer play like Tom and his friends, that they no longer have the freedom to go off in search of adventure ...*

7 E *brings back memories of my teenage years, when I lived in a house on a river bank.*

8 A *We learnt a lot about how hard life was for the gold prospectors and the girls were motivated to find out more.*

9 C *Being more modern than the rest ... the language is still fairly accessible for younger readers and there's less danger of them becoming frustrated with the style.*

10 E *... the first chapter, when Mole first meets Rat, provided the inspiration for the opening of my most recent novel Harvest Mouse.*

Unit 7   Value for money

Vocabulary 1: Shopping   Page 88

1

1 out-of-town   **2** corner   **3** brands   **4** own-brand
5 convenience   **6** range   **7** foodstuffs   **8** value
9 aisles   **10** trolley   **11** counter   **12** checkout   **13** till
14 cashier   **15** receipt

Listening 1: Sentence completion   Page 89

1

1 middle   **2** an outdoor market   **3** children
4 fresh meat   **5** (dead) animal(s)   **6** (the) well-known brands   **7** five times   **8** bakery/bread   **9** smell
10 (things) on impulse

Reading and Use of English: Gapped text
Pages 90–91

3

1 G   **2** C   **3** F   **4** E   **5** B   **6** A

Language focus 1: Present perfect simple
Page 91

2

a 4   **b** 1   **c** 2   **d** 5   **e** 3   **f** 1   **g** 2   **h** 4

3a

Present perfect	Past simple
yet	last summer
so far today	in September
in the last few days	two weeks ago
for the last two years	before I came here
over the last week	on my 10th birthday
already	when I was younger
this month	
since I got up	

Vocabulary 2: Paraphrasing and recording
Page 92

1

1 rid   **2** put   **3** for   **4** end   **5** through   **6** taken
7 all   **8** heart

2

Possible answers

b I feel they are forcing me to/making me try things on …

c I start sweating.

d I go to look for my size.

e I don't care if I look scruffy/untidy …

f This is sometimes caused by/the fault of the shop's fluorescent lighting.

Listening 2: Multiple choice   Page 93
2

1 B   **2** C   **3** A   **4** C   **5** A   **6** B   **7** C

Language focus 2: Expressing preferences
Page 93

2

1 come back later than wait

2 paying by cash to

3 to phone him rather than

4 not get

Vocabulary 3: Towns and villages   Page 94

1

2 pedestrian   **3** flats   **4** shopping   **5** office   **6** building
7 industrial   **8** housing

2

Positive: lively, bustling, pleasant, picturesque, prosperous, quaint

Negative: dull, run-down, shabby, depressing

Language focus 3: Present perfect continuous   Page 95

2

1a incompleteness – the book is not finished

b completed action – the book is finished

2a repetition – on a regular basis

b one occasion – they are not here now

3a focus on duration – the speaker considers *all day* to be important

b focus on completed action – the finished product rather than the duration is important to the speaker here

4a temporary – she is not staying with her on a permanent basis

b long term – this is not a temporary arrangement

3

1 've/have just heard   **2** have you been   **3** proposed
4 kept   **5** were   **6** have you made
7 've/have been saving   **8** 've/have both been working
9 've/have already saved   **10** have (you) been doing
11 've/have been studying   **12** failed

Writing: Email   Pages 96–97

1

A A formal style would be appropriate. The target reader is the director of a school. The style of the language in his email is also formal.

B An informal style would be appropriate. The target reader is a friend. The style of the language in his email is also informal.

2

a Yes, it is consistently formal.

b Yes, she mentions cost, shops and proximity to the school.

3a

A	B
less than twenty minutes	under thirty minutes
four supermarkets	five supermarkets
within easy walking distance of the school	you can cycle to the school

b

1 plenty/lots/loads   **2** thinking   **3** train   **4** get/travel
5 enough   **6** bit/little   **7** though/if   **8** But   **9** put
10 wait

4a

Openings and closings: *Dear Mr Simpson/Yours sincerely* in **A**; *Hi Rob/All the best* in **B**

The use of nouns in **A** (*the date of your arrival/a wide choice of/because of its location*) compared to verbs in **B** (*when you're coming/plenty of … to choose from/being in the centre*)

Informal words in **B** (e.g. *Thanks/really/enormous/a lot of*); more formal/neutral equivalents in **A** (*Thank you/very/very large/a great deal of*)

Latinate verb *tolerate* in A; phrasal verb *put up with* in **B** (though note that *look forward to* in **A** is a phrasal verb)

b

Dashes (*I'd definitely recommend the area – it's really lively*) and exclamation marks (*five supermarkets!*) are features of informal writing, which appear in **B**, but not in **A**.

c

Use of contractions in **B** (*you're/it's/it'd/Justa's/there's/can't*); no contractions in **A**

Ellipsis (omission of words) in **B** (*(I) hope this is useful/(I) Can't wait to see you*): no ellipsis in **A**

5

> **Sample answer**
>
> Hello Patrick,
>
> It was good to hear from you. You asked me about places to buy things so if I were you, I'd go and look at the shopping centre Amazing Prices. There are a few shops that you could try.
>
> The best place to buy your computer equipment is Technology World, where they sell from mobiles to televisions. If you go to the computer part of the shop you'll find everything you need. There are some decent and cheap printers.
>
> As for your clothes, go to Old Times, where you'll find old and modern clothes of all tipes. Go to Modern Clothes and you'll see some affordable and good quality clothes which are quite casual.
>
> It's a shame I couldn't be with you, but I expect I'll see you at summer.
>
> Best wishes
>
> Lara
>
> 135 words

Examiner's comment

Content: The letter is short and the writer could have added some introductory information in the first paragraph. However, all the questions are answered fully.

Communicative achievement: Although the opening comment could have been extended, the conventions of an informal letter are followed. The target reader would be fully informed.

Organization: Well organized into paragraphs. Simple cohesive devices used effectively, e.g. *as for your clothes.*

Language: Simple and complex grammatical forms used with control and flexibility, and errors do not obscure meaning, e.g. *they sell from mobiles to televisions, at summer, tipes.* There is a good range of appropriate expressions for the task, e.g. *good to hear from you, if I were you, I'd go, The best place to buy, If you go to the computer part of the shop you'll find everything you need, which are quite casual, I expect I'll see* and the writer shows a good knowledge of vocabulary *shopping centre, sell, decent, affordable, shame.*

Mark: Very good pass

Review 7   Pages 98–99

Vocabulary: Shopping

2 range   **3** value   **4** corner   **5** meat   **6** out-of-town
7 convenience   **8** own-brand   **9** brand   **10** goods

Reading and Use of English: Open cloze

1 is   **2** than   **3** to   **4** who   **5** despite   **6** was   **7** for
8 rather

Reading and Use of English: Transformations

1

1 c and e   **2** b and d   **3** a and f

2

1   the last time I spoke to
2   first time I have/'ve eaten
3   has/'s been playing tennis since
4   ages since he (last) saw/has seen
5   haven't/have not been swimming for
6   biggest supermarket I have/'ve (ever)

Unit 8   Up and away

Reading and Use of English 1: Gapped text
Pages 100–101

2

moving around, washing, sleeping, and a brief mention of eating (*chasing food through the air*)

3

Word or phrase	Possible student answers
(students may use gestures for some items)	
short-circuit	damage
wipes	some kind of cloth for washing
trickier	more difficult
chopped	cut

Dictionary definitions

short circuit *noun* [C]

a bad connection in the wires of a piece of electrical equipment, which prevents the equipment from working

short-circuit *verb* [T]

to make a piece of electrical equipment have a short circuit

wipe *noun* [C]

a small wet cloth used a single time for cleaning something

tricky *adjective*

difficult to do

chop *verb* [T]

to cut something such as food or wood into pieces

4

1 E   **2** B   **3** G   **4** A   **5** F   **6** D

Vocabulary: Sleep   Page 101

1a

1 falling   **2** nodding   **3** snoozing

b

going to sleep: *falling asleep, nodding off*
sleeping: *snoozing*

Additional material Page 204

1 get   **2** log   **3** in   **4** take   **5** stay

259

Answer key

Language focus: The future   Page 102

A Making predictions

1

a 3   **b** 1, 2 and 6   **c** 4 and 5

	Negative forms
will probably	*probably won't/will not*
may well*	
will	*won't/will not*
might	*might not*
could	*could not* (but note that the negative form changes the meaning to 'certainty' or 'logical impossibility')

**may well not* exists, but *may well* is normally only used in the positive

B Other futures

1 b   **2** d   **3** e   **4** c   **5** i   **6** f   **7** g   **8** a   **9** h

C Time linkers

1 before   **2** By   **3** until   **4** soon   **5** when

The present simple and present perfect simple are used after the time linkers to refer to the future.

D Further practice

A

1 is going to rain   **2** we're going   **3** we'll have to

B

4 takes off   **5** I'll get up   **6** we'll be driving

C

7 'm/am seeing *or* 'm/am going to see   **8** will last/is going to last   **9** 're/are only going to sign *or* 're/are only signing   **10** 'll/will have finished *or* 'll/will finish

D

11 shall we meet   **12** doesn't/does not start   **13** 'll get   **14** 'll probably see

Listening 1: Multiple choice   Page 103

1 A   **2** B   **3** C   **4** A   **5** B   **6** C   **7** B   **8** B

Vocabulary 2: Travel   Page 104

1a

1 journey   **2** flight   **3** travel   **4** cruise   **5** tour   **6** trip

2

1 holiday   **2** campsite   **3** stayed   **4** enjoy   **5** time   **6** fun   **7** excursion   **8** full   **9** away   **10** package

Listening 2: Multiple matching   Page 106

1 C   **2** F   **3** A   **4** H   **5** E

Vocabulary 3: Phrasal verbs   Page 106

1 catch on: begin to understand

2 head for: go somewhere

3 come up with: think of

4 turn out: attend/take part in an event

5 come across: meet (by chance)

6 get about: travel around

Word formation: Adjectives   Page 107

1

1 careful   **2** healthy   **3** additional   **4** dangerous   **5** impatient   **6** unpleasant   **7** attractive   **8** industrial

2a and b

-ous	-ful	-y	-al
dangerous	careful	healthy	additional
poisonous	peaceful	cloudy	industrial
mysterious	beautiful	hungry	original
humorous	successful	foggy	financial
			beneficial

-ent	-ant	-ive
impatient	unpleasant	attractive
different	ignorant	protective
apparent	tolerant	decisive
obedient	hesitant	descriptive

Reading and Use of English 2: Word formation   Page 107

1 significant   **2** numerous   **3** unusual   **4** distances   **5** impressive   **6** environmental   **7** inexpensive   **8** appearance

Writing: Essay   Pages 108–109

2

The fact that there are more opportunities to make new friends on a seaside holiday than in the countryside.

3a

Secondly, Another positive point is

b

Without doubt, which, whereas, but, also, therefore, because, In my opinion

4c

> **Sample answer**
> ....
>
> The best way to travel in my area is by car, which generally has more advantages from using public transport.
>
> Firstly, there are not trains and the busses in my area are not often. You can wait thirty minnutes to find a bus. They can be very slow and you can waist a lot of time going to a diferent place. In the car, you can travel more fastly to a variety of places.

Second point, although busses are not expensive to by tickets, they are not too clean so it is not nice to sit on them for long time. It is better to go to a place in the car because the car is more plesant.

Finally, the busses do not go to many diferent locations and you can have problems to go where you want. In the car you can decide what to visit in my area. It is not surprising that all of the people in my town use the car to go anywhere.

In my opinion, then, the car is the best way to travel in my area because it saves time, costs cheaply and you can go where you want.

Sinan Alpey

196 words

Examiner's comment

Content: Adequate coverage of 1 and 2 and candidate has added their own idea. However, the introduction is rather weak.

Communicative achievement: Register appropriate to the task. The reader would be sufficiently informed; however, the frequent inaccuracies would create a negative effect.

Organization: Clear paragraphing. Adequate use of simple linking devices e.g. *firstly, although, finally, in my opinion.*

Language: Although the frequent errors do not obscure meaning, they do distract the reader, e.g. incorrect prepositions *advantages from* (of), incorrect verb *busses in my area* (don't run very often) *are not often,* confusion with gerunds and infinitives *problems to find* (finding), incorrect comparative *more fastly* (faster), poor expression *busses are not expensive to by tickets* (bus fares are not expensive), problems with quantifiers *not too* (very) *clean, go anywhere* (everywhere), omission of indefinite article *for* (a) *long time,* There are also many spelling mistakes which have a negative effect, e.g. *minnutes, busses, waist, diferent, by, plesant.* Some variety of structures, e.g. *The best way to travel, although, better to go to a place, diferent locations, what to visit, It is not surprising,* some more complex collocation *you can waist* (waste) *a lot of time, a variety of places that, saves time.* However, in general the language is simple and contains frequent inaccuracies.

Mark: Pass

Review 8   Pages 110–111

Reading and Use of English: Transformations

1

2 a **3** f **4** b **5** e **6** d

2

1 are you planning to spend/on spending
2 on the point of saying
3 likely to get
4 not be able to stay/keep/remain
5 will probably have died by/may well have died by
6 soon as you come up

The future

2 away **3** for **4** be **5** much **6** to **7** a **8** well
9 of **10** is **11** not **12** on

Reading and Use of English: Multiple-choice cloze

1 D **2** B **3** A **4** B **5** C **6** B **7** D **8** A

Unit 9   Mystery and imagination

Reading and Use of English 1: Multiple choice   Pages 112–113

3

1 C *Laura felt the magnetic pull of the ocean beneath the black cliffs, and goose bumps rose on her arms.*

2 B *The tide was in and violent waves splattered the path. More than once, Laura had to leap to avoid a drenching.*

3 D *She almost didn't pick it up. The idea of finding a message in a bottle seemed ridiculous, like a joke or something. … Before she picked it up, she took a good look round in case the person who'd left it there was hanging around to have a laugh.*

4 A *Since the bottle was shiny and new and had obviously never been in the sea, old sea dogs could be ruled out.*

5 C *She put down the note while she zipped up her coat and pulled her scarf tighter.*

6 C *What if the writer was someone in real danger? What if she was their only lifeline and she ignored them and walked away?*

Vocabulary 1: Ways of looking   Page 113

1a

1 b **2** a **3** c

b

1 peer: look very carefully, especially because something is difficult to see
2 glimpse: see for a moment or not completely
3 glare: look at someone in a very angry way

2

1 glanced **2** gazed **3** staring **4** glimpse **5** glared
6 peered

Language focus 1: Modal verbs for speculation and deduction   Page 114

1

1a might have left, might have come

b can't have been

c must have done

2 *have* + past participle (the perfect infinitive without *to*)

3 could, may

Answer key

3
2 d   3 e   4 a   5 f   6 c

4
a present, continuous infinitive (*be* + present participle) without *to*

b present, infinitive without *to*

c past, perfect infinitive (*have* + past participle) without *to*

d past, (continuous) perfect infinitive without *to*

e past, perfect infinitive without *to*

f present, infinitive without *to*

Listening 1: Multiple choice   Pages 114–115

1 B   2 B   3 C   4 A   5 C   6 A   7 A

Word formation: Adverbs   Page 115

1
1 nervously

2 usually, extremely

3 regrettably

Add *-ly* to the adjective (e.g. *nervously*). This also applies to adjectives ending in *-l* (e.g. *usually*) or *-e* (*extremely*). However, if the adjective endings in a consonant + *-le* then omit the final *-e* and add *-y* (e.g. *regrettably*).

2
1 completely, solely   2 simply, gently   3 luckily, extraordinarily   4 scientifically, dramatically

3
1 wholly   2 shyly   3 fully   4 publicly   5 truly

4
1 Apparently   2 accidentally   3 increasingly
4 originally   5 daily   6 repeatedly   7 carelessly
8 unhealthily

Vocabulary 2: *Give*   Page 116

A Phrasal verbs with *give*

1
a give away

b give off

2
1 stop doing something you do regularly

2 allow oneself to be arrested by the police

3 give something (physical) to several people

4 give information to a lot of people

5 give something to a teacher; return

6 agree to something after initial resistance

B Collocations with *give*

1A
1 d   2 c   3 e   4 a   5 b

B
1 e   2 d   3 f   4 a   5 b   6 c

2
a 3 give great pleasure, 4 give a nasty shock

b 5 give an impressive performance, 6 give a lengthy speech

c 1 give one's best regards, 2 give full details

Reading and Use of English 2: Open cloze
Page 117

1 be/make   2 which   3 not   4 to   5 than   6 yourself
7 on   8 although/though/while/whilst

Listening 2: Sentence completion   Page 117

1 go hiking   2 summer   3 farmers   4 German
5 October   6 eight thousand/8000   7 setting   8 maps
9 ghost   10 song

Language focus 2: Question tags   Page 118

1
The subject and the auxiliary verbs in the main clause are repeated in the question tag but the order is reversed. Also, if the verb is affirmative in the main clause, it is negative in the question tag, and vice versa.

2
a Sentence 1 is a real question.

b In sentence 2 the speaker expects agreement.

The difference is in the intonation.

Rising intonation (↗) = real question

Falling intonation (↘) = expecting agreement

3
1 do you   2 will you   3 didn't you   4 is he   5 hasn't he
6 aren't I   7 can't you   8 shall we

4
1 You don't believe him, do you? ↗

2 You won't let me down, will you? ↘

3 You went away for the weekend, didn't you? ↗

4 He's not playing very well, is he? ↘

5 He's already passed the *First* exam, hasn't he? ↘

6 I'm right about that, aren't I? ↘

7 You can play chess, can't you? ↗

8 Let's phone Paul, shall we? ↗

Reading and Use of English 3: Multiple matching   Pages 118–119

3

1 C *Some of the beneficiaries wanted to meet the donor to express their gratitude.*

2 A *… there was unanimous approval of the intricate sculptures from all those lucky enough to view them on display.*

3 D *… one national daily, which asked readers to get in contact if they knew who the mystery benefactor was.*

4 B *What surprised them, however, was the huge interest shown by newspaper and radio journalists …*

5 C *There were a number of theories to explain who the donor was and why they might have given the cash away: an elderly person with no family to leave their money to, a criminal wanting to get rid of stolen money or a lottery winner trying to do some good.*

6 A *… the general view was that he or she should remain anonymous.*

7 D *I have recently been fortunate enough to come into quite a lot of money …*

8 B *… some residents expressed concern that the scarves might harm the trees and become unattractive with the effects of the weather.*

9 A *Each sculpture was carefully and suitably chosen …*

10 D *Believing it to be part of a marketing promotion, one beneficiary nearly threw the blank envelope away.*

Speaking: Collaborative task   Page 120

Useful language box
Task 1
A

1 on   **2** in   **3** for   **4** on   **5** out

B

1 is it   **2** wouldn't it   **3** do they   **4** haven't we
5 shall we

Language focus 3: Contrast linkers   Page 120

1

1 but   **2** Despite   **3** While (*or* Although)   **4** Although
5 However   **6** in spite

Writing: Review   Page 121

2

Abbey Road by The Beatles

3

a Yes.

Good points: *it still sounds as fresh as when it was first released in 1969; Lennon and McCartney, always a guarantee of quality music; my favourites are the two written by George Harrison; the Liverpool band's use of vocal harmony on the album is outstanding, and there's a good mix of fast and slow tracks, with one or two humorous ones as well.*

Bad points: *Ringo's contribution about the octopus is the weakest; the artwork … is tiny*

Recommendation: *The album has songs to suit every generation, from children to grandparents, so I'd recommend it to everyone.*

b Yes.

Paragraph 1: Introduction, reasons for buying the download

Paragraph 2: Good points

Paragraph 3: More good points and one bad point

Paragraph 4: Recommendation; concluding sentence, including a bad point

c Yes.
So, Despite, However, and, as well, but, so, Unfortunately, but

d Yes.

Vocabulary of music: e.g. *album, band, track, drummer, cover, compose, release*

Adjectives: e.g. *classic, scratched, fresh, gentle, outstanding, humorous*

Structures: e.g. *This classic album … has been in our family for over forty years; …it's been played so often that it's too scratched to listen to now; it still sounds as fresh as when it was first released; he was always a better drummer than a singer, wasn't he?; The album has songs to suit every generation.*

e The style is fairly informal, with contractions (*it's, there's*), a dash (– *gentle songs of love and hope*), exclamation marks (*we still have the cover from the vinyl version!*) and the use of direct address (*he was always a better drummer than a singer, wasn't he?*).

The style is appropriate: this is a school's English-language magazine so the readers will be other students.

4

> **Sample answer**
> ....
> I'd only been able to play this when I went to my friend Eli's house. So when I finally bought my own console it was the first game I bought. It involves you look after your own dogs, feed them, wash them, take them out for walks, and take them to competitions.
>
> I like it because if you have a dog, you can learn from this game, as it gives you useful information. Your dogs are given a number of accessories and toys which you can sell in order to buy others you would prefer having. Another way to be able to buy accessories is to enter competitions, were you can win money.
>
> There's nothing very bad to say about this game, but something that does frustrate me a little bit is that you can't go to more than 3 competitions in a day.
>
> I think it's a game for all ages, but it will probably appeal more to young people who like animals. You can buy it in any game shop.
>
> Elisa Pacheco
>
> 172 words

Answer key

Examiner's comment

Content: Full coverage of all information required.

Communicative achievement: Lively tone suitable for this type of review. Would inform the target reader, as well as hold their attention.

Organization: Well organized. Clear paragraphing.

Language: Minor inaccuracies with more complex language, e.g. *It involves you look (looking) after*. One spelling mistake *were* (where) which does not impede meaning. Good examples of accurate language use in often difficult areas. There is a wide range of simple and complex grammatical forms with control and flexibility, e.g. *I'd only been able to play, if you have a dog, you can learn from, dogs are given, in order to, prefer having, frustrate me a little bit, it will probably appeal more to young people*. Many examples of good vocabulary, e.g. *console, sell, look after, feed them, accessories, toys, appeal*.

Mark: Very good pass

Review 9   Pages 122–123

Vocabulary: Ways of looking

1 c   **2** d   **3** e   **4** f   **5** a   **6** b

Reading and Use of English: Multiple-choice cloze

1 B   **2** C   **3** D   **4** C   **5** A   **6** B   **7** B   **8** D

Reading and Use of English: Word formation

1 noisily   **2** traditional   **3** colourful   **4** evidently
5 suspicious   **6** shortly   **7** eventually   **8** mysterious

Reading and Use of English: Transformations

1 might not be playing

2 have given you great pleasure

3 may have given

4 give away a secret would *or* give a secret away would

5 'd/had better give/hand

6 caught/got/had a brief glimpse

Ready for Listening

Part 1: Multiple choice   Pages 124–125

2

A a blouse

Key words and expressions

It'll go really well with a skirt I bought last week.

The sleeves are a bit short, but if I wear a jacket over it …

Distractors

Cheaper than getting a dress …

It'll go really well with a skirt I bought last week.

3

1 C   **2** A   **3** A   **4** C   **5** B   **6** B   **7** C   **8** B

Part 2: Sentence completion   Pages 125–126

1

1 **False**: All parts of the listening paper are heard twice.

2 **True**

3 **True**

4 **False**: The maximum number of words you need to write is normally three.

5 **False**: It is not necessary to rephrase the words you hear.

6 **False**: You do usually hear the answers in the same order as the questions.

7 **False**: If you are having difficulty with a question, move quickly onto the next. You may miss later answers if you spend too long on one answer.

8 **True**: Spelling errors are accepted, but if the word is so badly spelt it is unrecognizable, then it may be marked wrong.

2

1 tea house   **2** several hundred   **3** isolated   **4** farmers
5 (local) Indians   **6** beautiful valley   **7** song and dance
8 (groups of) teachers   **9** (Welsh) flags   **10** chocolate cake

Part 3: Multiple matching   Page 126

1

Suggested underlining of key words

A I will need a <u>specific qualification</u> to do this job.

B I currently <u>combine</u> <u>work</u> with <u>studying</u>.

C I <u>disagree</u> with the <u>careers advice</u> I have been given.

D I <u>heard about</u> this job from <u>someone in my family</u>.

E I <u>do not really mind</u> what job I do.

F I think I have the necessary <u>personal qualities</u>.

G I am <u>not clever enough</u> for the job I would like to do.

H I am studying a <u>relevant subject</u>.

2

1 B   **2** H   **3** D   **4** A   **5** F   C, E and G not used

Part 4: Multiple choice   Page 127

3

C. Underline the whole of the first sentence.

4

A: Most of the people he works with are below average height. At one metre 84, he is above the average height of one metre 78 for British men.

B: We are told that he is taller than most, if not all, of the people in his studio, but we do not know if he is taller than most people in his profession.

5

2 B   **3** A   **4** A   **5** B   **6** B   **7** C

6

2 **A:** We are only told that tall people come from all over the country to stay in a hotel.

 C: Not mentioned.

3 **B** and **C** are both mentioned as problems but not the biggest.

4 B: People who make comments like 'What's the weather like up there?' think they are funny. Jenny does not.

   C: Jenny says that many fellow TPC members take offence, but she is used to it now.

5 A: They stand up straighter as they grown in confidence. No one encourages them to do so.

   C: Not mentioned.

6 A: Not mentioned. Jenny says 'I've never been very good at volleyball, but I always got picked for the university team when I was a student.'

   C: Not mentioned. The word 'job' is mentioned when she says 'you can get things off the top shelf that most other people have a job to reach.'

7 A: Not mentioned. Jenny merely compares the GB and Ireland club with those in America.

   B: No. People decide for themselves if they should join.

Unit 10   Nothing but the truth

Vocabulary 1: Crime and punishment
Page 128
A Crimes and criminals
1

2 shoplifting   **3** vandalism   **4** drink-driving
5 trafficking   **6** internet piracy   **7** identity fraud
8 burglary

2

2 shoplifter   **3** vandal   **4** drink-driver   **5** trafficker
6 internet pirate   **7** identity fraudster   **8** burglar

B Punishment

c to <u>acquit</u> someone of all charges (to state officially that someone is not guilty of the crime they were accused of)

d to order someone to pay a <u>£2000 fine</u> (a penalty of £2000 for breaking the law)

b to order someone to do 200 hours of <u>community service</u> (instead of going to prison, an offender has to work for the benefit of the community, e.g. picking up litter, cleaning walls of graffiti, etc)

e to give someone a <u>two-year prison sentence</u> (to send someone to prison for two years)

a to sentence someone to <u>life imprisonment</u> (in Britain, the maximum prison sentence)

Listening 1: Multiple choice   Page 129
2

1 C   **2** A   **3** B   **4** B   **5** A   **6** C   **7** B

Language focus 1: *Too* and *enough*   Page 129
1a

a nouns   **b** adjectives and adverbs   **c** before   **d** after

b

the infinitive with *to*

2

1 too quietly for me to
2 not tall enough to
3 aren't/are not enough eggs for
4 there were too many

Reading and Use of English: Multiple choice
Page 130–131

1 D   **2** C   **3** A   **4** D   **5** B   **6** A

Vocabulary 2: Paraphrasing and recording
Page 132
1a

1 blame   **2** far   **3** good   **4** hourly   **5** run   **6** available
7 own   **8** former

2

Possible answers

b Concentrated faces make the place feel busy.
c We always follow the law very closely in our work.
d It is not only women who are patient.
e People are more prepared to talk about their feelings to a woman.
f Clients do not want to take part.
g She smiles a little.

Language focus 2: Passives   Page 133
1a

1 *will not be accepted*
2 *could be done*
3 *not to be overheard*
4 *is called away*

b

to be, past

c

2 the clients   **3** her staff

1 The agent is obvious (the court officials) so does not need to be mentioned.
4 The agent is not known by the writer, or is not important in this context.

2

A be categorized
B will be/are going to be installed, has/have been criticized
C were increased, are/have been found, have been contacted, to be made
D were fined, was told, were/had been warned, would be taken, was not turned
E was being pushed, be attacked, being treated, was sent

Writing: Article   Pages 134–135

1

1 Personally   **2** Astonishingly   **3** Sadly
4 Unfortunately/Sadly   **5** Curiously   **6** Worryingly
7 Interestingly   **8** Happily

Answer key

4

a *A load of rubbish* [this expression can also be used to express disagreement or criticize something]

b *I'm sure the people of Brenton don't drop crisp packets and drink cans on the floor in their own home.*

c *So why do so many think it's acceptable to do so on the streets of our town?*

But surely they, more than anyone, want a town they can be proud of, don't they?

d *Incredibly, Clearly, Unfortunately, surely*

e *So, And, But* [Normally, these are used as conjunctions to link two ideas in the same sentence. Here they are used informally at the beginning of a sentence to link the ideas which follow with those in the previous sentence.]

f *But surely they, more than anyone, want a town they can be proud of, don't they?*

5

Paragraph 1: A criticism of some of Brenton's residents and their tendency to drop litter.

Paragraph 2: The serious nature of the problem in Brenton, and the impression left on tourists.

Paragraph 3: Suggested solutions.

Paragraph 4: A criticism of the council and a reason why they should take action.

6

> **Sample answer**
>
> Graffiti everywhere!
>
> Walls, schools, blocks of flats and offices – everywhere in my neighorhood is covered of graffiti. It's as an illness which has caught the buildings.
>
> Is it art? No, it is mostly untidy writing of young people who don't have nothing better to spend their time. It makes the town to look ugly and seem if somebody drop a can of paint on the area. When the young people would do it in their own house, their parents would get crazy. So it is difficult to understand why do they do it in the street.
>
> So what can be done to cure this illness? Obviously, the best thing is catch the people who do this kind of thing and make them to clean the building. In addition, if I were the council, I would make a special place, where it is allowed to paint the wall all what you want. Then the people will do graffiti there and not on the buildings.
>
> Perhaps they could also do a class of graffiti in order to become better. Then we could admire their work rather than see it like a problem.
>
> Klaus Fischer
>
> 190 words

Examiner's comment

Content: Full coverage of the questions.

Communicative achievement: The catchy style in which the article is written would hold the reader's attention. The reader would be fully informed; however, the writer has been penalized due to frequent inaccuracies.

Organization: The article is clearly divided into appropriate sections. The writer has used rhetorical questions and simple linking devices effectively, e.g. *obviously, in addition, perhaps*.

Language: Although the frequent errors do not obscure meaning, they do distract the reader. Some examples of inaccuracies are incorrect prepositions *covered of* (in) *graffiti*, problems with use of passive *which has caught the buildings* (which the buildings have caught), *where* (people were allowed) *it is allowed to paint the wall all what you want* (as much as they wanted), incorrect quantifiers *don't have nothing* (anything), problems with bare infinitive *It makes the town to look ugly* (town look), problems with prepositions and incorrect tenses *seem* (as) *if somebody drop* (had dropped), *like* (as) *a problem*, incorrect conditionals *When* (if) *the young people would do* (did) *it*, problems with indirect questions *understand why do they do* (why they do). Despite frequent inaccuracies, some complex language is included, e.g. *what can be done to cure, if I were the council, I would, make a special place, rather than*.

The writer also shows a good knowledge of vocabulary, e.g. *walls, blocks of flats, neighorhood, illness, untidy, drop a can of paint, cure this illness, admire*.

Mark: Good pass

Listening 2: Multiple matching   Page 136

1

to avoid punishment, to spare a friend's feelings, to keep secrets, to increase a child's power and sense of control

3

1 E   2 A   3 H   4 G   5 C   B, D and F not used

Vocabulary 3: Phrasal verbs   Page 137

1

show off:	behave in a way that is intended to attract people's attention and make them admire you
get away with:	manage to do something bad without being punished or criticized for it
get out of:	avoid doing something that you should do
find out:	discover a fact or piece of information
make up:	invent an explanation for something, especially in order to avoid being punished
come over:	visit someone in the place where they are, especially their house
run out of:	use all of something so that you do not have any left

Language focus 3: Passive of reporting verbs
Page 137

1

is believed he made up the story about being mugged

2

1 believed to indicate

2 are said to be trying

3 is considered to be

4 are thought to use

5 is known to have lied

Review 10   Pages 138–139
Phrasal verbs

1

1 ran   2 get   3 sort   4 find   5 fell   6 give

2

1 making   2 owned   3 taken   4 giving, put   5 bringing
6 Cheer

Reading and Use of English: Transformations

1 be kept free of

2 is given a warm

3 was paid (at) an hourly *or* was paid at the hourly

4 being left on their

5 did not/didn't deserve to be

6 not to blame for

Reading and Use of English: Multiple-choice cloze

1 D   2 A   3 B   4 C   5 C   6 A   7 C   8 D

Unit 11   What on earth's going on?

Vocabulary 1: Weather   Page 140

2

1 storm   2 rain   3 winds   4 sunshine   5 sea
6 clouds   7 showers

4

2 strong/gale-force winds

3 snow showers

4 angry-looking/thick clouds

5 Heavy/Torrential rain

6 calm sea

Listening 1: Sentence completion   Page 141

2

1 twenty-five/25 years   2 farmers   3 *Weather Signs*
4 high/higher   5 frosty   6 donkeys   7 hills
8 (the) grass   9 red sky   10 heavy rain

Language focus 1: *So, neither, nor*   Page 141

Neither and *so* are used when something is true for all people referred to in the sentence.

Neither is used with reference to grammatical negatives and *so* with reference to affirmatives.

Use the same auxiliary verb (e.g. *do, have, will, would*) that appears in the main clause (or the verb *to be* if that is the main verb used). e.g. *I'll read the book and so will Rita/but Rita won't.* Use *do, does* or *did* if no auxiliary verb appears in the main clause. e.g. *I went home and so did John/but John didn't.*

2

1 c   2 e   3 f   4 g   5 a   6 h   7 b   8 d

Reading and Use of English 1: Multiple matching   Pages 142–143

3

1 **C** *I couldn't put the novel down when I was reading it, and the film adaptation gripped me in the same way.*

2 **A** *… what impressed me most about this film was the quality of the lead performances.*

3 **B** *It's obvious from the start who will fall victim to a twister, and there are no surprises in the central love story, either.*

4 **D** *… the final scene might not be what you're expecting. It certainly didn't turn out the way I thought it would.*

5 **A** *… it was the positive opinions I'd seen online … that persuaded me to buy the DVD.*

6 **C** *The special effects are so well done, my first impression was that I was watching a real storm. And if I hadn't seen the special features on the DVD afterwards, I'd probably still think they hadn't employed any visual tricks.*

7 **E** *I always find it works better for me if I watch it during a storm or when it's snowing outside.*

8 **B** *… unlike in numerous other films of this genre which slowly build up to a dramatic climax, they appear from the very beginning.*

9 **E** *… it's all good fun, and as long as you see it as that and don't look for any deeper message, you should enjoy the film.*

10 **D** *…creating a number of unforgettable, if slightly disagreeable moments.*

Language focus 2: Conditionals   Page 144

1 *and* **2**

Zero conditional	*The Day after Tomorrow*
present simple, present simple	
First conditional	*Twister*
present simple, *will* + infinitive without to	
Second conditional	*The Day after Tomorrow*
past simple, *would* + infinitive without to	

267

Answer key

Third conditional   *Twister*

past perfect, *would* + perfect infinitive (*have* + past participle) without *to*

Mixed conditional   *The Perfect Storm*

past perfect, *would* + infinitive without to

3

Zero conditional: whenever

First conditional: a possible

Second conditional: future

Third conditional: past

Mixed conditional: present

4

The different modal verbs, *will, should* and *might*, express different levels of certainty on the part of the speaker.

a *will* expresses certainty: the speaker feels certain they will be home by six o'clock.

b *should* expresses probability: he/she thinks they are likely to be home by six o'clock.

c *might* expresses uncertainty or possibility: he/she is not certain, but thinks it is possible they will be home by six o'clock.

5

a long   **b** providing   **c** condition   **d** unless

6

1 If you'd asked me...   **2** ... if I find out ...
3 ... if she hadn't phoned ... **4** If I drink ...
5 ... I'll never go ...

Conditionals: Expressing regret   Page 144

Possible answers

1 If I hadn't gone skiing, I wouldn't have broken my arm.
2 If I hadn't committed a foul, the referee wouldn't have sent me off.
3 If I hadn't been using my mobile phone, I wouldn't have crashed into a tree.
4 If I hadn't gone out of the room, the cat wouldn't have eaten the fish.
5 If I'd worked harder, I would have got a better grade.

Note: In each of the above sentences, *might* can substitute *would* in order to express possibility rather than certainty. The negative auxiliaries *hadn't* and *wouldn't* are usually stressed but in the affirmative they are usually unstressed.

Vocabulary 2: *Put*   Page 145

1a

1 at   **2** down   **3** together   **4** with   **5** up

b

1 put at risk: endanger
2 put down: stop reading
3 put together: assemble
4 put up with: tolerate
5 put your feet up: relax

2

1 g   **2** a   **3** d   **4** e   **5** h   **6** b   **7** f   **8** c   **9** i

3

a put up   **b** put off   **c** put on

4

1 pressure   **2** effort   **3** money   **4** blame

Speaking: Collaborative task   Page 146
Useful language
Household waste

bottle bank

plastic containers

Dirty streets

dropping litter

cigarette butts

River and sea pollution

oil slick

dumping waste

Traffic pollution

biofuel cars

exhaust fumes

Climate change

global warming

greenhouse effect

Reading and Use of English 2: Gapped text
Pages 146–147

3

1 E   **2** A   **3** G   **4** C   **5** F   **6** B

Reading and Use of English 3: Open cloze
Page 148

3

1 This/The   **2** order   **3** if   **4** part   **5** such   **6** However
7 has   **8** without

Writing: Essay   Page 148

Sample answer

Without doubt, the environment is in danger and all people have a challenge to do something about it. However, even small things that individuals do can make a difference.

First of all, people can try to reduce pollution by taking public transport or by using less energy. Exhaust fumes from cars are a big threat to the atmosphere, so this is one way that an individual can make a contribution to helping the environment.

Secondly, we should try to recycle as much as we can at home in order to cut down on household waste. For example, if everybody brought their old bottles to a bottle bank instead of dumping them, there would have been less waste in the natural landscape.

Finally, individuals need to work together as a team. We should encourage each other to recycle more and conserve energy, and educate in our schools about the importance of taking care of our planet.

In conclusion, I disagree with the statement and I believe that individuals can definitely make a difference. If everybody tries a little bit, the result will be effective.

Fehér László

183 words

Examiner's comment

Content: Very good realization of the task.

Communicative achievement: Consistently appropriate format and register. The essay would have a positive effect on the reader, who would be fully informed.

Organization: The article is well-organized with suitable paragraphs and the writer uses linking expressions effectively.

Language: High level of accuracy. The writer uses a wide range of simple and complex grammatical forms with control and flexibility. Shows a very good knowledge of vocabulary related to the environment, e.g. *exhaust fumes, threat, atmosphere, recycle, household waste, bottle bank, dumping, waste, landscape, taking care of.*

Mark: Very good pass

Listening 2: Multiple choice   Page 149

1 C   2 A   3 C   4 B   5 C   6 B   7 A   8 A

Review 11   Pages 150–151

Vocabulary

A Weather

1

1 light rain/winds/showers   2 heavy rain/storm/showers
3 strong winds

2

1 c   2 f   3 h   4 a   5 d   6 b   7 e   8 g

B Put

1 up   2 on   3 off   4 on   5 up   6 off

Conditional sentences

1 stays, will/'ll probably   2 had/'d known, could have prepared   3 wouldn't do, paid   4 had/'d taken, would not/wouldn't be   5 will/'ll send, start   6 would/'d have done, had not/hadn't helped   7 usually works, feed
8 would/'d go, had

Reading and Use of English: Part 4 Transformations

1 if I hadn't/had not spoken
2 I would not/wouldn't have written
3 not help you unless you
4 as long as you give/hand/send
5 is being put at
6 is not/isn't calm enough for

Unit 12   Looking after yourself

Vocabulary 1: Food and drink   Page 152

1

1 fussy eater: someone who only eats the food they particularly like and refuses to eat anything else.

2 eat up: eat all of something
leave food on your plate: not eat all of your meal

3 chew: bite food into small pieces
swallow: make food or drink go from your mouth, through your throat and into your stomach
bolt down: eat food very quickly

4 sip: swallow a drink slowly a bit at a time
gulp down: swallow a drink very quickly

5 soft drink: cold, non-alcoholic drink
still drink: drink without gas bubbles
fizzy drink: drink with gas bubbles

6 drink straight from a bottle or a can: drink something without pouring it out first
drink from a glass: drink something having first poured it into a glass

Language focus 1: Countable and uncountable nouns A   Page 152

1

milk **U**   diet **C**   chicken **U, C** (for a whole one)
health **U**   chip **C**   chocolate **U, C**   meal **C** (**U** = animal feed)   pepper **C** (vegetable), **U** (spice)   spaghetti **U**
cake **U, C**

2

1 cheese, toast, cake, chocolate
2 cheese, toast, cake
3 spaghetti* (also *plateful*)
4 sugar, salt
5 salt
6 chocolate
7 jam
8 milk

*note that *spaghetti* is used with a singular verb in English

Listening 1: Multiple matching   Page 153

2

1 B   2 E   3 H   4 F   5 C   A, D and G not used

Answer key

Language focus 2: Countable and uncountable nouns B   Page 153

1

Just a few:	followed by a countable noun in the plural = a few glasses (of water)
Just a little:	followed by an uncountable noun = a little water

By saying *Just a few* she really means she wants *a lot*.

2

Speaker 1

a some   **b** any/much   **c** deal

Speaker 2

d lot   **e** little   **f** little   **g** some/several

Speaker 3

h piece   **i** few   **j** no/little   **k** many

Speaker 4

l plenty   **m** several/many   **n** no/few

Speaker 5

o number   **p** few   **q** much/any

Reading and Use of English 1: Multiple matching   Pages 154–155

3

1 B *… his curry is banana-skins curry, the skins filling in for what would normally be meat.*

2 D *… we also plan to set up a webcam to livestream what we do in the kitchen …*

3 C *Certainly the figures on waste are a cause for concern.*

4 A *And the reason we don't notice it is because that's the way we all cook – they simply cook like us, and, indeed, we cook like them.*

5 E *At a time when we are having to tighten our belts, we could all do with cutting down on the throwaway …*

6 B *… if he uses one part of a vegetable or fruit, he'll use the rest of it elsewhere, as long as it isn't harmful to health.*

7 A *… nearly all of the chefs waste food. Not consciously, but still they do it.*

8 D *… he'll teach kids … He is also targeting slightly older cooks.*

9 A *I used to watch and think: 'I could make a dish out of what you are throwing away alone.' So that's what he started doing.*

10 C *'I believe in spreading what knowledge I have of my type of low-waste cooking, I don't want to lecture people,' Jordan says. 'But I do want to try and show people there's another way.'*

Language focus 3: Reported speech   Page 156

1

The present simple changes to the past simple.

The present simple is also possible in the reported version, as the statement *'he doesn't want to lecture people'* is still true.

2

b She said she *had seen* him twice *that* day.

c He told me she *had been* living *there* for years.

d He said he *had spoken* to her *the previous* week.

e He told me he *had been* working *the day* before.

f They said they *had asked* her several times.

3

Direct speech		Reported speech
b present perfect simple	→	past perfect simple
c present perfect continuous	→	past perfect continuous
d past simple	→	past perfect simple
e past continuous	→	past perfect continuous
f past perfect simple	→	past perfect simple

4

Direct speech		Reported speech
will	→	would
may	→	might
can	→	could
must	→	had to

Would, might, could, should and *ought to* do not change in reported speech.

5

Direct speech		Reported speech
two days ago	→	two days before/earlier/previously
next month	→	the following month/the next month
tonight	→	that night/evening
this morning	→	that morning
now	→	then

Reading and Use of English 2: Open cloze   Page 156

2

1 little   **2** all   **3** than   **4** at   **5** which   **6** one/each
7 to   **8** no

Language focus 4: Reporting verbs   Page 157

2

advise	**offer**
(verb + object + infinitive with *to*)	(verb + infinitive with *to*)
order	refuse
urge	threaten

persuade ask

warn *promise

tell

remind

ask

encourage

recommend (and same patterns as *suggest*)

*can also take an object, e.g. *He promised me that he would...*

3
1 refused to clean her room
2 reminded him to take his sandwiches
3 threatened to call the police if I didn't turn my music down
4 warned/advised her not to take the car out (as/because/since the roads were very icy)
5 ordered/told him to get out of his office immediately
6 urged/encouraged/persuaded me to report the theft to the police

4
The infinitive with *to* is not used after *suggest*.

Vocabulary 2: Health matters   Page 158
1
A 1 heart attack   2 tooth decay   3 stomach ache
   4 blood pressure   5 ear infection
B 1 black eye   2 sore throat   3 stiff neck
   4 runny nose   5 sprained ankle

3
1 bandage   2 a plaster   3 prescription   4 plaster
5 injection

Listening 2: Multiple choice   Pages 158–159
2
1 C   2 B   3 A   4 B   5 A   6 C   7 A

Word formation: Nouns 2   Page 159
1
1 analysis   2 injury   3 complaints   4 pressure
5 advice   6 response

2
1 saying, meeting, building, advertising
2 pressure, departure, pleasure, signature
3 arrival, refusal, survival, approval
4 warmth, depth, truth, growth
5 flight, sight, weight, height
6 friendship, membership, championship, partnership

3a
2 loss, solution   3 success   4 choice   5 knowledge
6 speech   7 proof   8 belief, belief

Language focus 5: Reported questions
Page 160
1b
- auxiliary verbs *do, does, did* – disappear
- verb tenses – 'step back' a tense
- word order – the same in reported questions as for statements (subject + verb)
- yes/no questions – use *if/whether*
- punctuation – question marks are not used

2
1 how long she had been a doctor
2 what had made her decide to enter the medical profession
3 how many patients she saw each day on average
4 if/whether her friends often asked her for medical advice
5 if/whether she was planning to retire soon

Writing: Report   Pages 160–161
3a
1 well   2 here   3 but   4 where   5 This   6 as
7 However   8 which

b
1 In the paragraph on running, the writer refers to the promenade. He/She then begins the paragraph on cycling with *Cycling is forbidden on the promenade, but ...*
2 The writer finishes the paragraph on cycling by mentioning the views of the sea. He/She then begins the paragraph on cycling with *Swimming in the sea is not recommended, as ...*

4
Cycling
...your students can burn a few calories after class.
...with more superb views of the town and the sea.

Swimming
...there is a lake just outside the town, which is pleasant to swim in and less crowded than the town's swimming pool.

Conclusion
...your students will be able to do sport and enjoy beautiful scenery at the same time.

5

> **Sample answer**
>
> Report
>
> The aim of this report is to tell you the best places to eat cheaply in my area and say why. I will also say why, in addition to the reasons of cost I think the students will enjoy eating in these places.
>
> Where can you eat cheaply
>
> If I were you, I'd go to the shopping centre out of town. Here are many restaurants from different

Answer key

countries like Italian, Mexico, Chinese, Spanish and also Greece. In addition you eat very well and it is not espensive, you can do shopping or see a film in the cinema which is there. The students will enjoy to see a film after they eat.

Furthermore, I recommend you the area next the sea. Here are many good restaurants for eating fish and the prices are affordable. The best restaurant is 'Ocean Blue' where everything is blue, example chairs, tables, walls etc. The fish is catched local and is delicious. Also, the atmosphere is pleasant, friendly and lively.

Conclusions

To sum up, the students can eat tasty, delicious and cheap food in the shopping centre and next the sea.

Regina

186 words

Examiner's comment

Content: Full coverage of the information requested.

Communicative achievement: Although the report is slightly too informal, the tone is still polite and informative. The reader would be well informed.

Organization: The report is clearly divided into appropriate sections. Conventional linking devices are used adequately, e.g. *in addition, Furthermore, To sum up.*

Language: A number of errors, but none of which obscures meaning, omission of *there* (Here are many restaurants), confusion with gerunds and infinitives *enjoy to see*, omission of prepositions *next* (to) *the sea*, (for) *example chairs*, inaccurate past participle *catched*, incorrect word form *local* (locally), and one spelling mistake *espensive*. There is an adequate range of appropriate expressions for this type of task, e.g. *The aim of this report, Where can you, If I were you, I recommend.* The writer also shows a fairly good knowledge of vocabulary, e.g. *affordable, pleasant, friendly, lively, tasty, delicious, shopping centre.*

Mark: Good pass

Review 12 Pages 162–163

Reading and Use of English: Word formation

1 wholly   2 illnesses   3 choice
4 poverty   5 refusal   6 rising
7 unfortunately 8 discourage

Reading and Use of English: Transformations

1 have/'ve lost (some) weight since
2 advised Matt not to go
3 knowledge of English amazes
4 if/whether she knew how
5 offered to give Dawn
6 would not be (very) many

Collocation revision: Units 1–12

1 clothes   2 musician   3 (tele)phone   4 film
5 job/work   6 hair   7 town/neighbourhood/area   8 trip
9 give   10 sentence   11 wind(s)   12 drink

Reading and Use of English: Multiple-choice cloze

1 C   2 B   3 A   4 C   5 D   6 D   7 A   8 C

Ready for Speaking

Introduction   Pages 164–165

1

Part 1 b   **Part 2** d   **Part 3** a   **Part 4** c

2

Part 1

a No. Certainly, students should avoid trying to give over-complicated answers which cause them to become confused and so make unnecessary mistakes. However, very short one-word answers are usually inadequate and do not give the examiners a sufficient sample of language to assess. Students should therefore answer questions with appropriate detail.

b No. Long, pre-prepared answers will be interrupted by the interlocutor. As well as sounding unnatural they are often inappropriate to the question asked. Students may practise for this part of the test, but they should not try to prepare and learn long answers.

c Yes. Students will be nervous at the beginning but this part of the test is designed to relax them by asking questions on areas which are familiar to them.

Part 2

a No. Students are not required to describe the photographs in detail. They should compare them and then do the task which is given to them by the interlocutor and reproduced as a direct question above the photographs.

b Yes, as long as the student has tried to address both parts of the question. It is better to fill the minute and be interrupted than to run out of things to say before the allotted time finishes.

c Clearly the student should focus on the instructions that the examiner gives, though exam nerves often cause students to miss part of the instructions and it is perfectly acceptable for students to ask for them to be repeated. However, this is not really necessary as the second part of the interlocutor's instructions is printed in the form of a question above the photographs.

Part 3

a Good that the student had a lot to say. However, it seems that he/she may not have been respecting the rules of turn-taking, an important aspect of interactive communication. If students are paired with quiet, more reticent candidates, they should invite them to take part in the discussion by asking questions such as 'What do you think?' or 'What would you do?' Attempts to dominate the conversation will be penalized.

b No. As with Part 2, students should use the full amount of time allotted. The purpose is not to complete the task in the shortest time possible: rather, students should be aiming to provide enough relevant and appropriate contributions for the examiners to assess their English accurately.

c Yes. This student and his/her partner have clearly made full use of the time available. Student are not penalized if they fail to reach a decision, as long as it is clear that they are at least trying to do so.

Part 4

a Yes. Candidates should certainly be speaking more than the examiner! The implication here also seems to be that the candidates have been responding to each others' comments, something which is actively encouraged in Part 4.

b No. It is not only *what* you say but *how* you say it which is important throughout the exam. 'Nonsense, you must be mad' sounds rude and is not the best way to disagree with someone in a discussion such as this. Alternative expressions of agreeing and disagreeing are given on page 36 in Unit 3.

c No. Students should respond to questions appropriately and not try to divert the discussion to their favourite topic of conversation.

Part 1: Interview   Page 165

3

2 Christina has obviously come with a prepared speech. The interlocutor asks where she is from and, having answered the question, she begins to talk about her family.

3 He should develop his answers more, without pausing too much. He does improve by the end of Part 1, when he answers more confidently.

Part 2: Talking about photos   Page 166

2

1 Christina compares the photographs very well, using language such as *both pictures* and *whereas*. She addresses the second part of the task well, with a reasonable range of language (*get out of the towns or the cities where they live, in the open air, they can be lazy, peaceful*) and she successfully corrects herself when she says *in a camping* and *in the nature*.

Paolo does not actually compare the photographs at the beginning, though when addressing the second part of the task he does say that the people in both pictures are enjoying being with others. His range of language is good, particularly when speculating: *they must be enjoying themselves, it looks as if they are in a class, they might be listening to some music*, and he successfully corrects himself when he says *they are doing progress*.

Both candidates use fillers.

2 Christina gives a much more complete answer than Paolo, who makes no attempt to fill the 30 seconds he is given for this part.

Part 3: Collaborative task   Page 167

3

1 Christina asks Paolo questions to encourage him to speak.

Which one shall we start with?

It could be good fun, don't you think?

Now, what do you think about the concerts?

Do you agree?

I think nearly everyone will like this, don't you?

2 They both agree on the medieval fair. Christina's second choice is the dressing-up activity and Paolo's is the computer exhibition. At the end they are about to compromise by choosing the theatrical representations, as long as they are humorous.

Note the following words and expressions used by Paolo and Christina:

First task

I think it would appeal to all different types of people.

… it would also attract people of all ages.

It could be good fun.

I think it would bring in lots of families with young children.

This would be ideal for people who work near the museum.

I think they'd probably be more suitable for adults.

… nearly everyone would find them enjoyable …

Second task

I think Paolo made a good point earlier that …

… we both agreed that …

As I said before …

… we did both agree before that …

Part 4: Further discussion   Page 167

2

1a When answering the first two questions they do not interact at all, failing to respond to what each other says. Rather than a discussion, there is a series of short monologues.

b They interact much better in the second half of Part 4.

2 In the second half Christina helps the interaction by asking questions to involve Paolo: *What do you think, Paolo? Don't you agree?* and *Do you really think a robot could do all of our ironing for us?* and Paolo responds accordingly.

Unit 13   Animal magic

Vocabulary 1: The Arts   Page 168

1

1 classical **2** opera **3** stone **4** gallery **5** painting
6 novel

Answer key

2

Possible answers

music – musician, composer, conductor, orchestra, pianist, violinist, etc

literature – novelist, writer, author, publisher

art – artist, painter, art collector

opera – opera singer, tenor, soprano, cast, director

ballet – ballet dancer, ballerina, choreographer

sculpture – sculptor

Reading and Use of English: Gapped text
Pages 168–169

2

1 C   2 F   3 A   4 G   5 D   6 B

Vocabulary 2: Paraphrasing and recording
Page 170

1

1 changed   2 fetched   3 raises   4 doubt   5 freely
6 branched, taken   7 sensation   8 come

2

Possible answers

1 Animal rights activists were strongly opposed to his *Amazing Revelations*.

2 In 1994 people paid a lot of attention to *Away from the Flock*.

3 People say he painted only five himself.

4 This is not the first time artists have got others to do some of the work for them.

5 People will remember him most because of his art.

Language focus 1: Hypothetical situations
Page 171

A Wishes

2

a the past simple

b *would*

c the past perfect

3

a I wish I ~~would~~ **could** give up smoking.

b *I wish she could come to my party on Saturday.*
The speaker <u>knows</u> that she cannot come.
I hope she can come to my party on Saturday.
The speaker <u>does not know</u> if she can come or not.

4

1 could   2 didn't   3 hadn't bought   4 would
5 you'd listened

5

1 were   2 would stop   3 had/'d gone   4 had
5 would/'d make

274

B *It's time* and *would rather*

1

1 didn't   2 went

Listening 1: Multiple choice   Page 172

1 C   2 A   3 B   4 B   5 A   6 C   7 B

Word Formation: Suffixes *-ible* and *-able*
Page 173

1

a tarantulas   b rats   c ants   d pre-killed animals

2

1 un**predict**able   2 im**poss**ibility   3 incred**ibly**, comfort**ably**
4 respons**ibility**, valu**ables**   5 in**access**ible   6 consider**ably**

Language focus 2: Prepositions and gerunds
Page 173

1

a without   b like   c about

2

1 to   2 off   3 over   4 up   5 of

3

1 knowing how unhealthy

2 of getting rid of

3 instead of driving

4 result of his flight being

Vocabulary 3: Animals   Page 174

1

2 bat   3 bee   4 fox   5 lion   6 peacock   7 mouse
8 lamb   9 ox   10 owl

2

1 fly   2 horse   3 fish   4 cat, dog   5 bear   6 frog

3

a bird   b fish   c cat   d horse

Listening 2: Sentence completion   Page 176

2

1 monkeys   2 ten thousand/10 000   3 (one-)minute('s)
silence   4 stamps   5 (human) hand   6 New Mexico
7 flashing light   8 sixteen/16   9 half an orange
10 fingerprint

Vocabulary 4: Verbs followed by prepositions   Page 176

1

of, for

2

2 for, e   3 for, a   4 for, h   5 for, i   6 from, b
7 from, d   8 on, j   9 on, f   10 on, g

Writing: Email   Page 177

1

Range of language: the range of language is sufficiently varied and appropriate for this task, e.g. *… to get away from the city … the path that goes along the coast … it can get a bit windy … there are some good views from the cliffs.*

Style of the language: Appropriately and consistently informal, e.g. *You must be mad … It was great … Lots of people … I'd find it a bit boring … if you like that kind of thing.*

Use of paragraphs and linking words: The answer is clearly organized into paragraphs, although the closing comments are limited to a single word, *Bye*. There is a good range of linking devices, e.g. *I got a summer job **after that** so I could pay for my holiday to Greece, **where** I spent most of the time sunbathing … Anyway … Firstly/Secondly … Personally …*

Accuracy: Very accurate.

Relevance: The opening paragraph, whilst relevant, is overlong. The majority of the letter should be devoted to giving information about walking areas. In addition, the answer does not address the issue of wildlife mentioned in the question and this would be penalized in the exam.

Effect on the target reader: The target reader would not be sufficiently informed about areas where she could go walking and see interesting wildlife. The tone of the letter is also rather dismissive of walking and this would have a negative effect.

Sample answer

Hi Anna

Good to hear from you. I've finished my exams a week ago and I also went walking as I like nature aswell. I now quite a lot of places where you can go walking but I will only give you a couple of places.

Personally, I think that a lovely walking area is a path just outside the village of Alameda. The path is a bit rocky but not too steep. It's got some stunning views and you might catch sight of a vulture or two. Keep an eye out for eagles aswell.

Another walk is a coastal path in the south of Spain. People come here to observe dolphins and flamingos. It's a gentle circular walk which takes you round a nature reserve famous for its plants and colourful birds.

I hope this is usefull. Good luck in your exams.

Best wishes

Lara

146 words

Examiner's comment

Content: Full coverage of the information requested.

Communicative achievement: Suitably friendly informative tone. Reader would be fully informed.

Organization: The letter is clearly organized with suitable paragraphs and simple linking devices are used effectively.

Language: Minimal errors do not impede understanding, e.g. incorrect use of *ago* with present perfect. There are two spelling mistakes *now* instead of *know* and *usefull*. Has used more complex collocations accurately. Good range of appropriate expressions for this type of task *Good to hear from, Good luck in your exams, Best wishes.* Use of more complex collocations includes *Keep an eye out for, catch sight of a.* The writer also shows an excellent knowledge of vocabulary, e.g. *path, rocky, steep, stunning views, vulture, eagles, dolphins, flamingos, gentle circular walk, nature reserve.*

Mark: Very good pass

Review 13   Pages 178–179

Reading and Use of English: Word formation

1 peacefully   **2** remarkable   **3** originally   **4** responsibility
5 appearance   **6** proof   **7** unreliable   **8** statements

Vocabulary

A The Arts

1 portrait   **2** sculptures   **3** novel   **4** open-air
5 priceless   **6** playwright   **7** composer   **8** exhibition

B Animals

1
Lion

C Prepositions

1 to, to, for

2 on, for, without

3 for, to, to

4 for, of, for

Reading and Use of English: Transformations

1 I lived closer to

2 wish I had not/hadn't told

3 rather you did not/didn't wear

4 to playing the guitar the guitar well

5 prevented us (from) having

6 insisted on seeing

Unit 14   Mind your language

Listening 1: Multiple matching   Page 180

2
1 E   **2** C   **3** F   **4** H   **5** B   A, D and G not used

Answer key

Vocabulary 1: Phrasal verbs with *turn*
Page 181

1

reject

2

1 d   **2** f   **3** b   **4** e   **5** g   **6** a   **7** h   **8** c

3

a turn out   **b** turn up   **c** turn up   **d** turn over
e turn off   **f** turn off   **g** turn back   **h** turn into

Language focus 1: Compound adjectives
Page 181

1

The nouns are singular even though the number is plural.

2

1 five-minute   **2** English-speaking
3 blonde-haired, blue-eyed   **4** Italian-born
5 well-behaved

3

1 free   **2** time   **3** tempered   **4** brand/label   **5** down
6 haul/distance   **7** force   **8** air

Reading and Use of English 1: Multiple choice   Pages 182–183

2

1 C   **2** D   **3** C   **4** D   **5** B   **6** A

Vocabulary 2: *Make* and *do*   Page 183

1 do, make   **2** have/'ve made, doing/to do   **3** make, do
4 making, to make   **5** do, do   **6** to make, make
7 doing, do, do   **8** to do, to do, to make

Language focus 2: Expressing purpose
Page 184

A *In order to*, *so as to* and *so that*

2

so that + present simple/*can/will* = future

so that + *could/would* = past

3

Possible answers

1 … we can email her every day.

2 … to get a place near the stage.

3 … as to increase my chances of getting a job.

4 … I wouldn't have to do gym at school.

5 … to be nearer her parents.

6 … not to wake anyone up.

7 … I can go out afterwards.

B *In case*

2

Possible answers

1 … you have problems with the other one.

2 … it broke down again.

3 … you are burgled or there's a fire.

4 … I have to do overtime.

5 … I saw something good for my dad's birthday present.

6 … the alarm goes off by accident.

Listening 2: Multiple choice   Page 186

1 C   **2** B   **3** B   **4** C   **5** A   **6** C   **7** A   **8** B

Word formation: Suffixes *-ful* and *-less*
Page 186

1

a sleepless   **b** thankfully   **c** successful   **d** effortlessly

2

Noun	Positive adjective	Negative adjective
home	–	homeless
power	powerful	powerless
skill	skilful (Am* skillful)	unskilled
pain	painful	painless
point	–	pointless
delight	delightful	–
end	–	endless
harm	harmful	harmless
peace	peaceful	–
stress	stressful	unstressful
thought	thoughtful	thoughtless

*In the exam candidates should be consistent in their use of either American or British English.

Additional material Page 204

1 skilfully/skillfully   **2** carelessness   **3** thoughtful
4 uneventful   **5** painless   **6** cheerfulness   **7** pointless
8 homelessness   **9** peacefully   **10** harmless

Language focus 3: Ability   Page 187

1

1 to phone   **2** doing   **3** keeping   **4** come   **5** to solve

2

a be able to: there is no infinitive form of *can*.

b been able to: there is no past participle of *can*.

c was able to/managed to: for ability on one occasion in the past, *could* is not possible.

d unable: this word is an adjective, not a verb, so does not change its form.

e incapable: the negative prefix for this adjective is *in-*, not *un-*.

3

1 is capable of going

2 did not/didn't succeed in convincing

3 being unable to play

4 had been able to

5 incapable of turning

6 did not/didn't manage to buy

Reading and Use of English 2: Open cloze
Page 188

1

1 who   2 being   3 and   4 to   5 without   6 out
7 was   8 well

Writing: Letter of application
Pages 189–189

1

- The target reader is the Director of St George's House.

- The effect would not be positive. As well as making several requests concerning the school and the class (Manchester, the class size, idiomatic expressions) the applicant gives rather frivolous reasons for wanting to go to England: meeting a relative, clubbing, a base for travelling. This does not sound like a serious letter from someone asking for money and the application would probably not be successful.

3

Examples of other reasons:

- A course in the UK would help you pass the *First* exam.

- Your writing and grammar are fine but you would like to improve your fluency in speaking.

- You are going to study English at university next year.

- You are interested in meeting speakers of English from other countries.

- You will be working for two years overseas for a charity and English is a requirement.

Examples of further details relating to the other three reasons in the coursebook:

- A period of study in the UK would improve your chances of obtaining a job in your own country.

  I would like to work in the travel industry but my job applications are repeatedly rejected because of my level of spoken English.

- A recent illness has caused you to fall behind in your studies.

  I was absent from school for three months after a car accident and this has affected my chances of passing the First exam.

- You are interested in learning about British culture and the British way of life.

  I believe that knowledge of the culture would increase my enjoyment of the subject and provide an important context for my study of the language.

Review 14   Pages 190–191
Reading and Use of English: Multiple-choice cloze

1 C   2 B   3 A   4 D   5 A   6 C   7 C   8 B

Compound adjectives

1 twenty-pound   2 three-hour   3 short-sleeved
4 nine-to-five   5 high-speed   6 three-course
7 two-day-old   8 money-making

Reading and Use of English: Transformations

1 in order not to get   2 so as not to miss
3 in case it does not/doesn't   4 turned down an/the offer
5 make a complaint   6 made up your mind *or* made your mind up

Reading and Use of English: Word formation

1 performers   2 traditionally   3 competition
4 successful   5 extinction   6 useful   7 survival
8 popularity

Ready for Writing

Introduction   Pages 192–193
Extracts

A 5b   B 1   C 4   D 5a   E 2   F 3

Register

1

1 d informal   2 e formal   3 a informal   4 c formal
5 b formal

2

B Formal/neutral

  The linker, *however*, is fairly formal, and there are no contractions or phrasal verbs.

C Neutral

  There are no informal linkers, contractions or phrasal verbs, but neither is there evidence of any formal language.

D Formal

  The linker, *consequently*, is formal, as is the use of language such as *gained experience, in this field, well suited to the position*.

E Informal

  The writer addresses the reader directly with a question, and there are contractions in the second sentence.

F Formal

  The language used for making recommendations is formal: *is certainly to be recommended* and *it is advisable to*. The linker *However* is fairly formal and there are no features of informal language.

Marking

2 Content   3 Organization and cohesion   4 Register
5 Accuracy

Planning

2 e   3 c   4 d   5 a   6 f

Macmillan Education
4 Crinan Street, London N1 9XW
A division of Macmillan Publishers Limited
Companies and representatives throughout the
world

ISBN 978-0-230-44000-5 (+key edition)
ISBN 978-0-230-44005-0 (-key edition)

Text © Roy Norris 2013
Design and illustration © Macmillan Publishers
Limited 2013

Original design by Andrew Jones
Page make-up by xen, www.xen.co.uk
Illustrated by Ed McLachlan pp61, 92, 98, 145,
175; Matt Mignanelli pp11, 90, 132, 153, 174;
Julian Mosedale pp56, 80, 91, 121, 133, 151, 170,
191; Gary Wing pp75, 79, 95, 120, 161.
Picture research by Victoria Gaunt
Cover photograph by Getty Images/Graham
Monro/gm photographics

Author's acknowledgements
A big thank you to everyone at International
House, Madrid, who helped with piloting,
especially Steven McGuire, Kate Pickering,
Simon Mullan and Lee Williams. Thanks, also, to
Deborah Chilton, Faye Davies, Michael Gallagher
and Robin Martin for their contributions, and to
all the staff at Macmillan who have been involved
in the project. This book is dedicated to my wife,
Azucena, and daughters, Lara and Elisa, whose
enormous patience and understanding have been
so important throughout the whole process.
Thank you!

The publishers would like to thank all those who
participated in the development of the project,
with special thanks to Alice Lockyer, Debbie
Grossmann and the freelance editor.

The authors and publishers would like to thank
the following for permission to reproduce their
photographs:
Alamy/Glow Asia RF p25(t), Alamy/
BEAUTYFASHION p64(chef), Alamy/Adam
Burton p93(r), Alamy/CandyBox Images p157(3),
Alamy/Derek Croucher p148, Alamy/Corbis Cusp
p77(tl), Alamy/Patrick Eden p87(r), Alamy/Greg
Balfour Evans p88(1), Alamy/Martyn Evans
p119(bl), Alamy/Fancy pp6(2), 94(l), Alamy/liz
finlayson p114(b), Alamy/Hemis p157(2), Alamy/
Justin Kase z11z p127, Alamy/imagebroker
p141(tm), Alamy/Don Mason p205(l), Alamy/MBI
pp7(3), 137(2), Alamy/Jan Mika p130(l), Alamy/
moodboard p158(b), Alamy/Wavebreak Media ltd
p70(r), Alamy/Paul Melling p112, Alamy/ONOKY
– Photononstop p77(tmr), Alamy/Robert Harding
Picture Library Ltd p106(b), Alamy/philipus
p49(br), Alamy/Alex Segre p88(2), Alamy/
Benjamin Stansall p162, Alamy/Will Stanton
p30(tr), Alamy/ACE STOCK LIMITED p137(3),
Alamy/SuperStock p114(t), Alamy/Catchlight
Visual Services p137(1, 4), Alamy/Derek White
p140(br);
An Agent of Deceit by Chris Morgan Jones –
Cover image Brandenburg Gate © Mohamad
Itani/Arcangel Images. Man with Hat © Eduardo
Ripoll/Arcangel Images;
Anything for Love by Sarah Webb – Cover
illustration © Robyn Neild;
Brand X Pictures pp8, 158(t);
Bournemouth News and Picture Services
p122;
Courtesy of Apple pp30(tl, tm);
Corbis pp22(tr), 25(b), 117(t), 140(tr), 152(tr),
Corbis/engraving of Kitley House by R. Ackerman
1828 p52(c), Corbis/Bettmann p52(f), Corbis/Tom
Brakefield – The Stock Conne/Science Faction
p87(l, Call of the Wild), Corbis/Creasource
p105(3), Corbis and MACMILLAN\Haddon
Davies p152(tmr), Corbis/Imagesource p155,
Corbis/Sharie Kennedy/LWA p58(2), Corbis/
Beau Lark p59(3), Corbis/Will & Deni McIntyre
p38(b), Corbis/Tim Fitzharris/Minden Pictures
p117(b), Corbis/Ocean p154, Corbis/JLP/Jose

L. Pelaez p70(l), 182, Corbis/Geo Rittenmyer
p140(background), Corbis/Ariel Skelley/Blend
Images p185(l), Corbis/Soeren Stache/dpa
p26(tl), Corbis/Tatiana Markow/Sygma p49(bl),
Corbis/Bernd Vogel/ p64(hairdressers), Corbis/
Westend61 p59(4), Corbis/WK010310 p104; **City
of Edinburgh Council** p119(tl);
DigitalStock/Corbis pp108, 111;
Digital Vision p172(t, ct);
Empire and Barbarians by Peter Heather –
Cover photograph © Shutterstock;
Getty Images pp9(b), 12(l), 19(r), 22(br), 35(l),
36(tl), 77(tm), 188, 205(r), Getty Images/AFP
pp19(l), 26,(tml), 140(br), 180(r), Getty Images/
Alistair Berg p172(cb), Getty Images/Thomas
Brawick p10, Getty Images/Smith Collection p65,
Getty Images/Tim Draper p166(l), Getty Images/
Compassionate Eye Foundation/Steven Errico
p49(tr), Getty/Fox Images p86(The Adventures
of Tom Sawyer), Getty Images/Fuse p82,
Harrington p203(t), Getty Images/Martin Hartley
p85, Getty Images/Jason Hawkes p93(l), Getty
Images/Sports Illustrated p26(tr), Getty Images/
Lambert p36(tmr), Getty Images/Erin Patrice
O'Brien p51, Getty Images/Eyecandy Images
p77(tm), Getty Images/Marco Baass p130(r),
Getty Images/Muntz p58(1), Getty Images/
Science Faction/NASA p100, Getty Images/Nico
De Pasquale Photography p43, Getty Images/
Time File Picturesp176, Getty Images/British
Library/Robana p28, Getty Images/Thomas
Roetting p185(r), Getty Images/CARL IWASAKI
p36(tm), Getty Images/Jeff Rotman p7(4), Getty
Images/VisitBritain/Britain on View p6(1), Getty
Images/sot p157(1), Getty/Taxi p52, Getty Images/
Benjamin Tonner p141(tr), Getty Images/Digital
Vision p76, Getty Images/VisitBritain p109, Getty
Images/Chris Westwood p22(l), Getty Images/
Joan Woollcombe Collection p36(tr);
Greenpeace/Alex Hofford p146;
Imagesource pp64(surgeon) 103;
THE KOBAL COLLECTION/NEW
LINE CINEMA p46(d), THE KOBAL
COLLECTION/20TH CENTURY FOX
p143(b), THE KOBAL COLLECTION/
UNIVERSAL p143(cb), THE KOBAL
COLLECTION/AMBLIN/UNIVERSAL/WARNERS
p143(t);
Macmillan p9(c);
www.pagagnini.com p18(l);
Photodisc pp35(r), 140(tl), Photoshot/Fadi
Arouri p18(r), Photodisc/Getty Images pp31,135;
Photospin p172(b);
Plain Pictures/TatjaB. p128(l);
Rex Features/Image Broker p141(tl), Rex
Features/Monkey Business Images p157(4),
Rex Features/Huw Evans p26(cl), Rex Features/
c.20thC.Fox/Everett p46(c), Rex Features/c.
Warner Br/Everett p47, Rex Features/c.Universal/
Everett p142, Rex Features/Neale Haynes
p26(tmr), Rex Features/SAM PIKESLEYc p126,
Rex Features/RICHARD POHLE p49(tl), Rex
Features/Snap Stills p46(a), Rex Features/Ray
Tang pp168, 143(ct), Rex Features/c.Weinstein/
Everett p46(b), Rex Features/Eye Ubiquitous
p73, Rex Features/Richard Young p12(m), Rex
Features/KeystoneUSA-ZUMA p105(4);
Short Books (How to Get Things Really Flat)
p62;
Superstock/Ableimages p105(1), Superstock/
age footstock p106(t), Superstock/Cusp And
Superstock/age footstock p38(1), Superstock/
Blend Images p203(b), Superstock/Hans Blossey/
imagebro/imagebroker.net p94(m), Superstock/
Stock Connection p119(tr), Superstock/Corbis
p156, Superstock/Imagebroker.net p105(2),
Superstock/Kablonk p166(r), Superstock/
Image Source p152(tml), Superstock/Image100
p64(refuge collector), Superstock/NaturePL
p44, Superstock/Prisma p89(3), Superstock/
Radius p152(tl), Superstock/Superstock p36(tml),
Superstock/Tetra Images p12(r), Superstock/
View Pictures Ltd p94(r), Superstock/Westend61
p119(br);
Roy Norris p9(t);
Thinkstock pp64(receptionist), 77(tr),
Thinkstock/Photodisc p89(4), Thinkstock/Polka
Dot p128(r);
Weather Witch by Celia Dart-Thornton – Jacket
illustration © Julek Heller.

The authors and publishers are grateful for
permission to reprint the following copyright
material:
Adapted from website www.paganini.com,
reprinted with permission of the publisher;
Adapted from website www.rhythmofthedance.
com, reprinted with permission of the publisher;
Material used from website www.cirque-eloize.com;
Material used from website www.tapdogs.com;

Material from article 'Get the rugby high;
Rugby union' by Alison Kervin, copyright
© Alison Kervin 1999, first appeared in The
Times 29.09.99, reprinted by permission of the
publisher;
Material from article 'Digital detox: Why I pulled
the plug on my family' by Susan Maushart,
copyright © Susan Maushart 2010, first appeared
in The Independent 28.12.10, reprinted by
permission of the publisher;
Material from article 'Norwegian Boy Fends
Off Wolf Pack with Heavy Metal' first published
in SPIEGEL ONLINE, International 20.01.11,
reprinted by permission of the publisher;
Material from article 'A more commercial tune'
by Sarah Edgehill, copyright © Sarah Edgehill
2008, first appeared in The Independent 06.11.08,
reprinted by permission of the publisher;
Material from article 'Family member's yawns
are most contagious' by Nick Collins, copyright
© Nick Collins 2011, first appeared in The
Telegraph 08.12.11, reprinted by permission of
the publisher;
Material from article 'When the heat is on' by
Clive Tully, copyright © Clive Tully 1996, first
appeared in Country Walking 1996, reprinted by
permission of the publisher;
Material from article 'Yukutsk: Journey to the
coldest city on earth' by Shaun Walker, copyright
© Shaun Walker 2008, first appeared in The
Independent 21.01.08, reprinted by permission of
the publisher;
Material from article 'Life aboard the
International Space Station' by Ian Sample,
copyright © Ian Sample 2010, first published in
The Guardian 24.10.10, reprinted by permission
of the publisher;
Adapted material from 'Dead Man's Cove 6th
edn' by Lauren St. John, copyright © Lauren
St. John 2011, reprinted by permission of Orion
Publishing;
Material from article 'On your marks, get set
… get lucky' by Marie Winckler, copyright ©
Marie Winckler 2011, first published in The
London Evening Standard 20.07.11, reprinted by
permission of the publisher;
Material from 'World Famous Strange But
True' by Colin, Damon and Rowan Wilson, first
published by Magpie Books 1994, reprinted by
permission of Constable and Robinson;
From 'Nutureshock' by Po Bronson, published
by Ebury Press, reprinted by permission of the
Random House Group Limited and Curtis Brown
Ltd, Literary Agency US;
From 'Nurtureshock' by Po Bronson & Ashley
Merryman. Copyright © 2009 by Po Bronson.
By permission of Grand Central Publishing. All
rights reserved;
Adapted material from article 'The Trash Vortex'
taken from website www.greenpeace.org,
reprinted with permission;
Material from article 'Everything but the pips:
Arc Café is pioneering the vegetarian version of
zero-waste cooking' by Samuel Muston, copyright
© Samuel Muston 2012, first appeared in The
Independent 06.04.12, reprinted by permission of
the publisher;
Material from article 'Oldest goldfish Tish has
his chips at 43' by Paul Stokes, copyright ©
Paul Stokes 2009, first appeared in The Daily
Telegraph 07.08.09, reprinted by the publisher;
Material from article 'Learning the real local
lingo can be child's play' by Sarah Monaghan,
copyright © Sarah Monaghan 2006, first
appeared in The Daily Telegraph 14.06.06,
reprinted by permission of the publisher;
Material from article 'Everest next for the
climber who fell 1,000 feet- and survived' by
Lewis Smith, copyright © Lewis Smith 2011, first
appeared in The Independent 31.01.11, reprinted
by permission of the publisher.

Printed and bound in Thailand

2018 2017 2016 2015 2014
11 10 9 8 7 6 5 4 3